ELIZABETH'S SEA DOGS

How the English became the Scourge of the Seas

HUGH BICHENO

ELIZABETH'S SEA DOGS

How the English became the Scourge of the Seas

HUGH BICHENO

ADLARD COLES

LONDON · OXFORD · NEW YORK · NEW DELHI · SYDNEY

To Eileen Gunn and the Royal Literary Fund,
without whose timely support this book
could not have been written

and to

Ian Drury of Sheil Land Associates
Editor, literary agent and friend

ADLARD COLES
Bloomsbury Publishing Plc
50 Bedford Square, London, WC1B 3DP, UK

BLOOMSBURY, ADLARD COLES and the Adlard Coles logo
are trademarks of Bloomsbury Publishing Plc

First published in 2012 by Anova Books Ltd
First paperback edition 2013
First Bloomsbury Publishing edition 2014

A catalogue record for this book is available from the British Library

Library of Congress Cataloguing-in-Publication data has been applied for

ISBN: PB: 978-1-4729-6701-5; ePub: 978-1-8448-6190-3

2 4 6 8 10 9 7 5 3

Printed and bound by CPI Group (UK) Ltd, Croydon, CR0 4YY

To find out more about our authors and books visit www.bloomsbury.com
and sign up for our newsletters

CONTENTS

PROLOGUE

In January 1578, near the coast in northern Chile, a merchant snoozing in the shade of a tree woke from his siesta to find himself surrounded by a group of armed men. They seemed to be in high good humour, and were passing around 13 bars of silver taken from the saddlebags on his mule. They looked like Spanish soldiers, wearing the familiar morrions on their heads and thickly padded doublets, but they spoke a language he did not understand.

Their leader, a stocky man with piercing eyes set in a round head with reddish-brown curly hair, a light red moustache and a pointed beard, asked by gestures where the silver came from. The merchant replied that it came from the silver mine at Huantajaya. The strange men tried but could not pronounce the word. 'Want-a-what-ah?' asked one of them, and the rest fell about laughing.

After they departed, taking his worldly wealth with them, the merchant hurried back to the town of Tarapacá, where he reported the theft to the authorities. Not long afterwards a bonded drover arrived to report an ambush by the same group of strangers, not far from the town. They had stolen his team of eight llamas, each loaded with 100 pounds' weight of refined silver from the Huantajaya mine, enough to coin 12,800 pesos (pieces of eight) worth about £2,910 (equivalent to some £436,500 in 2010).*

Later a pinnace arrived from Valparaíso, far to the south, to report that a heavily armed ship manned by uncouth foreigners had raided the main port of Chile. They had stolen several tuns of wine from storehouses and had broken into more of the same on a ship in the harbour. Pausing only to get drunk, the foreigners looted the ship of everything portable, including a quantity of refined gold from the mines at Valdivia, further south at the fighting frontier with the fierce Araucano Indians.

* For further conversions see Appendix A: Sixteenth Century Inflation, Currency and Exchange Rates.

Worst of all, they profaned a crucifix made of gold and emeralds, tearing the golden figure of Our Lord from it. All agreed these outrages could only be the work of the dreaded *luteranos franceses*, the French Protestant enemies of God and Spain who had been raiding the American dominions of His Catholic Majesty King Felipe II for many decades.

Only later did they learn from Perú, where the foreigners raided the port of Callao before capturing a treasure ship on the high seas, that they had proudly identified themselves as *ingleses*, Englishmen, and that their stocky, curly-haired leader went by the fearsome name of *el Draque* – the Dragon.

WESTERN EUROPE IN 1560

0 100 200 300
miles

SCOTLAND
Edinburgh

Ulster

IRELAND
Dublin

Munster

ENGLAND & WALES
London

DENMARK

Netherlands (Spain)

Flanders

HOLY ROMAN EMPIRE

Normandy

Paris

Brittany

Saintonge

FRANCE

Franche Comté (Spain)

Swiss Confederation

Savoy

Milan (Spain)

Venice

Cantábrica

Navarre

Aragon

Genoa

Florence

PORTUGAL

Old Castille

Madrid

SPAIN

New Castille

Lisbon

Corsica (Genoa)

Rome

Sardinia (Spain)

Andalucia

Granada

Sicily (Spain)

Algiers

Tunis

Malta

© Hugh Bicheno

CHAPTER 1
THE WAY THEY WERE

B eyond basic physical attributes the Elizabethans were not much as we are today. We may visit their houses, view their portraits, read their words and believe our common humanity bridges the centuries that separate us – but it does not. The single fact that there were far fewer of them – about four million in England and Wales in 1600 compared to fifty-four million today – should warn us that their outlook on life was different to ours in ways we cannot comprehend.

They were perhaps an inch shorter than today's average 5 feet 9 inches/175 centimetres for men and 5 feet 3 inches/160 centimetres for women, with the sickly weeded out by high rates of infant mortality and – for the great majority – extremely unhygienic living conditions that selected for hardiness still further. The average life expectancy at birth for boys of landowning families was 31 years, improving to 40 if they reached their tenth birthdays, 45 at their twentieth and 50 if they reached their thirtieth. Girls had a ten percent higher survival rate through gestation, infancy and childhood (as they do, life-long, today), but during their child-bearing years (girls were legally marriageable at 12, boys at 14) puerperal sepsis sank the average life expectancy of Elizabethan women to about half that of men of the same age. Very few of either sex reached 75–80, today's *average* life expectancy at birth.

Contagious diseases such as smallpox, diphtheria, measles, scarlet fever and chickenpox did dreadful execution among children, and even those with strong immune systems could still be carried off by diseases almost unknown in relatively hygienic modern England.

The main scourges were lice-borne typhus; water-borne typhoid, cholera and dysentery (the bloody flux); flea-borne bubonic plague and air-borne pneumonic plague (together, the Black Death); mosquito-borne malaria (the ague); and a 'sweating sickness' (probably influenza) that disappeared after 1578. Tuberculosis was endemic and ergotism, caused by a fungal infection of rye arising from damp storage, added to the misery of scarcity following bad harvests. Open wounds invited deadly septicaemia and tetanus, and virulent syphilis had recently joined long-endemic gonorrhoea among the sexually transmitted diseases.

Only a serious health-food fanatic today could match the standard Elizabethan lower-class summer diet of barley bread, cheese, honey, fruit, a wide range of cultivated and wild vegetables, salted or dried fish, and only occasional meat. Fresh fish, crustaceans and shellfish were also cheap in coastal areas and along rivers. The modern foodie would, however, shrink from the copious use of eggs and lard in the commonest dishes. The upper classes ate white bread (manchet) and gorged on all kinds of meat and fowl, accompanied by high-cholesterol sauces and followed by butter-rich pastries, tarts and cakes made with refined sugar. Unremarkably, apoplexy (stroke) was a more common killer of the gentry than of the lower classes. Even so obesity was uncommon (among the laity), thanks to a very high level of physical activity – without which even fewer would have reached old age.

Dried, smoked or salted meats were the main sources of protein in the winter months, when all except the most robust animals were slaughtered because the problem of winter feed for livestock had yet to be resolved. For people, also, vitamin deficiency arising from a lack of fresh fruit and vegetables in winter made scurvy a winter disease on land, as well as the scourge of sailors on long voyages. The problem was compounded by the slide into the Little Ice Age that gathered pace during Elizabeth's reign, reducing growing seasons and making winters longer and more severe.

Elizabethan cooks used saffron, powdered sandalwood and spinach juice or parsley juice to add colour to soups, and dishes were cooked in ale, verjuice, wine and almond milk. To make preserved meats more palatable, even the humblest cooks used onions of many types, garlic, galingale, mustard, sage, marjoram, rosemary, fennel and rocket as well as many other plants no longer in common use. Cooks in wealthier households also used ginger, cloves and pepper imported from South East Asia, and aromatic or hot peppers from West Africa and America.

All levels of society knew that water, unless from a pristine source, was bad for your health and instead drank ale, also an important source of nutrition, brewed from malted barley by the addition of brewer's yeast. Hops gradually replaced the traditional mixture of herbs to counter the cloying sweetness of the drink, and also to act as a preservative by raising the alcohol content. 'Small beer' was a low-alcohol, safe alternative to water, but the longer lasting ales loaded on ships were of higher alcoholic content and it's safe to say that while the ale remained drinkable everyone aboard was at least mildly inebriated at all times.

Then as now, foreigners commented austerely on the English proclivity for drunkenness and consequent brawling. On festive occasions the lower classes might drink cider, perry and mead (honey wine), while the upper classes also regularly drank plain and fortified wines in astounding quantities, one reason why they tended to have what we now coyly call impulse management issues.

Although the common people dressed plainly, the upper classes spent small fortunes on their apparel. Prudent women at Elizabeth's court were careful to dress more modestly than the queen – but the men put peacocks in the shade. Male sartorial extravagance was so great that it impacted adversely on the nation's balance of payments and in June 1574 Elizabeth issued *Statutes of Apparel* in a vain effort to bring the preening under control. The wry preamble reads:

The excess of apparel and the superfluity of unnecessary foreign wares thereto belonging now of late years is grown by sufferance to such an extremity that the manifest decay of the whole realm generally is like to follow by bringing into the realm such

> *superfluities of silks, cloths of gold, silver, and other most vain*
> *devices of so great cost for the quantity thereof as of necessity the*
> *moneys and treasure of the realm is and must be yearly conveyed*
> *out of the same to answer the said excess, but also particularly the*
> *wasting and undoing of a great number of young gentlemen,*
> *otherwise serviceable, and others seeking by show of apparel to be*
> *esteemed as gentlemen, who, allured by the vain show of those*
> *things, do not only consume themselves, their goods, and lands which*
> *their parents left unto them, but also run into such debts and shifts*
> *as they cannot live out of danger of laws without attempting*
> *unlawful acts, whereby they are not any ways serviceable to their*
> *country as otherwise they might be.**

Elizabeth's *Statutes* explicitly confirmed the link between power and ostentation that was such a feature of the Renaissance. They gave detailed attention to what type of fur each level of nobility might wear, and what colour and type of silk was appropriate for each social station. Possibly as a result, the apparently plain clothing of the socially aspirant showed a high degree of skilled elaboration. In Cornelis Ketel's 1577 portrait, Martin Frobisher's seemingly plain apparel includes slashed white leather shoes, puffed Venetian breeches with looped knee borders in pickadil, a high-necked jerkin with skirt and wings tied by points, opening to show the padded peascod of a buttoned satin doublet with trunk sleeves and small figure-of-eight ruffs at neck and wrists.

The puffed breeches and peascod (a bulging abdominal device tapering to a point) marked a pronounced change from the massively padded upper body and jutting codpiece of Henry VIII's reign. The new fashion came from Italy, but as the poet Michael Drayton said of his own craft:

> *My muse is rightly of the English strain,*
> *That cannot long one fashion entertain.*

---

* In this and other quotations throughout the book, most spelling has been modernized.

Women emphasized the smallness of their waists with bodices narrowing to a point, and their hips, extravagantly, with hooped lattice-work farthingales that fully displayed their frounced, slashed and highly decorated skirts. Although it appears to have been coincidental, it's intriguing that English men ceased to exaggerate their masculine characteristics and began to emphasize their hips and bellies at about the time they were ruled first by Mary and then by Elizabeth, the first crowned queens of England. It even affected the development of armour, which one might have thought was strictly utilitarian but in fact always reflected upper-class fashion in clothing.

The portraits tell us how they chose to look when on show, but such elaboration was reserved for the court or for high social events. They 'dressed down' for everyday life in the country, away from the view of their peers or the general public. It was, of course, an overwhelmingly rural society. Only about six percent of the population lived in settlements of over one thousand inhabitants in Henry VIII's reign, rising to about ten percent by the end of Elizabeth's. Even so, the population of London trebled from 60–70,000 to over 200,000 during the 16th century. Other cities also grew, but much less: Bristol from 14,000 to 20,000; Norwich from 10,000 to 19,000; York from 10,000 to 12,000; and Exeter from 8,000 to 9,000.

There were some constants. It's fair to equate modern, property-price-enhancing 'green belt' legislation with late-16th century ordinances forbidding the building of new houses on less than 4 acres outside the boundaries of the City of London and the immediately surrounding, independently administered Liberties. Consequently the older urban area became one of the most crowded places on earth. In 1605 an estimated 75,000 lived in the square mile of the City – which would put it among the top ten most densely populated cities even today – while 115,000 lived in the Liberties; and with such density came extremely squalid living conditions and devastating epidemics.

However, at some still-to-be-defined point urban concentration reaches a critical mass that generates a sharper rise in productivity than numbers can explain. It permits increased specialization, makes it easier to combine with others for mutual benefit – what we now call 'networking' – but above all it facilitates the exchange of goods and services, while shared ideas speed innovation. Multiplying all these factors in the 16th century was movable-type printing, which recent research suggests may have added 60 percent to the rate of growth of every European city that became an early adopter of the technology. For London, the multiplier effect was further accentuated by the near monopoly held by the Guild of Stationers, which lasted until the end of the 17th century.

Perhaps the clearest illustration of the urban concentration effect was the rapid evolution of theatre, the main component of the 'English Renaissance', which came about because of intense competition among London companies. The first permanent amphitheatre – as distinct from inn yards or animal baiting pits – was built in the Liberty of Shoreditch by James Burbage in 1576 after the City expelled players in 1575. Rival establishments proliferated and by 1595 about fifteen thousand people a week (more than the entire population of York) were attending plays in London's theatres. Over a hundred playwrights scribbled frantically, often in collaboration, to keep up with demand. And out of this hothouse emerged such authors as Marlowe, Beaumont and Fletcher, Jonson – and Shakespeare.

And with them came modern English, a synthesis of dialects born of migration to London from all over England, spread by use in state administration and gradually standardized by printing. Mirroring the spirit of the age, a highly adaptable – and essentially lawless – common language emerged, quick to borrow from abroad or to coin new words to express novel concepts. The works of Shakespeare alone contain nearly 2,000 words not previously recorded. Some did not take, but most did and his legacy includes such basic words as *countless, excellent, hurry, majestic* and *radiance*.

Practical expressions of London's dynamism included Sir Thomas Gresham's commercial centre, built on a site made available by the City and the Worshipful Company of Mercers (Merchants) and named the Royal Exchange after Queen Elizabeth formally opened it in January 1571. It was modelled on the centuries-old *bourses* of the great Flemish trading centres and certainly owed as much to the disruption of trade with the Low Countries as it did to the phenomenon of urban concentration. But it marked the definitive supplanting of foreign by English trading houses in the management of the nation's commerce; and it served to affirm the ascendancy of a new class of merchants with a distinctively English – and not noticeably scrupulous – way of doing business.

Although the great majority, as always, knew little and cared less about anything beyond their parochial concerns, the upper classes in Elizabeth's time were more cosmopolitan than they are today. One reason was the greater exchange of personnel involved in trading relationships, another was that the break with the pan-European Roman church had taken place only a generation earlier, and Latin remained the lingua franca of all educated people across Europe.

The queen herself spoke Latin, French and Italian, and many of her courtiers were also polyglot. Although the custom became constrained during Elizabeth's reign because of the heightened risk of religious persecution, some still completed their education at mainland European universities, while continental fashions remained influential. There was, however, a cultural shift from medieval French to Renaissance Italian influence, already apparent in the latter half of the 15th century, which gathered momentum under Henry VIII and became complete under Elizabeth.

Under the cosmopolitan veneer, however, lay unique characteristics that distinguished English society far more from others than they do today. Although published in 1978, the painstaking scholarship of Alan MacFarlane's ground-breaking *Origins of English Individualism* has never been questioned, still less refuted. Yet it demolished the previously canonical view of medieval England as a peasant society where people were tied to the land by communal or familial obligations, akin to the norm in mainland Europe and in Scotland. MacFarlane found, instead, compelling evidence as early as the 13th century of a sizeable body of landless, free labour, and that land was a commodity owned by individuals – of either sex – who could buy, sell and bequeath it at will.

Although there's no documentary proof, it's reasonable to assume that these customs pre-dated the Norman Conquest of 1066. As they did in their simultaneous conquest of Sicily, the Norman invaders of England simply overlaid their authority on existing laws and customs, producing a fruitful synthesis. The roots of Anglo-Saxon civil rights probably lay in ancient Germany, but they were refined by a number of other historical circumstances, among them the contractual basis of feudalism, more comprehensively imposed in England than any other state.

But arguably the most influential factor was that, after 1066, the only invasions that led to a change in monarch took place during periods of near or actual civil war. Absent such conditions, there was no realistic threat of conquest by another power prior to the Spanish Armada in 1588, hence no need for a large military establishment. Consequently England's rulers were denied a standing army, the main driver of the absolutism that became the norm in mainland Europe. The country was also spared major domestic conflict from the end of the Wars of the Roses in 1485 until the start of the civil war in 1642, which was fought precisely to deny the theocratic absolutism to which King Charles I aspired.

The result was 'legal island', whose uniqueness was recognized to lie at the core of England's future economic development and rise to world power by thinkers from Montesquieu to Marx. Its principal manifestation in the 16th century, however, was the sort of widespread litigiousness today more associated with the United States. 'Money is like muck, not good except it be spread', wrote the great Elizabethan Sir Francis Bacon, and the incessant lawsuits in which landowning families were involved, alongside the competitive ostentation whose apogee was the building of grandiose country houses, acted to spread the wealth expropriated from the monasteries by Henry VIII.

The ancient roots of English individualism cannot be reconciled with modern academic dogma, but it was blindingly apparent to foreign observers. 'They have good ships and are greedy folk *with more freedom than is good for them*', wrote Ambassador Diego Guzmán de Silva to King Felipe (hereafter Philip) of Spain in 1565, explaining the determination of English merchants to trade with the Spanish Indies, by force if necessary. Philip did not need reminding. His experience as the highly unpopular consort to Queen Mary, Elizabeth's half-sister from Henry VIII's first marriage to Philip's great-aunt Catherine, can have left him in no doubt about the strain of disrespectful unruliness in the English character, and may help to explain the self-damaging stubbornness with which he refused to provide a safe channel in his domains for English commercial energy.

The single greatest difference between the English of Elizabeth's time and today was that they all believed they possessed an immortal soul, and religion played a correspondingly vital part in their lives. By the time Elizabeth came to the throne England had endured 30 years of bewildering assaults on what A. L. Rowse perfectly describes as 'the habits of mind, the usages, the penumbra of superstition and custom which was the religion of the people'. Mighty abbeys that had dominated communities for centuries were gutted and their brethren dispersed, revered statues of saints were destroyed, saints' days were abolished along with masses for the dead, pilgrimages were banned and liturgical changes had followed each other with bewildering rapidity – all for reasons even the elite could barely understand. Adding salt to the wounds, powerful landowners took advantage of the situation to enclose common lands. When sullen anger erupted into uprisings, they were suppressed with consummate bad faith and ruthless reprisals.

As a result of Wyatt's 1554 Protestant rebellion against the prospect of Queen Mary marrying the future King Philip II of Spain, Elizabeth was imprisoned in the Tower for two months, within a hundred yards of where her mother, Anne Boleyn, had been beheaded in 1536. Elizabeth's anxiety must have been all the more acute because Henry VIII's break with Rome was precipitated by his desire to divorce his first wife – Mary's mother – to make legitimate the child Anne was carrying. Although only an infant at the time, Elizabeth must surely have grown up traumatized by the knowledge that if she had been the male heir her father confidently expected, Anne's subsequent miscarriages would not have led to her judicial murder.

In the light of Elizabeth's later hesitancy over executing her scheming cousin Mary, Queen of Scots, it should be noted that at the time of Wyatt's rebellion Mary Tudor did not hesitate to order the execution of her blameless cousin Lady Jane Grey, urged to do so by Philip's father, the Emperor Charles V, to eliminate a focus for further Protestant unrest. Perhaps the most noteworthy aspect of Queen Elizabeth's personality is the sentiment fairly attributed to her by Sir Francis Bacon as 'not liking to make windows into men's hearts and secret thoughts', even though many Catholic hearts nurtured murderous hatred of her as the fruit of an unholy union that had torn England from the bosom of Holy Mother Church.

There was an urgent need for a compromise most could live with, and within the first year of Elizabeth's reign it was found in the form of communion established by the *religious* Act of Uniformity, which obliged all to attend church on Sundays – but did not force Roman Catholics to repudiate their faith. As the great Elizabethan scholar Joel Hurstfield put it, Elizabeth's government achieved a 'broad, ambiguous Anglicanism which, if it aroused only limited enthusiasm, would stimulate only a limited opposition'.

The *political* Act of Supremacy, which declared Elizabeth to be the Supreme Governor of the Church of England, forced any Roman Catholic who might seek religious or civil office to renounce allegiance to the Pope under oath. Mary burned otherwise loyal Protestants for *heresy*, but Elizabeth hanged, drew and quartered actively subversive Roman Catholics for *treason*. It was a crucial difference, reflecting her father's view that his break with Rome was a matter of sovereignty and not of theology.

Elizabeth's settlement was in keeping with the compromise reached at the 1555 Peace of Augsburg, which ended armed conflict between the Roman Catholic and Lutheran princes of the Holy Roman Empire. The principle, later graced with the Latin formula *cuius regio, eius religio*, established that the religion of the monarch should be the religion of his or her subjects.

Even though the papacy was her mortal enemy, and some of her ministers were fiercely anti-Catholic, Elizabeth refused to make common cause with other Protestant princes on the basis of religion. This was astute, as any religious call to arms risked re-opening domestic wounds. By laying the onus for disturbing the peace on her Roman Catholic enemies, Elizabeth came to represent stability in a highly uncertain world. England had become a more intolerantly Protestant nation by the end of her reign – but it was not she who forced the pace. This helped to spare her subjects the catastrophic effects of the religious polarization that occurred elsewhere in Europe.

Elizabeth was fortunate that by the time she came to the throne the worst effects of her father's legacy of inflationary wars had worked through the economy – although Elizabeth's ministers still needed to end the war with France embarked upon by Mary at the request of her husband Philip. Peace from 1559 made it possible to bring down inflation from 35 percent in 1550–60 to 15 percent in 1560–70, followed by slightly deflationary stability in 1570–80. Henry VIII's notorious debasement of the coinage (he was nicknamed 'Old Copper Nose' because the thin layer of silver on his coins first wore off the most prominent feature of the royal visage) had led to the hoarding or transfer abroad through trade of earlier, undebased coins – from which came one of the oldest 'laws' of economics: Sir Thomas Gresham's axiom that bad money drives out good.

Starting in Edward VI's reign all coins were re-issued with the correct amount of bullion. Elizabeth's government completed the process, with the further refinement of milling the edges of all gold and higher value silver coins to prevent shaving or clipping. Around a profile of the queen most of her coins bore an inscription in Latin that translates 'Elizabeth by Grace of God Queen of England, France and Ireland'. On the reverse, the inscription read 'I Have Made the Lord My Helper'. Around her profile on pennies – some of which bore dates for the first time – and on some sub-penny coins, there was the charming inscription 'Elizabeth by Grace of God a Rose without a Thorn'.

During Elizabeth's reign a river of silver from Potosí in Spanish America vastly increased the money supply worldwide, with the Spanish silver peso/piece of eight/thaler/dollar becoming the principal international unit of exchange. Both directly but more particularly through the economic growth facilitated by the rapid increase in liquidity, and in combination with soaring government spending on warfare, the additional money contributed to rising inflation, particularly in the price of staples. The influential political economist John Maynard Keynes (1883–1946) was to write of the 16th century that 'never in the annals of the modern world has there existed so prolonged and so rich an opportunity for the businessman, the speculator and the profiteer' – in a word, adventurers.

At the start of Elizabeth's reign a pound (£) had the equivalent purchasing power of £170 in 2010; by the time she died it had sunk below £100 – trivial by comparison with the shameless inflation that has characterized the reign of Elizabeth II, but startling at the time. However, the official poverty level in 2010 England was £17,310 p.a. for a household with two children; the equivalent purchasing power in 1560 was £101, beyond the wildest dreams of avarice for the vast majority in a society where a skilled worker would be happy to earn £18 p.a. By 1600 the equivalent to today's poverty line was £172, yet the rapidly growing population held wage increases below the rate of inflation. In contrast, delighted property owners saw the rents and cash price of their assets rising rapidly.

Some things never change, among them the tax aversion of the middle classes, no matter how much their houses have appreciated in value. Elizabeth and Sir William Cecil, her chief minister until 1598, chose not to try the loyalty of the gentry by raising their taxes, but even so her inherited debt was paid off by 1574. By the early 1580s a positive balance of about £300,000 had been built up, partly from a share of the loot from the guerrilla war waged by some of her subjects on Spanish and Portuguese shipping and dominions.

The full-scale war that ensued from the mid-1580s reversed the process, and when Elizabeth died the debt was back up to £350,000. It may not seem much to modern eyes, but it was a crushing worry for an elderly lady on a fixed income compelled to sell land to pay some of the bills; and it became an urgent incentive for her successor, Scots King James VI, who became James I of England, to end the war he inherited along with the debt. In contrast, when Elizabeth's great antagonist Philip II died in 1598 the Spanish crown owed over one hundred million gold ducats (£47.6 million – 136 times greater than Elizabeth's debt), with two-thirds of its revenues devoted to interest payments. Yet thanks to the silver bullion from Potosí Spain was still able to continue the war with England and the Netherlands, and to fight France as well.

That one can write of a 'middle class' in England but not in Spain points to another distinguishing feature of Elizabethan society, namely the community of financial interest among aristocracy, gentry and merchants. You could become a gentleman by creating lightly taxable wealth in England, but with few exceptions you could only be born a tax-exempt *hidalgo* in Spain, no matter how rich or poor your family might be. The tragicomic nobility of Cervantes's Don Quixote and Shakespeare's amusingly disreputable Sir John Falstaff illustrate the two societies' contrasting attitudes towards the rising importance of money and the corresponding decline in the status of aristocratic honour.

In 1583 the legal scholar Sir Thomas Smith published *De Republica Anglorum: the Manner of Government or Policie of the Realme of England*, written when he was ambassador to the French court from 1562 to 1566. Possibly struck by the absence of an equivalent class in France, he tried to define what the English meant by 'gentleman' at a time when it was easy to obtain the imprimatur of the College of Heralds in return for a fee. A generation earlier he would certainly have emphasized the knightly qualities of arms and horsemanship; but now Smith held that although study at the Inns of Court or of liberal sciences at the universities was desirable, a gentleman was anyone:

> … *who can live idly and without manual labour, and will bear* [afford] *the port* [style], *charge* [social responsibility] *and countenance* [appearance] *of a gentleman, he shall be called master, for that is the title which men give to esquires and other gentlemen.**

At the other end of the social scale, earlier in the 16th century a Venetian ambassador complained that 'there is no country in the world where there as so many thieves and robbers as in England, in so much that few venture to go alone in the country, excepting in the middle of the day, and fewer still in the towns at night, and least of all in London'. And this was *before* the population explosion later in the century that made so many indigent.

His words have been regularly echoed by visitors ever since, and it may be that there's a particular strain of larceny in English culture, impervious alike to punishment and attempts to establish 'causes of crime'. There was nothing specifically English, however, in the breakdown of the social controls that small communities exercised over their inhabitants when individuals moved to a more anonymous existence in the crowded metropolis.

Government itself was run on the understanding that office-holders would profit from their authority. Although it's hard to discern what constituted an excess of greed at the range of five hundred years, there were limits, and those who exceeded them might lose office, or – if their patron fell from power or withdrew protection – incur fines and imprisonment.

Abstract concepts of general welfare were not a feature of the age, but with regard to the poor we can see the laws changing to

---

* Reproduced, without attribution, from William Harrison's contribution to Holinshed's *Chronicles*. Harrison added the astute observation that it was a cheap way for monarchs to expand the taxpayer pool, which a newly minted gentleman 'doth bear the gladlier for the saving of his reputation'.

provide a more humane response. For all their faults the monasteries had provided a patchy social safety net and it took civil society many decades to create an alternative. At the start of Elizabeth's reign the law sanctioned whipping, burning through the ears, imprisonment and even execution for able-bodied beggars.

The introduction of a national Poor Law Tax in 1572 was recognition that many were unemployed and homeless for reasons beyond their control, while the 1576 Act required parishes to provide work for them. The 1597 Act for the Relief of the Poor required every parish to maintain an Overseer of the Poor, and the 1601 Poor Law codified previous provisions in a form that, although much modified, was not fully replaced until 1834. Balanced against these improvements in treatment of the poor, however, was a ferocious penal code that included disfigurement and amputation for quite minor offences, and punished any theft to a value of 5 pence or more by hanging.

Judicial torture took place in private but executions, including ritual disembowelments, were thronged public events. Other popular entertainments included hurling filth and stones at people with their head and hands locked into the stocks, and setting savage dogs on bears and bulls in special pits. The bull-dog that became a patriotic symbol for a later age was a very nasty animal indeed. When Shakespeare wrote 'Cry havoc and let slip the dogs of war', it was not a metaphor: war-dogs descended from the fierce animals used by the Roman legions, and more recently they had featured in the horrifying *Brevísima Relación de la Destrucción de las Indias* (Extremely Short Account of the Destruction of the Indies), published by Friar Bartolomé de las Casas in 1552.

The outstanding geopolitical fact of Elizabeth's reign is that with the loss of Calais in January 1558, ten months before her accession, England became a wholly island kingdom for the first time since 1066. The concept of the sea as 'a moat defensive', which Shakespeare put in the mouth of the dying John of Gaunt in *Richard II*, was 159 years premature. John was the duke of Aquitaine as well as Lancaster, and his coat of arms combined the castle of Castile, the lion of León, the lilies of France and the lions of England. Although English monarchs continued to style themselves kings or queens of France until 1801, the loss of Calais confirmed that England had become a marginal player in the affairs of Europe.

Thereafter, as Sir Francis Bacon later observed, command of the sea permitted England's rulers to 'take as much and as little of war' as they wished. Venice might formally renew her marriage vows with the Adriatic Sea every Ascension Day, but the union of England with the seas around her was more akin to a comfortable working cohabitation. With hundreds of ports and no place more than 70 miles/112 kilometres from the sea, what we might call 'maritime awareness' was a constant in English history. Even so, until Henry VIII's reign the monarchy did not maintain a significant force of royal ships, instead convoking vessels from English commercial operators or hiring them from abroad when needed.

Still, the king's majesty was to some extent invested in sea power well before the birth of the Royal Navy. In an age when symbols were extremely potent, magical properties attached to the gold angel coins first minted in the late 15th century, which showed St Michael slaying a dragon on one side – and a twin-towered carrack on the reverse. A century later Elizabeth's gold ryal showed her standing in a galleon, crowned, with a sceptre in her right hand and a globe in her left. An Elizabethan galleon appeared on the British halfpence coin until the venerable system of pounds, shillings and pence was abolished in 1971.

Prior to the advent of the railways in the 19th century trade or travel was faster, cheaper, and generally safer by sea or river than by land. Even so, shipwreck was always a possibility and piracy an ever-present threat. Julius Caesar's invasion of Britannia was a punitive expedition provoked by cross-Channel depredations against Roman Gaul, and the phenomenon reaches even further back in history.

Piracy develops wherever there's a combination of a seagoing culture, strong local autonomy, rich pickings off shore and no alternative employment offering comparable prospects of making a living. Like Willy Sutton, who robbed banks because that was where the money was, pirates tend to concentrate at geographic choke-points. Even during our period, much piracy took place in river estuaries, where small boats could slip from the shore at night to surprise the sleepy crews of anchored ships waiting to enter the river at dawn.

Taking a ship may have been easy, but selling the cargo required a well-developed covert infrastructure ashore. The minimum requirement was a secluded cove within easy range of a town where the goods could be sold on to merchants. The ideal was a port run by accomplice harbour officials and local magistrates, although of course the bribes they demanded greatly increased the overheads. The eternal problem is that corrupt officials do not stay bought and use their power to extort an ever-greater share of the proceeds.

In his landmark book *Barbary Legend* (1957), Sir Godfrey Fisher argued that the Barbary pirate strongholds of North Africa attracted adventurers from all over Europe and remained prosperous for so long not because they were lawless, but because they were precisely the opposite. Beyond a fixed share payable to the local authorities, captains were free to dispose of their prizes to competing buyers and above all were not subject to arbitrary arrest and the seizure of their ships. Those who operate at the margins of the law are happiest when those margins are clearly defined.

A culture akin to the Barbary pirate states began to develop on either side of the western reaches of the English Channel during the Middle Ages. The key ingredient was local autonomy, and how it would have developed became one of history's might-have-beens once that autonomy was ended when the Duchy of Brittany lost its independence in 1488, and was incorporated into the Kingdom of France in 1532. The Reformation further divided the English West Countrymen from the Bretons, who remained strong Roman Catholics while their cousins across the water settled into Protestant conformity after the Prayer Book Rebellion of 1549. Some, among them the young Francis Drake, were radicalized by that anti-Protestant rebellion and became bitter enemies of the Roman church; that enmity in turn was to form the basis of a new cross-channel community with the Huguenot sailors of Normandy, and also with those based in La Rochelle on France's Atlantic coast.

Although these communities shared the formative influence of facing the Atlantic, the English were far behind their French and Spanish peers in developing the skills necessary for oceanic navigation. Or to put it more accurately the English learned more slowly than the others from the Italian navigators who were the pioneers of Atlantic exploration.* Henry VII of England did sponsor John Cabot (Giovanni Caboto) to sail from Bristol in search of a north-west passage to the East Indies in 1497, but apart from a limited private effort out of Bristol there was no follow-up. The English fishing industry was concentrated on the East coast, facing the teeming North Sea, from where ships had sailed to fish the scarcely less abundant waters off Iceland since 1409.

English sailors finally did learn to sail across the Atlantic, and they did so just as their French mentors lost the impetus gained from almost continuous war against Spain between 1494 and 1559. French corsair activity, at the end almost entirely associated with the Protestant cause, peaked during the savage wars of religion that tore their country apart from 1562. Thereafter they lost the royal toleration and covert encouragement that had made them so formidable.

With their queen often a silent partner in their ventures, the Elizabethan maritime raiders inherited the mantle of the French corsairs, as England became the principal opponent of Spain's struggle to suppress the rebellion of the Netherlands, once a dependable source of wealth for the Hapsburgs and England's principal trading partner, now a bitter bone of political and religious contention. As we shall see, freedom to trade worked for peace, restrictions on trade for war.

So, while they were indeed very different to the present-day English, the most striking thing about the Elizabethans was how unlike they were to their own immediate ancestors. Every level of

* Portuguese fishermen actually crossed the Atlantic before any of the Italians, but they kept the information to themselves.

society had undergone transformative shocks, with new energies released. Although the day-to-day lives of the mass of the population still followed the age-old pattern of the seasons, the deep culture of English society proved peculiarly suited to a new age of uncertainty, where previously unimagined opportunities were opening in a vastly wider world.

It was a challenging environment, at once frightening and exhilarating, and the dynamic response of a relatively small number of bold men, including the cold-eyed servants of a studiedly charismatic monarch, generated the most exciting chapter in the relatively short period of purely English history.

CHAPTER 2
PRECURSORS

Hernán Cortés completed the conquest of Mexico in August 1521. Following the sack of Tenochtitlán, the Aztec capital, he set aside the pick of loot to send back to his master, the Hapsburg King Charles I of Spain, who was also the Holy Roman Emperor Charles V. Cortés consigned the treasure to Alonso de Ávila, one of his most trusted subordinates, who transported it to Havana in Cuba. There, Ávila and his priceless cargo boarded a ship under the command of Antonio de Quiñones, and sailed with two escorts for the transatlantic leg.

In June 1522 the ships made land-fall at the Azores, where Quiñones was killed by one of his officers in a fight over a woman. As the ships sailed on towards Seville they were intercepted by a flotilla of five French corsairs commanded by Jehan Fleury on the large (300 ton) *Dieppe*. The pursuit continued as far as Cape Saint Vincent, where the treasure ship and one of the escorts were captured. In addition to the treasure, Fleury captured Cortés's official report of the conquest of Mexico – and priceless navigation charts for the transatlantic crossing.

Fleury himself never made use of the charts – but he brought them back to the maritime entrepreneur Jehan Ango, recently created Viscount of Dieppe by his royal patron, the Valois King François I. Armed with the charts, Ango financed numerous transatlantic explorations and corsair expeditions that in the aggregate made the loss to Emperor Charles of the Aztec treasure seem trivial. But Fleury's coup had stung, and when he was captured by the Spanish in 1527 the emperor ordered him hanged, even though

Fleury's actions were acts of war authorized by his own king.

Such authorizations, issued in times of war to legitimize private commerce raiding against enemy shipping, traditionally differentiated what a later age called privateering from simple piracy. The same activity was authorized in times of peace by 'Letters of Marque and Reprisal', issued by a competent authority when a merchant was the victim of a foreign predator and was unable to obtain legal redress. In theory peacetime seizures were to obtain a pledge for redress; but they were more often cartes blanches to commit thinly – if at all – justified acts of high seas robbery in which the authorities in question were accessories before and after the fact.

It's as well to bear in mind that Fleury, on behalf of Ango and his royal patron, stole the Emperor's share of the treasure that Cortés looted from the Aztecs, who had extorted it in turn from the peoples they ruthlessly oppressed. It's footling to seek to distinguish among them according to today's selectively fastidious moral criteria.

Commerce raiding cannot be considered piracy if it took place with the approval of a nation's rulers. Although sometimes obliged to make restitution, those who took foreign ships – even when deaths resulted – were never treated as pirates in their own countries. Only those who preyed on their own countrymen risked prosecution, and of them only those without a powerful patron or the means to bribe magistrates might be hanged. That the English state could, if it wished, have taken a much firmer line was shown in 1573 after the ship bearing the Earl of Worcester on an embassy to France was plundered in the Channel. The Royal Navy promptly arrested hundreds of suspects, many from the freebooters' haven maintained on the Isle of Wight by the Vice Admiral of Hampshire, Sir Edward Horsey, although only three men identified as having robbed Worcester were hanged.

In 1499 Gian Giacomo Trivulzio, an Italian soldier of fortune soon to be made a Marshal of France, wrote the epigraph for the coming century in a letter to his employer, King Louis XII of France: 'To carry out war three things are necessary – money, money and yet more money'. François I, cousin to Louis XII and his

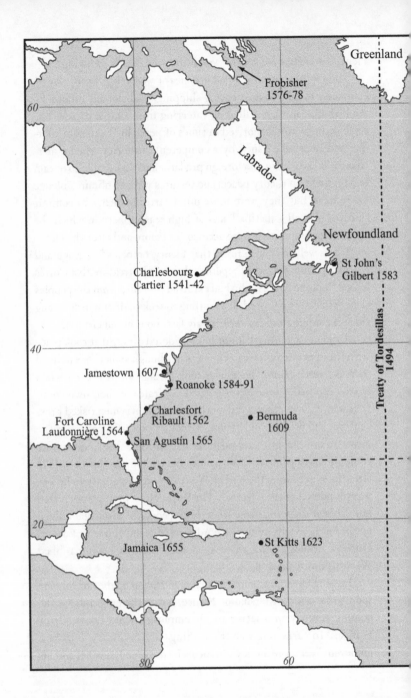

Greenland

Frobisher
1576-78

60

Labrador

Newfoundland

St John's
Gilbert 1583

Charlesbourg
Cartier 1541-42

Treaty of Tordesillas
1494

40

Jamestown 1607

Roanoke 1584-91

Charlesfort
Ribault 1562

Bermuda
1609

Fort Caroline
Laudonnière 1564

San Agustín 1565

20

Jamaica 1655

St Kitts 1623

80

60

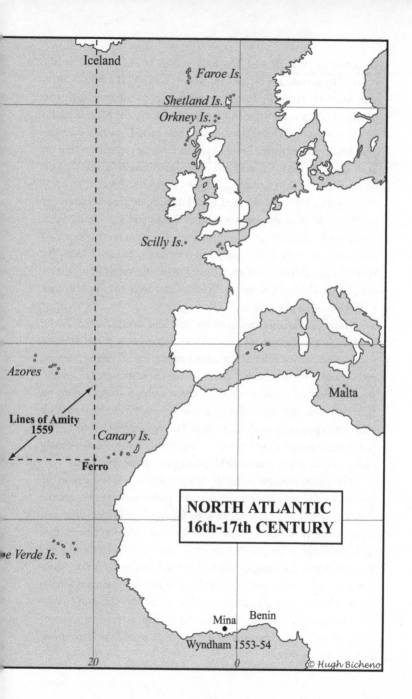

Iceland

Faroe Is.

Shetland Is.

Orkney Is.

Scilly Is.

Azores

**Lines of Amity
1559**

Canary Is.

Ferro

Malta

NORTH ATLANTIC
16th-17th CENTURY

e Verde Is.

Mina   Benin

Wyndham 1553-54

20   0

© Hugh Bicheno

successor in 1515, proved Trivulzio's adage to the point of bankruptcy. To sustain his bitter feud with Charles V, His Most Christian Majesty François I even entered into an alliance with the Muslim Caliph and Ottoman Emperor Suleiman the Magnificent.

François's son Henri II succeeded him in 1547 during a seven-year break in hostilities brought about by financial exhaustion on both sides. In 1551, when Henri judged that he could afford to do so, he renewed the Ottoman alliance and declared war. Charles V abdicated in 1556 and divided the Habsburg empire between his son Philip II of Spain and his brother Ferdinand I in Germany. A year later both the Spanish and the French crowns were compelled to default on their debts and peace was finally made in 1559. By that time, in addition to their financial woes, the Valois were threatened by the domestic religious divisions that were to cripple France until the end of the century.

Almost invariably defeated on land and overmatched in the Mediterranean, France enjoyed military success only in the Atlantic naval arena, which offered the added attraction of taking 'money, money and yet more money' directly from the Hapsburgs to replenish the depleted Valois coffers. An over-emphasis by historians on relatively well-documented state action has caused them to overlook that it was precisely in those areas of France where royal authority was most tenuous that the most – indeed the only – consistently effective military response to Hapsburg hegemony emerged.

The *guerre de course* – literally 'racing war' – was to become the quintessential weapon of a weaker naval power seeking to erode the fighting ability of a stronger rival by forcing it to disperse its maritime assets. In the 16th century, however, no such doctrine existed and commerce raiding by French adventurers cannot be shoehorned into some grand strategic vision. What it did offer the Valois kings was a welcome source of income that did not require royal investment. The principal downside was that it was very difficult to control. Letters of marque were no more than a tenuous form of taxation on a highly profitable activity that would still have prospered without them.

Intriguingly, commerce raiding as an element of state policy developed on both sides of the Channel as the result of seeking to impose a degree of central authority over the totally unregulated activity of descendants of the ancient Britons. The Armorican peninsula got its modern name of Brittany and its distinctive Brythonic language (akin to Welsh and Cornish) from Romano-British legionnaires and settlers displaced from Britain in the 4th and 5th centuries. In the early Middle Ages the peninsula was divided into three kingdoms, two of which – Domnonia and Cornouaille – took their names from the Britons who emigrated from Devon and Cornwall respectively. Brittany, Devon and Cornwall also shared the advantage of distance from the metropolis, which in the case of Brittany permitted an independent existence. Both sides of the Channel also offered numerous convenient harbours and shared a tradition of commerce raiding.

The tradition included the exploits of two remarkable women, Jeanne de Clisson (d. 1359) and the Duchess Jeanne de Montfort (d. 1374), both of whom waged war against French shipping in the Channel in alliance with England. Brittany used to be known in England as Little Britain, hence the name of the London street where the Duchy maintained its embassy. England lost more than a potential ally when Brittany lost its independence in 1488, because at a stroke France gained a strong naval presence in the Channel as well as some of the most experienced sailors in the world. When Henry VII sent troops to Brittany in 1489–92, this was understandably construed by French King Charles VIII as an attempt to recover lost geopolitical ground, and it worried him enough to make political concessions and pay an indemnity. That, however, was all Henry hoped to gain.

The dukes of Brittany profited from commerce raiding, but the danger of the tail wagging the dog was illustrated by the exploits of Jean de Coatanlem, lord of Kéraudy in the Bay of Morlaix, whose fleet of raiders so afflicted the merchants of Bristol that in 1484 they sent three ships to attack his base. He defeated them and then sailed to sack Bristol and take hostages. Duke François II of Brittany, who was anxious for an alliance with England, demanded that Coatanlem return the spoil; but instead he sailed to Portugal, where he became Grand Admiral before his death in 1492. In 1488 Duke François was defeated by French King Charles VIII at Saint-Aubin-du-Cormier and died not long afterwards, succeeded by his daughter Anne. The treaty signed in 1488 allowed Charles to oblige Anne to marry him, leading ultimately to the 1532 Edict of Union between Brittany and France.

The greatest Breton corsair base was the tidal island of Saint-Malo, on the border with Normandy, whose citizens declared an independent republic in 1490–93 and which remained a free port and a pirate haven until 1688. It was the home of René Duguay-Trouin, who ran a corsair fleet of 64 ships and in 1709 was made Lieutenant General of the Naval Armies by King Louis XIV after capturing more than 300 English and allied merchant ships. Saint-Malo also produced the last grand practitioner of the *guerre de course*, Robert Surcouf, who directed a fleet of corsairs against British shipping worldwide during the Revolutionary and Napoleonic period with a success that shone by contrast with the debacles of the French Navy, and who died fabulously wealthy in 1827.

Although the Bretons continued to play an active role in maritime exploration and commerce raiding, they lost their maritime pre-eminence to Normans operating out of Dieppe and the new port of Le Havre de Grâce (originally Franciscopolis) founded by King François I in 1517 on the right bank of the Seine estuary, and to Saintongeais sailing out of La Rochelle. Basque sailors from Bayonne and Saint-Jean-de-Luz were, as always, a law unto themselves, although their interests might coincide with those of the French monarchy from time to time. La Rochelle was already the most important French Atlantic port, but Dieppe owed its new prominence to the friendship between King François and the maritime entrepreneur and banker Jehan Ango, who financed the king's ransom after he was captured at Pavia in 1525.

Ango eventually controlled a formidable fleet of about 70 seagoing ships. When John III of Portugal confiscated one of his ships in

1530, Ango obtained letters of marque and reprisal from François I to embark on a personal naval war against Portugal – and won. In August 1531 John III agreed to pay 60,000 ducats in reparation in addition to the large amounts already looted from Portuguese ships and begged Ango to surrender the letters of marque and call off his corsairs. Nor was this the only way in which Ango acted as though he were a head of state. He also inherited from his father an ambition to found an overseas empire.

Ango *père*, also Jehan, was a very prosperous merchant, whose ships traded with the Ottoman Empire in the Mediterranean as well as with the British Isles and the Netherlands. In 1506 he financed a voyage of exploration beyond Newfoundland by Jehan Denys, followed by two ships in 1508 under Thomas Aubert, possibly accompanied by Giovanni da Verrazzano, seeking the same chimera of a North-West Passage to the Far East that had persuaded Henry VII of England to finance John Cabot's voyage in 1497. Portuguese, Breton and Norman fishermen had preceded them to the Grand Banks, but Denys and Aubert were the first to explore the mouth of the Saint Lawrence River with an eye to settlement. Remarkably these voyages, which in other countries would have involved royal patronage, were undertaken on the sole initiative of the older Ango.

Louis XII died in 1515 and the older Ango not long before, so Jehan Ango *fils* and François I came into their inheritance at about the same time. The younger Ango was fourteen years older than François, but they were both self-consciously 'Renaissance Men', further drawn together by the possibility of following up the older Ango's explorations to win an overseas empire to rival the Spanish. The son financed three further voyages by Verrazzano between 1523 and 1528, on the last of which Verrazzano was killed and eaten by Carib cannibals on the island later named Guadalupe. In 1534 François I commissioned and Ango financed the Malouin Jacques Cartier to explore the Saint Lawrence River, with instructions to find 'islands and lands where it is said there must be great quantities of gold and other riches'. It was a vain hope, and the only American

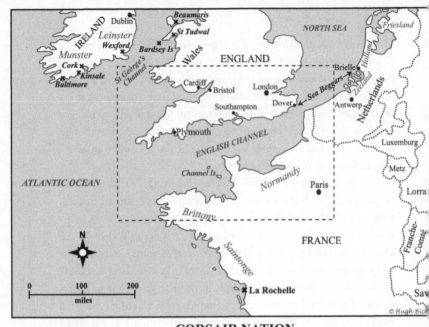

CORSAIR NATION

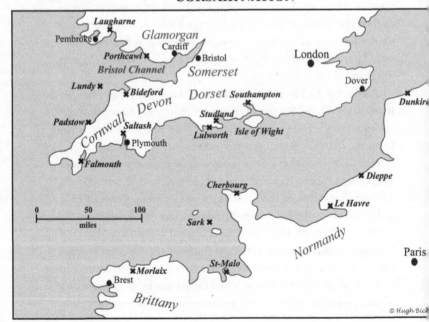

treasure François I ever saw was taken from Spanish ships and settlements, mainly by Ango's corsairs.

Ango lost interest in exploration after the 1534 expedition, but
his king did not. In January 1541 François I commissioned his friend
Jean-François de La Roque de Roberval to found the colony of New
France. The king provided three ships and appointed Cartier as the
navigator, but La Roque de Roberval was required to raise the finance. Cartier went ahead in May 1541 with 500 colonists and the
aim of building a fortified settlement on the Saint Lawrence, while
La Roque de Roberval remained behind to mortgage some of his
properties. He also embarked with the corsair Bidoux de Lartigue
to seize several English merchant ships. He finally sailed with a further 200 colonists in April 1542, crossing paths with Cartier who
was returning with what he believed were gold and diamonds, but
were only iron pyrites and quartz. The settlement endured two appalling winters, malnutrition, disease and Indian attacks until the
wretched survivors were withdrawn in 1543.

Meanwhile Ango continued to develop Dieppe, which became
the third city of France after Paris and Dijon. In most respects he
was a precursor of the Medici Lorenzo the Magnificent of Florence,
with the major difference that Lorenzo took over an already splen-
did city while Ango tried to build his own. Dieppe became a centre
for the arts as well as commerce, and in particular for a renowned
school of cartography; but its most distinctive feature was that it
was a nest of corsairs on a par with the Mediterranean Barbary
ports. In common with Tunis, Tripoli and Algiers, Dieppe drew adventurers from far and wide, and many English sailors discovered
the rewards of transoceanic trading and raiding on ships either
owned by Ango or in which he was an investor.

In 1527 one of Ango's ships manned by Englishmen and commanded by 'John Rut' (most likely the Scots-Norman John
Ross/Jehan Rotz), sailed into the harbour of Santo Domingo, the
capital of the Spanish Indies, claiming to have been blown off course
when seeking the North-West Passage. The settlers were eager to
trade, but the garrison fired a warning shot near the ship, forcing

Rut to withdraw. A few days later he landed a party of armed men at a nearby plantation, still seeking to trade but now also desperate for food. According to the plantation owner, when he virtuously refused to deal with them the men took the supplies they wanted by force and promised to return in greater numbers to exact revenge. The threat of force, whether real or not, was to become the standard excuse by which Spanish settlers and officials justified trading with French and English interlopers.*

It was not the first time the Spanish had fired on an English ship in the West Indies. In 1516 two ships under Sebastian Cabot and Sir Thomas Pert, Vice Admiral of England, sent by Henry VIII to look for possible lands to conquer, were fired on either at Santo Domingo or Puerto Rico even though Spain and England were firm allies at the time. Nothing came of the 1516 expedition, and after Rut the next incursion was by John Phillips in the *Barbara* out of Portsmouth, who sailed to the Indies with a French pilot in 1540. Off Hispaniola's Cape Tiburón Phillips took a ship loaded with sugar and hides, to which he transferred his crew because, he said, his own ship was leaking badly. He put the Spanish crew ashore, sank his old ship, and renamed the new one *Barbara*. The subterfuge did not survive the arrival of a formal claim by the Spanish owners and Phillips was arrested for piracy. No doubt he bought his way out.

The incidents of which records survive were surely just the tip of an iceberg – many more English sailors must have crossed the Channel to pursue more profitable careers than their own country offered, forerunners of the diaspora that was to make enterprising people Britain's greatest export for centuries to come.

Despite their common ancestry with their Breton counterparts, despite having more and better ports, and despite enjoying the backing of powerful local figures and a similar degree of freedom

* Rotz became Henry VIII's royal hydrographer in 1542, presenting him with the sumptuous *Boke of Idrography*, one of the greatest maritime atlases of the Renaissance. On Henry's death he defected to France with detailed maps of England and Scotland. In 1568 Charles IX's cosmographer declared that Rotz had been one of the foremost French navigators.

from central royal authority, the raiders of the English West Country and Wales seldom transcended local, small-ship piracy until well into the reign of Elizabeth. Probably the main reason for this asymmetry with the oceanic corsair culture that flourished across the Channel was that the rich flow of shipping between Spain and the Netherlands passed along the coasts of Saintonge, Brittany and Normandy, whose sailors were encouraged to attack it during France's almost continuous wars with the Hapsburg Empire.

Although England was almost as continuously at war with France and her ally Scotland, the pickings from Franco-Scottish trade were slim. Along the north-eastern coast and around the Irish Sea it was the Scots, often in what were little better than Viking longships, who more frequently preyed on English shipping. In 1533 they captured the *Mary Willoughby*, one of Henry VIII's new, purpose-built warships sent to curb the 'wild Scots' of the Western Isles, which went on to enjoy a successful career as a Scots corsair operating as far south as the Bay of Biscay. Professor Rodger illustrates the tokenism of Scots letters of marque and reprisal with the telling anecdote that in 1561 Captain Patrick Blackader (*sic*) took Portuguese prizes under a letter originally granted in 1476.

Most of the ships coasting the English West Country were sailing to or from English ports, and the sponsors of smuggling and piracy in the West Country were the last survivors of the medieval robber baron tradition rather than a reflection of the more modern, large-scale and capitalist phenomenon that developed across the Channel. Representative of the older tradition were the Killigrews, hereditary captains of Pendennis Castle. This was one of two forts built by Henry VIII to guard the mouth of the Fal Estuary, which together with Carrick Roads forms the most extensive deep-water harbour in Europe. The town of Falmouth grew up around the Killigrew family manor at Arwenack, equidistant from the castle and from the port of Penryn at the far end of the estuary, whose commercial development was permanently stunted by Killigrew-sponsored piracy. Yet during most of Elizabeth's reign the merchants of Penryn had no hope of redress because the Vice Admiral of Cornwall, whose duties included the suppression of piracy, was none other than Sir John Killigrew.

Killigrew's influence at court through close links with the queen's closest councillor Sir William Cecil enabled him to survive a long series of scandalous episodes. These included a charge that his mother led a boarding party to steal two barrels of pieces of eight from a Hanseatic League hulk off Falmouth, killing a commission merchant who tried to thwart her. In 1577 Sir John was found to have purchased stolen French wines from a pirate named Hix, but was allowed to settle the matter by paying the owners. In the winter of 1580–81 a Spanish vessel was dismasted in a storm and driven into Falmouth. According to the Spanish complaint, she was then plundered by Killigrew retainers during the night. The Privy Council ordered Sir John to restore the vessel and goods to their owners, and to render an account to the Council. Yet although he did none of those things, he seems to have suffered no adverse consequences.

In October 1588 he went too far. Again summoned to appear before the Privy Council, this time in the matter of a plundered Danish ship, the Council learned that he 'goeth up and down the country accompanied with divers lewd and disordered persons for his guard, armed with unlawful weapons to withstand those which should go about to apprehend him, contrary to all law and authority'. A warrant for his arrest was issued in March 1589, and in April he was stripped of his office. In July he was reported to be 'fleeing from place to place and cannot be taken, in contempt of all law and government'; yet in 1596 he was still Captain of Pendennis and still involved in piracy.

It was not until 1598 that Sir John Killigrew was finally imprisoned – not for piracy, but for treasonous dealings with Spain. So also Sir John Perrot, with a similar career as Vice Admiral of South Wales (where he maintained a private pirate cove at Laugharne) and as Lord Deputy of Ireland, who died in prison in 1592. Yet Perrot could not have prospered without paying off William and Henry Herbert, Earls of Pembroke, while Sir Henry Sidney, Lord President of Wales, took the same broad view of piracy in North and South

Wales. It's no coincidence that the Elizabethan officials most actively involved in piracy held high office in the counties enjoying the poorest land communications with London.

The last generation of robber barons flourished because, among the powerful and well-connected, any crime short of treason seemed minor during Elizabeth's reign. Thus a blind eye was turned to the nefarious activities of Sir Edward Horsey, Vice Admiral of Hampshire, under whose captaincy the Isle of Wight became a hub for corsairs of all nations, but who also served Elizabeth in a number of military and civil capacities at home and abroad. Likewise the extremely Protestant but no less larcenous Champernowne clan, who virtually owned the Vice Admiralty of Devon during her reign.

On the other side of the Channel, the great Jehan Ango bankrupted himself by financing the huge fleet of 128 ships and galleys sent by François I against England in mid-1545, which embarked some of the 50,000 troops assembled at Havre de Grâce for invasion. French royal ships were few but included two huge floating castles, one of which was lost to a catastrophic fire while the other ran aground and was lost in the Seine estuary. Under Admiral Claude d'Annebault, a landsman, the armada entered the Solent on 16 July and the English fleet of about 80 ships and a few small galleys retreated into Portsmouth.

During the ensuing confrontation the English vice flagship, the large but overloaded carrack *Mary Rose*, sailed out to attack the marauding French galleys. Heeling to starboard with her guns run out, water rushed in through the open gun ports and she sank with most of her crew trapped by the anti-boarding netting extended over the upper decks. The disaster had no effect on the outcome, because disease crippled the French fleet and it sailed away having achieved nothing. Henry VIII's loss became marine archaeology's gain when the remains of *Mary Rose* (most of which had been blown up as a hazard to shipping in the 19th century) were raised 437 years later.

Ango spent his last six years besieged by creditors at his Renaissance palace at Varengeville-sur-Mer, which boasts one of the largest dovecotes ever built — which in turn suggests that his fabled intelligence network must have made extensive use of carrier pigeons. But he had nurtured a generation of corsairs, and the assault on Hapsburg trade and dominions did not slacken with his death. Until well into the second half of the 16th century it was the French alone who were a headache for the Hapsburgs and a constant menace to Spanish settlers in the Indies.

In 1542 French entrepreneurs sent three flotillas totalling 20 ships to attack Spanish trade. One cruised the Azores and the Canary Islands, another lurked off Cape Saint Vincent, and the third, crewed by a mixed force of 300 French and Englishmen, sailed to raid the Spanish Indies, where it sacked the settlements of Cubagua and Santa Marta before holding Cartagena de Indias to ransom in 1543 for the sum of 35,000 pesos. Adding insult to injury the raiders then traded the stolen goods for food with the settlers of Cape La Vela, and looted neighbouring Santa María de los Remedios before sailing to Cuba to try, unsuccessfully, to seize Havana and Santiago, which were newly equipped with forts manned by arquebusiers sent from Spain. Denied similar protection, smaller settlements came to dread the sight of sails, for they were very seldom Spanish.

After the failure of the New France venture, La Roque de Roberval set out to recover his fortune by raiding in the Caribbean, where he sacked Rancherías and Santa Marta in 1543, attacked Cartagena de Indias in 1544, and Baracoa and Havana in 1546. Sadly, and presaging the future career of the Earl of Cumberland, he spent too much equipping and manning these ventures to make them profitable. By 1555, despite an appointment as the Royal Superintendent of Mines by Henri II, he was so deeply in debt that even his ancestral château was threatened with seizure.

In 1537 the Spanish initiated a policy of sailing to and from the Indies only in convoys of about twenty carracks escorted by war galleons. Every year one fleet would sail along the South American coastal settlements picking up mainly pearls, then to Cartagena de Indias to load emeralds and gold before sailing to Havana to rendezvous with another fleet that had sailed to Vera Cruz to load treasure extracted from Mexico. After crossing the Atlantic as far as the Azores, they were further escorted by the Ocean Fleet (*Armada del Mar Océano*), established in 1522 after Fleury's coup, for the perilous passage past Cape Saint Vincent to Cadiz.

The Greater Antilles (Cuba, Hispaniola and Puerto Rico), their gold and native population rapidly exhausted, languished under the new arrangement and turned to growing sugar cane (a crop imported from the Canary Islands) and culling vast herds of wild cattle for their hides. In due course Norman corsairs set up supply bases on Hispaniola to exploit the same resource and acquired the name *boucaniers* from the native term for the grill used to smoke beef over a fire pit.

In 1544 Charles V and François I concluded the Peace of Crépy, in which the Emperor abandoned his ally, Henry VIII of England. This led directly to the French invasion attempt the following year and further undermined the traditional Anglo-Spanish alliance, already strained by Henry's divorce of Charles V's aunt Catherine and his break with Roman Catholicism. But it was also a watershed in the development of oceanic raiding, because the French corsairs simply ignored their king's sincere effort to abide by the terms of the treaty, for which he even sacrificed France's Ottoman alliance. Once again, as Coatanlem had done in Brittany fifty years previously, the tail wagged the dog and uncontrolled maritime hostilities made renewed warfare between the Empire and France almost inevitable.

Added to which, conversion to Calvinism by the Norman and Saintongeais corsairs added the element of religious fanaticism to what was already a ruthless conflict. It's tempting to believe that they became Huguenots because of a deep hatred of the Spanish upholders of Roman Catholic orthodoxy, resulting from the refusal of the Spanish authorities to grant the corsairs the rights of combatants when at war; yet the Bretons and Basques, faced with the same provocation, remained true to the old religion. While the causes may be diffuse the effects were not: the conflict now became as cruel on the French side as it had always been on the Spanish, while laying the basis for common cause between French and English Protestant sailors in the decades to come.

That said, the driving force continued to be the lure of Spanish American treasure, which drew investors to finance the corsairs. In 1550 some Bordeaux merchants without previous experience in the business hired veteran captain Menjouyn de La Cabanne to command the *Sacre* with 80 men on a voyage to raid the Indies. He captured a Portuguese caravel on the way and left it as a floating warehouse off the island of Dominica (home to ferocious Caribs and hence not settled by the Spanish) while he prowled off the port of Santo Domingo, returning periodically to off-load plunder from nine prizes. When the holds of both ships were bursting with loot, he sailed back to his delighted investors. La Cabanne was further graced by fortune because war with Spain broke out again in 1551 and he was given command of a royal ship by King Henri II, who had succeeded his father François I in 1547.

Under Henri II for the first time we see royal ships under orders to raid the Caribbean. The first such expedition was by three large royal ships in 1553 under the command of François Le Clerc, known as *Jambe-de-Bois* (Peg-Leg), with Jacques de Sores and Robert Blondel. They were accompanied by three private venture ships of similar size and four smaller ones, carrying 800 men. The expedition marauded around Puerto Rico and Hispaniola and was hugely profitable, but Le Clerc and Sores returned at daggers drawn and Sores's expedition the following year, with three ships and 300 men, was a private venture. He took Santiago de Cuba in July 1554 and spent three months in possession of the town, coming away with 80,000 pesos.

Returning the following year Sores took Havana, once again intending to remain until the paroled governor could collect the ransom he demanded. Instead the governor gathered forces and counter-attacked by night. Sores and most of his men escaped and regrouped, but the Spanish slaughtered the French sick and wounded. Sores promptly killed 30 Spanish hostages in reprisal, but that was just the start. He then took back the town and sacked and burned it so comprehensively that when another French corsair flotilla arrived three months later they found nothing worth looting and sailed away.

The governor, no doubt seeking to mitigate his own culpability, reported back to Spain that Sores had profaned the churches, and this was to become a leitmotif of Spanish accounts of corsair raids, rather unquestioningly repeated by modern historians. Looting inevitably involved the stripping of gold and silver from churches, but provincial officials had every reason to attribute satanic powers to the men who defeated them (La Roque de Roberval was called 'Roberto Baal'). After all, France was once more allied with the Ottoman Empire, so tales of priests martyred and churches defiled by the Huguenot enemies of the true church were eminently believable.

England's adoption of the *guerre de course* made a strong but false start in the later years of Henry VIII's reign. Letters of marque had been issued against the French in two previous wars, but at the start of the third war (1542–46) Henry proclaimed a blanket authorization that went further than even the French kings in making commerce raiding an act of state policy.

Behind this precedent-setting proclamation there was a backstory of venomous informal warfare between Ango's Dieppe and the traders of Southampton, in particular one called Robert Reneger. Two petitions made to the High Court of Admiralty in the late 1530s describe attacks on Southampton ships in which the French corsairs expressed particular enmity towards Reneger for his attacks on Dieppe shipping. It's not difficult to imagine Ango's fury as the technique he had employed so successfully was turned against him. That anger almost certainly lay behind his ultimately ruinous backing for the 1545 French invasion attempt during which *Mary Rose* sank, which he must have conceived as a massive punitive expedition against Southampton.

There's more than a hint that Henry VIII may have seen Robert Reneger as his Jehan Ango, if not before then certainly after the exploit of 1 March 1545 that gave the Southampton captain a firm claim to being the first of the English sea-dogs. On that day Reneger, in command of two ships and a recently captured French prize, took *San Salvador*, a Spanish carrack coming from the Indies, off Cape Saint Vincent. The cargo of gold, silver, pearls, hides and sugar was valued at 19,315 ducats.

The timing alone is suggestive, coming as it did at the first practical occasion (winter intervening) since Emperor Charles V concluded the Peace of Crépy with King François I on 18 September 1544, leaving his ally Henry VIII to face France alone. Henry, by now morbidly obese and covered in boils, had spent his patrimony and the money from selling off monastic lands – and also incurred heavy debts – to make himself a player on the European stage. His towering fury at being treated as if of no account by Charles V is well documented; yet he was still a Renaissance king who knew better than to lash out in anger. It's entirely possible that Henry informally assured Reneger that he would suffer no adverse consequences should he capture one of the emperor's treasure ships.

Reneger knew better than to put much faith in unwritten royal assurances, so he concocted a plausible cover story for his premeditated action. First he took a French ship in the Spanish port of San Lúcar de Barrameda, making sure the Spanish authorities were fully aware of his illegal act (while prudently remaining offshore) by offering local merchants the return of any of their goods that were in the French ship. Upon his refusal to surrender the illegally taken prize, the authorities seized another of Reneger's ships, docked in the harbour, from which we may assume he had previously removed the crew and anything else of value. He then sailed to Cape Saint Vincent to intercept the incoming treasure ship *San Salvador*, of whose imminent arrival he had learned in San Lúcar.

That, of course, is not the version of events Reneger rushed home to give the Privy Council. According to him, the French prize was taken on the high seas and the seizure of his own ship by the authorities of San Lúcar was an act of unprovoked aggression to which he responded by seizing the first Spanish ship he encountered, which just happened to be a treasure ship. Reneger's tale did have the virtue of connecting all the dots, but it still required willing suspension of disbelief by the Privy Councillors, taking their lead from the king.

The loot was stored in the Tower of London and Charles V's ambassador reported that Reneger swaggered about the court and was treated as a hero. In sum, although there's not and probably never was a documentary 'smoking gun' to prove the king's complicity, strong circumstantial evidence argues that the entire episode was intended to repay Charles V for the insult of Crépy, and as a warning that England's sailors could do him just as much harm as the French.

It was a warning the Emperor did not, in the first instance, choose to heed. On Charles's instructions his heir and regent in Spain, the future Philip II, ordered the goods of all English merchants in Spanish ports seized. This was an order of magnitude more serious than the embargo on English traders Charles himself had recently imposed on the Flemish ports in retaliation for English captains with letters of marque seizing supposedly French goods from Spanish ships in the Channel. It put Charles in the wrong, as it breached the terms of the treaty governing trade between the two countries, reaffirmed as recently as 1543, which forbade reprisals before the sovereign of the injured party had made a formal demand for redress from his fellow monarch.

One of the odd aspects of relations between Renaissance rulers was that while they often sought secretly to undermine each other, even to the point of encouraging assassination, they made a show of paying scrupulous attention to the letter of the law. The Emperor could not hope to prove that Henry was responsible for the illegal act of his subject Reneger; Henry, however, could and did claim the moral high ground when Charles V openly breached the terms of the lately concluded treaty.

Perhaps to bolster Henry's pose of injured innocence, in May 1545 – two months after Reneger's coup – the Privy Council called upon William Hawkins, father of the famous John Hawkins, and his business partner the mayor of Plymouth to account for a recent seizure of goods from a Spanish vessel in the Channel, as promptly reported by the Spanish owner of the goods, who had been aboard at the time. Hawkins and his partner alleged, in fact correctly, that the goods were French and therefore a legitimate prize (the two countries being at war), but for once the Council brushed the justification aside. When it transpired that the goods had been sold while the matter was *sub judice*, William was judged in contempt and sent to prison, though so briefly that we may safely conclude it was all for show. It certainly exercised no deterrent on dozens of English captains led by those, mainly West Countrymen, lately dispossessed of their Spanish goods, who correctly perceived that Henry's benevolence towards Reneger was a nod as good as a wink.

The quid pro quo for official tolerance of their attacks on Spanish shipping was that they should serve in the Navy Royal (the convocation of armed merchantmen that provided the bulk of the kingdom's naval strength in an emergency), as they did to oppose the French invasion fleet in the Solent in mid-1545. Reneger alone contributed *Trinitie Renneger* under his command (200 tons and 120 men), *Jamys Runygare* and *Gallyone Runygare* (each 110 tons and 80 men), *Galigoe Renneger* under his brother John, *Renneger's Pynnes* (pinnace) and the smaller *Shallop Rennerger* and *Marlyne*, the latter probably the French prize taken at San Lúcar de Barrameda. In addition Reneger must have gifted Henry the pinnace *Trego Ronnyger*, which appears in the Anthony Roll, an illustrated catalogue of Royal Navy ships drawn up in 1546.*

Henry's calculation was that unless he were to emulate the Emperor's treaty-breaking act by ordering the seizure of Spanish ships and property in English ports, Charles could not escalate the conflict even though both sides knew that the Spanish ships taken by force at sea and brought into English ports were acts of informal retaliation. Nor would Charles wish to do so, as it would give the French and English an incentive to sink their differences and ally against him. Accordingly the Reneger incident was pursued through legal channels and a face-saving solution was at last agreed in 1548, after the death of Henry VIII, under the Regency Council

* The distinction made here between Navy Royal and Royal Navy is anachronistic but convenient to emphasize the slow transition of the fighting navy from a semi-feudal to a permanent establishment. Tons are 'tons burden' (see Appendix D) unless otherwise specified.

presided over by the Earl of Somerset, Lord Protector of King Edward VI, who was still a minor.

Reneger, who three years after his seizure of the *San Salvador* had still made no restitution, continued to play his hand superbly. First he negotiated the notional value of the seized cargo down to 11,800 ducats – 6,000 to be repaid immediately and 5,800 after eight years under security – in total some 7,500 less than the original claim. The key to this negotiation was the manner in which he caused the Emperor and the merchants whose goods he had taken to doubt each other's good faith. Then he raised part of the down payment by subscription from the English merchants whose goods had been seized in Spain. But the master stroke was to request the return of the gold, silver and pearls that he had given to Henry VIII. It's most unlikely he should have done this without being given assurances that there would be no adverse consequences.

As to why Somerset might wish Reneger to request the return of the treasure, one should never underestimate the subtlety of Renaissance statesmen. It was not at all in Charles V's interest to be obliged to take official cognisance of Henry VIII's role in the incident. When the Council let it be known that the treasure had been quietly returned to Reneger, it was probably an elaborate charade to convince Charles V's ambassador – and perhaps also any members of the Council who did not know better – that Reneger lacked the means to settle the claim in full because the proceeds from his coup had mainly accrued to the late king, and that it would be undiplomatic to pursue the matter further.

The security for the balance was provided by the Council in the form of lead taken from the roofs of the expropriated monasteries, sold to Reneger at a favourable price and on easy terms of credit. Again, this was interpreted by Charles V's ambassador as a bribe – and as further proof that the Council was anxious to cover up Henry VIII's role in the incident. If it was a double bluff, it succeeded admirably. The Emperor decided to take what was on offer and close the books on the incident, judging it best not to embarrass the English court further.

In fact, Reneger was very far from being impoverished. Not only did he still possess his fleet, but he had also purchased the manor of Broughton and other lands from his patron, Henry VIII's Lord Chancellor Thomas Wriothesley (Earl of Southampton from 1547). Although Wriothesley's loss of office and expulsion from the Council in 1548 had nothing to do with the Reneger incident, the Emperor's ambassador was either told or convinced himself that it represented further proof that Edward VI's Council was making a clean break with the past; against which we must set the fact that Somerset's Council appointed Reneger Controller of the Port of Southampton, and that his declared wealth more than doubled between 1545 and 1550.

Whether or not Henry VIII had it in mind to make Reneger his Ango, and whether Edward VI's Council believed that he had, or simply judged it convenient to pretend that they did in their dealings with the Emperor, the fact that the Southampton merchant became conspicuously wealthy as a result of seizing a Spanish treasure ship, and remained so with the apparent connivance not only of Henry VIII but also of the succeeding regime, set a precedent and an example that could not fail to inspire like-minded merchant captains.

Under Edward VI the losing war with the Franco-Scottish alliance limited official toleration of attacks on Imperial shipping (Spanish and Flemish) to the looting of any demonstrably French cargoes they were carrying. Under Mary the most notable Protestant corsairs transferred to ports in Brittany and Normandy, while thanks to her marriage to Philip there was a sufficient resurgence of traditional Anglo-Spanish trade to permit the West Country merchants to make money without resorting to arms. But the stage was fully set for confrontation when the politico-religious tension between the two countries reasserted itself with a vengeance under Elizabeth.

CHAPTER 3
PREREQUISITES

The evolution of naval predation from piracy through semi-official corsair activity to the *guerre de course* conducted as an adjunct to warfare by permanent fighting navies corresponds to the theme of Thomas Hobbes's 1651 political treatise *Leviathan*, which can be summed up as the view that a single shark is greatly to be preferred to a swarm of piranha. To develop the piscine analogy, indiscriminate pirates were piranha and the shark was the Royal Navy, with the more focused corsairs in between the two. A disproportionate amount of Elizabethan historiography has been devoted to the shark, whereas it was the privately financed corsairs that took the war to the queen's enemies and came together to provide the great majority of the Navy Royal in times of national emergency.

In biology a shoal swimming in a coordinated manner is said to be a 'school', exhibiting collective intelligence and purpose, and the development of maritime activity in the 16th century closely resembled an evolution from shoal to school. The state directed and dominated the process in Portugal and Spain, while in France it was mainly a free rider. In England the development of the Royal Navy by Henry VIII and his offspring permitted the state to play a bigger naval role than it did in France. Although the word 'synergy' springs irresistibly to mind, it must be used with caution. The Tudor state was more dependent on the sea-dogs than vice-versa; and while in some respects it facilitated schooling, in others it thwarted the process from a well-founded fear of losing control.

Henry VIII's chief minister Thomas Cromwell tried to make the administration of the state more efficient, but in general the changes that came about were conservative and incremental. One clear exception was the creation late in Henry's reign of the permanent institutions of the Royal Navy, which was innovative and unusually far sighted. What emerged was a deterrent uniquely suited to England's population and financial resources, and that ability to 'punch above their weight' that remains the consoling conceit of her rulers today. Nor did it stop there: once the English state made a major investment in ships it became involved in more general naval activities, which was of benefit to the greater English maritime community. But arguably the more significant outcome lay in the intangible naval 'consciousness raising' among the ruling class.

In his benchmark *Safeguard of the Sea*, Professor Rodger identifies the building of storehouses at Erith and Deptford on the Thames and the creation of a new post (later separated into two) of Comptroller and Keeper of the Storehouses in 1512–14 as the first steps to giving the Royal Navy a permanent establishment. Other new offices were created in 1545, the whole being formalized in April 1546 with individual letters patent issued to the Clerk of the King's Ships (the oldest office, dating from the 14th century), the Comptroller, the Keeper of the Storehouses, the Treasurer of the Admiralty, the Master of Naval Ordnance, the Lieutenant of the Admiralty, and the Surveyor and Rigger of Ships. Although no formal corporate body was created, these patents were the foundation of what became known as the Navy Board, which lasted until 1832.

In June 1550 further letters patent were issued by Edward VI's Privy Council appointing a Surveyor General of Victuals for the King's Ships and Marine Affairs to work under the Lord Admiral or the Navy Board. But the key development came in January 1557, when Queen Mary's Privy Council placed the Navy Board under the Lord Treasurer with the Treasurer of the Navy as his deputy, and decreed an annual £14,000 to support the building and repairing of ships, provisions of all kinds, and the wages and food of seamen. The establishment of regular funding (the 'Ordinary') marked the true birth of the Royal Navy as a permanent department of state and was not the least of several highly positive administrative legacies that Queen Elizabeth inherited from her half-sister.

Barring the vastly superior Venetian establishment, whose bureaucracy reflected the ruling families' wise assumption that each would rob the others blind unless strictly supervised, no other European state enjoyed a comparable naval – or, indeed, military – administration during the 16th century. Characteristically, the English organization was a hybrid that integrated state and private interests. As Rodger explains: 'It was more in the nature of an informal partnership, not of equals but of parties neither of whom could do without the other, and each of whom could exploit the arrangement to his own advantage'. The state had the benefit of officials drawn from the ranks of experienced shipowner-captains and merchants; they, in turn, not only enjoyed the guaranteed profits that have always accrued to defence contractors but could also charter royal ships for private ventures.

Much has been written about royal investment to encourage the development of new industries under Henry VIII, with particular emphasis on gun foundry and ship construction. The state sponsored development of iron gun foundry and the consequent decline in price of the smaller calibre guns (expensive bronze was lighter and remained the preferred metal for larger guns) must have reduced the expense of outfitting an armed merchantman or corsair; but there's no evidence that the cost or availability of naval artillery was ever a limiting factor.

Likewise the Royal Navy's move away from the 'high-charged' carrack, with its tall towers at bow and stern, to the slimmer, faster and more manoeuvrable galleon followed the lead of the private raiders even before the 1578 appointment as Treasurer of John Hawkins, the pioneer of 'armed trading' with the Spanish Indies. Even during Hawkins's tenure, the finest vessel to join the Royal Navy was the flagship *Ark Royal*, built (as the *Ark Ralegh*) as a private venture by Sir Walter Ralegh (his own most consistent spelling), and taken in part repayment of his large outstanding debts to the queen.

The English raiders, in turn, were simply following the lead of their French peers. The most famous of the Elizabethan galleons was the *Pelican*, later renamed the *Golden Hind*, in which Francis Drake completed his 1577–80 circumnavigation and which was put on public display in Deptford for nearly a century afterwards (a replica floats proudly in Southwark to this day). Yet, tellingly, she was modelled on the typical French corsair design.

The signature of the galleon was that it incorporated the forward firing guns of the Mediterranean galley and the heavy stern armament of the carrack. The abolition of the tall bow castle of the carrack (and the effect of the wind on it) pointed to the development of new battle tactics. No longer was the aim to come alongside and board the enemy ship; rather – although it was still essential to gain the weather gage – improved speed and manoeuvrability permitted the galleon to attack on a curving course, firing the bow, side and stern guns sequentially before wearing out of range to reload. An opponent might still be boarded, but the possibility now existed to induce surrender by gunfire alone.

The galleon was deeper than the galley and narrower than the carrack, typically with a waterline length three times its breadth. The fore and main masts were square rigged, while the mizzen and (if fitted) the fourth or bonaventure mast were lateen rigged, with a single spar mounted diagonally. This was a compromise, already seen in the later carracks, of the power before the wind of the square rig and the better performance into the wind and steering qualities of the lateen-rigged caravels. The first portrayal of the characteristic rigging and crescent-shaped superstructure of the galleon is to be found in Gillaume Le Testu's 1555 *Cosmographie Universelle* commissioned by King Henri II, the last and greatest product of the Dieppe school of cartography founded by Jehan Ango.

The English surpassed their French teachers within a generation chiefly because French society turned savagely inward during the 1560s. Even so, in some areas the English never caught up: the French continued to design better ships until steel replaced wood.

French failure at sea relative to the English was never due to technical inferiority; it came about chiefly because of different geopolitical imperatives. England could be threatened only by sea, either directly or through the Scottish bridgehead enjoyed by France from 1295 to 1560. In contrast France had vulnerable land frontiers to defend and faced a greater naval threat in the Mediterranean than on its Atlantic and Channel coasts. The first consideration greatly favoured the emergence of absolutism; the second gave French monarchs no pressing reason to encourage the Atlantic corsairs to school rather than swarm.

The rivalry with France should not be permitted to obscure the fact that both the French and English were far behind the Portuguese and the Spanish, not only in the size of their merchant fleets (measured both in the tonnage of individual ships and in absolute numbers), but also in developing the science of oceanic navigation. The first manual on the subject in English was a translation of a work originally published in Seville in 1551 by Martín Cortés de Albacar. A copy was brought to England by the pioneering maritime explorer and future Queen's Pilot designate Steven Borough. It was translated by Richard Eden, secretary to the queen's chief minister Sir William Cecil, and published in 1561 as *The Arte of Navigation*. Cortés's preamble, addressed to Emperor Charles V, claimed that:

> *I am the first that have brought the art of navigation into a brief
> compendiousness, giving infallible principles and evident
> demonstrations, describing the practice and speculation of the
> same, giving also true rules to Mariners and showing ways to
> Pilots by teaching them the making and use of instruments, to
> know and take the altitude of the Sun, to know the ebbing and
> flowing of the sea, how to order their cards and compasses for
> navigations, giving them instructions of the course of the Sun and
> the motions of the Moon; teaching them furthermore the making
> of Dials both for the day and for the night, so certain that in all
> places they shall show the true hours without default. And have*

> *likewise declared the secret property of the lodestone, with the*
> *manner and causes of the Northeasting and Northwesting*
> *(commonly called the variation of the compass) with also*
> *instruments thereunto belonging.*

The Spanish word *carta* can mean either 'card' or 'chart'. From the context it's evident that Cortés meant 'chart' and the fact that it was translated as 'card' is significant, because the English were slow to adopt charts. Cards were little outline maps portraying relatively short journeys, typically around the British Isles and across the Channel and, as William Bourne bitterly observed in the 1578 edition of his book *A Regiment for the Sea*, even cards were derided and mocked by the majority of English sailing masters, for reasons to which we shall return.

The principal navigational device was a disc marked with the cardinal points aligned with a needle magnetized by rubbing it with a lodestone – a piece of the naturally occurring mineral called magnetite – and rotating around a central point in a compass. The problem Cortés claimed to have solved was the allowance that had to be made for the lodestone pointing to magnetic north, which is at variance with geographic or 'true' north by a number of degrees, depending on where on the Earth's surface the compass reading is taken. In fact his solution was flawed, as argued by Borough himself in his 1581 *Discourse of the Variation of the Compass, or Magnetical Needle*. Cortés was also over-optimistic in claiming to have solved the matter of accurate time-keeping, essential for calculating longitude; mariners would have to wait another two hundred years for a reliable sea-going chronometer.

Nonetheless, until Borough brought back a copy of Cortés's book for Eden to translate there had been no works published in English about the revolution in maritime navigation that had taken place over the preceding century. Perhaps more remarkable is that Borough's visit to the navigation school in Seville took place at the invitation of Queen Mary's long-absent consort, by that time King Philip of Spain, during the last year of the queen's unhappy life.

Thereby hangs a story of the best-laid plans of mice and monarchs.

As Mary's consort, Philip encouraged English maritime explorations seeking North-West and North-East passages to fabled Cathay, in the hope that they would succeed and find sufficient outlets for their energies at the expense of the Portuguese monopoly of trade with the Far East – and stay away from the Spanish American dominions. At a time when England and Spain were allied in war against France, Philip invited Borough to visit Seville; but by the time Borough returned to England, Cortés's book in hand, Mary was dying, and under her successor the old Anglo-Spanish alliance rapidly unravelled. It would not have been the first, nor by any means the last time that a hegemonic power equipped an ally with the means to become a more effective enemy.

But is that what happened? For obvious reasons historians tend to ascribe more importance to published ideas than to those spread by example or word of mouth, and this can be misleading. At the death of Henry VIII few in England knew it was possible to fix a ship's position when far from land by means of celestial observation and mathematical calculation. But by the time the *Arte of Navigation* was published there were many more, thanks to the efforts of the Privy Council that ruled in the name of the young King Edward VI. In 1547 the Council hired away Spain's Pilot-Major Sebastiano Caboto, once and now again Sebastian Cabot, who was not only a highly experienced oceanic navigator but also privy to all the navigational secrets of the Spanish Empire.

Sebastian was the son of John Cabot, who had made the first of England's few contributions to the European voyages of discovery by sailing to North America in the 50-ton caravel *Mathew* in 1497 under Letters Patent from Henry VII. Sebastian followed in his father's wake in 1508–09, leading a private expedition to find the North-West passage, which he believed he had found before being forced to turn back by his crew. In 1516, as we have seen, he and Sir Thomas Pert were warned off by cannon fire at either Puerto Rico or Santo Domingo, and sailed home. Discouraged by lack of support in England, Sebastian sought employment in Spain, where he was soon appointed a member of the Council of the Indies.

With the rank of captain general he led an expedition in 1525 that was supposed to take settlers to the Moluccas, therefore involving what would have been the second circumnavigation of the world. Instead the venture degenerated into a deadly imbroglio over his insistence on exploring and settling the River Plate. On return to Spain in 1530 he was convicted of a number of serious offences, including the death by marooning of his senior officers, but was saved from the more severe consequences by the personal intervention of Charles V.

Cabot's move to England was coincident with the successful diplomatic solution of the Reneger incident, and it would be unwise to assume that he transferred his allegiance when he changed his address. To the contrary, he retained the favour of Philip, the Emperor's regent in Spain, and continued to enjoy the title and emoluments of his Spanish office. It should come as no surprise, therefore, to find that Cabot, while sharing his navigational skills with his new employers, encouraged them to develop trade with the Mediterranean, with Muscovy, with the Guinea coast of Africa – everywhere, in fact, except the American possessions of His Most Catholic Majesty, about which he was as well if not better informed than any other man.

One of the ordinances laid down by Sebastian Cabot after he moved to London was so crucial in moving English mariners from swarm to school that it merits citing in full:

> *Item, that the merchants and other skilful persons in writing shall daily write, describe and put in memory the navigation of each day and night, with the points of observation of the lands, tides, elements, altitude of the sun, course of the moon and the stars, and the same so noted by the Master and Pilot of every ship to be put in writing, the Captain General assembling the masters together once every week ... to put the same into a common ledger, to remain a record for the company: the like order to be kept in*

proportioning of the cards, astrolabes, and other instruments
prepared for the voyage.

The company referred to was the joint stock 'Merchant Adventurers of England for the discovery of lands, territories, isles, dominions and signories [domains] unknown', whose first expedition in 1553 saw two ships icebound and their crews, including expedition leader Sir Hugh Willoughby, frozen to death. Richard Chancellor in the third ship enjoyed better fortune and returned to promote the formation of the Muscovy Company, which was to break the burdensome monopoly on Baltic pitch, hemp, timber and masts previously enjoyed by the Hanseatic League. Not only did this reduce the cost of ship-building and outfitting in England, it also meant that English traders felt more free to compete for trade in the Baltic, because less inhibited by fear of commercial reprisal by the Hansa.

The evident continuity between Sebastian Cabot's influence over English maritime development under Edward VI and the policy later pursued by Philip as Queen Mary's consort strongly suggests that both were part of a subtle long-term strategy. The immediate purpose would have been to defuse the volatile situation created by Henry VIII and Reneger, compounded by Philip's own serious error in retaliating indiscriminately against all English merchants. The longer-term aim would have been to discourage English captains from following the predatory example of the French corsairs.

It would appear, therefore, that this was one of those rare best-laid plans that did *not* 'gang agley'. It bought Charles and Philip twenty precious years, during which the situation in England might well have developed to their advantage, before the growing tension between the two states could no longer be contained. Spain was immeasurably stronger by the time hostilities escalated to open war at sea, and by then no longer had to deal with the state-sponsored French *guerre de course*.

Nor did the skills the English acquired from Sebastian Cabot and Cortés's manual significantly increase their ability to attack Spanish possessions in America. The transatlantic routes to and from the Spanish Indies were, if not signposted, at least clearly indicated by the clockwise currents of the North Atlantic Gyre and the prevailing winds. A stick thrown into the ocean off La Palma, the westernmost of the Canary Islands, will eventually wash up on the Leeward Islands of the Caribbean. The tricky part was sailing along the South American coast and among the islands of the Caribbean, and for that even the skilled navigator Francis Drake continued to use foreign pilots until the day he died.

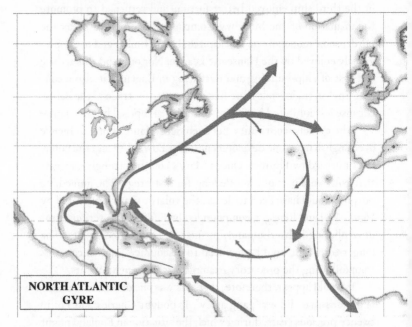

NORTH ATLANTIC
GYRE

By contrast explorers sailing to North America required greater oceanic navigational skills, not least because the Gyre and prevailing winds tended to push them into taking the 'great circle' route long before the algebraic formula to plot it accurately on Mercator's projection was established in the 1590s. It's reasonable to assume that the greater technical skill required to overcome those powerful natural phenomena, as well as the absence of gold, silver and gems, explains why successful colonization of North America got under way only a century after the main islands and the southern coast of the Caribbean were settled, and the Aztec and Inca empires of Mexico and Peru had been conquered.

The man who did the most to equip the English with the necessary skills for these more northerly voyages was John Dee, the Muscovy Company's chief consultant on scientific navigation. Dee was part of a network of brilliant European intellectuals, including Gerard Mercator and several others devoted to the development of scientific navigation. All of them – particularly Dee – owed a major intellectual debt to the Portuguese mathematician Pedro Nunes, who in 1537 first demonstrated that a rhumb line or loxodrome, a line crossing all meridians of longitude at the same angle (or a ship maintaining a constant bearing) would describe a spiral on the earth's surface.

In his 1570 mathematical preface to the first English translation of Euclid's *Elements*, arguably the most influential scientific textbook of all time, Dee argued that mathematics provided the key to all of human arts, among them:

> *The Art of Navigation, demonstrating how by the shortest good way, by the aptest direction, and in the shortest time, a sufficient ship, between any two assigned places may be conducted: and despite all storms and natural disturbances, how to use the best possible means to recover the place first assigned. It is easy to know what need the Master Pilot has of other arts, here before recited: as of hydrography, astronomy, astrology, and horometry, presupposing continually the common base and foundation of all: namely arithmetic and geometry.*

The Master Pilot, Dee continued, could use mathematics to calibrate and if necessary make his own navigational instruments, including 'the proportional and paradoxal compasses (of me invented in 1559 for our two Muscovy Master Pilots, at the request of the Company)', and should 'be able on globe, or plane to describe the paradoxal compass and duly to use the same to all manner of purposes, whereto it was invented'. Among Dee's disciples were the explorers Francis Drake, John Davis and Walter Ralegh, the compiler and popularizer of English voyages Richard Hakluyt, and the astronomer-mathematicians Thomas Digges and Thomas Harriot, the last of whom was so talented that Ralegh hired him as his personal mathematics tutor immediately upon graduation from Oxford.

Thus we know that Drake, who had served a long and varied apprenticeship at sea, was also among the very few trained scientific navigators in England, a point underlined in his famous speech to the members of his expedition at San Julián in June 1578 when he asked those who wanted to turn back how they thought they could get home without him. But Thomas Cavendish is the only famous Elizabethan sea captain whose maritime career was entirely enabled by scientific navigation skills.

In the early 1580s Cavendish received instruction in the theory of navigation from Thomas Harriot in Ralegh's house, but he had never even been to sea before 1585 when he bought a small ship to join Ralegh's 1585 expedition to Virginia – also his tutor Harriot's first time at sea. Yet the following year Cavendish built his own ship and set out to sail around the world, which he accomplished nine months faster – and having acquired greater loot – than Drake in his circumnavigation of 1577–80. Alas for his historical standing the epic of the Spanish Armada had intervened just weeks before his return, and Cavendish enjoyed little of the adulation showered on his predecessor.

Drake delivered the comprehensive and illustrated notes he made of his circumnavigation to the queen, after which they disappeared. Although some of his charts and technical information were disseminated, the suppression of Drake's log meant that few Englishmen tried, and only Cavendish succeeded, in emulating his achievement. The question is whether Cavendish's confidence in scientific navigation set him apart – and by a process of deduction we may conclude that it was. There was no shortage of bold English captains, the dangers involved in the circumnavigations were not much greater than in any long voyage and the potential rewards were mouth-watering. It was also open to others to hire men who had sailed with Drake, as Cavendish did. It follows that the barrier to a full-scale English assault on the Spanish in the Pacific must have been a generalized lack of the necessary navigational skills to make proper use of the many charts available.

For clarity's sake it's best to differentiate between navigation and pilotage. Pilotage was a skill or craft, learned through practical experience of coastal sailing, and involved the systematic observation of landmarks to provide positional fixes, coupled with offshore soundings to establish the depth and the consistency of the sea bed as revealed by lines attached to lead weights with their tips coated in tallow. A crucial component of the pilot's art was knowledge of tides and of shoals within river estuaries. Pilotage was mainly acquired through apprenticeship, although for the literate there were also written sketches and observations collected in pocket books – known as rutters – that might be passed on from master to apprentice.

The art became freely transferable only with the advent of printing. The first *portolano* was printed in Venice in 1490 and once again the English lagged far behind. Their first printed rutter was a 1528 translation of *Le routier de la mer*, originally printed at Rouen in 1502, which gave the sailing directions for the western Atlantic coast down to Cadiz. A rutter of the coasts of the British Isles was not added to the meagre list until 1541, and even then was based on a Scots manuscript from the early 15th century. English sailing masters, clearly, were averse to sharing their acquired knowledge, which underlines the significance of Sebastian Cabot's above-cited ordinance.

The oldest surviving rutter of native English origin is a manuscript roll (6 inches wide by nearly 3.5 feet long/ 15 by 105 centimetres) dating from 1539, which has a roughly sketched companion pilot's chart. It was commissioned by Henry VIII because the court could find no reliable sailing directions for the Texel channel and the Zuider Zee to reach Harderwiijk, whence he wished the royal fleet to bring his fourth bride, the famously dowdy Anne of Cleves. The reason these documents survive seems to be because they were not used, as Anne crossed from Calais to Dover. It's highly unlikely that there were no pre-existing English rutters for the dangerous waters off the Frisian Islands and in the Zuider Zee, leading one to assume that their owners did not wish to share them even with their king.

Possibly as a result of this costiveness, freely transferable scientific navigation overtook traditional pilotage to such an extent that in his old age Sir William Monson (d. 1643) lamented that 'since I [first] served in the Narrow Seas I find so great a difference between the masters of that time and this that I may compare it to an ancient art, that in the long continuance of time has been forgotten and lost for want of use'. Intriguingly, he contrasted the 'ignorantly adventurous' sailing masters of his youth with their 'providently cautious' successors, which is not what one would expect. It seems that improved navigational skills did not necessarily act to liberate the adventurous, but may rather have inhibited them through a better understanding of the difficulties involved.

The same knowledge-hoarding tendency may explain why it took so long for what is best described as 'armed trade' with Spanish America to gather momentum. At the death of Henry VIII, few in England seem to have been aware of the epochal geographical discoveries made by explorers sponsored by the Portuguese and Spanish courts since the latter decades of the preceding century. The first book in English to describe the new geography was taken from Sebastian Munster's 1544 *Cosmographia*, translated from the Latin by Richard Eden and published in 1553. This was followed by the 1555 edited translation from the Latin, again by Eden, of the great compilation of voyages by the Italian-born historian Pedro Mártir de Anglería. Originally published in Spain under the general title of *Decades* between 1511 and Pedro Mártir's death in 1525, they were printed together for the first time in 1530, and included narratives of the first English voyages by John and Sebastian Cabot.

The sub-title of Eden's borrowing from *Cosmographia* urged the 'diligent reader' to 'see the good success and reward of noble and honest enterprises, by which not only worldly riches are obtained but also God is glorified and the Christian faith enlarged'. Lest the diligent reader should fail to get the message, Eden wrote a long preface to the *Decades* in which he expatiated on the profitability of sea exploration. He selected from Pedro Mártir's narratives both to excite the imagination with florid descriptions of the newly discovered lands and also to inform by including practical observations by such as Amerigo Vespucci about astral navigation in the southern hemisphere, where the Southern Cross constellation replaced the Pole Star as the most important point of reference.

It bears repeating that from 1552 Eden was secretary to Sir William Cecil (Lord Burghley from January 1572), who was Secretary of State in 1550–53 under Edward VI and 1558–72 under Elizabeth, then Lord High Treasurer from 1572 until his death in 1598, and during his last eight years also Lord Chancellor and Lord Privy Seal. Like any successful courtier Cecil was a master of what has been crudely reified as 'nudge theory' by the American political economist Richard Thaler. In 1559 Spanish Ambassador de Feria reported that Elizabeth 'must have been thoroughly schooled in the manner in which her father conducted his affairs. She is determined to be governed by no one'. Guided, however, she was – very tactfully – by Cecil. It's in keeping with what we know of Cecil that Eden should have been acting on his instructions in producing the books; accordingly we may take them as an indication of the subtle role of state policy in 'schooling' the English mariners.*

Cecil knew that the expansive maritime mentality he was seeking to cultivate would eventually come into conflict with Spain and Portugal, because in 1481 and 1493 Popes Sixtus IV and Alexander VI had issued bulls declaring the world divided between the two Iberian monarchies. Spain and Portugal in turn negotiated the 1494 Treaty of Tordesillas, which agreed a pole-to-pole dividing line running 370 leagues (1,110 nautical miles) west of the Cape Verde

* In a 1576 book dedicated to Burghley, Thomas Digges was the first English scholar to embrace the heliocentric explanation of the solar system proposed by Copernicus and called for a mathematical reformation of navigation.

Islands, with Spain claiming all lands to the west and Portugal all lands to the east. The Spanish further, tacitly, limited their claim in the Americas to the lands south of a line of latitude through the Canary Islands, hence their eagerness that the English – then an ally – should explore and settle north of it.

Cecil did not accept this division and bluntly told the Spanish ambassador in 1561 that the Pope had no authority to divide up the world. Five years later, on behalf of the Privy Council, he explicitly rejected a Spanish note stating that trade with 'West Indies Continent and Islands' was forbidden without licence from the King of Spain, which both parties knew would not be forthcoming. It's incorrect, therefore, to see Cecil as a 'dove' at Queen Elizabeth's court in the matter of conflict with Spain: strategically, he was as much a 'hawk' as anyone else. But he was also chief minister to an extremely indecisive monarch, and loyally worked to keep her options open as long as possible.

In recognition that the uncontrollable corsair phenomenon had contributed to the breakdown of previous treaties between the two kingdoms, the negotiators of the 1559 Peace of Cateau-Cambrésis between Philip II of Spain and Henri II of France – who was killed in a jousting match staged to celebrate the peace – informally agreed on 'lines of amity' beyond which the nefarious activities of their subjects should not compromise the peace. They were the lines of longitude and latitude that passed through Ferro, the westernmost of the Canary Islands. East and north of the lines the treaty was binding on the signatories; west and south of them it was up to Spain to enforce her monopoly.

A separate agreement between Henri II and Elizabeth I simply confirmed the English loss of Calais, to which the queen was not resigned and which led to further hostilities in 1562–63. It was only after that last spasm of traditional cross-Channel warfare that the concept of 'no peace beyond the lines' became significant for the English.

The final prerequisite for the sea-dog phenomenon was that the traditional English cloth trade was in decline and the Spanish denied

English traders new outlets in the American colonies, which were very far from adequately served by the annual *flotas*. Also, taking a lead from their highly sectarian king, the Spanish authorities became increasingly hostile towards well-established English traders in the Atlantic islands and in Spain itself simply because they were Protestants – or, if still Catholic, because they refused to denounce their own English monarch. Spanish producers and merchants protested in vain that they were the greater losers – the Inquisition did not care.

This self-damaging intolerance was a natural outcome of the brutal stupidity that had led the Spanish monarchs to expel (to the enormous benefit of the Ottoman Empire) the Jews who handled much of their commerce, which metastasized under Philip II into the expulsion even of those Muslims and Jews who had embraced Christianity, and who made up the majority of Spain's artisan class. Philip not only wanted a window into men's hearts and secret thoughts – he and his religious minions anticipated the totalitarian communist tyrannies of the 20th century by affirming that they were uniquely equipped to uncover even the heretical thoughts that men might *unknowingly* harbour.

Added to which was the grating arrogance noted by the Venetian ambassador to Philip's court in 1581: 'The only noteworthy thing about them is a certain loftiness and dignity which in Italy we call 'Spanish composure' and which makes all foreigners hate them. They let it be known that not only is there no other people which bears comparison with them, but that everyone should be grateful to be ruled by them'. Typically, the *Pax Hispanica* imposed on Italy after the 1559 Peace of Cateau-Cambrésis generated resentment even among the local rulers who benefited from it, as noted by the Spanish Governor of Milan in a 1570 dispatch to Philip II:

> *In Italy there is no state, no power, no prince, nor man who owns a castle nor one who does not, who desires the maintenance and increase of Your Majesty's states; and all are past masters in giving good words and pretending the contrary. I do not know*

> *whether there is any one in the whole world who is subject to the*
> *Spanish nation and empire and who is devoted to them, but does*
> *not rather abhor their name. And this is much more the case in*
> *Italy than in any other part of the world.*

Finally, Philip's principal attention throughout most of his reign was focused on mainland Europe and the Mediterranean. Although in retrospect we can see that winds and currents dictated a strategic stalemate in the Mediterranean, Philip could not have been expected to perceive it when the Muslim tide that once swept over much of Iberia had ebbed only as far as the North African coast. As a result he took too long to appreciate that England, the small, backward kingdom he had thought to acquire by marriage, might mount a serious challenge to his domination of the Atlantic.

Philip believed he was God's agent in opposing the spread of Protestantism as well as Islam. 'May God give you life and health', he wrote to one of his courtiers, 'because you are involved in His service and in mine, which is the same thing'. His more cosmopolitan Burgundian father had agreed to tolerate Protestantism in return for peace in Germany. Philip, born and raised in Spain, could not do the same in the Netherlands or in his dealings with England because he identified fully with the crusading ethos of his Spanish kingdom, forged in the long centuries of the Reconquest.

Both the Ottoman and the Spanish Hapsburg Empires began their long declines during the 16th century because, under Suleiman the Magnificent and Philip II, they became repressive theocracies. The hostility of their respective religious establishments towards social change as well as to the emerging scientific understanding of the world and the cosmos ultimately doomed their societies to stagnation. However, 'ultimately' is seldom of concern to rulers overwhelmed by daily calls on their attention.

Although there was no causal relationship between the new knowledge and Protestantism, once people begin to question established authority in one sphere, they will do so across the board. God's agency apart, Philip also threw all the resources of his poorly integrated empire into the battle against change because if he had not done so the empire would have fallen apart from its own internal contradictions, as he acknowledged in 1590:

> *Everybody knows about the great, continuous and unavoidable expenses that I have incurred for many years to defend our holy Catholic faith and to conserve my kingdom and lordships, and how that they have grown immensely through the war with England and the developments in France; but I have not been able to avoid them, both because I have a specific obligation to God and the world to act, and also because if the heretics were to prevail (which I hope God will not allow) it might open the door to worse damages and dangers, and to war at home.*

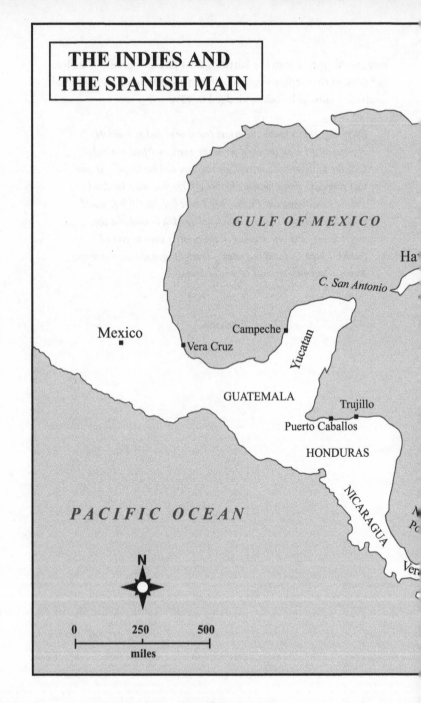

THE INDIES AND THE SPANISH MAIN

GULF OF MEXICO

Ha

C. San Antonio

Mexico

Campeche

Vera Cruz

Yucatan

GUATEMALA

Trujillo

Puerto Caballos

HONDURAS

PACIFIC OCEAN

NICARAGUA

N
Po

Ver

N

0   250   500
miles

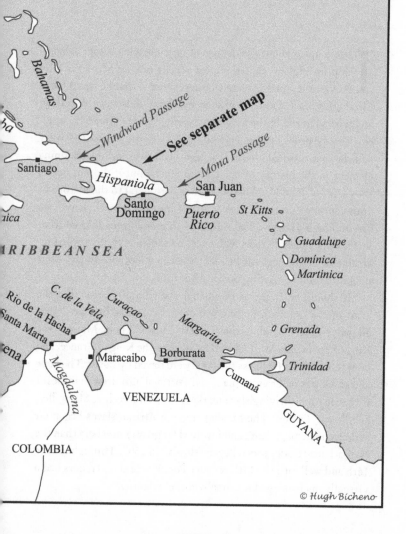

Bermuda

Caroline
Augustín

ATLANTIC OCEAN

Bahamas

Windward Passage

See separate map

Mona Passage

Santiago

Hispaniola

San Juan

Santo
Domingo

*Puerto
Rico*

St Kitts

...ica

...a

CARIBBEAN SEA

Guadalupe

Dominica

Martinica

C. de la Vela

Curaçao

Rio de la Hacha

Santa Marta

Margarita

Grenada

...ena

Magdalena

Maracaibo

Borburata

Cumaná

Trinidad

VENEZUELA

GUYANA

COLOMBIA

© *Hugh Bicheno*

CHAPTER 4
JOHN HAWKINS

It says much about the demise of once-thriving Tudor scholarship in England that the most recent biography of Sir John Hawkins is a prissy tome whose premise is that he was 'Queen Elizabeth's Slave Trader', written by Harry Kelsey, an American archivist so mired in the modern obsessions of the American academy that he projects them back to the 16th century. African slavery and the institutional racism that replaced it was indeed a defining element in the history of the United States; but it did not define the career of John Hawkins and it was peripheral to the history of 16th-century Europe. In the context of his time it would have been astounding if Hawkins had refrained on moral grounds from what was always a brutal trade. Sadly, had he shown such principled restraint he might perhaps be mentioned in a footnote today – but nobody would be writing books about him.

It should be borne in mind that the administration and the army of the Ottoman Empire was entirely manned by slaves, that all galley fleets including those of His Most Catholic Majesty the King of Spain, His Most Christian Majesty the King of France, and even those of His Holiness the Pope were rowed by slaves. The Pope and the kings of France, Spain and Portugal also drew significant revenues from thriving slave markets in Civitavecchia, Marseilles, Seville and Lisbon. The Muslim trade in African slaves began far earlier, ended much later, and involved far greater numbers than the transatlantic trade, which began (slowly) in 1502. Throughout the 16th and well into the 17th century Portuguese slave traders had a virtually unchallenged monopoly in the Atlantic.

It's therefore grotesque to suggest that Hawkins initiated the transatlantic slave trade. Nor was he by any means the first English merchant to blur the line between trade and plunder in defying the Iberian trade monopolies. Sailing out of Portsmouth on behalf of a London syndicate with two leased royal ships and the syndicate's 150-ton *Lion*, the ex-Barbary pirate Thomas Wyndham attacked Portuguese ships and settlements along the West African coast in 1553–54. Ignoring the advice of his Portuguese pilot he stayed too long, contracting malaria and learning at the cost of his own life – and that of three-quarters of his 160 crew – to 'beware, beware the Bight of the Benin, for few come out though many go in'.

John Lok of London followed in 1554–55 with less violence and much lower mortality – although he abandoned the young Martin Frobisher, sent ashore as a hostage during negotiations with a local governor, who spent many months in Portuguese captivity. This time the formal protest by John III of Portugal to Queen Mary was supported by her husband Philip II of Spain. Mary formally prohibited the Guinea trade and even tried to enforce the ban, but William Towerson of Plymouth ignored it in 1555–56 and again in 1556–57 with a flotilla of three ships led by his own 120-ton *Tiger*. During the second voyage he encountered a French ship under Denis Blondel (presumably related to the Robert Blondel who raided the Caribbean with François Le Clerc and Jacques de Sores in 1553) and they allied to fight a Portuguese fleet and to attack the native town (Dondou) protected by São Jorge da Mina, the principal Portuguese fortified trading post on the Guinea coast.

According to his own account, Towerson was invited by a native chief he called King Abaan to establish an English fort in his territory to rival Mina. In the spirit of 'If you can't beat 'em, join 'em', Treasurer of the Navy Benjamin Gonson leased two royal ships – the 300-ton carrack *Minion* and the *Christopher* – to Towerson for his last voyage in January 1558, during which he fought not only Portuguese but French ships along the Guinea coast. Although his crew refused to sail into the lethal Bight of Benin, so many became disabled by disease that he had to abandon his own *Tiger*, while the

Christopher and her depleted crew were lost at sea.* When *Minion* returned with only 12 men fit to work in October 1558, it was the end of Towerson's involvement in the Guinea trade.

But not the crown's. From the beginning of her reign Queen Elizabeth and her chief minister Sir William Cecil took a robust line, rejecting Portuguese protests with the sharp rejoinder that if the Portuguese monarchy was sovereign over the Guinea coast, then it should forbid its subjects to trade with the English. They also initiated a new policy of using royal ships for commercial ventures. Previously the crown had leased them out for a fixed amount and a bond against damage or loss, but starting in mid-1561 they were loaned as an investment against a percentage of the profits. *Minion* was loaned several times to syndicates for armed trade with Guinea, the first time in an abortive attempt to set up an English fort in King Abaan's territory. Each time these expeditions returned with crews depleted by disease and with the scars of gun battles against Portuguese ships – but all returned with profitable cargoes of gold, ivory and savoury peppers.

Slaves were another matter, as at this time Spain was practically the sole buyer, not only fixing the price but also requiring that slaves destined for Spanish America should be registered, and a 20 percent royal duty paid on them at the *Casa de Contratación* in Seville, which involved long delays sailing against wind and current with what was a very perishable cargo. Portuguese traders chafed under these irksome restrictions, which opened the door to third-party smugglers. Hawkins was the first English merchant known to have sailed the triangular trade route to Guinea and the Caribbean.

But the greater novelty was that while he could not have collected slaves from West Africa or sold them in America without the secret connivance of local officials, with each voyage he became more insistent on *formal* recognition of his right to trade in flagrant violation of Portuguese and Spanish ordinances whose validity, as

* A 400-ton Bremen hulk of that name was acquired for the Royal Navy in 1545 and sold in 1555, and another of 800 tons was bought from London merchants in 1560, but was not used and last mentioned in 1563. This cannot have been either.

we have seen, was rejected by the English court. He was not content to play the smuggler and was trying to force open a new market for *legal* trade. Since such a course of action involved higher risks with less certainty of personal reward, the assumption must be that he acted from the start with the encouragement of Sir William Cecil.

Was Cecil seeking to nurture an English Ango? The combination of limited royal revenues and England's military–strategic situation called for a self-financing fleet of large ships, such as would have been required for transatlantic trade. From Henry VIII's time the crown had been paying a bounty of 5 shillings for every ton over 100 to encourage ship owners to build bigger ships, conditional upon their not being sold abroad so that they could serve in the Navy Royal when convoked – but finding a profitable use for them could be a problem.

In 1581 the first Levant Company had 14 ships between 200 and 350 tons, but complained that Venetian and Ottoman demands were squeezing their profits and that the ships were too big to be employed in other commercial activities. Perhaps – although one suspects special pleading. But ships of that size were, of course, ideal for the transatlantic trade. It's consistent with Cecil's efforts to create a cadre of oceanic navigators that he should always have had in mind the military-strategic as well as the fiscal advantages of opening up the Spanish American market to English trade.

Added to which, John Hawkins does not fit the sea-dog profile. He was not a hungry new man but a well-established and prosperous merchant who enjoyed strong – and legal – commercial connections with the Spanish Canary Islands. Why would he put that at risk by embarking on a mad-cap adventure with a strong possibility of being killed in battle or executed by the authorities on both sides of the Atlantic? He was a mature man of 31 when he made his first voyage to Spanish America and his financial backers included not only his future father-in-law, Treasurer of the Navy Benjamin Gonson, but also the Surveyor of the Navy Sir William Wynter and a syndicate of London merchants. When, prior to Hawkins's second voyage, the Spanish ambassador to the Court of

Saint James expressed concern that he might contemplate piracy, Cecil replied that Hawkins was not only an honest man but rich as well, and that all he wished to do was trade. As far as Philip II was concerned there was no difference – which was to prove a serious error of judgement.

France was England's natural enemy, as proved by the centuries of war between the two nations, and Philip might have cemented the old alliance by allowing English traders regulated access to his American dominions. After all, San Lúcar de Barrameda, the principal Spanish port for English trade, was at the mouth of the Guadalquivir River leading to Seville and the *Casa de Contratación*, which by royal decree controlled all trade with America. It would have been the thin end of a wedge, but preferable to making an enemy of a nation that could attack his vital seaborne communications with the Netherlands, where he was fighting to retain control of his second most important revenue source after Castile.* Granting the English a regulated permit to trade with the American market would, at the very least, have bought him some time, and would also have helped ensure good behaviour on the part of English traders.

But Philip could not do that because of the religious question, which led his secular and religious officials to persecute English traders in Spain even though Anglo-Spanish trade had always been complementary, with the balance favourable to Spain. Meanwhile the war in Flanders had interrupted trade with Antwerp, historically the principal outlet for English exports. Geostrategically it did not make sense to deny the English compensation in America, especially since they would supply the colonies with goods Spain herself could not provide. As Ambassador Guzmán de Silva reminded his master, the English had good ships and would seek profits regardless.

In sum, absent the matter of religion, Philip had little to lose and much to gain by accommodating the English. Cecil, who had

* Castile was all of Spain except Aragon and Navarre. Crushingly taxed Sicily also produced more royal revenues than the Indies monopoly, which accounted for about one-fifth of all royal revenues during Philip II's reign.

trimmed his sails to the abruptly shifting religious wind under four monarchs, may have had difficulty believing that Philip could be adamant in a policy so evidently harmful to his own interest. Much of the indecision attributed to Elizabeth with regard to unleashing the sea-dogs can as easily be interpreted as the graduated armed diplomacy of her Secretary of State, designed to make Philip be reasonable and see things his way.

In order to achieve a clearer picture of the times, researchers have to raise their eyes from the archives to encompass the wider context. The most that any document can reveal is what the author wished to achieve by writing it, and to accept it at face value is naive. Beyond that general consideration, prudent rulers did not (and do not) give written or even face-to-face oral instructions to commit illegal acts. Instead they let those called upon to perform them know indirectly that if those acts are successful – and if the perpetrators are discreet – they may expect a substantial reward; and that if unsuccessful but still discreet, they will be sheltered as far as possible from adverse consequences. The modern term for the technique is 'deniability' and the Reneger incident illustrates how it may have been used as a means of informal communication.

If, instead of blithely believing that Hawkins undertook his slave-trading ventures as a free agent suicidally seeking to force the hand of his own government as well as the Spanish, we assume instead that he wished to survive and prosper in the service of the most powerful man in England, then his actions and the rest of his career require no further explanation. With regard to his later negotiations to lead a fleet in the service of Spain, this was to include some royal ships: how was he going to do that without official support? In addition, Hawkins would have been a fool to believe that he could have secret dealings with the heavily surveilled and spied-upon Spanish ambassador in London. Hawkins was worldly wise and intelligent, so it follows that he acted at all times with Cecil's knowledge and consent.

In October 1562 Hawkins sailed from Plymouth on *Saloman* (140 tons), accompanied by *Jonas* (40 tons) and *Swallow* (30 tons).

His first stop was Tenerife in the Canary Islands where his local partners, the Ponte family, supplied the ships with food and water – and also with the pilot Juan Martínez, who would guide them to the Portuguese outposts on the West African coast and then across the Atlantic. At Sierra Leone, in his own words, Hawkins 'got into his possession, partly by the sword and partly by other means, to the number of 300 negroes at the least, besides other merchandise'. What were those 'other means'? Portuguese traders alleged that he captured five or six of their caravels *on the high seas*, with cargoes of cloves, wax and ivory as well as 400 slaves.

Yet some, if not all of these ships sailed with him across the Atlantic, and could not have done so with English crews – Hawkins sailed with less than 100 men because overcrowding generated the diseases that were the greatest danger on long voyages. Another interesting question is what happened to the trade goods he loaded in Plymouth. He sent the *Swallow* home, with his cousin Francis Drake aboard, loaded with the other allegedly looted goods, and there could not have been room for many slaves as well as English trade goods on the remaining two ships. If Hawkins was wise enough to avoid overcrowding with regard to his crew, who sailed for a share of the profits and cost him only food and drink, he would surely have taken even greater care not to overcrowd the slaves, who represented a significant investment and could be sold for a handsome profit.

It's clear that most if not all of the trade goods were exchanged for the merchandise shipped home on the *Swallow*, and that most of the slaves remained on board the caravels, which were sailed by their own crews under their own captains. 'Partly by the sword', in this scenario, would have been a mainly-for-show threat of violence to provide the Portuguese with an alibi for not only evading the Spanish royal tax but also saving the greater loss of time and wastage involved in sailing against wind and current to Seville. It follows that the local officials and traders in Sierra Leone were willing accomplices and that the deal was fixed in advance, probably by Pedro de Ponte.

And so it continued. In April 1563 the Anglo-Portuguese flotilla arrived on the northern coast of Hispaniola and did brisk trade with the Spanish settlers in Puerto de Plata, Monte Christi and Isabela. When news of this reached officials in Santo Domingo, the capital of the Spanish Indies, they sent a troop of cavalry under Juan Bernáldez. His report claimed that he seized two of the interlopers and that after an armed skirmish Hawkins requested a parlay, at which point Bernáldez demanded that Hawkins pay the licence fee and duty on the slaves he had sold. Hawkins made a counter-offer of a hundred slaves in lieu of the fee and duty and for the return of his two men, in return for permission to sell the remainder. When this was rejected Hawkins sweetened the pot with one of the caravels, at which point the stalwart Bernáldez reasoned that he had done all he could and issued a licence which, as he emphasized in his report, was valueless since he lacked the authority to issue it.

And the three bears. Clearly a hundred slaves was the previously agreed bribe and Bernáldez's role was to be seen by the local settlers to be trying to uphold the sovereign rights of Spain. Bernáldez is a name very much associated with the Canary Islands, and Canarians were very prominent in the settlement of the Indies; so the most likely explanation is that the whole thing was arranged in advance by Hawkins's partners in Tenerife. Further evidence of extensive collusion came when Hawkins loaded part of the hides and sugar paid in exchange for the slaves onto two ships in Isabela harbour owned by the Martínez family* of Seville, and sent one to Lisbon and the other to Seville under Thomas Hampton, who had left Plymouth as captain of the *Swallow* but remained with Hawkins when she was sent back from Sierra Leone. The remaining Portuguese caravels also parted company at this point.

Alas, one of the officials in Santo Domingo, motivated by hatred of Bernáldez, denounced the deal to the *Casa de Contratación*, which alerted the authorities in Lisbon. The two ships were seized on arrival but, strangely, Thomas Hampton was not arrested and soon

---

* The same surname as his pilot – it is, however, as common as 'Smith', and Fernández as 'Jones'.

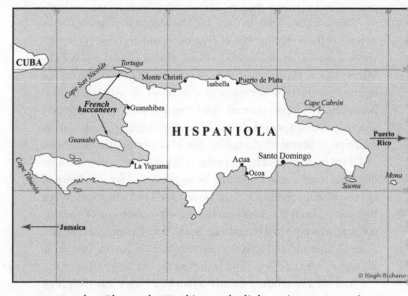

returned to Plymouth. Hawkins made diplomatic representations to recover the (inflated) value of the confiscated cargoes, claiming that he had only arrived at Hispaniola because blown off course; but that tale was at least as old as Rut/Rotz in 1527 and was a gesture to give cover to his Iberian accomplices. The ships would have been returned to the Martínez family because they had allegedly been taken by force and the cargoes probably found their way to the intended recipients' prior payment of larger than usual bribes to the customs officials. One wonders what happened to the whistle-blower in Santo Domingo.

During his return voyage Hawkins stopped at Tenerife to share profits and confer with his partners. A little local difficulty when officials confiscated some of Hawkins's goods on instructions from the mainland was resolved when the merchandise was entrusted to Pedro de Ponte for safe keeping. He returned it to Hawkins when next they met – but he must have been appalled by the circumstances: while the first voyage had involved Hawkins's own small ships that traded regularly with the Canary Islands, he returned with a flotilla including one of the largest warships in the Royal

Navy. If the aim had simply been illicit profit, it was a crass blunder to attempt it again in such a big ship, flying royal banners to boot. Local officials would be compelled to send urgent dispatches to Madrid reporting the presence of such a force, and the possibility of obtaining bribed cooperation would have been greatly reduced.

Although he misrepresented the manner in which the first voyage had been conducted in his written report and in conversation with such as Richard Hakluyt, it's most unlikely that Hawkins would have dared conceal the truth in private meetings with his highly placed backers, who now included the queen's Master of the Horse and long-time favourite Robert Dudley, Earl of Leicester; William Herbert, Earl of Pembroke; and Lord Admiral Edward Clinton. They would have realized that the kind of covert deal Ponte had put together was not indefinitely repeatable and certainly would not bear the weight of a significantly larger-scale enterprise.

What was a quandary from the perspective of a profit-seeking merchant would have looked very different to Sir William Cecil, who was playing for higher stakes. Possibly the Portuguese and Spanish officials had suggested that it would be easier for them to justify their notional surrender if Hawkins returned with something that could credibly be described as overwhelming force; but by permitting him to use an ostentatiously large royal ship Cecil unmistakably raised the ante. Even though a thin layer of deniability was maintained, the next voyage would be semi-official and Philip II would not be able to treat it as one more random act by uncontrollable English pirates.

On 18 October 1564 Hawkins set sail from Plymouth aboard *Jesus*, a 700-ton Hansa hulk acquired from Lübeck by Henry VIII in 1545 and refitted as a war carrack, followed by Hawkins's own ships *Saloman*, *Swallow* and the 50-ton *Tiger*. This was the second time the queen had used *Jesus* as a loan investment through Dudley and Herbert. By an almost theatrically symbolic coincidence Hawkins's flotilla encountered *Minion*, on her last independent voyage to Guinea, immediately offshore. They were to meet again at El Ferrol after weathering a violent storm in the Bay of Biscay, in which *Minion* became separated from the royal pinnace *John Baptist* and Hawkins from his own *Swallow*. No more is known about *John Baptist*, but *Swallow* rejoined Hawkins at Tenerife, where the local militia turned out to oppose what they thought was an invasion until Hawkins, recognizing one of the Pontes among them, went ashore to reassure them.

After refitting, watering, and stocking up on supplies, the flotilla sailed for West Africa on 15 November and, after raiding two African Muslim principalities on the way down, arrived at a Portuguese outpost where Hawkins bought two caravels loaded with slaves on Christmas Day. Advised that he might profitably raid a nearby native village against token opposition, he took 40 armed men ashore but unexpectedly ran into ferocious resistance, being driven back to his boats with the loss of seven killed, including the captain of *Saloman*, having captured only ten natives. To round off a very bad day, many of the rest of the landing party were wounded and it was probably their blood in the water that provoked a shark feeding frenzy in which he lost five more men.*

Hawkins spent a further month on the Guinea Coast acquiring slaves from Portuguese traders, whose claims to have been forcibly dispossessed of their cargoes and some caravels were forwarded to London three-and-a-half years later. Such singular lack of urgency argues either that the authorities in Lisbon never believed a word of the claims, or else that pressure from Madrid forced them to concoct a belated cover story for an officially winked-at breach of the irksome conditions imposed on them by the hated Spanish. Given the semi-official nature of his enterprise, it defies belief that Hawkins would have made unprovoked war on the King of Portugal's subjects.

After being becalmed for three weeks and then enduring a violent storm, the flotilla arrived off the 'cannibal island' of Dominica on 9 March 1565. Although by now smallpox had decimated the

---

* As an aside, the word 'shark' entered the English language as a result of Hawkins's voyages. In Hakluyt's *Principal Navigations* Hawkins himself refers to 'many sharkes or Tiburons' – *tiburón* being the Spanish name for the beasts.

fierce Caribs, their reputation lingered and the Spanish had not established settlements on the string of small islands running in a crescent from Puerto Rico to the Venezuelan coast. The ships replenished their water supply and sailed on to a disappointing reception at the pearl island of La Margarita, where the settlers sold them fresh meat but would not trade for slaves or other goods, and where officials tried to persuade Hawkins's Spanish pilot to desert. There was no attempt by Hawkins at 'armed trading', which is significant in the light of what followed.

His next stop was Borburata on the Venezuelan mainland, where he negotiated in a desultory manner with the local settlers. This was odd; Borburata was notoriously hospitable to smugglers, so frequented by French corsairs that in 1553 the Spanish authorities ordered its complete evacuation, as they were to do eventually along the entire northern coast of Hispaniola. However, the tempo picked up after the governor arrived ten days later. He was another member of the Canarian Bernáldez clan and, like the one on Hispaniola, he went through a charade to disguise his collusion, obtaining testimony from some of the settlers that he was acting under duress and once again issuing a licence while specifying that he had no authority to do so.

Hawkins ripped it up, perhaps because he had been led to expect something more, but he obtained proof that he had paid 1,600 pesos duty on the slaves he sold, most to Bernáldez himself, and even accepted a promissory note from him for 600 pesos to be cashed at Río de la Hacha, his next stop. There, after a show of resistance, the local commander Miguel de Castellanos declared the town open and business was so brisk that the settlers gave Hawkins shopping lists for his next visit.

Not the least intriguing aspect of this episode is that the eyewitness account by the Plymouth merchant John Sparke in Hakluyt's *Principal Navigations* matches Bernáldez's testimony to his superiors, which suggests that the pantomime was conducted as much for the benefit of Hawkins's own people – who included London as well as Plymouth merchants accompanying their own merchandise – as it was to provide a suitable cover story for Bernáldez. One can only speculate what the two sharps were up to, but it's reasonable to suspect that the merchants as well as Hawkins's backers were being short-changed in plain sight.

If so, they were more credulous than Bernáldez's superiors, who concluded that the threats of violence, hostage-taking and apparent negotiation under duress at Borburata and later at Río de la Hacha were a pre-arranged farce. The excuse of trading under threat became so hackneyed that the Spanish authorities, demonstrating an unexpected gift for irony, began to refer to contraband as *rescates* (ransoms).

In the midst of Hawkins's lively sojourn at Borburata, the Norman smuggler Jean Bontemps (literally, 'Good-time John') arrived with his own cargo of slaves and trade goods and, after the two captains conferred, Hawkins brought his business there to a conclusion and made way for the Frenchman. Of course, the fact that *Jesus* had enough guns to blow Bontemps's little flotilla out of the water might explain the cordiality of their encounter; but if further proof were required that Hawkins was trying to achieve more than mere profit, it's the difference between his insistence on official recognition of his activities and Bontemps's regular, low-key operation.

Having sold all his slaves and merchandise, Hawkins sailed to the island of Curaçao, where he purchased 1,500 wild cattle hides, then sailed to Jamaica where he had promised to drop off his pilot and interpreter, Cristóbal Llerena, whom he had allegedly freed from captivity in Guinea. Or at least that was one of several explanations Hawkins gave. Llerena did not recognize the coast of Jamaica and stayed aboard. Also allegedly rescued from captivity in Guinea – and here come those three bears again – was the Dieppois Martin Atinas, who just happened to have been a member of a French settlement expedition to Florida led by Jean Ribault in 1562. And this same settlement just happened to be Hawkins's next landfall, after sailing in the Florida Straits – or to put it another way, downwind of the treasure ship assembly port of Havana – for two weeks.

If Hawkins had captured a treasure ship the result would have been like the Reneger incident all over again. It's vanishingly unlikely that he had authority from Cecil to do such a thing, but the possibility cannot be dismissed that the Earl of Leicester may have encouraged him to seize the opportunity should it present itself, seeing it as a means to undermine his rival Cecil's Spanish policy while also enriching himself and his doting but penurious queen. Hawkins, certainly, would have known that Reneger was made for life after his exploit, and he may have calculated that his government could not disown him if he did the deed while in command of one of the queen's largest warships.

We cannot know because no treasure ship ventured into his area of operations and, needing water, he sailed on to the French outpost – Fort Caroline at the mouth of today's St Johns River – where the Huguenot commander René Goulaine de Laudonnière regarded his arrival with understandable reserve. England had but recently gone to war with France, seeking to exploit the first of the French religious civil wars to recover Calais, only to have the Huguenots sink their differences with the Catholics and unite with them to expel the English. It cannot have been reassuring to have a large English warship appear off his little settlement, but all was amity once Hawkins made himself known, as Huguenot corsairs were able to use Plymouth as a resupply base thanks to the good offices of his brother William.

Finding the settlers destitute, Hawkins relieved their more pressing needs and offered to ship them home. Laudonnière did not know whether France and England were currently at war, and feared that Hawkins might 'attempt somewhat in Florida in the name of his mistress', so he declined the offer and asked if he could buy a ship instead. Hawkins sold him *Swallow*, his smallest ship, taking four guns and a supply of ammunition in exchange for the weaponry on board, plus a promissory note for the ship herself.

It does not seem likely that Cecil would have approved of providing the French with the means to prey on Spanish treasure ships riding the Gulf Stream along the Florida coast, but he could hardly object to a merchant getting a good price for his own property. Hawkins also had much to gain by cementing his family's friendship with the Huguenots, who posed the greatest threat to shipping of any nationality in the Channel and the eastern Atlantic. He succeeded in doing so: years later Laudonnière wrote that he was 'a good and charitable man, deserving to be esteemed as much of us all as if he had saved all our lives'.

Which he had; but not for long. On 28 August 1565, exactly a month after Hawkins's departure, Jean Ribault arrived from France on a resupply mission with 600 new settlers; simultaneously Pedro Menéndez de Avilés, the newly appointed *adelantado* of Florida, arrived from Spain with 800 troops and settlers and orders from Philip II himself to exterminate the French. After rough weather foiled an attempt to close with Ribault's ships, Menéndez sailed 40 miles/64 kilometres) south and disembarked his landing party at what became the settlement of San Agustín and is today St Augustine. While Ribault sailed south in pursuit and into a hurricane that destroyed his fleet, Menéndez marched north under the cover of the same storm, captured Fort Caroline and slaughtered 140 settlers, sparing some 60 women and children. Only Laudonnière and about 40 others escaped and managed to get back to France, presumably on *Swallow*.

Menéndez went on to bluff Jean Ribault into surrendering the men who had got ashore from the wreck of his fleet, and then ordered their throats slit. A second cold-blooded massacre two days later brought the death toll to about 500. Menéndez hung their bodies on trees and put up a sign saying, 'Not as Frenchmen but as Lutherans'. French sailors did not appreciate the distinction and thereafter were merciless towards the Spanish. Specific vengeance was taken by the Catholic Dominique de Gourgues, who sailed to Fort Caroline from Bordeaux in April 1568, took it with the help of Indian allies and then hanged the garrison, putting up a sign saying 'Not as Spaniards but as murderers'.

Two years later, off La Palma in the Canary Islands on 17 July 1570, the furiously Protestant Jacques de Sores took a large Portuguese carrack bound for Brazil and sent shock waves through the

Catholic world by the malevolence he showed towards 40 Jesuit missionaries led by Fr Ignacio de Azevedo, who were thrown overboard along with all their crucifixes, relics and pictures of the saints. In September 1571 Jean Capdeville, one of Sores' lieutenants, accompanied – according to French naval historian Charles de La Roncière – by Richard Grenville's 240 ton *Castle of Comfort*, captain unknown and sailing under Huguenot letters of marque, took another Portuguese carrack in the same area. The new Viceroy of Brazil, Luis de Vasconcelos, was killed in the battle, and after the carrack surrendered, 15 more Jesuits were hurled into the ocean.

Despite riding the Gulf Stream, contrary winds held up Hawkins's return and he had to pause off Newfoundland to fish for cod to feed his crew. Encountering two French fishing boats, he bought their catch and finally arrived at Padstow in Cornwall on 20 September 1565, eleven months after setting out from Plymouth. On 23 October *Jesus* was returned to the Earls of Leicester and Pembroke, who spent £500 refitting her. Everybody got rich, and if Hawkins got notably richer than the other investors, nobody begrudged it. As usual he had lost no men to shipboard diseases and his reputation as a skilful, careful but above all lucky commander was affirmed. In addition he was granted a coat of arms: 'sable, on a point wavy a lion passant or; in chief three bezants and for a crest a demi-Moor, proper, in chains'. The slave was loosely roped, not chained, in a later version of the escutcheon, and then disappeared. Although Hawkins published a pamphlet in 1567 boasting about slave raiding in alliance with local chiefs, as time passed and he grew more respectable he would have wished to blur the manner in which he became a gentleman.

For his book Kelsey uncovered some fascinating documents relating to contacts between Hawkins and Spanish Ambassador Guzmán de Silva following the second voyage, but failed to see that they make sense only in the context of an overall strategy of trying to persuade Philip II of the advantages of permitting the English to trade with Spanish America. It's called negotiating with threats, which in this case involved Hawkins professing interest in Guzmán's pet project of taking prominent English captains into Spanish royal service to fight in the Mediterranean, while warning the ambassador that many of his men now knew their way to the Indies and would go with Hawkins or without him. Thus the ambassador was made aware that in addition to Hawkins's four ships in Plymouth, George Fenner was preparing three ships for a long voyage in Portsmouth.

After agonizing over breaching what he believed was the confidentiality of his dealings with Hawkins, Guzmán made an official complaint and Hawkins was, in modern parlance, bound over to keep the peace. Nonetheless the Plymouth flotilla sailed on 9 November 1566, fulfilling Hawkins's warning that those who had sailed with him were now capable of going without him. Yet another charade, of course, as Hawkins never had any intention of going himself. Having married Benjamin Gonson's daughter Katherine, he was in the process of moving to London, where he continued his cultivation of Guzmán de Silva.

The flotilla sailed under John Lovell, a man of total confidence in the Hawkins organization, who had been actively involved in their trade with the Canary Islands. The flagship was once again the Hawkins brothers' 140-ton *Saloman*, with their distant cousin Francis Drake on board as an able seaman, joined by a new, 80-ton *Swallow*, replacing the ship of the same name they had sold to Laudonnière. Their Plymouth partners were represented by James Hampton in the 140-ton *Paul* with his brother Thomas (he of the amazing 1563 'escape' from Seville), and by Robert Bolton on the 40-ton *Pascoe*.

The journey was a carbon copy of Hawkins's second voyage: slaves obtained from Portuguese traders in Guinea who reported how they had valiantly resisted the outrage; resupply without trade at La Margarita; then elaborate pantomimes in Borburata and Río de la Hacha to sell the slaves while officials postured for the benefit of the reports they would be writing about the incidents. There were, however, some significant departures from the script. When Lovell arrived in Borburata he found Jean Bontemps already there, and they made a joint representation to the governor, offering 100 slaves 'for the royal treasury' in exchange for permission to sell another 200. But Bernáldez had been replaced and his successor refused to deal with them at all, leaving Lovell and Bontemps to make individual arrangements with the local merchants.

Despite the censure he had received for being so accommodating during Hawkins's last visit, Miguel de Castellanos was still the Treasurer at Río de la Hacha. This time, however, when Bontemps arrived he was met with a show of armed resistance, as was Lovell when he sailed in a few days later. Castellanos claimed that all the settlers who had given Hawkins shopping lists in 1565 now loyally turned out to fight the evil pirates and drove them off with many casualties. So disheartened was Lovell by this, Castellanos continued, that he unloaded 96 old and sick slaves on the other bank of the river and sailed away. He hoped that his superiors would permit the brave citizens of Río de La Hacha to keep them, he wrote.

Lovell sailed on to Hispaniola and returned to Plymouth in September 1567, with some fifty unsold slaves on board *Swallow*. Hawkins was disappointed and attributed the lower than previous profits to Lovell's lack of subtlety. It was certainly a major error of judgement to become associated with a Frenchman following the deepening of Franco-Spanish animosity as a result of Menéndez's Florida massacre, let alone a smuggler as notorious as Jean Bontemps. We may doubt, however, whether even Hawkins could have overcome the loss of Bernáldez at Borburata and the fact that Castellanos was on such thin ice that he felt obliged to be seen to prevent by force of arms a repeat of the flagrant 1565 bazaar – although the tale of the old and sick slaves was such a transparent fabrication that it's a mystery how he got away with it.

CHAPTER 5
SAN JUAN DE ULÚA

W̲e come now to Hawkins's third voyage and a watershed in Anglo-Spanish relations, after which Cecil's nuanced approach became less tenable, gradually giving way to outright predation largely uncoordinated by the state. By the time Lovell returned, Hawkins was almost ready to sail on *Jesus* with Robert Barrett as master, now accompanied by *Minion* under John Hampton, the 150-ton *William and John* under Thomas Bolton, the 50-ton *Judith* and the 33-ton *Angel*, to which Hawkins added *Swallow* and her cargo of slaves. She must have been in remarkably good condition to permit such a rapid turnaround after a year-long voyage. *Judith* was probably commanded by 27 year-old Francis Drake from the start – she certainly was by the time the flotilla reached the Americas.

A little earlier, on 30 August 1567, a Spanish fleet sailing from Flanders to Spain under the Flemish Baron DeWachen entered Plymouth harbour, allegedly blown off course by bad weather. When DeWachen tried to enter the inner harbour, where Hawkins's flotilla lay, his ships were fired on by the fort guarding the entrance and by Hawkins' ships. DeWachen sent a messenger to the mayor of Plymouth, who directed him to 'the queen's ships' and their commander, John Hawkins, who bluntly told him that in the absence of contrary instructions from 'my mistress' he would regard any attempt to get into the inner harbour as a hostile act. Hawkins invited DeWachen aboard *Jesus*, where he entertained him royally. Subsequently a number of (presumably Protestant) Flemish prisoners condemned to the galleys escaped from one of the Spanish ships –

freed by English sailors, said DeWachen; by their fellow countrymen in the Spanish fleet, said Hawkins; by collusion, say I.

In the light of what was to happen a year later, it was unfortunate that Cecil should have written to Hawkins to express the queen's displeasure at his action. 'I had rather Her Highness found fault with me for keeping her ships and her people, to her honour,' Hawkins replied, 'than to lose them to the glory of others'. Then he added a cryptic comment: 'I know they hate me and yet without cause for they are the better of me by great sums, and I the worse by 4000 ducats', the debt 'not unknown to the ambassador of Spain. I hope one day they will make me recompense of their own courtesy'. This was the amount Hawkins was to have received in return for leading an English fleet to fight for Philip II in the Mediterranean, Guzmán de Silva's ambitious project to defuse the rising naval rivalry between the two nations. It's absurd to believe that this was the first Cecil learned of the scheme: common sense indicates that Hawkins acted with his prior approval at all times.

The flotilla sailed on 2 October 1567 and four days later was scattered by a violent storm in the Bay of Biscay. Hawkins admitted that 'we set our course homeward, determining to give over the voyage', but when the weather broke on the 11th he reversed course, hoping to be reunited with the others at the Canary Islands. *Minion*, *Swallow* and *William and John* reassembled at La Gomera, while *Jesus* and *Angel* sailed to Santa Cruz on Tenerife, where it became apparent that the Hawkins brothers' peaceful trading days with the islands were over. Obedient to instructions from Madrid the militia turned out in force and remained mobilized and watchful throughout his stay.

Realizing that his bridges were burned, Hawkins no longer bothered to go to Mass, as he had always diplomatically done in the past during his visits. However, unlike Lovell the previous year, he punished any member of the crew who showed disrespect for the Catholic church. It was an anxious time for him also because for several days he had no news of his missing ships. When he learned that three of them were at La Gomera he sailed at once to join them, and encountered the late-arriving *Judith* on the way. It was, perhaps, an unfortunate accident that when he departed Santa Cruz, one of the guns fired in an exchange of salutes with the fort proved to be shotted, and demolished a house.

Hawkins's confidential report of the voyage to Cecil, which the Secretary of State chose to have published in May 1569, was clearly edited by someone a great deal more literate than the nominal author, and displays the marvellous economy of language that characterizes Elizabethan English at its best. The following is representative:

> . . . *all our ships, before dispersed, met in one of those islands, called Gomera, where we took water and departed from thence the 4th day of November towards the coast of Guinea, and arrived at Cape Verde the 18th of November, where we landed one hundred and fifty men, hoping to obtain some negroes; where we got but few, and those with great hurt and damage to our men, which chiefly proceeded from their envenomed arrows; although in the beginning they seemed to be but small hurts, yet there hardly escaped any that had blood drawn of them but died in strange sort, with their mouths shut* [a symptom of tetanus, also known as lock-jaw], *some ten days before they died, and after their wounds were whole; where I myself had one of the greatest wounds, yet, thanks be to God, escaped.*

Hawkins's partners in La Gomera had complained of a recent raid by French corsairs and warned him that they had sailed on to West Africa. Reading between the lines, when Hawkins arrived at Cabo Blanco he found that the French had (genuinely) plundered his Portuguese suppliers and scuttled their caravels, which forced him to make up the shortfall by trying to capture slaves himself. Near Cape Verde he met up with six French ships trading at another settlement. Five of them had letters of marque from the Huguenot Admiral Gaspard de Coligny, but the sixth did not. Hawkins decided it had been involved in the raids on La Gomera and Cabo Blanco and took it, putting his own men on board and transferring the French crew to *Jesus*. One of the other French captains, Paul Blondel on *Don de Dieu* (Gift of God), was granted permission to join Hawkins' flotilla.

Here, as in the case of Martin Atinas in 1564, we have another allegedly chance encounter between Hawkins and an amenable Huguenot. In this case the bounds of credulity are further tested by the fact that the French ally of the Plymouth merchant William Towerson in the 1557 raid on São Jorge da Mina was Denis Blondel, likely another member of the same extended family as Paul. Neither Towerson's nor Hawkins's accounts of their dealings with their French peers in West Africa are convincing, and the truth they were trying to conceal may have been a degree of planned collaboration they did not wish their government to know about.

In December 1568 claims from Portuguese traders totalling a ridiculous 70,000 ducats were submitted by the Portuguese ambassador in London, some of them alleging trading under threat. However, Hawkins's need to collect slaves for himself did bring about a genuine armed conflict on the São Domingo (today's Gambia) River, where a landing party led by Robert Barrett raided and burned the village of Cacheo and had to fight its way back with about 100 captives through an army of natives led by Portuguese. Hawkins retaliated by plundering two Portuguese ships moored in the river, taking one with him to Sierra Leone, where he looted two more. He had already lost his secure base in the Canaries; now the Portuguese connection was unravelling and he had collected less than 150 slaves.

With his men sickening and time running out, Hawkins received an emissary from an African chief requesting his assistance in an attack on an enemy village, 'with promise that as many negroes as by these wars might be obtained, as well of his part as of ours, should be at our pleasure'. On 15 January 1568 a joint attack was made on a place 'very strongly impaled and fenced after their manner', and Hawkins lost six men killed and 40 wounded before they set fire to the village and the defenders fled. 'We took 250 persons, men, women and children, and by our friend the king of our side there were taken 600 prisoners, whereof we hoped to have our choice, but the negro (in which nation is seldom or never found truth) meant nothing less; for that night he removed his camp and prisoners, so that we were fain to content us with those few which we had gotten ourselves'.

The flotilla, augmented by the two French ships and two caravels, one salvaged from those scuttled at Cabo Blanco and the other taken on the Santo Domingo River, sailed for America on 3 February and did not make landfall at Dominica until 27 March. When they reached La Margarita their request to trade cloth for provisions was welcomed with open arms, as the settlement had been sacked the previous year by vengeful Huguenot corsairs. The governor even gave Hawkins a certificate of good conduct when he left on 9 April. After that things went rather worse than they had for Lovell. At Borburata the governor wrote to say he could not allow Hawkins to trade because 'I saw the governor my predecessor [Bernáldez] carried away prisoner unto Spain for giving licence to the country to traffic with you at your last being here'. A 'ransom' was duly arranged with local merchants, but the governor prevented the deal going through.

At Río de la Hacha the great survivor Miguel de Castellanos 'had fortified his town with divers bulwarks in all places where it might be entered, and furnished himself with a hundred arquebusiers, so that he thought by famine to have enforced us to have put on land our negroes, of which purpose he had not greatly failed unless we had by force entered the town; which (after we could by no means obtain his favour) we were enforced to do, and so with two hundred men brake in upon their bulwarks, and entered the town with the loss only of eleven men of our parts, and no hurt done to the Spaniards, because after their volley of shot discharged, they all fled'.

Castellanos's own report to Madrid claimed no more than a skirmish in which one Englishman was killed and two wounded. Nor does the story of eleven men killed jibe with the rest of Hawkins's account, which states that (my italics) 'partly by the Spaniards' desire of negroes, *and partly by friendship of the treasurer*, we obtained a secret trade; whereupon the Spaniards resorted to us by night, and bought of us to the number of two hundred negroes'. So, if the exaggeration was not the product of residual loyalty to his accomplice, what purpose did it serve? The only obvious explanation is that he wanted to impress Cecil with how valiantly he had tried to force open the door to legal trade.

At Santa Marta, a new stop, the governor settled for a few cannon shots over the village and a show of force by Hawkins at the head of 150 armed men, after which he issued a licence and for two weeks the local dignitaries often dined on board while the English (and presumably the French) were entertained ashore and even performed some public works for their new friend. Commercially, all was profitable sweetness and light and it must have been with reluctance that Hawkins sailed on 13 July for Cartagena. There, the governor made it clear that Hawkins could not enter the inner harbour by firing a salvo of ill-aimed shots from the fort guarding the narrow entrance; but no attempt was made to prevent him replenishing his water supply on the island enclosing the outer harbour, where he left trade goods in payment for a hundred jars of oil and twenty of wine deposited there.

However, when he sailed away Hawkins still had about 70 slaves as well as a considerable quantity of cloth unsold on board his ships. The voyage had not been an outstanding success although at this point, their hold space no longer required for the slaves that had been sold, the crew of the French corsair seized near Cape Verde were put back aboard their ship and permitted to sail away, while the caravel seized at the São Domingo River was scuttled. The six original ships, along with Blondel's *Don de Dieu* and the caravel salvaged at Cabo Blanco, sailed around the western point of Cuba and into a hurricane. 'There happened to us, the twelfth day of August, an extreme storm, which continued by the space of four days, which so beat the *Jesus* that we cut down all her higher buildings; her rudder also was sore shaken and, withal, was in so extreme a leak that we were rather upon the point to leave her than to keep her any longer; yet, hoping to bring all to good pass, sought the coast of Florida, where we found no place nor haven for our ships because of the shallowness of the coast.'

Some historians have cast doubt on this, citing the fictional storms that so frequently blew English merchants, including Hawkins, to the Indies across the Atlantic or south from Newfoundland; but the telling detail is that Hawkins did, indeed, feel obliged to reduce the windage on *Jesus* by demolishing her fore and after castles, proof of which is that all the light, anti-personnel guns with which they would have been fitted were found in her hold when the Spanish captured her. As to her seams opening so wide that 'fish swam upon her ballast', that was hyperbole: a leak that big would have overwhelmed her pumps whether the fish fouled them or not.

William and John became detached and made her own leisurely way back to England, in fact arriving well after Drake and Hawkins. All we know about the intervening months is that the ship stopped at an unidentified port, where Captain Bolton picked up a man who said he was the captain of a Spanish ship taken by French corsairs off the Yucatán Peninsula. He gave his name as Juan de Mendoza and said he was from a wealthy family that would pay to have him back safe. It transpired that this was not his name, and that nobody was prepared to pay for his return. His real name may have been Juan de Salvatierra and he was to spend several years a prisoner in Dublin, where Bolton dumped him, trying desperately and in the end successfully to attract enough attention to himself to get sent home as part of a convoluted negotiation for a prisoner exchange in which John Hawkins was closely involved. As to why *William and John* should have lingered around Ireland, it's reasonable to assume the crew indulged in a little piracy to compensate themselves for the failure of Hawkins's venture.

For lack of alternative Hawkins found himself obliged to moor his flotilla at San Juan de Ulúa, an island a little offshore from Vera Cruz – the gulf port serving Mexico City, which was in turn by far the most important Spanish settlement in America. A justifiably nervous Hawkins 'took in our way three ships, which carried passengers to the number of one hundred, which passengers we hoped should be a means to us the better to obtain victuals for our money and a quiet place for the repairing of our fleet'. On 16 September, being greeted with a ceremonial gun salute followed by a boat-load of dignitaries who were appalled to find themselves in the presence of the dreaded *Juan Canes* (John Dogs), he learned that they were expecting the annual *flota* from Spain daily; and that his ships were occupying the only safe mooring in the event of the strong north winds that frequently swept the Gulf. Already moored at the island were twelve hulks reportedly loaded with '200,000 livres in gold and silver'. This is believable: it was what the annual *flota* came for, and the port authorities would have had it ready.

Although subsequently the Spanish turned it into a major, bastioned fortress, in 1568 San Juan de Ulúa was an inverted L-shaped island with a fishing village on the northern point and a 300-foot/90-metre rampart crossing the southern end, with 26 large mooring rings cemented into it. A sketch made 20 years later (no major work intervening) by the military engineer Bautista Antonelli

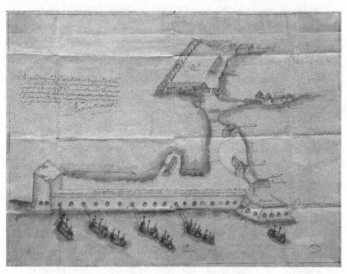

Antonelli sketch of San Juan de Ulúa.

shows a square tower with guns on it at the western end of the rampart and a large customs building, aptly known as the 'House of Lies', set in a semi-bastion at the eastern end.

Ships were moored bows-on at a prudent distance, with anchors cast off astern to prevent being driven against the wall by wave action. Rather than crowd the moorings, a second row of ships was moored to the sterns of those tied up at the wall, leaving ample space between the files. The sketch shows two small doors leading to a narrow walkway at the foot of the rampart, but any bulk loading and unloading must have been by lighters from the shore or among the moored ships.

If one draws a Venn diagram with the following circles: take care of the queen's ships – do not be the cause of damage to the King of Spain's ships – open the door to legal trade – make a profit ... the reasons for Hawkins's subsequent decisions become clear. Had he been a simple predator, he would have held on to the hostages and moored close to the hulks. He chose instead to show good faith by ostentatiously doing the opposite, while sending two of the hostages to Mexico to explain his presence and to request permission to remain long enough to repair his ships and resupply.

What might have come of that became moot when the Spanish *flota* of two galleons (*El Salvador* and *Santa Catalina*) and eleven carracks hove into view the very next morning, confronting Hawkins with the need to decide which was the lesser of two evils:

> ... *either I must have kept out the fleet from entering the port (the which, with God's help, I was very well able to do), or else suffer them to enter in with their accustomed treason, which they never fail to execute where they may have opportunity ... If I had kept them out, then had there been* [a] *present shipwreck of all the fleet, which amounted in value to six millions, which was in value of our money 1,800,000 livres, which I considered I was not able to answer, fearing the Queen's Majesty's indignation in so weighty a matter. Thus with myself revolving the doubts, I thought rather better to abide the jutt of the uncertainty than the certainty. The*

uncertain doubt was their treason, which by good policy I hoped
might be prevented; and therefore, as choosing the least mischief, I
*proceeded to conditions.**

Hawkins sent Robert Barrett, the Spanish-speaking master of *Jesus*,
to negotiate terms. He returned with the news that the flagship *El
Salvador* was carrying Martín Enríquez, the new viceroy of Mexico,
'so that he had authority, both in all this province ... and in the sea,
who sent us word that we should send our conditions, which of his
part should (for the better maintenance of amity between the
princes) be both favourably granted and faithfully performed'. This
was music to Hawkins's ears because suddenly the possibility of re-
deeming a lacklustre voyage and also achieving his larger mission
seemed within his grasp. Perhaps for that reason he failed to attach
sufficient weight to the rest of the Viceroy's 'many fair words', in
which he said that 'passing the coast of the Indies, he had understood of our honest behaviour towards the inhabitants, where we
had to do as well elsewhere as in the same port'.

The heavy irony of 'our honest behaviour towards the inhabitants' was not lost on Hawkins, who commented 'the which I let
pass'. He should not have done so; ignoring the implicit warning
led him to overplay his hand, demanding 'victual for our money,
and licence to sell as much ware as might furnish our wants, and
that there might be of either part twelve gentlemen as hostage for
the maintenance of peace, and that the island, for our better safety,
might be in our own possession during our abode there, and such
ordnance as was planted in the same island, which was eleven pieces
of brass [bronze], and that no Spaniard might land in the island
with any kind of weapon'.

Stripped of polite verbiage, Enríquez had enquired whether it
was Hawkins' intention to engage in armed trading – and when
Hawkins insisted on retaining control of the rampart and its guns
and also demanded 'license to sell as much ware as might furnish

* Whoever corrected Hawkins's syntax did not do likewise with his mathematics: six million
pesos, itself a wildly inflated overestimate, was roughly £1,364,000.

our wants', he confirmed that it was. The Viceroy might have consented to running repairs and resupply if Hawkins had offered to pay cash, arguing that custom and treaty obliged him to lend assistance to the storm-damaged ships of a nation with which Spain was not at war. But Enríquez had not even begun to 'make himself the Indies' (fill his pockets) and there was no chance whatever that he would guarantee his immediate recall to face an irate Philip II by granting Hawkins a licence to trade.

After much toing and froing the *flota* finally came to mooring on 21 September when, pausing to order the fleet's military commander, Francisco de Luján, to destroy the interlopers, Enríquez prudently departed for Mexico. 'Easier said than done', Luján and Antonio Delgadillo, the commander at Vera Cruz, must have muttered. The two galleons and the merchant ships of the *flota* were tied up at the western end of the mooring, separated from Hawkins's ships at the eastern end by the treasure hulks. They were under the guns of the tower and there may have been more along the rampart, all manned by Hawkins's men.

Still, the two officers were products of the most effective military machine since the Roman Empire and did not waste time. During the night Delgadillo loaded his militia on lighters in Vera Cruz and rowed towards the unprotected north-western side of the island. Meanwhile 150 arquebusiers and sword and buckler men moved from Luján's flagship to *La Margarita*, a large hulk nearest to *Minion*, which was moored to the stern of *Jesus*. The English sailors failed to notice when the Spanish switched the mooring cable of the ship now packed with soldiers to the same ring as *Jesus* and drifted slowly towards the two English carracks.

In the morning of 23 September the English opened fire far too late on the approaching hulk and were soon engaged in hand-to-hand fighting. Some smart work saw *Minion* cast off and pull away on her stern anchors, after which Luján's soldiers attacked *Jesus*. The detailed Spanish report on the location of the guns on *Jesus* reveals that Hawkins had brought his big guns (2 bronze cannon perier, 1 iron demi-cannon perier, 2 bronze culverins, and 3 bronze and 2 iron demi-culverins*) to the upper deck. Although they were distributed to balance the weight from side-to-side, in the aggregate they would have made an already top-heavy ship even more unstable in any kind of sea. Accordingly he must have done this at the mooring to exploit the height of the big carrack in order to menace the Spanish galleons over the intervening hulks. It's equally clear that Luján and Delgadillo designed their attack to neutralize the overwhelming English advantage in artillery.

In the event their plan met with only partial success. On the other side of the rampart Delgadillo's men swarmed ashore and swept through Hawkins's men on the island, putting them to the sword and taking control of the guns on the tower and along the rampart. The panicked survivors fled to the *Jesus* just as her crew cut loose and began to pull her out into clear water. Once clear, the carracks vengefully turned their big guns on *El Salvador* and *Santa Catalina* at point blank range, sinking one and setting the other on fire. It was difficult to sink big wooden ships with gunfire, and the loss of his flagship must have come as a shock to Admiral Juan de Hubilla. The other Spanish ship sunk in the engagement was *La Margarita*, riddled by both *Minion* and *Jesus* as they pulled away.

Elsewhere little *Angel* was sunk by gunfire, but *Swallow* and the caravel were easily taken by Delgadillo's militia, which argues that they were moored nearest the rampart and lightly manned. *Don de Dieu* and *Judith* did not fall to the first rush, either because they were moored astern of the others or because their crews were more alert. Tying together the facts that only four Frenchmen were captured, that *Don de Dieu* was later sold for the value of her guns and metal work and that if Paul Blondel made it home it must have been on *Judith*, the likeliest scenario is that for some reason – probably damage from the guns on the rampart – he could not get his ship away, and so set fire to her after transferring most of his crew to Drake's ship, the only one of the five smaller vessels to escape.

* See Appendix C: Naval Artillery.

Jesus was unseaworthy and now so severely battered by the guns on the tower that Hawkins realized she could go no further, 'whereupon we determined to place the *Jesus* on that side of the *Minion*, that she might abide all the battery from the land, and so be a defence for the *Minion* till night, and then to take such relief of victual and other necessaries from the *Jesus* as the time would suffer us, and to leave her'. That time was curtailed when Luján's flag captain sent two fireships against them and, according to Hawkins, no sooner had he transferred to *Minion* than her crew panicked and cut loose from *Jesus*, abandoning the supplies and most of the men on board her.

But not the jewels, gold, silver and pearls acquired by trade: in Hawkins' grossly inflated claim for losses he itemized 57 slaves, 30 bales of linen, 1,000 pieces of dyed cloth and several smaller amounts of trade goods – but in valuables only 'a little sack with 600 pesos gold and silver'.

There followed the most quoted passage in Hawkins's account: 'The most part of the men that were left alive in the *Jesus* made shift and followed the *Minion* in a small boat, the rest, which the little boat was not able to receive, were enforced to abide the mercy of the Spaniards (which I [am in no] doubt was very little); so with the *Minion* only, and the *Judith* (a small barque of 50 tons), we escaped, which barque the same night forsook us in our great misery'.

The credence that historians have given to this accusation is extraordinary, especially since it was contradicted by survivor Job Hortrop in the account he published after 23 years in Spanish captivity. The unexamined premise is that little *Judith* could have relieved the overcrowding that was the source of the 'great misery' on *Minion*, which clearly *Judith* could not have done even if she did not already have Blondel's crew aboard.

The most obvious explanation is also the most likely: Hawkins took all the easily portable valuables with him from the *Jesus* to the *Minion* and ordered her to cast off, abandoning the men on *Jesus* to their fate. When some of the desperate men managed to row to *Minion*, he was obliged to take them on board. Hortrop's account is that Hawkins, on finding that *Judith* could accept only a few more men, told Drake to make his own way home. He would have done so for the same reason he abandoned the men on *Jesus*: they could not contribute to his survival and might imperil it. The self-pitying accusation against Drake – made in confidence to Cecil – was designed to distract attention from his own coldly pragmatic behaviour.

When Hawkins finally returned to Plymouth there were only 15 survivors of the more than two hundred men who sailed away from San Juan de Ulúa with him – yet he had managed to keep some of the valuable slaves on *Minion* alive while the crew starved. Of his four objectives, Hawkins had failed to save the queen's ship *Jesus*, he had inflicted severe damage on the King of Spain's ships, and he had spectacularly failed to open up Spanish America to legal trade. But he did make sure that he would not be out of pocket, while the number of people who might claim a share had been greatly reduced, including several of the other Plymouth merchants who might have returned to dispute his version of events as well as his accounting.

The evidence is strong that Hawkins was seriously discredited by the episode. He had to wait nine years before he achieved public office and a further ten years for his knighthood. By contrast, far from it being the case that Drake's career was 'haunted' by his alleged abandonment of Hawkins, he emerged with his reputation so greatly enhanced that not long after the disaster at San Juan de Ulúa William Hawkins entrusted him with command of a further voyage to Spanish America. In contrast John Hawkins undertook only one more such expedition, jointly with Drake 25 years later when they were both well past their best, which was a total failure even before shipboard disease claimed the lives of both men.

Hawkins concluded his account with a valedictory declaration that to do justice to 'all the misery and troublesome affairs of this sorrowful voyage' would have required the skill and time employed by John Foxe in writing his massive *Book of Martyrs*, first published in 1563. Hawkins and his unknown editor did well enough, in a few short paragraphs summarizing a horrendous crossing: 'We wandered in an unknown sea by the space of fourteen days', he wrote, from which we may conclude that not the least of his losses at San

Juan de Ulúa was the Portuguese pilot who took him there in the first place. *Minion* was allegedly so short of supplies that in that first fortnight 'hunger enforced us to seek the land; for hides were thought very good meat; rats, cats, mice and dogs, none escaped that might be gotten; parrots and monkeys that were had in great prize [that is, expected to command a good price in England], were thought there very profitable if they served the turn of one dinner'.

The hunger so graphically described certainly came later, but Hawkins needed to bring it forward in his narrative to explain why half the men on *Minion* chose to be put ashore, when the possibility still existed of obtaining supplies from some other Spanish settlement. That they should have preferred to hope for mercy from the Spanish or the possibility of encountering friendly natives indicates that they had no confidence in Hawkins's ability to get them home, and suggests something akin to mutiny.

On 8 October a hundred men were duly abandoned somewhere near San Francisco de Campeche on the Yucatán peninsula. Hortrop wrote of an emotional farewell from their captain, yet according to Hawkins he and fifty of the men remaining with him were also on land to replenish the ship's water, when a violent storm nearly sank *Minion*. A number amounting to half his remaining crew was certainly not required for routine watering, so a more likely explanation is that Hawkins was guarding against hostile acts by the men he had put ashore with not a weapon among them. Once good weather returned it took him a month to get out into the Atlantic, and a further six weeks to make landfall in northern Spain.

From his own account, therefore, either Hawkins was a poor navigator or else there was an explanation for the extraordinary delay in leaving the Gulf of Mexico that he wished to conceal from Cecil; on past form that would have been a failed attempt to capture a treasure ship in the Florida Strait. By now seriously short of food, he sailed north to take the great circle route back to England but, 'growing near to the cold country our men, being oppressed with famine, died continually, and they that were left grew into such weakness that we were scarcely able to manoeuvre our ship'.

Faced with contrary winds and with his men dropping from exposure, Hawkins sailed south to Pontevedra, near Vigo, where many of his starving men died of what today is medically recognized as 'refeeding syndrome' after gorging on meat. Defeated by a storm in his first attempt to sail home across the Bay of Biscay, in the end Hawkins only managed to get *Minion* back to Mounts Bay in Cornwall on 24 January 1569 thanks to men and supplies on two ships sent by William Hawkins when he learned of his brother's plight.

It must have been a huge relief to find that in his absence Anglo-Spanish relations had deteriorated so greatly for other reasons that the battle at San Juan de Ulúa could not be blamed for the collapse of Cecil's policy. Not long after Hawkins sailed on his ill-fated third voyage, Elizabeth's government became involved in supporting the revolt in the Netherlands, which came close to being crushed after Fernando Álvarez de Toledo, Duke of Alba, arrived with a large army in 1567 and set about brutally suppressing religious and political dissidence.

The presence of the all-conquering Spanish Hapsburg army just across the Channel was a palpable threat, but there was little Elizabeth could do except permit the 'Sea Beggars' (corsairs of all nationalities under letters of marque issued by William, Prince of Orange, the leader of the revolt) under their ruthless and flamboyant leader William II de la Marck, to operate out of English ports. Bearing in mind that as recently as 1563 the French religious factions had sunk their differences to expel the English from Le Havre, England could not afford to risk war with Spain, the only useful ally she might have in the event of renewed war with France.

That consideration ceased to be paramount when the third French war of religion broke out in the summer of 1568. Catholic leagues across the country launched pogroms against the Huguenots, causing their leaders Admiral Coligny and Louis de Bourbon, Prince of Condé, to flee the court to La Rochelle, where once more they unleashed the *guerre de course* to raise funds for their cause. It soon became a pan-European war with Spanish, Papal and Tuscan troops serving under the Duc d'Anjou for the Catholics, and German Calvinist militias and mercenaries serving under Condé. William of Orange attempted to intervene, but with his unpaid troops on the point of mutiny he had to accept Charles IX's offer of money and free passage out of the country.

It was greatly in England's interest that France should remain divided. After Count Palatine Wolfgang of Zweibrücken was killed in battle, Condé was able to retain the services of the count's mercenary army thanks only to a loan from Queen Elizabeth, with the Queen of Navarre's jewels as security. But Condé himself was killed at Jarnac in March 1569, and the Huguenot army was crushed at Moncontour in October. Coligny resorted to a punitive *chevauchée* across the south and up the Rhone valley, but it was the exhaustion of royal credit that forced Charles IX to agree to peace and the reinstatement of Huguenot rights in August 1570. Perhaps more than at any other time in history, war during the Renaissance was nakedly a test of financial rather than military power, and the startling fact is that despite losing the land battles, the Huguenots won the money war.

They were able to do so thanks to support from England, which included permitting the Huguenot corsairs to operate out of English ports against Spanish shipping. The back story was that in November 1568 a Spanish fleet carrying gold bullion worth over £85,000 for the Duke of Alba to pay his restless troops in the Netherlands was driven into Plymouth by Huguenot corsairs. This was to leap from the frying pan into the fire, as Devon under Vice Admiral Sir Arthur Champernowne was wholly given over to support of the Huguenot cause and Sir Arthur's closest English collaborator was William Hawkins of Plymouth, who had lent one of his own ships to the great Huguenot corsair Jacques de Sores. Accordingly, when the queen took possession of the bullion it was to prevent her subjects from conniving with Sores to steal it.

However, when informed by their local representative that the bullion was still the property of the King of Spain's Genoese bankers, she decided to borrow it herself.* Alba promptly ordered

* She repaid the full amount, with interest, which was more than the Genoese bankers could expect from Philip II.

the arrest of all English ships in Netherlands ports and then, as he had over the Reneger incident, Philip II put himself further in the wrong by ordering all English ships in Spain impounded as well, only to find himself the loser when Elizabeth ordered the seizure of the larger number of Spanish ships in English ports, including any sailing offshore. Ironically, this confrontation played out with neither monarch aware of the battle that had taken place at San Juan de Ulúa in September. When news did filter back, it hardened attitudes on both sides.

With the Princes of Condé and of Orange freely issuing letters of marque to English captains, Elizabeth and Cecil had no need to do so, thus maintaining deniability but also foregoing the revenues they might have had in the interest of not letting the corsair tail wag the policy dog. The queen limited herself to general denunciations of corsair activity without, at this time, taking action against them. To do so would have been incoherent, given that she was already supporting the Huguenot cause directly. In December 1568 royal ships under Admiral Sir William Wynter landed arms and ammunition at La Rochelle under cover of escorting the annual wine convoy to Bordeaux.

Even after she felt compelled to deny the Huguenots the use of English ports, support for their cause continued to flow to La Rochelle and attacks on Spanish shipping continued under a tacit understanding that the English bearers of Huguenot letters of marque – the Champernowne-Hawkins combine well to the fore – would take care of the Channel while Sores and his men operated along the Atlantic coast.

Consequently John Hawkins was not called upon to explain himself when *Minion* finally limped into Plymouth. On 13 February 1569 ten Spanish merchant ships en route from Spain to the Netherlands were driven into Plymouth Sound by contrary winds. The next day *New Bark* under Philip Budockshide sailed out flying the flag of Saint George to inform them that in view of the embargo between the two countries they must submit to arrest, and shepherded them into Ashwater. Only then did Budockshide reveal that he was sailing with letters of marque from the Prince of Condé. *New Bark* was jointly owned by the Hawkins brothers and Champernowne, who in his capacity as Vice Admiral arrested half the ships in the name of the queen, and awarded the rest to himself and his partners as private shipowners. In accordance with their letters of marque, they sent the prizes to La Rochelle for disposal.

The official reason for the queen acting against the Huguenots operating out of English ports was that on 10 December 1569 Sores sortied from Portsmouth to capture the large Venetian carrack *Justiniana*, sailing to London with a cargo of silk, sugar and wine, and on the way to La Rochelle captured the even bigger Venetian carrack *Vergi*, sailing to London with a cargo of cloth, lead, tin and pewter. Sores's coup threatened the valuable trade between England and Venice and when the Queen of Navarre refused her demand that the prizes be released, Elizabeth had no choice but to act against the Huguenot corsairs.

Sores was already in the process of transferring his base of operations to La Rochelle and his actions were seen as a parting act of disrespect to his English hosts. Perhaps it was – he may have harboured a grudge over the English attempt to exploit the first war of religion to recover Calais. The Queen of Navarre's refusal to make amends is more easily explained by the fact that the 900 ton *Vergi*, renamed *Huguenotte* and heavily armed with both her own guns and those from *Justiniana*, became much the strongest ship in the official Huguenot fleet and was instrumental in breaking the Catholic blockade of La Rochelle in July 1570, the final straw that broke Charles IX's ability to continue the war.

The English background to these events was that in October 1569 the Ridolfi Plot to murder Elizabeth and put the captive Mary, Queen of Scots on the English throne was uncovered. Penetrated from the start by Cecil's agents, it involved secret funding from the ex-Inquisitor General Pope Pius V and, through their ambassadors, the complicity of the kings of France and Spain. It was followed almost immediately by the rebellion of the earls of Northumberland and Westmorland, whose twin aims were the overthrow of Elizabeth and the restoration of England to the Catholic faith. Their campaign quickly degenerated into farce, but the unamused queen ordered savage reprisals.

Thus by the time Sores seized the Venetian carracks, Elizabeth had reason to believe that the boil of domestic Catholic subversion had been lanced and that she did not need the Huguenot corsairs as well as the Sea Beggars to help protect her from a cross-Channel invasion by the Duke of Alba, the essential ingredient in both the Ridolfi Plot and the rebellion of the Northern earls. On 25 February 1570, as though to confirm her confidence, the frustrated Pius V issued the vindictive bull *Regnans in Excelsis*, which declared Elizabeth deposed and absolved her subjects of any allegiance to her, which both Philip II and Charles IX deplored as of dubious legality and wholly counter-productive effect. In the words of a great French statesman of a later age, it was worse than a crime – it was an error.[*]

Although it dashed Cecil's hope of forcing Philip II to let the English trade with America, San Juan de Ulúa was not particularly significant when measured against the geopolitical background. The deterioration in Anglo-Spanish relations resulting from Philip II's implacable hostility towards all things Protestant made it natural for England to ally informally with those who could help to keep the Spanish threat away from her shores. The operational ties and cross-fertilization among English seafarers, Sea Beggars and Huguenot corsairs were a natural consequence of this, fed by the loss of traditional markets and the denial of new ones by the Spanish and the Portuguese.

However, the treachery of Viceroy Enríquez and the vile subsequent treatment of the English hostages and captives from the third Hawkins expedition, culminating in the burning at the stake of Robert Barrett, the master of *Jesus*, was crucial to the evolution of the sea-dog phenomenon in another way. In the 47 years since Fleury first attacked the flow of treasure across the Atlantic, the only Englishman to follow his lead had been Reneger. During the

[*] Pius V's tomb is decorated with relief carvings celebrating the extremely bloody defeats of the Huguenots at Mercontour and the Ottomans at Lepanto. He was declared a saint in 1712.

same period, while French investor syndicates had financed numerous raids against the Spanish Indies, not one had sailed from England. That was now going to change, not as an act of government policy but because San Juan de Ulúa persuaded the Hawkins and Wynter brothers that peaceful trade was a chimera – and it made Francis Drake a mortal enemy of Spain.

CHAPTER 6

DRAKE AND OXENHAM

When Drake sailed into Plymouth on 20 January 1569, William Hawkins sent him to London with a letter for Cecil, Drake's first contact with the court. We can be sure that Drake and Blondel did not take four months to cross the Atlantic, as the supplies on little *Judith* would have run out even more quickly than they did on *Minion*. Possibly they sailed to Blondel's home port of La Rochelle to get him another ship and were delighted to find they could prey on Spanish shipping under Huguenot letters of marque. A history of previous collaboration would add credence to Hortrop's belief that Drake and Blondel joined forces in a subsequent Caribbean raid. Also, if Drake returned to Plymouth with a shipload of loot it would explain why he was able to marry in July that year, and why later the same year William Hawkins sailed with him to Guinea on the 50-ton *Brave*. Returning home himself on a smaller ship, Hawkins sent Drake on to complete the triangular voyage to the Caribbean.

Drake went on to become the avatar of the triumph of Protestant English individualism over the termite swarms of Hispano-Popish imperialism, which until relatively recently defined a major element of English national consciousness. He was undoubtedly heroic: bold, fearless and blessed with good fortune. Furthermore he was born into obscurity and achieved greatness; started dirt poor and died wealthy; consorted with the highest in the land without losing the common touch; and – so important in the English preoccupation with class – he moved in cosmopolitan circles but remained true to his roots.

Cornelis Ketel's famous 1580 portrait celebrating Drake's circumnavigation shows a man who did not take himself too seriously, a little gamecock in a bright red suit whose twinkling eyes gently mock his grandiloquent pose. In old age the wrinkles on his face were those of one who smiled and laughed a lot, an endearing feature not often found in portraits of his contemporaries.

He was also sly, casually cruel, no more honest than he had to be, boastful and inclined to swagger. In sum, he was a 'wide boy', from whom you would be ill-advised to buy a used galleon – which, while it may tarnish the halo a patriotic posterity painted around his head, simply enhances his roguish attractiveness. Posterity also tried to portray him as a great military commander, which does not hold up to even casually sceptical scrutiny. The evidence is clear that his secretive and idiosyncratic style of leadership was only effective at the single-ship or small-flotilla level where he could emphasize, as brutally as necessary, that not only the hopes of profit but also the very survival of the men under his command demanded unquestioning obedience.

A brilliant opportunist, Drake was temperamentally unsuited to lead any enterprise that required working to a plan, which sometimes led to conflict with less talented subordinate commanders as strong willed as himself. He was hardly unique in this: naval command during the Renaissance was akin to herding cats and from time to time admirals of all nationalities felt compelled to hang recalcitrant captains as an example to the rest. Drake, however, behaved more like one of those insubordinate captains than an admiral. Although later generations tried to portray him and Hawkins as co-founders of the Royal Navy, his talent and aspirations simply did not run in that direction. Instead, his strengths and his failings confirm him as the epitome of the English talent for 'muddling through', the other side of the coin that makes 'English planning' an oxymoron.

English corsair activity was insignificant by comparison with the French until the 1570s, and only surpassed it in the 1580s because at last there was open, if still undeclared war with Spain and the English authorities freely issued letters of marque. On the other side of the Channel the assassination of Coligny in 1572 and the immediately following nine-month siege of La Rochelle, in which the French crown finally had the wit to pay the corsairs of Brittany, Saint-Malo and Dieppe to fight against the Huguenots, broke the mainspring of the *guerre de course* against Spain. The French maritime challenge to the Spanish and Portuguese monopoly in America slowly ebbed away because, without the official backing enjoyed by such as Ango, Le Clerc, Ribault and Sores, French corsair activity reverted from school to swarm.

Hesitantly, the English took up the baton, led by Drake. The degree to which he was inspired by the French example is hard to assess. Perhaps someday a French scholar will discover details of his association with Blondel – but we do know that the man who gave Drake his first independent command was William Hawkins, who was more closely associated with the Huguenot corsairs than any man in England. It also seems likely that Drake's 1573 meeting with Gillaume le Testu in Panamá planted the seed of his 1577–80 circumnavigation. That he became the heir of the French corsair tradition is unarguable – what has been overlooked is the degree to which he learned from them directly.

The absence of Spanish complaints argues that Drake's 1569–70 voyage was a low-key smuggling venture in the style of Jean Bontemps. However, his next Caribbean voyage in 1571 (the year Bontemps was killed) was on behalf of a syndicate in which the highly placed Wynter brothers joined the Hawkins brothers, as they had for the slaving voyages. Drake sailed in the 25-ton pinnace *Swan*, one of three English ships (one of them a mother ship for two pinnaces) that took part in a purely piratical raid on Panamá in league with French corsairs who may have included Paul Blondel. By now Drake must have spoken French fluently, which was to prove a useful ability.

In *Sir Francis Drake Revived*, published by Drake's namesake nephew in 1626, the claim is made that the voyages of 1569–71 were a reconnaissance for the 1572–73 raid, which gives food for thought. Since the mid-1550s the main stream of bullion from America to

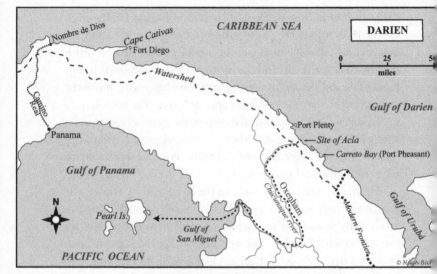

DRAKE AND OXENHAM 1572-1577

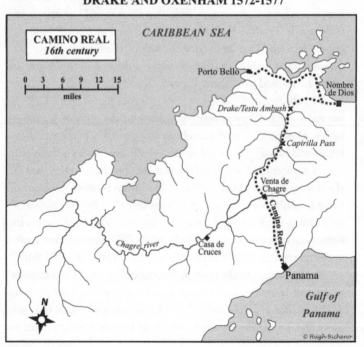

Spain came from the mountain of silver at Potosí in Upper Perú (today Bolivia), whence it was brought by mule down to Callao, the port of Lima, thence by ship to the Pacific port of Panamá. From there it was carried across the isthmus by mule to the Caribbean port of Nombre de Dios, where it was collected by the annual *flota*. Although preceded by a decade of small-scale French smuggling activity, the Anglo-French raid in 1571 was the first such outright attack on Panamá, whose shallow coastal waters and shifting sand banks had previously deterred the oceangoing corsair ships. The combination of a mother ship and pinnaces that was employed in 1571 was designed to overcome the problem.

Given the political uncertainties it's most unlikely that either Drake or his backers would have planned the 1571 voyage either as Drake's corsair apprenticeship or as a trial run for the 1572–73 raid: but that is what it turned out to be. When the three ships returned bulging with loot, they paused before entering Plymouth to establish whether England and Spain had patched up their differences since they sailed. They had not: Anglo-Spanish diplomatic and trade relations were not officially restored until 21 August 1574, when the Treaty of Bristol was signed.

Thus a window of opportunity remained open for the first major English raid on Spanish America, and Drake was not only eager but now very able to lead it. In Panamá he had rowed up the Chagre (today Chagres) River towards a place called Casa de Cruces 20 miles/32 kilometres) from the city of Panamá, where he mistakenly believed that bullion was loaded on boats as an alternative to the overland mule trains (*recuas*). He had also made contact with one of the escaped slaves called 'feral cattle' by the Spanish (*cimarrones*, later anglicized to 'Maroons'), who had intermarried with the Amerindians and established free communities in the jungle, from which they waged merciless guerrilla warfare against their hated former masters. Finally, he had left a cache of stores at 'a fine round bay of very safe harbour' he named Port Pheasant, 'by reason of the great store of those goodly fowls [great currasows] which he and his company did kill and feed on'.

In 1610 a Spanish report of John Oxenham's 1577 raid stated that 'some English ascended the river of Puertofaisanes [Port Pheasants] from the North Sea [Caribbean] and entered the Rio Indios which flows into the South Sea [Pacific], carrying material for launches which they put together and began to rob the sea'. If the reference to 'the river of Puertofaisanes' is correct, then Carreto Bay is the most likely candidate, as the stream flowing into it rises a few hundred yards from the source of an important tributary of the river known today as the Chucunaque, which drains into the Pacific at the Gulf of San Miguel.

Oxenham was also reported to have crossed from Acla, an abandoned settlement at the place from which Vasco Núñez de Balboa set out for the first European crossing of the isthmus in 1513 – although he is also said to have started from 'Carreta'. Oxenham could not have hidden his ship at Acla, which is on a promontory between two streams, and probably he did indeed set out from Carreto Bay, where he concealed his ship, but went to Acla in the pinnaces and crossed from there.*

Camino Real (Royal Road) was rather a grand name for a 50-mile/80-kilometre path carved out of dense jungle from Panamá on the Pacific coast to the ports of Nombre de Dios and Porto Bello on the Caribbean coast. Although said to be wide enough for two carts to pass, the fact that the Spanish continued to use mule trains to transport the bullion from Perú confirms that it was simply a roughly cobbled track. Water flow in the Chagre was highly unpredictable – it drains the central highlands and, until tamed by the artificial Gatún Lake created by the US Army Corps of Engineers as the keystone for the Panamá Canal, constituted more of an obstacle than an alternative for trans-isthmian travel. It was therefore unguarded, and a well-established smugglers' route. Drake saw it as a means to get men and guns close to Panamá, by-passing the Caribbean coastal range. He tried repeatedly but was never able to

* Acla is in the middle of an inset stretch of coast between Mulatupo Bay and Caledonia Bay, the latter named for the calamitous 'Darien Scheme' colony of 1698–1700 that bankrupted Scotland and brought about the 1707 Act of Union.

mount such an attack – that was left to his great successor Henry Morgan, who took an army of corsairs up the Chagre to defeat the garrison and sack Panamá in January 1671.

The 1572 expedition consisted of three components. The first ship to sail was commanded by James Garrett, who had been the mate of the *Minion* in her ill-starred voyage to and from San Juan de Ulúa and who sailed for the Hawkins–Wynter syndicate. James Rance, master of *Saloman* in Lovell's voyage and of *William and John* in Hawkins's third voyage, either left after Drake or was overtaken by him. Rance was not sailing for Hawkins this time, however. He commanded a ship belonging to that friend of all corsairs Sir Edward Horsey, Vice Admiral of Hampshire.

Drake sailed as an investor in his own right, being at least co-owner with John Hawkins and probably outright proprietor of the two ships with which he departed Plymouth on 24 May 1572 . They were his flagship, the 40-ton *Pascoe*, which had sailed under Robert Bolton in Lovell's voyage, and the *Swan*, in which Drake himself had sailed in 1571 and now under the command of his brother John. Another brother, Joseph, sailed with them. Having found that even the 25-ton *Swan* drew too much water for Darien's shallow coastal waters and mangrove-lined inlets, Drake had three smaller pinnaces, each of about 10 tons, prefabricated and then disassembled to be packed in his ships' holds. He had 46 men on *Pascoe* and 26 on *Swan*, double the number Hawkins thought healthy, but apart from *Pascoe*'s 50-year-old master they were all under 30 and selected for robustness.

Drake's passage to the Canaries was so rapid that he did not stop and sailed straight on to Dominica, arriving on 28 June. This was a sensationally fast crossing – 35 days – which meant that he did not need to stop for stores and alert the Spanish before reaching Port Pheasant on 12 July. There he found a message from Garret incised on a lead tablet and nailed to a tree that seemed to doom the expedition:

> *Captain Drake, if you fortune to come to this port, make haste away, for the Spaniards which you had with you here last year*

> *have betrayed this place, and taken away all that you left here.*
> *I departed from hence this present 7 of July, 1572. Your very*
> *loving friend, John Garrett.*

Drake ordered the construction of a pentagonal log fort within which his carpenters put together the prefabricated pinnaces, which he named *Lion, Bear* and *Minion*. No sooner had work begun than Rance arrived with a prize – a shallop carrying mail. As soon as the pinnaces were assembled all five ships sailed north-west to a cove in the Isle of Pines (not to be confused with the much larger Isle of Pines off the south-west coast of Cuba), which was named Port Plenty (see Map, page 114) by the relentlessly optimistic Drake and which became the new base of operations.

On the basis of Drake's future form we may be sure that relations with Rance deteriorated rapidly. Horsey's captain was an older and more experienced sailor, but Drake had twice as many ships and men, and with them the right to command. It's clear that Rance chafed at taking orders from Drake, as he went his own way soon afterwards. Drake must have been glad to see him go; the enterprise was a high-stakes gamble, too steep for prudent employees like Rance and Garrett.

At the Isle of Pines Drake found two *fragatas* from Nombre de Dios and learned from their crews, if he did not know already, that the annual *flota* had been and gone a month earlier and that Nombre de Dios would probably be treasureless and sparsely populated. Nonetheless, Drake insisted on leading a raid against the port, taking the three pinnaces, the shallop and all the men except for 20 who remained with Rance to guard the ships. It took five days, probably under oars and hugging the coast, to cover the relatively short distance. On 28 July, when they arrived close enough to make a night approach, Drake set the men ashore on an island (today called El Porvenir) off Cape Cativas, issued them with weapons and rehearsed how the attack was to be carried out.

According to *Sir Francis Drake Revived* his biggest concern was a battery of heavy guns that the men captured at the Isle of Pines said was on a hill overlooking the harbour, so he led one column to neutralize it while the other was supposed to take the town. In fact he found the guns near the shore and dismounted them, but Drake still went up the hill, where he found nothing. The element of surprise was lost because the second column was delayed and by the time Drake entered the town the militia was formed and ready.

> *But the soldiers and such as were joined with them, presented us with a jolly hot volley of shot, beating full upon the egress of that street in which we marched; and levelling very low, so as their bullets ofttimes grazed on the sand. ... having discharged our first volley of shot, and feathered them with our arrows ... we came to the push of pike,* so that our firepikes [a pike with an explosive head] *being well armed and made of purpose, did us very great service.*

Drake's trumpet signaller was killed and he himself was shot in the leg by the only volley the militia fired before the English charged them and they fled. They soon found a house full of silver bullion in bars, but Drake dared not risk having his men encumbered should the Spanish counter-attack:

> *... our Captain commanded straitly that none of us should touch a bar of silver; but stand upon our weapons, because the town was full of people, and there was in the King's Treasure House near the water side, more gold and jewels than all our four pinnaces could carry: which we would presently set some in hand to break open, notwithstanding the Spaniards' report of the strength of it.*

A report of an imminent attack on the pinnaces sent them rushing back to the beach, where Drake passed out from loss of blood. The leaderless men gave up the attack and pulled away, joined by an escaping slave called Diego. It will come as no surprise to anyone with even a casual interest in military history that a night amphibious assault by untrained men on an unknown shore was chaotic, and that despite early success it failed when command and control was lost.

What glowers from the page is the ferocity of the English response when fired on, which had the result of sparing them greater casualties. The Spanish militia had many killed and wounded, whereas the trumpeter was the only English fatality and Drake one of the few wounded. It was a serious wound, yet he recovered quickly, and on the way back to the Isle of Pines sent his brother John in one of the pinnaces to find out if the Chagre River was navigable.* As soon as he had his men back Rance sailed away, no doubt with a triumphant 'I told you so' as a parting shot.

John Drake's report on the Chagre was presumably discouraging, because his brother took the little flotilla east across the Gulf of Darien to attack Cartagena de Indias instead. Once again a bold night attack in the pinnaces came up empty because the only Spanish ship in the inner harbour ran herself aground and cavalry appeared to prevent the English looting and burning her.

At this point *Swan* was lost – according to *Sir Francis Drake Revived* as the result of deliberate sabotage by Drake in order to redistribute her crew among the pinnaces, with John Drake coming aboard *Pascoe* as captain. This story is so bizarre that one is inclined to believe it, and it does fit the pattern of Drake taking drastic action to tighten his grip when he detected wavering and discontent. A further indication that the men were surly is that he now sailed his ships to the Gulf of Urabá for two weeks of rest and relaxation.

On 5 September 1572 he sent John and Diego with *Pascoe* and *Lion* to make contact with the Maroons in Darien while he took *Minion* and *Bear* back along the coast past Cartagena to sail up the Magdalena River in search of supplies and loot. Although the river was the principal means of communication with the interior he found nothing worth stealing and it was only after he returned to the Caribbean that he was able to capture two well-laden *fragatas*, which he added to his fleet.

* The rainy season runs from May to November. Drake would have wanted to know if the Chagre was flooding.

He then returned to the Isle of Pines and distributed the supplies to a number of caches on the mainland and on several small islands, such that they would survive even if the Spanish discovered Port Plenty. When John and Diego rejoined him it was with news that the Maroons were eager to combine forces, and on their advice he moved his base of operations to the island off Cape Cativas, where he cannibalized the captured *fragatas* to build a log fort he named in honour of Diego.

To concentrate Spanish attention elsewhere, Drake now took his flotilla to raid Cartagena again, capturing two merchant ships in the mouth of the harbour. Unable to sail them out, he looted and destroyed them. He then tried the Magdalena River, again fruitlessly, and finally made an appearance off Santa Marta, drawing fire from the fort. By now supplies were low and his men once more surly, but 'of God's great mercy' he fell on a fat cargo ship and morale was restored. The sequence of events is highly reminiscent of a similar occasion 150 years later, wonderfully recorded in his log by the famous Golden Age pirate Edward 'Blackbeard' Teach:

> *Such a day, rum all out – our Company somewhat sober – a damn'd confusion among us! – rogues aplotting – great talk of separation. So I look'd sharp for a prize – such a day took one, with a great deal of liquor on board, so kept the Company hot, damn'd hot, then all things went well again.*

Returning to Fort Diego, Drake learned that his brother John had been killed in a failed attack on a *fragata*. It seems clear that he was now marking time until traffic on the Camino Real picked up in anticipation of the annual *flota*. Unfortunately many of his crew fell ill from the virulent yellow fever that made Darien as infamous as the Bight of Benin. Among the dead was his second brother, Joseph. In desperation Drake ordered the ship's doctor to perform an autopsy, which found a swollen liver and a 'sodden' heart but, of course, no indication that it was the result of mosquito bites.

Even though his men were reduced to half their original number, Drake remained indomitable. Informed by the Maroons early in January 1573 that the annual *flota* had arrived, he decided to march across country, guided by the Maroons, to a point on the Camino Real where he hoped to intercept a mule train of Peruvian treasure. This must have been near Venta de Chagre, but Drake believed it was called Venta Cruz, confusing it with the smugglers' haven towards which he had rowed with his French associates in 1571.

Thirty Maroons trailblazed for Drake and seventeen of his own men, with John Oxenham as second in command. On the way, after passing through a well-ordered and prosperous Maroon village, his guides pointed out a tall tree from which he could see both the Caribbean and the Pacific. Drake 'besought Almighty God of his goodness to give him life and leave to sail once in an English ship on that sea', to which Oxenham replied that unless Drake 'beat him from his company he would follow him by God's grace'.

Informed by the Maroons that a bullion mule train was about to set out from Panamá, the raiders set an ambush on the road before Venta de Chagre, only for the trap to fail because a seaman called Robert Pike found a bottle of brandy, got drunk, and staggered into the road. It's unlikely that his shipmates took him with them as they retreated along the Camino Real, plundering a mule train of less valuable cargo and finally looting and burning the warehouses at Venta de Chagre before once again cutting across country to regain their pinnaces and return to Fort Diego. From there the pinnaces fanned out looking for loot and supplies. Drake failed to find anything to the west and had to sink one of his pinnaces for lack of crew, but Oxenham returned from the Colombian coast with a 20-ton *fragata* full of needed supplies, which Drake added to his now very thinly manned fleet.

Then on 23 March 1573 came one of those encounters that seem so improbable yet happened so frequently in the age of discovery. At Cape Cativas Drake met the great French cosmographer Gillaume Le Testu with 70 men in the 80-ton *Havre*. Le Testu had been appointed Royal Pilot by Henri II in 1556 but became a

Huguenot corsair at the outbreak of the Wars of Religion. Imprisoned in 1569 he had only recently been pardoned by King Charles IX, so the most likely explanation for his appearance at Fort Diego is that he had been sent to chart the coast of Central America, as he had the eastern coast of South America in 1551–52. He told Drake that Admiral Coligny had been murdered six months earlier, on 24 August 1572, in the infamous St Bartholomew's Day massacre in Paris that signalled the start of a frenzied nationwide pogrom against Huguenots.

Le Testu had popularized a fictitious southern continent he called 'Java la Grande' in his atlases, which were still highly regarded. Drake surely knew of him by reputation and they would naturally have discussed the southern continent, and probably also Coligny's failed attempts to found French colonies in the southern hemisphere, in which Le Testu had been involved. The Frenchman would have felt no loyalty to Charles IX or perhaps even to France following the St Bartholomew's Day massacre, and may have regarded collaboration with Drake as a first step towards obtaining the patronage of such as the Hawkins and Wynter brothers for further exploration and Protestant colonization.

Whatever his longer-term hopes, he was receptive to Drake's plan to intercept a bullion mule train near Nombre de Dios, where the Spanish would have dropped their guard. They agreed on a daring raid along a stream that ran between Nombre Dios and Porto Bello, attacking from a bay with many islands to conceal their approach. Telling the pinnaces to return for them in four days' time, Le Testu with 20 and Drake with 15 men plus a number of Maroons struck inland along the stream. When they reached the Camino Real five miles south-west of Nombre de Dios on 29 April, Maroon scouts reported the imminent arrival of a lightly guarded caravan of almost 200 mules.

Soon they could hear the tinkling of mule bells, and Drake's prediction that the Spanish would not have advance scouts out so close to their destination proved correct. Surprise was complete, but even so there was a bitter battle before the Spanish soldiers were driven off, during which the Maroons and the French suffered casualties including Le Testu, who was severely wounded. The spoil of nearly 30 tons of bullion was far beyond the capacity of the raiders to carry, so they took the gold, worth an estimated 80,000–100,000 pesos, and buried most of the silver for later recovery. Le Testu could not travel and remained behind with two men.

On return to the mouth of the stream Drake found Spanish *fragatas* waiting offshore. Resourceful as ever, he constructed a raft and paddled to one of the outer islands, where he was able to attract the attention of his own pinnaces. Under his command they presumably drove off the *fragatas* then picked up the rest of the ambush party and the loot, while Drake sent a larger number back to recover Le Testu and the silver. They returned with only a small portion of the buried silver to report that the delay caused by the *fragatas* off the rendezvous point had proved fatal for the Frenchmen, who were captured and tortured to reveal where most of the silver was hidden. Le Testu had been decapitated and his head taken back to Nombre de Dios for display in the marketplace.

The *Havre* sailed back to France immediately after the division of the loot. Drake sailed back to Port Plenty and sent the pinnaces to raid for supplies on the Magdalena River, from which they returned with another *fragata* that Drake decided to keep. After giving their guns and ironwork to the Maroons, Drake burned the remaining pinnaces and, after careening *Pascoe* and the two captured *fragatas* to clear marine infestation and apply a new coat of tallow, set sail sometime in early July, arriving back in Plymouth on Sunday 9 August 1573. They had been gone for over fourteen months, so long that everyone had given them up for dead, and the parsons of Plymouth saw their congregations decamp *en masse* when word of Drake's return spread.

At a conservative estimate the venture returned with 100,000 pesos in cash and specie alone. Drake would not have maintained the popularity he enjoyed in Plymouth if he cheated his investors, or his crew, or the dependants of those who died – but he was fully entitled to the lion's share as admiral and proprietor, while the two *fragatas* more than compensated for the lost *Swan* and pinnaces. Historians are naturally drawn more to Drake's circumnavigation, but he would not have been the natural choice to lead it were it not for the robustness, intrepidity, intelligence and, above all, the inspirational leadership and dogged determination he displayed in the face of constant setbacks and almost unimaginable hardship in 1572–73.

He was also a supremely lucky individual, as he returned not long before Elizabeth's and Philip II's representatives agreed the Convention of Nijmegen, ratified by the Treaty of Bristol in August 1574, which restored Anglo-Spanish diplomatic and trade relations and ushered in a period of official disapproval of attacks on Spanish shipping. The back story was that when Elizabeth closed her ports to the Sea Beggars, who had unwisely failed to share their loot with her, they seized Brielle in Zeeland on 1 April 1572 and re-opened the land war in the Low Countries, undoing Alba's brutally effective pacification.

This was followed by the Treaty of Blois between France and England of 22 April 1572, the realization of Alba's worst fears and a triumph for Sir Francis Walsingham, Elizabeth's ambassador in Paris. Unfazed by the Saint Bartholomew's Day Massacre, the queen used the leverage of the French alliance to obtain excellent terms from Alba at Nijmegen, her principal 'concessions' being the withdrawal of English troops from the Netherlands, which she wanted to do anyway, and the denial of bases to the Sea Beggars, which she had already done.

Even so, Drake's voyage had been a nakedly piratical venture without even the fig leaf of letters of marque from Orange or Coligny, and he prudently refrained from drawing further attention to himself for the next three years, confining himself to legal trading with his three small ships.

He also employed them in support of the Earl of Essex's 1575 campaign in northern Ireland, during which he became friendly with the earl's retainer Thomas Doughty. It was a genocidal, expensive and largely futile campaign in which Drake's ships were instrumental in the attack on the Rathlin Island supply base of corsair and perennial pain in the English neck Sorley Boy MacDonnell, where over five hundred people – mainly women and children – were massacred. Drake must have made a profit, for he ordered a new 150-ton galleon to be built in 1576 incorporating all that he had learned from operating alongside the French corsairs.

The new galleon was to be christened *Pelican*, a bird believed to provide her young with blood by wounding her own breast when no other food was available, thus a heraldic symbol of the Passion of Christ and the Eucharist. More to the point, in 1574 Nicholas Hilliard painted his famous 'pelican portrait' of Queen Elizabeth in which a pelican pendant accompanied her usual pearls for purity and Tudor roses for unity. Whether Drake saw the portrait or not, he would have known that it was the queen's fondest conceit that she gave her life's blood (money) for her people. The choice of name tells us that Drake intended his new ship to be the means of providing his sovereign with a notable transfusion, an unexpectedly subtle and courtly gesture from one of such humble origins.

The intervening years were filled with unpiratical projects and expeditions intended to win England new markets, which need not concern us. The West Country mafia continued to send out raiders under foreign letters of marque, but in the summer of 1574 they also produced the only 'schooling' proposal of the period. Cousins Richard Grenville and William Hawkins, on behalf of 'certain gentlemen of the West Country, desirous to adventure ourselves and our goods', requested a patent for the 'discovering, traffic and enjoying for the Queen's majesty and her subjects of all and any lands, islands and countries southward beyond the equinoctial [equator]' that were not already claimed by Christian princes. 'Ships of our own are well prepared', Grenville urged, and the company included men 'to whom the passage thither is almost known'.

One of the ships was the powerful *Castle of Comfort*, bought from Thomas Fenner of Chichester for the purpose, but the company notably did not include Drake. The mathematician Thomas Digges was included among the sponsors, perhaps seeing the journey as an opportunity to prove his faith in properly scientific navigation, but he was just respectable window dressing. However peaceful the stated intention, the fact that Grenville and Hawkins were the leading proponents meant that while the expedition might find new lands and establish new colonies, it would certainly involve predation on Spanish ships and settlements in the southern cone of South America.

Grenville unsuccessfully wooed John Oxenham as one of the men 'to whom the passage thither is almost known', and it's thanks to his later testimony in Spanish captivity that we know as much about the Grenville–Hawkins project as we do. Oxenham declared that he had seen the letters patent issued by the queen, but they were later revoked because she 'had heard that beyond the Strait of Magellan there were settlements made by the Spaniards, who might do them harm'. The statement has the authentic ring of queenly irony – of course her well-founded apprehension was that Grenville would do the harming.

So it was that the only outright English raid on Spanish America between 1573 and 1579 was an entirely unofficial venture by John Oxenham himself, no doubt with every assistance short of overt sponsorship by Drake. Oxenham sailed from Plymouth on 9 April 1576 in a 100-ton ship with two disassembled pinnaces and several veterans of Drake's raid among his 57 men, which was close to the Hawkins' optimum of one man per two tons for long voyages but not enough to replicate Drake's exploit. Like his mentor, Oxenham did not bother to obtain letters of marque, on the face of it a strange decision because, although the Spanish did not respect them, such licences offered their bearers some protection from legal consequences should they come before an English court. Clearly men risen from the ranks like Drake and Oxenham sailed with the do-or-die attitude that if they were successful they would be able to buy their way out of trouble, and if not they would be past caring.

Oxenham returned to Port Pheasant, built another stockade behind which to assemble the pinnaces, and from that moment onwards barely put a foot right. First he sailed the pinnaces past

Nombre de Dios to attack a *fragata* off the coast of Veragua and was beaten off with losses, thereby alerting the Spanish authorities without relieving his supply situation. On returning to Port Pheasant he found the Maroon Diego, who had been such a valuable ally for Drake, waiting for him with the bad news that it would be impossible to repeat Drake's bullion caravan exploit because the mule trains were now heavily escorted and routinely preceded by advance parties on the look-out for ambushes.

It must have been Diego who suggested striking inland to the village of a Maroon chief known as Mozambique Luis, where they would be taken care of and from which they would be able to descend a large river to raid the defenceless Pacific coast of Darien with the full support of Mozambique Luis's men. This must have appealed powerfully to Oxenham and the other veterans of the previous voyage, who would have been aware of Drake's ambition to use the Chagre River to attack Panamá. They do not appear to have had difficulty persuading the rest of the company to abandon the original plan and to embark on what was an extraordinarily high-risk alternative.

The ship was made light by removing all her guns and cargo (logically also her top-masts and rigging) and run into an inlet where she could be camouflaged among the trees, while the cargo of trade goods and all except two small guns were buried. From there, as previously speculated, the company probably sailed the pinnaces to Acla for a rendezvous with Mozambique Luis's Maroons, who would have provided porterage for the guns and other stores across the watershed to their village, while the pinnaces were concealed in one of Acla's streams.

From September 1576 to February 1577 Oxenham's men stayed first at the Maroon village and then at a camp further downstream on a tributary of the Chucunaque River, where they built a 45-foot pinnace with timber and tools stolen by the Maroons from a Spanish lumber yard on the Gulf of San Miguel. Meanwhile, following the failed attack off Veragua, *fragatas* had been sent out from Nombre de Dios to locate the mother ship from which the pirate pinnaces must have sailed. Given that they knew Drake had used it they must have looked very carefully at Port Pheasant and found the ship, guns and trade goods, probably also some of the men left to guard them, from whom they would have extracted information that led them to the pinnaces at Acla.

Unaware that his retreat had been cut off, Oxenham set off with most of his men and six Maroon guides down the river to the Gulf of San Miguel, and from there to the Pearl Islands, where they set up camp. During their stay on the island they stole the pearls gathered by the local Indians and allegedly tortured and murdered a Franciscan friar. If true, this is the only occasion when English sailors displayed the sort of anti-clerical ferocity common among their Huguenot peers.

The Pearl Islanders sent word to Panamá, where the Governor already knew there were pirates operating in the Gulf of Panamá. In a matter of a few days Oxenham's company had captured a ship from Ecuador carrying 60,000 pesos of gold as well as wine and bread, and then another from Perú carrying 100,000 pesos of silver ingots, more than Drake had managed in a year of operations.

The Spanish reaction was swift. The Governor of Ecuador sent a flotilla under Pedro Ortega Valencia, and the Viceroy of Perú, Francisco Álvarez de Toledo, sent another under Diego Frías de Trejos. Ortega sailed to the Pearl Islands but found the pirates gone. The islanders told him they had sailed towards the Gulf of San Miguel, and on the way Ortega encountered the two pirated cargo ships, their crews busy making good the damage done to their rigging by Oxenham's men. Sailing up the river, Ortega came to the junction of three tributaries and was about to give up the chase when he noticed chicken feathers floating down one of them.

Ortega followed the stream, and after four days found the pirates' pinnace pulled up on the river bank, with six men guarding it. The Spanish killed one and captured the others, who were tortured to reveal where the rest had gone with the treasure. Ortega now knew that he outnumbered the pirates and raced after them. Less than 2 miles/3 kilometres along the trail he was delighted to find all the treasure under a mound of freshly dug earth. The weight had proved too burdensome for Oxenham's men, who had made little progress through the jungle before they fell to squabbling over how to proceed. After wasting a great deal of time they decided to bury it, intending to return with Maroons to help them carry it across the watershed.

Ortega called off the pursuit in order to get the silver bullion and gold safely back to Panamá, but the pirates came to him instead. Advised by Maroons that the Spanish had discovered the treasure, Oxenham's men charged back along the trail so noisily that Ortega had plenty of time to set up an ambush. Against trained troops, ferocity was not enough. Eleven pirates were killed and seven captured against only two Spanish killed.

Ortega tortured his captives to obtain the full story before returning to Panamá, where the authorities were quick to appreciate the danger posed by the Maroon–pirate alliance. Ortega returned to wage a two-year campaign against the Maroons, leading columns of soldiers into the jungle to burn their crops and villages until in 1579 the surviving Maroons accepted resettlement in one location where they were granted a considerable degree of self-government in return for acknowledging Spanish sovereignty and agreeing to return escaped slaves in future.*

The first (1589) edition of Hakluyt's *Principal Navigations* stated that Oxenham's raid also caused Philip II to send two galleys for the protection of the Darien coast, which took 6 or 7 French ships 'and after this was known there were no more Englishmen or Frenchmen of war that durst adventure to approach that coast until the present year 1586'. A fort was also built at the mouth of the Chagre and the isthmus was not attacked again until Drake returned in 1595.

When Oxenham's remaining men regained the Maroon village, they learned their ships were lost. Although relations between the two groups had become strained, the Maroons helped them get to

* The British were to reach exactly the same arrangement with the Maroons of Jamaica in 1737.

the coast and gave them the tools to build another ship. However, yellow fever soon thinned their ranks to eighteen, including Oxenham, ship's master John Butler, the pilot Thomas Sherwell and five cabin boys.

Nemesis caught up with them in the form of Frías de Trejos's troops from Perú, who took over the pursuit from Ortega and found the Maroon village, burning it and capturing 40 of the inhabitants, who were sold into slavery. In September they tracked down Oxenham and his remaining men, who were taken back to Panamá and convicted of piracy. Ten men were hanged in the main plaza, the cabin boys spared to become the governor's house servants, and Oxenham, Butler and Sherwell were sent to Perú, where they were prisoners of the Inquisition.

During interrogation in Panamá Oxenham gave his age as 42. It was noted that he was 'coarse of speech ... of grave demeanour, much feared and respected and obeyed by his soldiers'. Perhaps in captivity; but indiscipline no less than a serious underestimation of the speed and effectiveness of the Spanish reaction had doomed the enterprise. Although letters of marque would not have saved them, it's significant that the Spanish took pains to establish that no such authority existed, which left the Englishmen with no defence against the charge of piracy.

The Inquisitors were oddly hesitant to release Oxenham and his two officers to the civil authorities for execution, perhaps because they could not decide whether they should be hanged as pirates or burned as heretics. In February 1579 Drake learned that his comrades were still alive when he attacked Callao, the port of Lima. He sent a Spanish captive with a message for the governor threatening reprisals if the men were not released, but could not follow through on the threat. The three men were finally hanged in early November 1580.

CHAPTER 7

AROUND THE GLOBE

As Harry Kelsey has pointed out at length in his biography of Drake, few of the documents concerning the circumnavigation are first-hand. One unimpeachable source is a badly charred document dating from mid-1577 discovered by Eva Taylor and published in 1930, which confirmed that the venture was a standard Elizabethan joint-stock enterprise formed for the following purpose (Taylor's reconstructions of text lost to fire are in bracketed italics):

> [*Francis Drake ... shall enter the Strait of Magell*]anas [*lying in 52 degrees of*] the pole, and [*having passed therefrom into*] the South Sea then [*to sail so*] far to the northwards as [*xxx degrees seeking*] along the said coast af[*orenamed like*] as of the other to find out pl[*aces meet*] to have traffic for the vent[*ing of commodities*] of these her Majesty's realms. Where[*as at present*] they are not under the obedience of [*any Christian*] prince, so there is great hope of [*gold, silver*], spices, drugs, cochineal, and [*divers other*] special commodities, such as may [*enrich her*] Highness' dominions, and also [*put*] shipping a-work greatly. And [*having*] gotten up as afore said in the xxx [*degrees*] in the South Sea (if it shall be thought [*meet*] by the afore named Francis Drake to pro[*ceed so*] far), then he is to return by the same way homewards as he went out. Which voyaging by God's favour is to be performed in 12 months, all though he should spend 5 months in tarrying

upon the coasts, to get knowledge of the princes and
countries there.

This may be the most intensely analyzed document in English history, so it is with caution that I draw attention to the phrase 'and
also put shipping a-work greatly', and suggest that it reflects the
overriding desire to increase trade of the queen's principal minister
Sir William Cecil, Baron Burghley since 1571 and Lord Treasurer
since 1572. The possible significance will soon become apparent.

The principal capitalists were: Drake himself with £1,000; Surveyor of the Navy Sir William Wynter with £750; Clerk of the
Queen's Ships George Wynter with £500; and John Hawkins with
£500. Subscribers whose influence clearly counted as much or more
than whatever investment they made were: Secretary of State Sir
Francis Walsingham; the queen's confidant and later Lord Chancellor Sir Christopher Hatton; her most favourite Robert Dudley, Earl
of Leicester and Lord Admiral; and the previous Lord Admiral, Edward Clinton, Earl of Lincoln. Notably absent were the London
merchants, who were prospering from the re-establishment of normal relations with Spain.

The presence of Hatton among the high-placed sponsors is the
key to understanding the genesis of the venture. On or shortly before the death in 1575 of his patron Walter Devereux, Earl of Essex,
Drake's new friend Thomas Doughty became Hatton's secretary
and interested him in Drake's proposal to raid Spanish ports along
the Pacific coast of America. As the entry on Hatton in the *Dictionary of National Biography* perfectly puts it: 'Hatton was a consummate player of a game which Elizabeth adored, that of courtly love.
His role was that of the perpetual suitor, who forever worships an
earthly goddess with unwavering devotion – a devotion that cannot
be fulfilled but never wanes'.

In return the queen showered him with benefits to relieve his
constant indebtedness, of which the most significant in the context
of Drake's voyage was the gift in 1576 of the Isle of Purbeck and
Corfe Castle in Dorset, the revenues from which came almost en-

tirely from being the most notoriously pirate-infested place on the south coast. Hatton's deputy sent servants every day to the pirate ships moored in Studland Bay to collect 'gifts', and claimed a share of all transactions in Studland market, where exotic goods stolen from ships of all nationalities were openly traded. His appetite duly whetted, Hatton must have been highly receptive to Drake's project.

Even so, why Drake and not Grenville, whose 1574 proposal to sail south of the equator could be considered the precursor of Drake's voyage? Grenville's timing was poor, as at that time his project would have threatened the conclusion of the Treaty of Bristol; but in addition Drake was much the more experienced seaman, with a proven record of bringing ventures through adversity to a profitable conclusion. The crucial difference, however, may have been that while responsibility for the actions of either man could be denied, the commoner Drake had the added merit, from the queen's point of view, of being disownable in a way that Grenville, who was old-money gentry and also a Member of Parliament, could not be.

Drake recalled that when Walsingham 'showed me a plot [chart] willing me to set my hand and to note down where I thought [the King of Spain] might be most annoyed', he told him 'some part of my mind' but refused to put anything in writing, saying that 'Her Majesty was mortal and that if it should please God to take her Majesty away it might so be that some prince might reign that might be in league with the King of Spain and then will my own hand be a witness against myself'.

What he wanted was some guarantee that he would not be thrown to the wolves if diplomatic circumstances changed. Walsingham, according to Drake's account, then arranged a private audience with the queen, who told Drake that she 'would gladly be revenged on the King of Spain for divers injuries that I have received'. But, she said, the whole matter must be kept secret so that the king should not learn of it and 'gave me special commandment that of all men my Lord Treasurer [Burghley] should not know of it'. The inference Drake drew was that Burghley might betray the venture in the interest of maintaining good relations with Spain;

yet the queen may simply have been using a rather girlish device to bind Drake to her by sharing the 'secret' that she was ignoring authority-figure Burghley's advice.

An innocent in the ways of the court, Drake would not have known that there was no possibility Burghley could be kept in ignorance. He also seems to have been too overawed to insist on being given reassurance that he would not be sacrificed as a pawn in the diplomatic game. Despite his frequent later affirmations to the contrary he was not given the get-out-of-jail-free card of a commission from Elizabeth, who refused even to allow one of her ships to be used. She did, however, invest in the venture, laundering the money through Hatton.

Hawkins put together a cover story of a trading voyage to Alexandria that convinced nobody, least of all the Spanish ambassador, one of whose informants at Westminster – presumably one of the many agents Walsingham used to disseminate disinformation – told him that the real target was the Caribbean. Meanwhile Hatton asked Doughty to go on the voyage to look after Hatton's interest. Hatton would not have told Doughty to keep the matter secret from Burghley, as both would have known it was impossible. Accordingly Doughty thought nothing of giving Burghley a chart of the proposed voyage,which, when he mentioned it during the trial to which Drake submitted him many months later, sealed his fate.

The key to untangling the back story is to bear in mind that that all at court, the queen included, were accomplished dissemblers who would never have dreamt of revealing their true thoughts and intentions. It's not at all improbable that Burghley and Walsingham constructed a deep cover story about a supposed 'war party' (the backers of the venture) and a putative 'peace party' represented by Burghley, and then had Hawkins concoct his superficial cover story so that the Spanish ambassador should be more inclined to believe the deep one. The purpose, as in any good-cop/bad-cop routine, would have been to make the Spanish regard Burghley as the lesser of two evils.

The great French historian Fernand Braudel argued that 1577 marked the end of the Mediterranean-centric world, mainly because it was the year that the Spanish and Ottoman empires agreed an informal truce that lasted until 1584. They did so to free their hands to deal with more defeatable enemies. Despite suffering a seemingly annihilating defeat at Lepanto in 1571, the Ottomans swiftly rebuilt their galley fleet and soon reversed all the Spanish gains in the Mediterranean. Philip's allies dropped away and he reluctantly concluded that there was no hope of breaking the stalemate for as long as the Christian world remained divided. The Ottomans also judged that the jihad would have to be suspended while they dealt with the schismatic Shi'a regime in Persia. Protestants and Shi'as alike were rightly appalled when the two empires formalized the truce in February 1578.

Despite ordering church bells rung to celebrate Lepanto, Elizabeth knew that Ottoman attrition of Spanish power was an important factor in her own survival. Her representatives at the Porte lobbied tirelessly against the truce, but geopolitical reality could not be denied indefinitely. The Ottomans still looked favourably on the Protestants because, unlike the followers of the 'evil-doer they call Papa', they did not worship idols (statues or images of the saints). The Ottomans also believed that Protestants denied the Holy Trinity, which they saw as a blasphemous denial of the singularity of God.* This was not enough, however, to offset the constant aggravation of attacks by Protestant corsairs on Ottoman shipping, yet another example of the corsair tail wagging the policy dog.

Another factor that may have influenced Elizabeth to initiate covert warfare was that in 1577–84 there was a lull in the French Wars of Religion, and during 1574–79 the Spanish seemed to be running down the war in the Netherlands. Following on Philip II's first default on debt interest payments in 1575, his army in the Netherlands mutinied and brutally sacked Antwerp, which brought about the union of the Catholic and Protestant provinces against Spanish rule. When Juan de Austria, the king's half-brother

* William de La Marck's Sea Beggars wore crescent moon medallions with the inscription 'Better Turk than Papist'.

and victor of Lepanto, arrived as governor in February 1577 he issued a 'Perpetual Edict' agreeing to withdraw Spanish troops from the Netherlands.

At the same time the belief took root among English Catholics that Juan would invade England and marry Mary, Queen of Scots, which Walsingham took seriously enough to attempt to have him assassinated. An overreaction, perhaps, as Juan could only have invaded England if he first pacified the Netherlands, which was beyond his power. But even if Elizabeth's courtiers had known with certainty that it was all a rather pathetic delusion, they would have been remiss to ignore the possibility that the implacable Philip II might use the immense resources freed up by truces in the Mediterranean and the Netherlands to strike at England.

Failure to attach sufficient importance to the broad strategic context has led some to conclude that Drake's expedition to the South Seas was simply a piratical venture sponsored by a penurious monarch and greedy courtiers, and that the objectives set out in the charred memorandum were just window dressing. This is to impose a linear construction on people who thought more laterally than we do today. There was no certainty that the venture would succeed and they could not have anticipated how profitable it would prove to be – yet there was no doubt that it would be a highly provocative act. At a time when the strategic balance had tipped against England, sending Drake into the Pacific might well have appealed to all of them, Burghley included, as a timely gesture of defiance and a renewed warning that England made a better friend than an enemy.

The flotilla that sailed from Plymouth in November 1577 was larger than any Drake had commanded before, with the added complication that the company of 160 men included a number of gentlemen who came along to look out for other investors' interests. Doughty, his brother John, a lawyer called Leonard Vicary and John Thomas, the captain of the 30-ton carrack *Marigold*, came for Hatton. The Wynters recruited the crew of the 80-ton carrack *Elizabeth* and her tender, the 15-ton bark *Benedict*, commanded by George

Wynter's son John. Walsingham's observer appears to have been the chaplain, Francis Fletcher. John Hawkins sent his brother's namesake son William.

Drake brought his brother Thomas and young cousin John. Divided command was a recipe for disaster and Drake knew it, but he had to accept it to get the backing. The flagship was his own 150-ton galleon *Pelican*, carrying two disassembled pinnaces and powerfully armed in French corsair style with seven demi-culverins on each side plus two in the bow and two in the stern. He also provided the 50-ton supply carrack *Swan*. Only *Pelican*'s hull had horsehair and pitch sandwiched between double planking, a necessary defence against the teredo shipworm (actually a clam) that infested the Caribbean and was assumed, incorrectly, to be found in equal concentration in all warm waters.

The voyage got off to an ill-omened start when the flotilla ran into a storm that drove the ships back, partially dismasting *Pelican* and *Marigold*. They set sail again on 13 December but two weeks later had only reached Mogador, off the coast of Morocco. There, while one of the pinnaces was being assembled, Drake lost a man to Moorish raiders. As the flotilla sailed along the West African coast they looted three Spanish fishing boats and three Portuguese caravels, exchanged little *Benedict* for a 50-ton Spanish ship renamed *Christopher*. Drake then set out for the Portuguese Cape Verde Islands, arriving off Praia on the main island of Santiago on 30 January 1578. Despite gunfire from the fort he captured the *Santa María*, a large ship loaded with wine and other stores commanded by Nuño da Silva, who unwisely admitted to knowing the coast of South America very well.

Drake set the crew adrift in the pinnace, but kept Silva – to whose later interrogation by the Spanish authorities we owe some key insights – and appointed Thomas Doughty to command *Santa María*, renamed *Mary*, with Thomas Drake as his deputy. The crew got into the wine, leading to a dispute that culminated in Doughty accusing Thomas of theft. There followed a furious altercation on the flagship in which Francis accused Doughty of seeking to undermine his authority, which ended with the Drake brothers together on *Mary*, presumably to restore order, leaving Doughty on *Pelican*.

As the voyage progressed Drake became more and more enraged towards Doughty, and it's hard to escape the conclusion that Drake determined relatively early that he had to get rid of him. The most deadly suspicion was that Doughty wanted to undermine his authority in order to sabotage the venture, but we should not lightly dismiss Drake's belief that Doughty was a conjurer or Jonah, as sailors have always been ruled by superstition. It could be that the damaging storm at the start of the voyage and the contrary winds that denied him his usual rapid transit to the Canary Islands were seen by Drake as evidence of a curse. That suspicion deepened after the flotilla reached the coast of Brazil, along which thanks to Nuño da Silva a rapid passage might have been made were it not for storms that twice scattered the ships. Doughty was the obvious candidate, as Drake knew he dabbled in the arcane and kept a diary in Latin, which Drake could not read.

The flashpoint came on 17 May 1578 at the river known as Deseado in today's Argentina. Having previously reduced Doughty to command of the lowly *Swan*, whose master and crew took their lead from their admiral and treated him with contempt, Drake now ordered the supply ship stripped of her metalwork and burned. Doughty exploded in rage, accused Drake of having reneged on their partnership agreement, and declared that he had lost all confidence in his leadership. Drake struck him and had him tied to the mast. There was no way back from that.

Following a false start, after which Drake also disposed of the ex-Spanish *Christopher*, the remaining ships sailed to San Julián Bay, the place where Magellan hanged one of his mutinous captains and marooned another along with a troublesome priest in April 1520, six months into the first circumnavigation. The blackened beams of Magellan's gallows were still to be seen as Drake convened a court of all the company ashore. He assured Vicary, the lawyer, that he would not seek the death penalty, and it's possible he had not yet made up his mind; but after Doughty admitted that he had given Burghley a chart of the voyage, Drake determined that he must die.

Everything suddenly made sense to his fevered mind: the queen had hinted that her Lord Treasurer might betray the venture to Philip II, so what would be more natural than for Burghley to instruct Doughty to sabotage it? There was no question of letting Doughty live, because even if he were sent back to England in chains, Burghley would free him and use him to blacken Drake's name to the queen.

Given that the accounts of the trial were written by men hostile to Drake, the remarkably eloquent words they attributed to him are probably an accurate reflection of what he said. Summing up the case against Doughty, he reportedly spoke as follows:

> *My masters, you must judge for yourselves whether or not this fellow has tried to undermine my authority, for no other reason than to abort this voyage; first by taking away my good name and altogether discrediting me, and then by taking my life, which being taken what would then become of you? You will be reduced to drinking one another's blood, and as to returning again to your country, you will never be able to find the way. Now, my masters, consider what a great voyage we are about to make, the like of which was never made out of England, by which the least in this fleet shall become a gentleman. If this voyage should not proceed — which I do not see how it possibly could if this man lives — the simplest here must appreciate what a reproach it will be, not only to our country but especially to us. Therefore, my masters, let they who think this man deserves to die hold up their hands, and let they who think he does not deserve to die hold down their hands.*

The show of hands against him, Doughty asked to be carried to Perú and put ashore, but Drake replied that he could not answer to the queen if he did so — that is, he believed Doughty would give the Spanish full details of the origin of the venture. Then Drake asked if anyone would undertake to keep him safe from Doughty. The condemned man desperately appealed to John Wynter, who said he would. Drake replied that Doughty must be kept under hatches and all the ships must return home, and if that was what the company wanted they should say so. 'God forbid, good General', cried out Drake's supporters, and those with dissenting thoughts wisely did not voice them.

After Doughty was executed on 2 July 1578, Drake held up the severed head and spoke the traditional words 'behold the head of a traitor'. The effect on the assembled company can readily be imagined, but terror can only command obedience and Drake needed enthusiastic support. John Wynter, the third among equals, must have been fingering his own neck nervously, and Doughty's friends and supporters were left in no doubt that Drake regarded them as enemies.

What followed is generally regarded as Drake's command moment, when he took hold of the venture and made it his own, thereby ensuring its success. Once again summoning the entire company ashore, he announced that all the officers appointed by the shipowners were relieved of command. After a dramatic pause he reappointed them in his own right as commander of the expedition by authority of the queen. There followed the most famous speech of all:

> So it is, my masters, that we are very far from our country and friends; we are surrounded on all sides by our enemies, for which reason we are not to value any man lightly, because we cannot find another even if we would give ten thousand pounds for him. Therefore we must redress the mutinies and discords that have grown among us, for by the life of God even to think about it has disordered my wits. We have such quarrelling between the sailors and the gentlemen, and such grumbling between the gentlemen and sailors, that it drives me mad even to hear it. But, my masters, I must have this put behind us; for I must have the gentlemen haul and draw with the mariner, and the mariner with the gentleman. Let us show ourselves to be of one company, and let us not give occasion to the enemy to rejoice at our dissolution and failure.

> *I would know if there were someone who would refuse to set his*
> *hand to a rope, and I know there is none such here. As gentlemen*
> *are very necessary for authority's sake in the voyage, so I have*
> *shipped them for that purpose – and to some further purpose; and*
> *yet though I know sailors to be the people most resentful of*
> *authority in the world, even though disorderly without authority*
> *over them, yet I need them too. If there are any here who wish to*
> *return home, let them speak up, and here is the Marigold, a ship*
> *I can very well spare. I will give those who choose to return in her*
> *whatever authorisations I can, either by way of letters or in any*
> *other way; but let them be sure to return homeward, because if*
> *I find them in my way I will surely sink them. You have time to*
> *think about it until tomorrow, but for now I swear that I must*
> *speak to you plainly: I have undertaken something that I do not*
> *know how in the world I can carry out; it is a greater burden than*
> *I can bear alone, and thinking about it has driven me to distraction.*

Nobody was foolish enough to take him up on his offer, transparently intended to smoke out malcontents. Abandoning Nuño da Silva's old ship *Mary* at San Julián, on 17 August Drake's *Pelican*, John Wynter's *Elizabeth* – now crewed by the men who had supported Doughty – and *Marigold* , still commanded by Hatton's man John Thomas, set out to round the continent of America into the South Seas. At some point in the following days Drake renamed his flagship. The new name was *Golden Hind*, honouring the crest on the coat of arms of Sir Christopher Hatton. Perhaps it was to show that he meant no disrespect by beheading Hatton's secretary and terrorizing the rest of his men. In the immortal words of *The Godfather*, it was not personal: it was just business.

The weather gods were not appeased by the human sacrifice, and after struggling through the Magellan Strait the flotilla emerged into a violent storm in which little *Marigold* was lost with all hands and *Elizabeth* became separated from *Golden Hind*. Wynter later declared that he wanted to sail on to an agreed rendezvous in the Moluccas, but his crew demanded he return home.

It was not until late October that Drake was finally able to sail northwards along the South American coast, by which time he had lost some of his scurvy-weakened crew to exposure. Putting in to one of the islands off Tierra del Fuego, Drake sent men ashore to bring back plants, which were boiled and served to the sick mixed with wine to disguise the bitter taste. The symptoms of scurvy disappeared and he lost no more men. The expedition was now down to one ship and the company to fewer than half the 170 who had set out; but with those weak of body and will weeded out, the remainder were totally loyal to Drake and tightly knit by their long struggle against the elements.

Drake did try to fulfil his obligation to find places 'not under the obedience of any Christian prince' with which the English might profitably trade, but gave up after an encounter on 25 November with Mapuche natives on the island of Mocha who were indeed independent – because they were lethally hostile to any Europeans who landed there. Two of Drake's men were killed, another two mortally wounded, and he himself was hit by an arrow under the right eye.

After that he reverted to type and plundered his way along the Spanish settlements of the coast of Chile, as recounted in the prologue to this book inspired by the broad humour of the account in *The World Encompassed*, published in 1628 by Drake's namesake nephew. Although based on the notes of the chaplain Francis Fletcher, it's interspersed with passages that read like anecdotes recounted by Drake himself. The raid on Valparaiso harbour took place on 5 December 1578 and may well have 'made' the voyage financially, as the Spanish were to claim for losses totalling 200,000 gold pesos. Even allowing for the usual exaggeration, it was enough to explain why Drake became jocular for the first time since setting out – although the stolen tuns of wine no doubt also contributed to making *Golden Hind* a happy ship as she sailed along the coast, guided by rutters and a pilot seized from a ship in Valparaiso harbour.

At a bay near Copiapó in northern Chile Drake ordered the remaining pinnace assembled, and careened *Golden Hind* for much-needed scraping and tallowing. As he now planned to raid Callao, the port of Lima, he also had the demi-culverins brought up from the ship's ballast, where they had been stowed since San Julián. It proved an unnecessary precaution, as there were no other warships on the Pacific coast and the merchant ships, if armed at all, carried only swivel guns.

On 5 February 1579 Drake raided the port of Arica, where he obtained a little loot but came away with a ship, and on 9 February at Chule, the port of Arequipa in Perú, he had to content himself with stealing a treasure ship that to his chagrin had been emptied of its cargo when a warning from Arica preceded him. He lacked the men to crew the extra ships and set them adrift at sea, the purpose of the exercise being to prevent them sailing ahead of him to warn Callao, where he confidently expected to 'make himself the Indies'.

He was to be disappointed. There were nine ships in the harbour, but none contained anything very valuable. Learning from captives that Oxenham, Butler and Sherwell were prisoners of the Inquisition in Lima, and lacking the manpower to sail the ships away, Drake had their moorings cut in the hope that they would drift out to sea, so that he could use the threat of sinking them to obtain the release of his old shipmates. Unfortunately the ships ran aground in the harbour and all he could do was to send a message to the Viceroy threatening reprisals if the men were killed. As we saw at the end of the last chapter, this may have prolonged their miserable existences for another year.

Viceroy Francisco Álvarez de Toledo, whose prompt action had doomed Oxenham in 1778, reacted no less quickly on this occasion. He ordered all the ships in Callao to pursue, but none were equipped to challenge *Golden Hind* and several were improperly ballasted, so they returned to port. The furious Viceroy then ordered two ships to be fitted out for war with good pilots, 120 soldiers, and his son Luis in titular command, backed by the explorer and historian of the Incas Pedro Sarmiento de Gamboa, to whom we owe many of the details that follow. The ships left Callao on 27 February and sailed towards Panamá, where Sarmiento de Gamboa thought Drake would strike next.

SIR FRANCIS DRAKE IN 1580

The portrait by Cornelis Ketel with the quintessential sea-dog smiling wryly.

QUEEN ELIZABETH IN 1574 – THE PELICAN PORTRAIT
The pendant reflects her view that, like the mythological pelican, she gave her own blood
to feed her subjects.

KING PHILIP II OF SPAIN IN 1580

With the Rosary ever-present in his hand, his only adornment is the
Burgundian Order of the Golden Fleece.

ELIZABETH'S EYES AND EARS
(*LEFT*) Sir William Cecil, 1st Baron Burghleigh.
(*ABOVE*) Sir Francis Walsingham.

ELIZABETH'S FAVOURITES

(*TOP*) Robert Dudley, Earl of Leicester (1576); (*ABOVE*) Robert Devereaux,
Earl of Essex (*c.* 1587); (*RIGHT*) Sir Walter Raleigh (*c.* 1583).

SIR JOHN HAWKINS
The only true likeness, dated 1591.

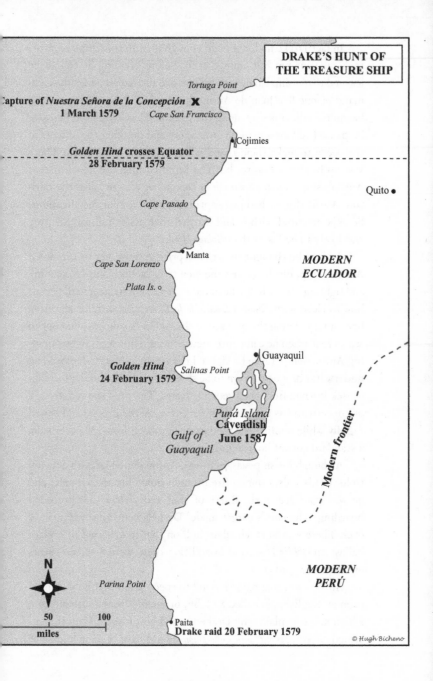

DRAKE'S HUNT OF
THE TREASURE SHIP

Tortuga Point

Capture of *Nuestra Señora de la Concepción* ✖
1 March 1579

Cape San Francisco

Cojimies

Golden Hind **crosses Equator**
28 February 1579

Quito •

Cape Pasado

MODERN
ECUADOR

Cape San Lorenzo

Manta

Plata Is. ○

Guayaquil

Golden Hind
24 February 1579

Salinas Point

Puná Island
**Cavendish
June 1587**

*Gulf of
Guayaquil*

Modern frontier

N

MODERN
PERÚ

Parina Point

50   100

miles

Paita
Drake raid 20 February 1579

© Hugh Bicheno

In fact Drake no longer had enough men to contemplate an attack on Panamá, but immediately before arriving at Callao he learned that a ship laden with bullion had just sailed under the command of one San Juan de Anton, heading for Panamá. Drake now began to stalk this ship along the coast and at Cojimies in Ecuador he paused to loot a prize, half-hanging and dunking the officers in the ocean to make them reveal where treasure was hidden. There was no hidden treasure, but the terrified men did confirm that Anton's ship, *Nuestra Señora de la Concepción*, was just over the horizon. As the ship he had just captured was of similar specifications, he experimented with it and learned that under full sail his prey was likely to be faster than *Golden Hind*.

At first he thought to arm the prize and use her to run down Anton's ship, but he lacked the men to crew both ships for sailing and fighting. Accordingly he opted instead for a stratagem to permit him to close with *Nuestra Señora de la Concepción* without alarming her captain. Tying the pinnace to *Golden Hind*'s side he sailed out to sea so that when he came into view he would not seem to be pursuing Anton's ship. Once he sighted the target's sails he deployed an underwater drogue to seem to be slower than he was under full sail, a trick learned from the French corsairs. The prey showed no sign of concern and as night fell Drake cut away the drogue and closed rapidly while sending the pinnace to approach from the other side, a standard corsair boarding technique.

Although his ship was unarmed, Anton defied Drake's demand to lower his sails. Cannon fire brought down his mizzen mast and he was wounded in the flurry of shot and arrows that preceded boarding. The ship's cargo 'made' Drake's venture several times over. There was so much silver bullion that it was used to replace ballast on *Golden Hind*, and in addition there were fourteen chests of silver and gold coins.

Anton's unusual name has led to speculation that he may have been an Englishman called St John, originally from Southampton, which might explain why Drake treated him royally. Why the unarmed *Nuestra Señora de la Concepción* should have become known as

'Cacafuego' (Shitfire – although to be pedantic that would have been *Cagafuego*) is a puzzle. A 17th-century Dutch print of the encounter showing *Golden Hind* identified as *Caca Fogo* and Anton's ship as *Caca Plata* (Shit Silver/Money) points to a possible origin of the nickname as a Spanish sailor's rueful comment on the relative merits of the two ships, misunderstood by English seamen.

An expansive Drake gave Anton many gifts and also a safe conduct letter should he encounter John Wynter, John Thomas, or two other invented names, signed 'with a very heavy heart' at being separated from them and indicating that he still hoped to be reunited with them. Kelsey thinks the note was simply disinformation to cause the Spanish to panic at the prospect of four other pirate ships loose on their ocean. Against which the phrase 'I will fulfil the decision that we made together to return to our own country' seems to confirm Wynter's statement about an agreed rendezvous in the Moluccas.

Half the note consists of pious invocations that must have had the Spanish authorities scratching their heads for hidden meanings but which point to a profound psychological change in Drake, who seems to have become convinced that his good fortune was an unquestionable sign that he enjoyed divine favour. He spoke very freely with Anton and later captives of a rank that made it certain his words would be repeated to the authorities, and the motivation he ascribed to himself ran the gamut from legitimate reprisal for San Juan de Ulúa through a licence granted by Queen Elizabeth to fulfilling a mission from God. The captives also noted that he conducted divine services on *Golden Hind*, usurping the chaplain, and that his men held him in awe.

Sailing past Panamá up the coast of Central America, Drake took more prizes and raided Isla de Cano, Realejo, Sonsonate and finally Guatulco in Mexico. Loot included charts of the Manila galleon route across the Pacific, a shipload of silks and fine china, several black slaves and 'a proper negro wench' to service the crew, plus a heavy gold chain and 7,000 pesos in silver and other valuables taken from the local landowner at Guatulco. Here he put ashore the

Portuguese pilot Nuño da Silva, who had not been able to contribute much to the voyage since the passage of the Magellan Strait, and who informed the Spanish authorities that Drake intended to return to England by the Strait of Anian, the western end of the North-West Passage that so many English expeditions had failed to find from the east. The Spanish did not believe a word of it.

It was a double bluff because Drake did continue to sail north, seeking a suitable place to careen the leaking *Golden Hind* and make her sound for the journey across the Pacific, and also to kill time until the season (October and November) recommended on the charts he had seized. There was also the matter of identifying places that might 'enrich her Highness' dominions, and also put shipping a-work greatly', which made sailing clear of areas settled by the Spanish doubly attractive. He did careen the ship somewhere near modern San Francisco, but the tale of Drake being crowned by the local inhabitants, whose chief swore fealty to Queen Elizabeth, reads too much like earlier Spanish accounts of simple native people treating them like gods to be credible.

On the other hand, wherever it was must have been fertile because 'there were herds of deer by a thousand in a company' and it would have been impossible to find such a place along the California coast that did not have native inhabitants, as it was the most densely populated area of pre-European North America. Also, as the 19th-century gold rush was to show, there was indeed 'no part of earth here to be taken up, wherein there is not some probable show of gold or silver'. Lastly, there's no reason to doubt that Drake laid formal claim to the territory of Nova Albion on behalf of Queen Elizabeth, as described by one of his men:

> *At our departure hence our General set up a monument of our being there, as also of her Majesty's right and title to the same; namely a plate, nailed upon a fair great post, whereupon was engraved her Majesty's name, the day and year of our arrival there, with the free giving up of the province and people into her Majesty's hands, together with her Highness' picture and arms in*

a piece of six pence of current English money, under the plate,
whereunder was also written the name of our General.

In 1936 a brass plaque purporting to be this plate was discovered in Drake's Bay, a little to the north of San Francisco, with a chiselled inscription as described and dated 17 June 1579. Forty years later microscopic and metallurgical analysis proved that it was of recent manufacture: it seems that what was originally intended as an amusing hoax by local historians got so swiftly out of hand that they did not dare admit it.

Drake spent more than two and possibly as many as three months crossing the Pacific. His voyage was so long because he missed what are today's Marshall Islands and the Federated States of Micronesia, and only made landfall at the Palau archipelago. Obviously he must have loaded a sufficient store of dried meat, grain and wood for the oven in California, but it's astonishing that the limited water storage on *Golden Hind* could have kept 70 men healthy for such a long period in the tropics.

At Palau, furthermore, trading with natives in dugout canoes degenerated into an ugly stand-off resolved by sinking one of the canoes with a cannon shot, so there cannot have been an opportunity to refill the water casks. There would have been rain, but the only certain way the water could have been eked out for so long was by the exercise of a collective self-discipline one does not associate with Elizabethan sailors; further proof – if any were needed – of Drake's exceptional leadership.

And on he went. Somewhere south of Mindanao, where he did refill the water casks, he attempted to take a passing ship for supplies but was foiled when his bow guns misfired and the ship escaped to shallow water where he could not enter. Pausing to bring up the guns he had stored in the ballast for the oceanic crossing, he eventually reached the small, actively volcanic island of Ternate in the Moluccas, an Islamic sultanate that was the focus of native resistance to the Portuguese, yet another sign of Drake's outstandingly good luck. The sultan welcomed him with enthusiasm but when invited aboard he politely refused, as did Drake when invited to dine with the sultan ashore. But he did engage in legal commerce for the first time, trading English linens for spices and supplies, and departed with ten tons of ginger, black pepper and, mainly, cloves.

The next stop was an uninhabited island off the Celebes, where he stopped to careen *Golden Hind* once more to remove the marine infestation built up since California. Here he also put ashore the black slaves he had taken at Guatulco 'with rice and seeds and fire to populate the place', for the woman Maria was by now heavily pregnant. Beyond the fact that the treatment of Maria was cruel even by contemporary standards, sailors traditionally regarded it as very ill-omened to have women aboard. Given that Drake was as superstitious as any, the only obvious – and bleak – explanation for having offended against the taboo by taking her on board in the first place is that Maria was regarded as a domestic animal.

Not long afterwards, on 8 January 1580 under full sail, *Golden Hind* ran hard aground on a coral reef with no bottom found off her stern to a depth of 300 fathoms. Several guns, six tons of cloves and much of the supplies acquired at Ternate went overboard, but the ship would not budge. Abdicating his role as warrior priest, Drake called on Chaplain Fletcher to lead the crew in prayers for salvation. Fletcher must have thought they were surely doomed, for the subject of his sermon was that the stranding was God's judgement for the killing of Doughty and all the other evil they had done on the journey, of which the treatment of Maria was only the most recent.

God suspended sentence, however, and sent a strong wind that blew them off the reef. Drake immediately moved to undo the harm done to his authority by the plain-speaking chaplain and had him chained to a hatch cover while he pronounced excommunication on him. This was clearly heavy-handed mockery designed to take away Fletcher's dignity and with it the sting of his sermon. But Drake also forbade him to mingle with and talk to the men on pain of hanging, and forced him to wear a placard saying he was 'the falsest knave that liveth'.

Drake stopped twice on the island of Java, once to replenish supplies and the second time at a major port with at least three and probably more rajahs in residence. They would trade only for the best linens and for the silk stolen at Guatulco, and one account states that it cost Drake goods to the value of £4,000 to load *Golden Hind* with enough rice, yams, live chickens and dried beef to see them home. The hospitable local women also gave the crew syphilis, known as 'the French pox', which the sailors believed could be cured by exposing their suppurating genitals to the sun. The mind shrinks from imagining the scene on the deck of *Golden Hind* as she sailed away.

It took at least as long to cross the Indian Ocean as it had the Pacific, and by the time *Golden Hind* reached the Cape of Good Hope she was desperately low on water. Drake could not find anywhere to land, but the situation was resolved by a heavy and prolonged downpour. The next stop was Sierra Leone, which they reached on 22 July 1580. Kelsey cites Spanish documents to the effect that Drake also put in at La Rochelle, which would have been a very sensible thing to do. He could have had no idea of the state of diplomatic relations between London and Madrid, but he could be quite sure that the Huguenots would, as always, be at war with Spain.

They were indeed, with the seventh war of religion under way. From Drake's point of view the situation in the Netherlands had also developed most satisfactorily. Don Juan de Austria and his nephew Alessandro Farnese (became Duke of Parma in 1586), who was appointed governor when Juan died of typhus in October 1578, had unpicked the fragile unity between the Protestant and Catholic provinces. A new Spanish army had arrived in the Netherlands and the Protestants were once again on the defensive. England was once more committed to the traditional policy of keeping the King of Spain tied down elsewhere by supporting the Huguenots and the Dutch Protestants.

Finally, the oceanic balance of power had been fundamentally altered by the union of the crowns of Castile and Portugal following the death on 31 January 1580 of King Henrique. He was known as 'the Chaste' because, being a cardinal of the Catholic Church, he died without issue, as had his grand-nephew and predecessor Sebastian, who was killed in 1578 leading an idiotic crusade in Morocco. A short, sharp military campaign by the Duke of Alba secured for Philip II the throne to which he was the legitimate claimant, overthrowing the pretensions of the illegitimate Dom Antonio, Prior of Crato. As when the kingdom of France acquired Brittany 92 years earlier, the union of the Iberian monarchies posed a serious threat to England. The Spanish Empire now extended around the globe and at a stroke Philip II had more than doubled his naval assets in the Atlantic, gaining the services of some of the best oceangoing ships and the most experienced sailors in the world.

All indicators were that it was safe to go home, and Drake sailed into Plymouth on 26 September 1580. The timing of his return was more fortunate than he could have dreamed. The diplomatic situation was dominated by the possibility that the queen might marry François, Duke of Anjou and Alençon, the youngest son of Henri II and Catherine de' Medici and next in line to the French throne should his brother Henri III fail to produce an heir. Although a Catholic, Alençon had sided with the Huguenot leaders Condé and Henri of Navarre to bring about the Edict of Beaulieu in May 1576, which represented the high-water mark of the Huguenot cause.

Lord Burghley strongly advocated a dynastic marriage between Elizabeth and Alençon, and in 1579 François came to come to London to press his suit in person. He was 22 years her junior and she seems to have been genuinely fond of him, even writing a sad little poem when he departed in 1581, the first stanza lamenting the conflict between her heart and her head:

> I grieve and dare not show my discontent,
> I love and yet am forced to seem to hate,
> I do, yet dare not say I ever meant,
> I seem stark mute but inwardly do prate.
> I am and not, I freeze and yet am burned,
> Since from myself another self I turned.

Also in 1579 Alençon was invited by William of Orange to become the hereditary sovereign of the United Provinces, and three days after Drake sailed into Plymouth the Dutch States-General (with the exception of Zeeland and Holland, who were to proclaim themselves an independent republic in 1581) pronounced him Protector of the Liberty of the Netherlands. The geopolitical advantages of the match explain Burghley's enthusiasm but, at 46, it was likely that Elizabeth would not survive a pregnancy, leaving the Catholic Mary, Queen of Scots as her successor. Elizabeth was better advised (by the same group of councillors with whom she had invested in Drake's voyage) that a Catholic marriage ran too great a risk of re-opening domestic religious divisions.

Still, the possibility that the marriage might take place had the useful effect of causing Philip II to say and do nothing that might push the queen into Alençon's arms, which meant that his response to Drake's depredations was low key. Elizabeth made the connection explicit when she went aboard *Golden Hind* for a gala celebration in April 1581. She produced a gilded sword and joked that she had come to cut off Drake's head, then handed it to the Marquis de Marchaumont, the man entrusted with maintaining the courtship in Alençon's absence, to knight him instead.

Long before that, discretion and deniability had gone out of the window when the queen learned that her profit from the venture was going to be enormous. As soon as Drake arrived she ordered the treasure secured by royal officials and for Drake to ride to London and report to her in person. After a six-hour interview, during which Drake gave her samples of the loot as well as his detailed log and a world map showing the course he had sailed, Elizabeth almost committed the error of ordering the treasure to be taken to the Tower. Perhaps this was Burghley's idea, with an eye to using it as a bargaining chip; if so, it stood no chance against cupidity. Walsingham, Hatton and Leicester swiftly pointed out to their royal fellow investor how unwise it would be to take responsibility for it, not least because the Spanish would probably acquire a copy of the inventory.

Thus if Drake was a thief, then the queen and many of her courtiers were receivers of stolen goods. Since this could not be, it followed that Drake was not a thief and thus deserving of honour. The queen became fond of Drake and referred to him as 'my pirate', yet that poses the far from trivial question – within the legal framework of that time – of whether an act committed with the approval of the supreme legal authority can be considered a crime at all. Simply put, if he was hers, he was not a pirate. He did not possess any authority from her during the voyage, although he said he did and repeatedly told Spanish captives that his actions were in legitimate reprisal for losses suffered at San Juan de Ulúa. Like Oxenham, had he been captured he would have had no defence against the charge of piracy. However, by knighting him Elizabeth retrospectively legitimized his actions and sharply reminded Philip II that his servants had attacked her ships, flying her flag at San Juan de Ulúa, when they were seeking to trade.

A Spanish term for forcible trade is *plata o plomo* – silver coins or lead bullets. The message sent to Philip II from the deck of *Golden Hind* in April 1581 was 'commerce or corsairs'.

CHAPTER 8
NOT GOOD HAPP BY SEA

The queen's share of Drake's loot proved to be as great or greater than her entire annual revenues from tax and crown lands combined.* As they had after Hawkins's second voyage, but on an unimaginably larger scale, everybody involved got rich, Drake most of all. He may have become the most cash-wealthy man in the country and was able to pay premium prices to buy prime real estate. He paid his cousin Sir Richard Grenville £3,400 for his magnificent Buckland Abbey estate, midway between Plymouth and Tavistock, and bought several other manors. He also purchased a large portfolio of Plymouth properties from William Hawkins, with more than enough left over to become a major merchant shipowner – and to give the queen extravagant gifts.

The purchase of Buckland was a necessary precondition for becoming a gentleman, itself a precondition for knighthood. He was granted a coat of arms comprising 'Sable, a fess wavy between two stars Argent' and the motto *Sic Parvis Magna* (Greatness from Small beginnings). Once again it was the crest that told the more interesting story: 'Upon the terrestrial globe a ship under sail drawn round the same with golden hawsers by a hand appearing from clouds Proper, on the mainmast a star Argent, and in the ship a wyvern [a two-footed dragon] Gules [red], its wings spread, looking towards the hand, motto: Auxilio Divino [Divine help].'

* The total sterling value of Drake's loot was about £600,000, of which at least £265,000 in coined silver went into the royal coffers as well as an unspecified amount of uncoined silver and most of the jewels.

Francis Drake's coat of arms.   Bernard Drake's coat of arms.

The crest appears to have been a pointed joke by the queen (whose own red Tudor dragon had four feet) at the expense of Sir Bernard Drake of Ashe, whose arms bore a red wyvern alone and who haughtily denied Francis Drake of Tavistock any right to have used the blazon engraved on the silverware he took around the world. By instructing the heralds to put a little wyvern on board the galleon, furthermore looking up to the hand holding the golden hawsers (a none too subtle reminder that arms came from above), Elizabeth not only mocked Sir Bernard's snobbery but also the whole pretentious business that chivalric arms had become.

Needless to say, attempts by John Doughty to obtain legal redress for the execution of his brother did not prosper. When he persisted, he was falsely accused of conspiring to murder Drake along with the representative of the Spanish merchants seeking restitution for Drake's depredations. Both were thrown in jail, and John Doughty may have died there. However galling it was, Doughty should have had the common sense to realize that he was not going to be permitted to rain on Drake's parade. John Stow's *Annales of England* confirms that after the signal favour shown by the queen,

Drake's 'name and fame became admirable in all places, the people swarming daily in the streets to behold him, vowing hatred of all that durst mislike him'.

So – in the light of the enormous wealth, honours and popular apotheosis won by Drake, why did his voyage prove so strategically sterile? There was no attempt to build on his claim to Nova Albion, it took another twenty years to follow up on his trading contacts in the Far East, and only Cavendish replicated his circumnavigation. In his 1967 extended essay *Drake's Voyages*, Professor Andrews remarked on 'the extraordinary proliferation of projects for trade, plunder and colonization that marked the period from 1578 to 1584', concluding that the absence of wholehearted state support, financial commitment and strategic co-ordination doomed it to being an outburst of 'militant but largely ineffectual energy which eventually found expression in the open sea-warfare of 1585'. In other words, contrary to what earlier generations of scholars portrayed it as being (taking their lead from Richard Hakluyt's *Principal Navigations*) it did not lay the foundations for the English/British maritime supremacy that won a world-girdling empire.

Indeed; but every age has its blinkers. For one writing in the mid-1960s, when it was still just possible to believe that state planning represented progress, it was a knee-jerk assumption that 'strategic co-ordination' by the state would have produced a more positive outcome for England. With all the respect due to a great scholar, this is a case of *quandoque dormitat Homerus*: the greater the involvement of the state in any enterprise, the more certain that it will be characterized by incompatible objectives, incompetent execution and systemic corruption.

In practical terms, even leaving aside the intractable problem of herding cats, the unpredictability of the weather and the epidemics that proliferated any time men were massed together made it highly likely that any grand naval scheme would be ruinously expensive and strategically nugatory. It's perfectly clear that only the very limited role of the state permitted Elizabethan England to produce an affordable fleet that proved numerous and strong enough to defeat a supreme effort to achieve 'strategic co-ordination' by experienced and talented commanders in the service of Renaissance Europe's greatest military power.

As we have seen, Cecil tried to play an indirect role by seeking to open up the Atlantic trade route that would have encouraged merchants to build large, dual-purpose ships, only to see it fail at San Juan de Ulúa. It's a stretch too far to argue that official connivance in piratical activity was designed to produce a cadre of aggressive English sea captains, and to hasten the trend to larger, well-armed merchant ships that could defend themselves, operate as corsairs, or serve in the Navy Royal when required. Those developments did take place, but the unchecked corruption and unpredictability of government officials acted as a drag on the process.

Until the appointment of Julius Caesar (born Julius Adelmare) as its sole judge in 1587, the English High Court of Admiralty was an expensive farce that failed to satisfy legitimate claims, did little to deter piracy and did not even function to tax the activity it so signally failed to control. Caesar's great achievement was to replace the rancid county commissions with a self-financing central Admiralty Commission empowered to search out and prosecute piracy nationwide.

Context is everything, and he could not have achieved this revolution in the administration of justice if Elizabeth's government had not, at last, adopted the *guerre de course* as state policy in 1585. With letters of marque in one hand and a noose in the other, Caesar was better able to regulate corsair activity and to clamp down on common piracy based in England. There was nothing he could do about Ireland, but in that he was not alone. He was no saint, but he was less venal than his predecessors. Of course the self-financing power vested in the Admiralty Commission invited the extortion and other abuses that came to characterize the office under his successors; but initially it proved a classic example of the Hobbesian shark being preferable to a swarm of piranha.

The Yorkshireman Martin Frobisher is usually grouped with John Hawkins and Francis Drake because the three of them commanded independent squadrons under Lord Admiral Howard of Effingham in the iconic battle against the Spanish Armada in 1588. It's difficult to understand how Frobisher rose to such prominence, as his previous achievements were meagre when compared to his fellow squadron commanders. Although well born he was uncouth and only semi-literate, and his early career as an inept, low-rent pirate motivated by hatred against the merchant class that had abandoned him in Guinea in 1554 should have ended on the gallows. Yet in 1570 he was released from prison, where several well-founded warrants had placed him, thanks to the interventions of Lord Admiral Sir Edward Fiennes de Clinton and the queen's principal adviser Sir William Cecil, and he continued to enjoy the favour of Cecil for the rest of his often murky career. As James McDermott observes in his witty and altogether exemplary biography of Frobisher:

> ... the traffic in illicit goods undoubtedly created points of contact which circumvented the social norms, particularly as the middle-men excluded from its transactions – the merchants involved in legitimate trade – comprised the 'middle' classes through whom most commercial intercourse necessarily flowed. These contacts, once established, did not dissipate with a handshake or the delivery of stolen goods; they remained, if dormant, ready to be resurrected when other, greater causes required. Even allowing for the excellent work done to date, there is much that may yet be written about this great, black economy and the wider social and political implications that grew from its anonymous processes.

Much may indeed be written but, as in the case of MacFarlane's seminal work on English individualism, the conceptual framework proposed by Charles Tilly in 1985 – that Renaissance state-making and the process whereby crime becomes organized are indistinguishable – is not one with which state-dependent scholars are at all comfortable. Nonetheless, it's much easier to understand the period if one can accept the slightly hallucinatory vision of Good Queen Bess as the Godmother, the Privy Council as her Consiglieri, senior county officials as Capiregimi – and that all contemporary governments were similarly constituted.

Frobisher's release from prison was just another of Cecil's recruitments of shady characters who might prove useful in the future. The warrants were not revoked, so in modern intelligence parlance Frobisher became a 'controlled asset'. His immediate employment in command of a small flotilla on a poacher-turned-gamekeeper anti-piracy patrol in the Irish Sea may have been an indirect signal to the queen's favourite Robert Dudley, Earl of Leicester. Sir Henry Herbert, a Dudley partisan, had very recently succeeded to the earldom of Pembroke, and Cecil may have judged it an opportune moment to remind him that the tidy income his family derived from Welsh piracy could be curtailed if Cecil chose. Frobisher's orders may have been simply to cruise along the coast and visit pirate haunts to make sure the message was understood. This would explain why, despite not capturing a single pirate ship, he was rewarded with a lucrative transport contract to supply the army sent to suppress the first Desmond rebellion in southern Ireland. Subsequently Cecil used Frobisher as an agent provocateur in several characteristically intricate plots.

The *Dictionary of National Biography* entry for Sir Edward Horsey, the corsair-friendly Vice Admiral of Hampshire and Captain of the Isle of Wight, states that in 1571 he equipped a hulk for Frobisher to use in Ireland. Hulks were heavy, unwieldy ships and Horsey must have prepared what a later age called a 'Q-ship', outwardly a helpless merchantman with which a pirate ship would grapple only to discover that its prey concealed a large complement of well-armed troops. The stratagem was used by the joint Comptroller of the Navy William Borough to capture the celebrated Purbeck-based pirates Clinton Atkinson and Thomas Walton (a.k.a. Purser) in 1583.

So it was as Cecil's agent and not as a failed pirate that Frobisher became involved in a 1574 initiative to discover the mythical North-

West Passage to the fabled Far East. The driving force was Michael Lok, the brother of John Lok who had abandoned the young Frobisher in Guinea. Michael was the London agent of the Muscovy Company, which enjoyed a royal patent on any new northern trading routes and markets and whose members were unenthusiastic about any enterprise that might dilute their monopoly. Their resistance was overcome by pressure from the Privy Council fronted by Ambrose Dudley, Earl of Warwick, the devoted older brother of the queen's favourite.

Lord Treasurer Burghley, Secretary of State Walsingham, the latter's son-in-law Sir Philip Sidney, and Lord Chamberlain Thomas Radclyffe, Earl of Sussex, joined the Dudley brothers as the venture's sponsors, lending mainly their names. The joint stock offering raised little more than half the outlay of £1,614 for the voyage and Lok had to fund the rest, also paying off Frobisher's debts to prevent him being put in debtors' prison. With such limited finance the expedition was equipped with two 30-ton barks and a 7-ton pinnace instead of the three carracks originally envisaged. The barks *Gabriel* and *Michael* had crews of 17 and 12 respectively and the pinnace had three. *Gabriel* carried elaborate navigational equipment supplied by John Dee, consultant on scientific navigation to the Muscovy Company, and by Steven Borough, who had brought Martín Cortés de Albacar's navigational treatise back from Seville in 1558.

Frobisher did not know how to use any of it and depended on Christopher Hall, master of the *Gabriel*, and on the expedition purser Nicholas Chancellor, son of the late founder of the Muscovy Company Richard Chancellor, who had drowned in a 1556 shipwreck. On 7 June 1576 they set sail from Dartford in the Thames on what was a fool's errand. The enterprise was based on Mercator's world map of 1569, which showed a northern sea accessed through a passage between the southern tip of Greenland, which was shown at 66°, six degrees north of its true position, and a peninsula called 'Estotilant' jutting from the North American mainland between 61° and 65°. Also between those latitudes, east of Estotilant and south of Iceland, Mercator had drawn an imaginary island called

'Frislant'. So, after sailing to Shetland at 60°, Frobisher sailed west by north expecting to get a clean shot at the North-West Passage. After two weeks the little flotilla reached the southern tip of Greenland, which they naturally identified as Frislant. Sailing on into what is today called the Davis Strait the pinnace was lost in a violent storm and shortly afterwards *Michael*'s crew decided to desert, returning to England to report that *Gabriel* had been lost with all hands.

Far from it: Frobisher brought the bark through the storm and sailed to the south-eastern coast of what is now known as Baffin Island – but which on his return was named by the queen herself 'Meta Incognita' – stopping briefly at a small island offshore from which sailing master Hall brought back an intriguing black rock containing glittering particles. Sailing on through towering icebergs, the bark entered what is now known as Frobisher Bay in mid-August and sailed along it without reaching the end, wrongly concluding that it was a strait. The expedition did encounter Inuit hunting parties in kayaks, who after an initial period of wary friendliness abducted five of Frobisher's men. Frobisher tried to get them back by seizing one Inuk and his kayak, but was unable to communicate the idea of an exchange.

He sailed for home on 27 August and after surviving yet another terrifying storm reached Harwich on 2 October. A week later *Gabriel* sailed up the Thames with a globe supplied by Lok tied to her bowsprit. In the brief period before he died of pneumonia, Inuk caused great excitement, his seemingly Mongolian features confirming that the expedition had come very close to Asia. Also, before setting off home, Frobisher had climbed a mountain and saw 'two headlands at the furthest end of the straits and no likelihood of land to the northwards of them and a great open sea between them', which Michael Lok told the world was the Strait of Anian between America and Asia. Both men must have known it was no such thing – Frobisher had not sailed nearly far enough west – but they also knew that nobody ever became rich by underselling their product.

Lok took the black rock to several assayers until finally one of them said it contained gold. He wrote a letter to the queen with this information and even though Walsingham had the rock tested and confirmed that it was worthless, Elizabeth chose to make a loan investment of the 200-ton carrack *Aid*, which dwarfed *Gabriel* and *Michael*. This sign of royal favour alone would have produced sufficient courtier backing for a second voyage of exploration, but as news of the alleged gold spread, the purpose of the expedition was redefined and 'the captain more specially directed by commission for the searching more of this gold ore than for the searching any further of the passage'. Lok raised £5,150, enough to recover his costs on the first voyage and to finance the second.

The only confirmed likeness of Frobisher was painted at this time by the Dutch artist Cornelis Ketel, who sought to accentuate the raw aggression in Frobisher's face and posture by painting him with an elaborate pistol in his right hand and his left arm tensed around his sword. The unknown artist who had portrayed the psychopathically violent Sir Richard Grenville at the age of 29 managed to capture the arrogant deadliness in his eyes; but Ketel saw that Frobisher was a wary, volcanically dangerous man, and thanks to his skill we can see it too.

The expedition sailed on 31 May 1577 with Edward Fenton* sailing for the Earl of Warwick as captain of *Gabriel*, Gilbert Yorke for Lord Admiral Clinton as captain of *Michael* and the voyage's chronicler, George Beste, sailing for Christopher Hatton as Frobisher's deputy on *Aid*. Three 'goldfiners' also came along and only if their findings proved negative was Frobisher to send *Aid* back and explore further in the two barks. Meta Incognita was sighted on 16 July and after once again weaving through icebergs the 'strait' was found. No deposits were found on the original island and on the southern shore, where another contact with the Inuit ended with five of them shot dead, a woman and infant abducted, and Frobisher with an arrow in his buttocks.

* Like John Hawkins, Fenton was married to a daughter of Treasurer of the Navy Benjamin Gonson.

A bay on the northern shore proved more fruitful, and a base was set up on an island within it named for the Countess of Warwick. In three weeks 160 tons of rocks were loaded and by mid-September the expedition was back in London. There followed a classic example of the madness of crowds. Even though extensive tests revealed that if gold was present in the rocks – and no assayer was prepared to state that it was – it was in very low concentrations, this merely served to persuade investors that a large fleet should be sent to bring back enough to refine a worthwhile amount of gold in expensive, new, purpose-built furnaces. Although he was later to be accused of perpetrating a fraud by many, most vociferously by Frobisher himself, Lok himself invested far more than he could afford.

A fleet of 15 ships, four of them recruited by Frobisher himself, sailed on 31 May 1578, exactly a year after the second. Frobisher was commanded to load as much 'ore' as possible and to leave 100 men to hold the newly claimed country, but he was also permitted to sail further along the Passage with two barks. The organizers paid tribute to the exceptional powers of leadership he had displayed in the first two voyages by stipulating that he must return to lead the fleet back. Nature conspired to test those powers to the limit. After making landfall at 'Frislant' (in fact, southern Greenland) the fleet ran into pack ice and thick fog, in which the 100-ton *Dennys* was lost to an iceberg. At this the crew of the Ipswich bark *Thomas* mutinied and turned back, but the rest followed Frobisher's lead.

The fog caused Frobisher to make the only useful geographic discovery in the whole enterprise when, on 7 July, the fleet was swept by a fast-moving current into the 'Mistaken Straits', now known as the Hudson Strait. Once the fog cleared, he realized that this was a far more important waterway than the one he had explored previously. He was sure he had found the true North-West Passage, but after leading the fleet a further 200 miles/320 kilometres into the Mistaken Straits he dutifully turned back to the bay that bears his name and to Countess of Warwick Island.

Here we have the reason why Burghley – indeed any superior officer – would prefer Frobisher to Drake. The West Countryman had a flair the Yorkshireman lacked, but in the same circumstances he would have slighted the authorized mission to pursue the possibility of greater glory. To which we must add Frobisher's ability to impose his will on a large fleet of ships, each commanded by a man as proud and obdurate as he. Of course he was physically more imposing than Drake and the man who glowers from Cornelis Ketel's portrait did not need to prove that you crossed him at your imminent peril – but those are not uncommon qualities among history's great commanders.

Under his direction mining proceeded apace and by the departure date of 31 August the fleet had loaded 1,136 tons of ore. Having lost the prefabricated housing shipped on the *Dennys*, Frobisher did not proceed with the plan of leaving an occupying force. Edward Fenton built a small stone and lime-mortar house to test how it would hold up through the coming winter, and also left an oven containing baked bread, bells, mirrors, knives and pictures for the Inuit, 'the better to allure those brutish and uncivil people to courtesy'. Apart from the Inuit, the next person to visit the island was the American explorer Charles Hall in 1861–62, whose findings confirmed Beste's account.*

Once again Frobisher kept his fleet together through vile weather but on return to London they found that the black-rock bubble had burst. Frobisher had departed London as the heir to Christopher Columbus and returned to find himself suspected of conspiracy to defraud. Lok had already been obliged to submit his accounts to an official audit and, pausing only to dump the worthless ore at the foundry in Dartford (where samples were taken in the 1930s and the flecks of 'gold' proved to be yellow mica), a furious Frobisher demanded another to fasten the blame solely around Lok's neck, in which he was successful. The total call on investors, mostly for expenses associated with the third voyage and building the smelting plant, had risen to £17,630, with the outstanding balance of £3,658 sufficient to bankrupt and imprison Lok.

---

* See http://www.civilization.ca/cmc/exhibitions/hist/frobisher/frsub10e.shtml for the archaeology of Countess of Warwick's Island, now known by its Inuit name of Kodlunarn.

It's tempting to see the whole Lok–Frobisher fiasco as the product of another Burghley 'nudge' in the direction of finding a peacefully profitable outlet for English maritime energy. Whether it was or not, it rapidly degenerated into a get-rich-quick scheme that obliterated the longer-term objective of plotting a hypothetical North-West Passage. It's mildly surprising that hard-nosed London merchants let themselves be swept away by a highly speculative gold-rush, but not that they were reluctant to invest in further exploration. Even if the Passage did exist, they knew that it would be closed by ice for 8–9 months of the year and highly hazardous even in high summer. These were men who required a new ship to pay for itself on its first voyage because the uncertainties of normal sea travel were so great. The very faint chance that the black ore might be gold-bearing was a better bet than risking ships and cargo in iceberg-infested seas.

Lurking in the background of everyone's calculations was the growing realization that the idea of competing with the Spanish and Portuguese for oceanic trade was a chimera, at best a long-term investment that could not compensate for declining returns from traditional European markets in any useful timeframe. Alongside that thought another was becoming irresistible – that 'like dealing', the polite euphemism for piracy, was a far more certain way of sharing in the wealth of the Indies. The next English oceanic debacle dramatically confirmed that the two could not co-exist.

Frobisher had only two official employments over the next two years, one of them in the fleet at the 1580 siege of Smerwick Fort in Ireland in 1580, where a group of mercenaries hired by the Pope was butchered. He was not, however, idle and it must be assumed that he was permitted to restore his finances through unlicensed corsair activity; which he did so successfully that in 1581 he invested in, and was chosen to lead, a voyage to the Moluccas around Africa sponsored by a consortium led by Robert Dudley, Earl of Leicester; Sir Francis Drake; Secretary of State Walsingham; and the Southampton merchant and corsair investor Henry Oughtred.

The four men had originally come together to exploit the circumstance that Terceira in the Azores refused to accept Philip II as the new king of Portugal and supported the claim of Dom Antonio. Their plan, at first cautiously encouraged by the queen, was for a joint venture with Dom Antonio and the French to garrison the Azores as a base from which to interrupt the flow of silver from America to Spain – which they all believed would severely curtail Philip II's politico-religious ambition. In the event, Elizabeth's reservations and the strong opposition of Burghley and the London merchants trading with Iberia prevented significant English participation, although 11 small English ships including two of Drake's joined the expedition. Given the green light by the French regent, Queen Mother Catherine de' Medici, 58 ships carrying 6,000 mainly French soldiers under the command of the Italian *condottiere* Filippo di Piero Strozzi sailed from France in June 1582 intending to seize the islands of São Miguel and Santa María.

The thud of the next domino to fall echoed around Europe. On 26 July 1582 Strozzi's fleet was crushed off São Miguel by 60 ships and 8,000 men under the command of Philip II's admiral Alvaro Bazán, Marquis of Santa Cruz, whose strongest ships were the great Portuguese galleons only recently added to the Ocean Fleet that for the previous 60 years had proved inadequate to police the waters between the Azores and Spain. Despite using the line-abreast tactics of Mediterranean galley warfare, Santa Cruz prevailed over corsair galleons commanded by men who had become accustomed to defeating Iberian ships relatively easily.

In 1583 Santa Cruz followed up with a massive amphibious operation – 98 ships and over 15,000 soldiers – that conquered Terceira for Philip II. 'I know not what limits any man of judgment can set on his greatness', wrote a gloomy Burghley in 1584, concluding that England would now certainly fall prey to Philip's 'insatiable malice, which is most terrible to be thought of, but most miserable to suffer'. There, in a nutshell, was the reason why Burghley worked indefatigably to find alternatives to confrontation: he did not think England could win.

Sadly for the advocates of appeasement over the centuries, weakness is unfailingly provocative. Burghley did nothing to put off the evil day by preventing English participation in what was the only clear opportunity to diminish the adverse geopolitical impact of the union of the Spanish and Portuguese crowns. For once, it would have been in England's interest to operate in concert with France and, by urging Elizabeth to refuse to do so, he ensured that when the day came England would have to stand alone against the might of Spain, the very outcome he most dreaded.

The Moluccas venture was probably doomed by being born of the frustration of the Azores project. Frobisher's patience was rapidly eroded by squabbling between Drake's men, many of them veterans of the circumnavigation, who regarded the stated objective of the journey as simply a cover story for a raid on Spain's Pacific colonies, and the representatives of the Muscovy Company,* who demanded guarantees that no raiding would take place. Faced with unacceptable constraints on his freedom of action, Frobisher resigned in early 1582. Command devolved to his deputy, the Dudley brothers' man Edward Fenton, who had been Frobisher's lieutenant during the 1578 voyage. Thus a leader with a proven record for bringing difficult but clearly defined missions to a successful conclusion was replaced by one who thought he could 'muddle through' but lacked the authority to carry it off.

The expedition consisted of two large, heavily armed ships, the 340-ton *Galleon Leicester* commanded by Fenton with William Hawkins's 22 year-old namesake son aboard as his lieutenant, and the Muscovy Company's 250-ton *Edward Bonaventure* under Luke Ward, who wrote a fair account of the voyage. Sailing with them was the 70-ton pinnace *Francis* commanded by John Drake, a young cousin raised in Francis Drake's household since the age of 10 who had sailed with him on *Golden Hind*, and another bark that joined later as a supply ship. After long delays the flotilla sailed from Southampton in May 1582, and by the time it reached the coast of Africa Fenton showed signs of mental deterioration, announcing his intention to seize and make himself king of the remote island of St

* Ironically including William Towerson, whose voyages to Guinea in 1555–58 set the pattern for predatory trading that he was now so anxious to prevent.

Helena. His hallucinatory behaviour so closely matches that of Cavendish on his last voyage that one wonders if both may have been afflicted by ergotism, a product of mouldy rye bread.

Fenton's expedition almost crossed with perhaps the most outstandingly disastrous voyage of the 16th century. Pedro Sarmiento de Gamboa, whom last we saw vainly seeking to intercept Drake off Panamá in 1579, was sent by Viceroy Álvarez de Toledo to survey the Straits of Magellan and then to report to the King on the question of fortifying them. Early in 1580 Sarmiento found Tierra del Fuego natives with European cloth they had obtained from two ships, which may have been Drake's. When he reached the Cape Verde islands he learned that the Portuguese had captured five Englishmen, who said they were part of a fleet of ten ships 'fitted out by a great lord in England', which had been to the Straits and then returned along the coast of Brazil looking for a port suitable for 1,000 colonists aboard the 900-ton flagship, which Sarmiento believed may have been the large English ship the Portuguese reported wrecked on Terceira in the Azores in November 1579.

There's no corroboration for any of this in English sources, which does not necessarily mean that there was no such expedition – although whenever one comes across a round figure like 1,000 it's always best to mentally substitute 'big number'. There simply *were* no 900-ton English merchant ships, and the loss of one even half as big would certainly have been recorded. The most likely explanation is that Sarmiento strung together every piece of information and rumour he could in his report to Philip II, in which he urged the king to fortify the strait against any further hostile incursions. Philip entrusted him with the task and early in 1582 he sailed with a huge fleet carrying over 2,500 sailors, soldiers and settlers commanded by Admiral Diego Flores de Valdés (later Medina Sidonia's chief of staff in the 1588 Armada) with the double purpose of overawing Philip's new subjects in Brazil and establishing a permanent garrison in the strait.

After a long lay-over at Rio de Janeiro the fleet sailed again in November and suffered every conceivable misfortune and delay, such that Sarmiento was unable to establish the Magellan Strait outpost until February 1584. There was vicious disagreement between Sarmiento and Flores, mutinies, and hangings. Ship after ship was lost and the soldiers and settlers were abandoned to their fate after Sarmiento's desperate efforts to obtain resupply for them were defeated by storms.

Bad luck continued to dog Sarmiento, who was captured off Terceira in the Azores in 1586 by *Mary Sparke* and *Serpent*, two of Sir Walter Ralegh's pinnaces. Released by Queen Elizabeth with a safe conduct to bear a 'letter of peace' to Philip II, he was captured by Huguenots when crossing France and remained a prisoner until his king paid a ransom of 6,800 ducats and four horses for him in 1589. Four years later he was made Admiral of an Indies *flota*, but died within days of the *flota*'s departure from Lisbon.

Back in 1582, although they had missed the optimum months for the voyage, Fenton's ships sailed across the Atlantic to the coast of Brazil, from where the wind and current of the South Atlantic gyre would give them the best shot at rounding the Cape of Good Hope – or so the merchants were told. However, it seems Fenton's true intention was to follow the route Francis Drake had taken through the Strait of Magellan – until he captured a Spanish ship and learned about Sarmiento's expedition.

On 21 December, after heated arguments over which course to follow, John Drake deserted the expedition and sailed south. Unfortunately he wrecked *Francis* in the River Plate estuary and after many vicissitudes was happy to surrender to Spanish captivity. The remaining ships sailed to São Vicente (which shares an island with today's better known Santos, the port of São Paolo) hoping to find a market for the merchandise intended for the Far East.

Duly overawed by Flores's fleet, the Portuguese were unwilling to trade even before three Spanish warships sailed into the harbour and tried to board the English ships, which sank one and severely damaged the other two at little cost to themselves. It was the end of the line for the merchants on *Edward Bonaventure*, who sailed back to England the next day. *Leicester* sailed on to offend the Portuguese further at Spirito Santo before returning to England on 29 June 1583, with William Hawkins in irons after coming to blows with Fenton and drawing a knife on him when the expedition commander announced a new plan to make himself king of Newfoundland.

And that was that as far as the prospects of peaceful trade with Brazil were concerned, as the elder William Hawkins, aged 63, found when he stopped for water and supplies at the Cape Verde Islands later that year with a flotilla of six ships, including two of Francis Drake's and his own 300-ton *Primrose*. The Portuguese launched a surprise attack and inflicted serious loss on the English, who encountered the same fierce hostility when they reached Brazil. Hawkins had to console himself with a run to the Caribbean, where he profitably disposed of his goods as a tolerated smuggler.

Humphrey Gilbert must come near the top of anyone's list of Elizabethan failures – not so much for the depth of his failure as for the height from which he plunged. Walter Ralegh, who rose higher and fell further, was his half-brother, both born of the remarkably fecund Katherine née Champernowne from her marriages to Otho Gilbert and Walter Ralegh *père*. When one considers that they were also related to Richard Grenville, the suspicion arises that there may have been some unique genetic trait common to the inbred gentry of Devon, for they seem to have produced a statistically improbable number of strikingly good-looking, highly intelligent and self-destructively rash individuals.

Gilbert's great-aunt Katherine Astley (or Ashley) was Princess Elizabeth's adored governess and later First Lady of the Bedchamber. Thanks to her he entered his future queen's service in 1554, when he was seventeen, and Elizabeth remained fond of him for the rest of his stormy life. He showed an early interest in maritime exploration but most of his early career was devoted to military activity, in particular an outstandingly brutal role in the suppression of the 1569 Desmond rebellion in Ireland, in which he slaughtered men, women and children indiscriminately, and forced those who wished to surrender to walk between rows of severed heads – for which service he was knighted.

In 1572 Gilbert commanded a force of English volunteers sent to support the Dutch rebels, a mission perfectly described by Professor Andrews as 'requiring diplomatic tact and discretion as well as military skill, all of which he conspicuously lacked'. For the next few years he devoted himself to personal affairs that evidently bored him to distraction for in 1577, riding the same wave of anti-Spanish feeling that sent Drake on his circumnavigation, he submitted two proposals to the queen on how she might harm the King of Spain. They were insanely ambitious. He asked for letters patent to discover new lands, but only as cover for the real intention of sailing to Newfoundland to capture or destroy all Spanish, Portuguese and French ships, the proceeds from which would finance further expeditions to capture Cuba and Hispaniola – and the annual treasure fleet.

The queen gently pointed out that what he proposed exceeded the military capacity of her entire realm. Nonetheless in June 1578 at Walsingham's urging she awarded Gilbert letters patent that granted him six years to discover lands not already in the possession of a Christian prince, which he and his heirs could hold by absolute right forever. The last paragraph sternly abjured him not to 'rob or spoil by sea or by land, or do any act of unjust and unlawful hostility to any of the subjects of us, our heirs, or successors, or any of the subjects of any king, prince, ruler, governor or state being then in perfect league and amity with us'.

Despite this prohibition, Gilbert's first attempt to use the letters patent was as cover for a 10-ship raid on the West Indies later in 1578, which he proved unable to control and which degenerated into desultory piracy around Ireland. Only Walter Ralegh in his own 100-ton *Falcon*, bought from the queen, sailed into the Atlantic in search of prizes, seemingly without success. The fiasco seriously impaired Gilbert's personal finances, which never recovered, and the queen spoke for many when she commented that Gilbert was 'of not good happ by sea'.

Gilbert's next attempt to assert his rights in November 1582 involved a joint-stock company based in Southampton whose investors were to have exclusive rights to trade with the lands he had not yet identified, still less occupied. The new scheme involved an agreement with leading English Catholics anxious to escape rising recusancy fines to set up a colony of their co-religionists in the New World on eight-and-a-half million acres gifted by Gilbert. The Vatican was appalled at the prospect, as it threatened to dry up the water in which swam the Jesuits sent by Rome to subvert Elizabeth's kingdom; which, no doubt, explains why Walsingham was keen on the project. The project foundered on the adamant opposition of their church and the government's insistence that would-be Catholic emigrants must pay recusancy fines before they went.

Determined to create the fiefdom allowed by his letters patent before the expiry date, Gilbert went ahead with a greatly reduced plan of colonization and on 11 June 1583 sailed out of Southampton on the 120-ton *Delight* under its owner William Winter (not to be confused with Sir William Wynter), followed by Walter Ralegh's 200-ton *Bark Ralegh*, owner-captain and tiresomely pious voyage chronicler Edward Hayes in the 40-ton *Golden Hind*, another 40-ton ship called *Swallow* that Gilbert had taken from the famous pirate John Callice, and Gilbert's own 10-ton frigate *Squirrel*. Hayes wrote:

> *We were in number in all about 260 men; among whom we had of every faculty good choice, as shipwrights, masons, carpenters, smiths and such like, requisite to such an action; also mineral men and refiners. Besides, for solace of our people and allurement of the savages, we were provided of music in good variety not omitting the least toys, as morris-dancers, hobby-horse, and May-like conceits to delight the savage people, whom we intended to win by all fair means possible. And to that end we were indifferently furnished of all petty haberdashery wares to barter with those simple people.*

Hayes seems to have been the only captain on the expedition who shared Gilbert's enthusiasm. *Bark Ralegh* dropped out after two days at sea, unconvincingly citing lack of supplies, and Callice's men on *Swallow* parted company for a while to loot an English fishing bark on her way home. On arrival at St John's, Newfoundland, Gilbert was obliged to flourish his royal commission to overcome a blockade by Spanish, French, Portuguese and English fishing boats united under an English admiral who feared – from the company he was keeping, for *Delight*'s master had attacked Portuguese fishermen at St John's the previous year – that he was just another pirate. On 5 August Gilbert went ashore to annex the harbour and all land within 200 leagues of it in the name of the queen. His colonizing ambitions lay further south, but it was prudent to validate the letters patent at the first opportunity.

By doing so he established the first English possession in the New World, demonstrating effective sovereignty by issuing licences to the fishermen for the use of the shore areas they had been using to dry fish for decades. The rent in kind went to supply his poorly provisioned ships. In a bizarre ceremony he promulgated laws to the bemused fishermen as though he already ruled over a settled colony, and put up a post bearing a lead plaque embossed with the royal arms. The fixity of Gilbert's purpose (and, no doubt, his glaring eyes) evidently awed the fishermen, for they voiced no objection at this trampling of their customary rights.

The monument that now stands at the place states that by doing so Gilbert 'founded Britain's overseas empire'. Well, no. Ireland, for obvious geopolitical reasons, absorbed England's colonizing energy under Elizabeth, with much of the horror of the Spanish conquest of America but none of the riches. Elizabeth indulged the grandiose ambitions of men like Gilbert and Ralegh but invested neither money nor expectations in their endeavours. She needed a quick return on any investment she made to pay expenses she could not avoid – in particular, securing the flanks of her realm across the Channel and the Irish Sea. Hakluyt and his many successors implanted and cultivated the idea that England's destiny lay overseas, but the empire was eventually won by establishing and maintaining a global naval supremacy that was far beyond the capability of Elizabethan England.

After sending his many sick and disaffected sailors home in *Swallow*, on 20 August 1583 Gilbert sailed south on little *Squirrel*, with

Delight and *Golden Hind* in attendance. Nine days later *Delight* ran aground at Sable Island, off the coast of Nova Scotia, and was lost with most of her crew and all of Gilbert's charts and mineral samples from Newfoundland, which he believed contained silver. Now fully sharing the queen's view of their leader's happ, the men in the remaining ships demanded to go home. Near the Azores they ran into heavy seas, 'breaking short and high pyramid wise', and at midnight on 9 September the lights on *Squirrel* went out forever. When Hayes last saw Gilbert he was reading a book in the frigate's stern and called out, 'We are as near to heaven by sea as by land', an echo of a famous line from Sir Thomas More's *Utopia*.*

He was 44 years old when he died. The only likeness of Gilbert drawn from life is a crude depiction of him as a younger man, with the inaccurate statement 'drowned in the discovery of Virginia' added later. What redeems the poor artistic merit of the portrait is the inclusion of Gilbert's personal motto, the very modern *Quid Non* – 'Why Not?', thus drawing attention with words to the restless spirit that the artist was unable to capture in paint.

Gilbert's two sons, John and Raleigh, together with his brother Adrian Gilbert and half-brother Walter Ralegh, remained involved in the colonization of the New World. In February 1584 Adrian Gilbert obtained Letters Patent to continue the search for the Northwest Passage, and the following month Walter Ralegh obtained the same to explore and colonize farther South, which gave birth to the Roanoke voyages dealt with in the next chapter. John Gilbert accompanied Ralegh on his voyage to Guiana in 1595 and against Cadiz in 1596, during which he was knighted by the Earl of Essex.

Raleigh Gilbert saw his father's ambition brought to fruition as one of the eight men granted Letters Patent by King James I in 1606 for the London Colony and the Plymouth Colony. In May 1607 ships under Christopher Newport sent by the London Colony founded Jamestown in Chesapeake Bay, Virginia, which survived to become

---

* 'He that hath no grave is covered with the sky: and the way to heaven out of all places is of like length and distance.'

the first permanent English colony in the New World. The first Plymouth colony – in which Raleigh Gilbert sailed – and the second did not put down roots, but he remained closely involved in the colonizing efforts that eventually gave birth to the permanent settlement of New England.

That the expedition leading to the first permanent settlement was led by Christopher Newport provides an irresistible segue from the theme of this chapter to the rest of the book for, as we shall see, over the previous 20 years he had been one of the most successful English corsairs. Until Spain and England made peace in 1604 the energy required to make a success of overseas settlement was fully absorbed by the demands of war instead, and it was only because of its war-making potential that the last colonial enterprise of Elizabeth's reign was allowed to proceed.

CHAPTER 9
CHEVAUCHÉE

The geostrategic balance continued to tip against England during the early 1580s. In the Netherlands Farnese's relentless pressure won back the Channel ports of Dunkirk and Nieuport in 1583, and Dutch resistance was decapitated when an assassin killed Prince William of Orange in Delft on 10 July 1584. Three weeks earlier, with the death of Elizabeth's one-time suitor the Duke of Anjou, the Huguenot Henri of Navarre became the legitimate next-in-line for the throne of France, which guaranteed that France would remain too divided to counterbalance Spain.

Worse, in December Duke Henri of Guise, already in receipt of a secret subvention from Philip II, signed the Treaty of Joinville by which he openly enlisted the Catholic League in Philip's counter-reformation in return for an annual subsidy. In due course this led to the 'War of the Three Henrys', which saw Guise and his brother murdered on the orders of King Henri III in December 1588 and the king himself assassinated in July 1589, leaving the third Henry, of Navarre, to bring the Wars of Religion to an end by converting to Catholicism while establishing official toleration of Protestantism and protection for the Huguenots.

Diplomatic relations between England and Spain were severed in January 1584 when the Spanish ambassador Bernardino de Mendoza was summarily expelled. Once a lieutenant of the Duke of Alba in the Netherlands, Mendoza had plotted ceaselessly against Elizabeth from the time of his appointment in 1578. The final straw was his involvement in the Throckmorton plot, a conspiracy penetrated by Walsingham from its inception, in which English

Catholics were to prepare the way for an invasion by Farnese, after which Mary, Queen of Scots would be placed on the throne.

Walsingham, desperate to persuade the queen that war with Spain was inevitable, presented her with irrefutable evidence that Mendoza had acted with the express authorization of Philip II and that the Duke of Guise was also deeply implicated. Immediately after his expulsion Mendoza was appointed ambassador to France, where he was far more successful at keeping his king's enemies at each other's throats than he had been in England.

It was against this backdrop that the extraordinarily good-looking Walter Ralegh became one of the leading sea-dogs. In March 1584, undeterred by his half-brother Humphrey Gilbert's failure, he obtained similar letters patent to explore and settle lands south of Gilbert's grant, a region he was to name Virginia to flatter the queen. It was what he did best, and in a few short years it had made him a wealthy man, knighted and named Lord and Governor of Virginia. Like Hatton he knew how to play the game of courtly love, and although the story of laying his cloak on a puddle for Elizabeth to walk over is apocryphal, the elegant poems he wrote for her would have moved even one less susceptible to gallantry than she. Thus his poem 'A Farewell to False Love' renounced all previous emotional entanglements, implicitly wiping the slate clean for devotion to the queen.

Ralegh's project was better adjusted to geopolitical realities than Gilbert's. Although the temperate area he chose offered far better prospects of eventually producing cash crops, the primary purpose of the proposed plantation was to provide a self-sustaining base from which corsairs could operate against the Spanish treasure convoy route, far enough away from the Spanish garrisons in Florida to rule out an overland attack. An initial reconnaissance by two of Ralegh's servants, guided by a sinister Portuguese pilot called Simão Fernandes, returned to report a land flowing with milk and honey, populated by natives who, while constantly at war with each, were well disposed to their overseas visitors, in proof of which two of them, Manteo and Wanchese, were brought back to England.

Unlike their Inuit predecessors they survived to be presented at court, and to teach Ralegh's house mathematician Thomas Harriot their Algonquin language.

The report, of course, was a sales pitch, as was the *Discourse of Western Planting* written by Ralegh's friend Richard Hakluyt for the eyes of the queen and Secretary of State Walsingham.* While not acceding to Ralegh's request that she formally adopt the project, the queen did make a loan investment of her newly acquired 150-ton galleon *Tiger*, previously Sir William Wynter's private corsair *Sea Dragon*. The queen also released the experienced soldier Ralph Lane from duty in Ireland to lead the 600 men who were to be landed. Further investment followed from Walsingham, the new Lord High Admiral Charles, Baron Howard of Effingham, and several merchants. Investment in kind came from Ralegh's cousin Sir Richard Grenville, who was to lead the expedition, and from the maritime neophyte Thomas Cavendish who, as previously noted, bought the 50-ton *Elizabeth* for the purpose while still learning navigation from Harriot.

In *The Roanoke Voyages* David Quinn suggests there may have been some overall co-ordination, presumably by Burghley, of the Ralegh–Grenville expedition and two other plans. One of these was a follow-up voyage by Bernard 'Wyvern Gules' Drake on his first – and only – corsair venture in *Golden Ryall*, in which he was authorised to raid the Newfoundland fisheries on his way back from resupplying the Roanoke outpost. The other was a grand raid on the Caribbean led by Francis Drake. If so it was the last attempt by the government to impose strategic coherence on the corsair activity that exploded from 1585 onwards. The model should have been the simple flat tax imposed by Coligny to keep the Huguenot cause alive, but there was not the same sense of shared and imminent peril, nor enough respect for royal authority, to do the same in England.

---

* In full, its title is *A Particuler Discourse Concerninge the Greate Necessitie and Manifolde Commodyties That Are Like to Growe to This Realme of Englande by the Westerne Discoueries Lately Attempted, Written in the Yere 1584.*

There was, of course, no question about the primary purpose of an expedition led by Grenville, who turned to raiding even before establishing the base at Roanoke Island, within the outer line of barrier islands off the coast of modern North Carolina. The expedition took the traditional route to the Caribbean, but was scattered by a storm. By the time *Tiger* reached the southern coast of Puerto Rico on 20 May 1585 Grenville had already taken several small prizes. He put Lane's men ashore to build a stockade within which to assemble a pinnace and, joined by Cavendish's *Elizabeth*, spent a month marauding the Mona Passage and the coast of Hispaniola. Although he took a few small ships and held them to ransom, he was surprised to encounter little hostility and much willingness to trade, and so was able to load livestock and plants for the Roanoke outpost without having to fight.

When *Tiger* reached her destination in mid-July she ran aground and sprang a leak when negotiating the barrier islands, spoiling the dry goods for the outpost. Accordingly Lane was left with little more than a hundred men and promises that resupply would shortly arrive. It did not because by now open warfare had begun and Bernard Drake was sent straight to Newfoundland to capture or destroy the Iberian fishing fleet. Ralegh's 240-ton *Roebuck* and pinnace *Dorothy* also reached Roanoke, but owner-captain George Raymond's *Lion* of Chichester never rejoined and, pausing to leave 32 men on the barrier island of Croatoan, sailed off to join Bernard Drake's Newfoundland raid. They returned with 20 prizes and 3,000 tons of dried cod, having done serious and lasting damage to the Spanish and Portuguese fishing industries, for which Bernard Drake was knighted.

Grenville more than paid for the whole enterprise by taking the 300-ton *Santa María de San Vicente* near Bermuda, while Cavendish and Ralegh's ships made independent return journeys in the hope of taking prizes of their own. Grenville declared the value of his prize to be £15,000, the bereft owners said it was £50,000. All we can say with certainty is that every corsair captain returning from a successful cruise had to calculate the minimum that would keep his investors happy, while his victims on the other hand had every incentive to exaggerate their loss against the remote possibility that they might recover some proportion of it through legal channels.

In theory the proceeds from the sale of a captured ship and its cargo were divided among investors, owners and officers, with a relative pittance left over for the sailors, whose compensation came from the right to loot everything except the cargo on boarding the prize. This was simply to recognize a fact of life – soldiers storming a town enjoyed the right to sack it for the simple reason that any officer who tried to stop them was likely to be murdered. However, the integrity of the cargo was probably only respected when it was bulky, and of course the 'chested treasure' that warmed the heart of Queen Elizabeth was particularly vulnerable. A handful of silver pesos represented more than a year's wages for a skilled artisan, and a like amount of gold ducats or jewels could set up that rare being, a provident sailor, for life.

We find in daily experience that all discourse of magnanimity, of national virtue, of religion, of liberty, and whatever else hath wont to move and encourage virtuous men, hath no force at all with the common sailor in comparison of spoil and riches.

Thus the stone thrown by Sir Walter Ralegh from within the glass house of what motivated him and every other gentleman to embark on maritime adventures. Beneath the hypocrisy, however, lay the cold truth that it was only the prospect of hitting the spoil jackpot that led men to embark on highly dangerous and entirely contingent corsairing ventures. A captain who failed to take prizes risked, at best, difficulty in crewing his next voyage – at worst he might face mutiny.

Only abject misery can explain how anyone would volunteer to crew the queen's ships. Although in theory sailors serving in the Navy Royal in 1588 were paid 7s.6d. per month, in practice they were paid late or not at all and had little prospect of spoil. The only certain payment was in kind: accommodation on board was better than sleeping in the street or in dosshouses, and while the food and drink was usually rank and sometimes poisonous, the alternative might be starvation.

By the time the Roanoke adventurers and the Newfoundland raiders returned to England, the gloves had come off when, on 26 May 1585, Philip II ordered the seizure of all foreign ships in Spanish ports (in fact, mainly merchant ships from Holland and Zeeland, which did a brisk trade with Spain throughout the revolt) to serve in an unspecified expedition. Since this could only be intended either to deliver the coup de grâce to the Netherlands revolt or else to attack England directly, the Privy Council issued the first blanket authorization of letters of marque since 1542, when Henry VIII had done so as an explicit act of state policy in conjunction with declaring war on France. Burghley was already resigned to war, but Philip's initiative converted the powerful London merchant lobby from opposition to a vengefully enthusiastic embrace of the *guerre de course*.

Elizabeth never made a *de jure* declaration of war against Spain, but did so *de facto* on 10 August 1585 when she signed the Treaty of Nonsuch, whereby she undertook to send 5,000 foot soldiers and 1,000 cavalry under Robert Dudley, Earl of Leicester, to relieve the siege of Antwerp and to provide an annual loan of 600,000 florins (£100,000) to sustain the Dutch revolt.

As surety the ports of Brielle in Holland, and Flushing with nearby Rammekens castle on Walcheren Island in Zeeland, were 'placed in the hands of such governors as it shall please her Majesty to appoint until she shall be completely repaid'. The 'cautionary ports', as they were known, were at the mouths of major estuaries from which an invasion of England might be launched if the Spanish succeeded in gaining control of the river systems. Elizabeth firmly rejected an offer to become Governor General of the (not very) United Provinces and was furious when Dudley, desperate to co-ordinate the disparate forces losing piecemeal against Farnese, accepted the title in January 1586.

The first great public-private military venture of Elizabeth's reign emerged from this turmoil. In preparation since late 1584, and originally intended as an expedition to the Moluccas, on 14 September 1585 Sir Francis Drake sailed from Plymouth at the head of seven large and 22 small ships carrying 2,300 infantry. The military commander, Walsingham's stepson Christopher Carleill, joined at the last minute on the 200-ton London ship *Tiger* – the queen's smaller and newer ship of the same name was still at sea under Grenville. It was a joint-stock enterprise in which the queen contributed £10,000 as well as two ships, whose generously assessed value gave her a stake of £20,000 in a total stock of a little over £60,000. Other major investors were Drake himself (£7,000, including at least five ships), Robert Dudley (£3,000, two large ships), John Hawkins (£2,500, four or five ships) and William Hawkins (£1,500, one or two ships). Sir William Wynter, the Earl of Shrewsbury and Lord Admiral Howard also sent ships, and Sir Walter Ralegh invested £400.

This was by far the largest fleet and royal investment so far sent out against Spain, and Drake at last achieved his ambition to sail as a queen's admiral. The downside of the commission was that it brought with it indecisive and incompatible instructions that accreted to produce operational incoherence. Drake was to liberate English ships detained in Spanish ports, yet they no longer were by the time he sailed because Philip, too late, had tried to undo his blunder by releasing them. Drake was also supposed to intercept the annual *flota*, which would have required prolonged cruising that would be fatal to the troops packed aboard the ships. Finally he was to raid the Spanish Indies and attack important Spanish settlements, which as far as Drake was concerned was the real purpose of the voyage. There can be little doubt that he had the bullion chokepoint of Panamá in his sights, but circumstances were to prevent him, once again, from realizing his ambition.

The greatest disadvantage of the royal commission was uncertainty about whether the expedition would be permitted to sail at all. Elizabeth never appreciated that fully manned ships cost as much sitting in harbour, consuming the limited amount of food that race-built galleons could store, as they did at sea. Nor, in common with Philip II, did she realize that prolonged inactivity greatly multiplied both desertions and the strong possibility that epidemics might cripple a fleet before it could set sail. Consequently as soon as Drake had his full complement of sailors and soldiers, a modicum of supplies and a favourable wind, he departed because the leaders of the expedition were not, as Carleill put it, 'the most assured of her Majesty's perseverance to let us go forward'.

In addition to Carleill, Drake had the support of Martin Frobisher as Vice Admiral on John Hawkins's new 300-ton *Primrose* and the veteran Thomas Fenner as his flag captain on the 400-ton royal ship *Elizabeth Bonaventure*. With his chaplain Philip Nichols as secretary the three men formed Drake's council for the duration of the voyage, and such evidence as we have indicates that they worked well together. This would not have been the case if Walsingham's son-in-law and queen's favourite Sir Philip Sidney had succeeded in joining the venture, a divided command disaster in the making that Drake averted by warning the queen, resulting in Sidney's recall on the eve of departure.

The main sources for the voyage are a log kept for Carleill by one of his lieutenants and an account written by Walter Bigges, captain of a company of infantry, and continued by someone else after his death at sea in April 1586. Consequently we know a great deal more about the land operations than we do about how the fleet was handled at sea, although the detailed sailing instructions and the negative evidence of the absence of important dispersions, desertions, or accidental losses argues that Drake wisely delegated day-to-day fleet management to the proven skill of Frobisher.

The only evidence of command discord found by Kelsey in his diligent search for anything that might discredit Drake came about when Nichols gratuitously offended the already bruised pride of Francis Knollys, Dudley's brother-in-law and captain of the 400-ton *Galleon Leicester*, who was third in naval command but excluded from the council. While Frobisher returned from the journey coldly determined never to serve under Drake again, Thomas Fenner was happy to do so in the 1587 Cadiz raid. The tie-breaker is the private opinion of Drake formed by that true Renaissance man Carleill, an intellectual from a powerful London merchant family who was also an immensely experienced soldier and sailor: 'I cannot say that I ever had to deal with a man of greater reason or more careful circumspection'.*

In all there were 25 named ships, 15 of them of 100 tons or greater, and at least 8 unnamed small pinnaces plus the *Duck*, a 20-ton galliot (see Appendix B) under John Hawkins's illegitimate son Richard, for close inshore work. George Wynter's son Edward was the captain of the queen's *Aid*, rebuilt as a 220-ton galleon since she had served as Frobisher's flagship in 1577, while Sir William Wynter's new 140-ton *Sea Dragon* was to have been commanded by the elder William Hawkins but in the end sailed under a contract captain. Instead the younger William Hawkins sailed as captain of his uncle John's 150-ton *Bark Hawkins*. George Talbot, Earl of Shrewsbury, sent his veteran corsair ship the 200-ton *Bark Talbot* (later used as a fireship against the Armada) and Lord Admiral Charles Howard of Effingham sent one of his private raiders, the 140-ton *White Lion*.

Walsingham is not listed as a stockholder, but he had invested considerable political capital in backing Drake and in turning him away from his first conception, which was a voyage to the Moluccas, sending him instead on the naval equivalent of the medieval *chevauchée*, a punitive expedition designed to demonstrate that an enemy prince could not protect his possessions. Thus the fleet's first stop was at some islands off Bayona at the mouth of Vigo Bay, where it remained from 27 September to 11 October doing a little light raiding and forcing the Governor of Galicia to assist in watering and (paid) resupply. The matter of the detained English ships was cleared up within a few days of arrival and as Drake later admitted in a rueful letter to Burghley, the second of two annual American treasure *flotas* sailed to safety while he was anchored at Bayona.

---

* Carleill fought with distinction in the Netherlands in 1573–77 and again in 1581–82, played an important part in the defence of La Rochelle in 1577, commanded a fleet in the Channel in 1583 and held senior commands in Ireland.

So why did he remain so long? First of all it demonstrated that he could close one of Spain's most important Atlantic ports at will. But there may have been a second reason, reminiscent of how he raided alternately between the coasts of Colombia and Panamá in 1572–73. He may have calculated that his outrageous defiance of Philip II's authority at Vigo would cause the Spanish to pull back the Ocean Fleet and leave the *flotas* unescorted. If so he achieved his aim, as confirmed by a letter from Admiral Santa Cruz to Philip II in which he admitted complete uncertainty about Drake's intentions. However, the second *flota* unexpectedly did not remain at the Azores waiting for its escort, and when Drake learned that it had reached Cadiz he sailed away from Galicia to the Canary Islands. Because a stratagem did not work does not necessarily mean it was ill conceived.

Strong seas prevented a landing at La Palma in the Canaries on 3 November, where the fleet was also greeted by accurate artillery fire. One 3-pounder shot nearly changed history when it 'struck atwixt our General's legs, standing in his gallery with Captain Frobisher and Captain Carleill standing of the one side and Captain George [Barton] on the other, the splinters of the plank whereon they stood hurt George a little but there was no more hurt done by it being a minion shot'. They sailed past La Gomera, judging it too poor to be bothered with, and a landing party led by Drake at El Hierro on 5 November also found there was nothing worth looting. After cruising to Cape Blanco on the African coast, the fleet next made landfall on 17 November at Santiago Island in the Cape Verde group, also known as Praia from the name of its largest town.

During the voyage from Vigo, Drake had circulated written instructions for the land forces, presumably drafted by Carleill, to correct the indiscipline that had marred landings at Vigo. Carleill was a genuinely honest man, proof of which is that after a lifetime of distinguished service he died poor and owed a considerable amount of money by a queen who assumed he was as big a thief as the rest of her loyal servants. His instructions bear witness to his integrity: all spoil was to be surrendered to a single individual on each boat or pinnace whose duty it was to deliver it to 'such Captains as are of best account in the fleet', who were to keep it in chests locked with four or five keys.

> *For as much as we are bound in conscience and required also in duty to yield an honest account of our doings and proceedings in this action and that [by] her Majesty shall be appointed and persons of credit shall be assigned unto whom such portions of goods of special price as gold, silver, jewels or any other thing of moment or value shall be brought ...*

Thus when Frobisher and Carleill, both of whom spent years seeking full payment for their service in 1585–86, signed off on Drake's accounts at the end of the journey, it confirmed that standard corsair operating procedure was suspended on this voyage. This must have come as a nasty shock to almost everybody in the fleet, particularly those captains judged not to be of 'best account', which may explain why Drake tried to soften the impact by signing the circular 'your loving friend'. He was a very wealthy man and this journey, the first he had been allowed to make since the circumnavigation, seems to have been his bid for respectability. Although the voyage did not quite pay for itself, if one factors in the millions of pesos Philip II was afterwards obliged to spend to remedy the military weaknesses it revealed, as well as the significant damage it did to his prestige, the balance for the national interest was as hugely positive as Secretary of State Walsingham could have wished it to be.

The cruel logic of the *chevauchée* was displayed on Santiago, with Praia thoroughly sacked and partially burned and the inland settlement of Santo Domingo also burned to extort a ransom. Fifty bronze guns were taken along with enormous quantities of stores, and seven ships in the harbour were plundered and cut adrift. A complete caravel found in a shipyard was disassembled and loaded.

Something else they took with them, as a result of gawking at the wretched patients in what they did not realize was a quarantine hospital, was the pneumonic plague at that time ravaging the Iberian mainland. This was not the highly contagious and invariably fatal strain of the Middle Ages but an attenuated form that did not kill all it infected yet left the survivors seriously debilitated. Between 300 and 500 of Drake's men died and at least as many more were disabled, leaving him with insufficient men to realize his dream of conquering Panamá.

Before departing Drake hanged two of his men, one for murder and the other, a steward on either *Aid* or *Talbot*, for sodomizing two cabin boys – which is odd, because that's what cabin boys were for. Perhaps the steward was a rapist, but it may be significant that every account mentions that there were *two* boys, so perhaps the man's downfall was the result of a rivalrous triangle.

Drake also replayed the psychodrama that had led to the beheading of Thomas Doughty in 1578 by requiring his officers to swear an oath of allegiance to the queen and to himself as her deputy. The exercise seems to have been designed to force a confrontation with Francis Knollys and his gentlemen. In her profound analysis of the documentary evidence, Mary Keeler suggests Drake distrusted Knollys because he and his brother Henry had deserted Humphrey Gilbert's 1578 expedition; it's also possible Drake let it be known that he did not consider Knollys one of the captains of 'best account'. However, Knollys's refusal to take the oath also revealed an insufferable belief in his own social superiority, and Chaplain Nichols added fuel to the fire by goading some of Knollys's followers into expressing disloyal sentiments.

Drake reacted with an ominous echo of San Julián. He confronted them and snarled that they 'did nothing but sow sedition and by means of their factions he stood in fear of his life'. On the same day as the hanging of the steward, Drake called a general assembly ashore in the shadow of the gallows. Whatever the next act was going to be was cut short when a false report of enemy sail on the horizon sent everybody racing back to their ships, but not before he had dispersed Knollys's entourage to other ships and stripped him of his authority as rear admiral.

Bearing in mind that this occurred before the epidemic struck, it seems likely that in preparation for announcing what was likely to be a contentious decision to attack Panamá, the whole exercise was designed to make every man in the fleet, regardless of rank, acutely aware that Drake regarded dissent as a potentially capital offence. He may have coldly decided to make an example of Knollys, whose father was Treasurer of the Royal Household and who chafed at being subordinate to a parvenu. In what was both a carefully staged leadership statement and also a highly personal reaction to Knollys's snobbery, Drake humiliated him and made him a pariah.

On New Year 's Day 1586, the expedition arrived off Santo Domingo on Hispaniola, once the capital of Spanish America. While the fleet kept the few defenders looking out to sea, Carleill disembarked 1,000 men some distance away and attacked the poorly fortified landward side. He took it with the loss of one man and his army then fanned out to loot the town, joined by escaped galley slaves. The defenders also gave up the Ozama fort, which commanded the entrance to the inner harbour, without a fight. It was the oldest military work in America, an old-fashioned keep that could not have held out for long once Carleill got some guns ashore – but such was the demoralization of the local garrison that they did not even impose that slight delay on the invaders.

Most of the townspeople had fled, taking as much of their worldly wealth with them as they could carry. After three days they sent a representative to negotiate a ransom for their homes. Drake demanded a million ducats and when it was not forthcoming began burning the town block by block in the usual style. It took three weeks to convince him that Santo Domingo was a shadow of its former self, and that the best offer its wretched inhabitants could scrape together in cash, personal jewellery, and church ornaments amounted to 25,000 ducats.

During the negotiations Drake directed his men to sack every church and religious establishment in the town, but the story about him hanging two friars in retaliation for the murder of a negro servant appears to have been invented by Thomas Cates, the editor of

A Summarie and True Discourse of Sir Frances Drakes West Indian Voyage, an account (otherwise based on Bigges's diary) that was published in four languages in 1588–89.

At the Governor's house they found an elaborate escutcheon with the royal arms above a terrestrial globe on which stood a rampant horse, the scroll from its mouth reading *Non Sufficit Orbis* (the World Is Not Enough), which Drake kept despite attempts to ransom it. The *Summarie* commented:

> ... *if the Queen of England would resolutely prosecute the wars against the king* [note lower-case] *of Spain, he should be forced to lay aside that proud and unreasonable reaching vain of his, for he should find more than enough to do, to keep that which he had already, as by the present example of their lost town they might for a beginning perceive well enough.*

Perhaps it's simply a product of changed usage over time, but to the modern eye 'if' and 'would' imply that, despite being part of the largest fleet ever to sail to the West Indies, Bigges believed the queen was not yet resolutely prosecuting the war.

Before leaving, Drake took two Spanish ships of 400 and 200 tons, which he renamed *New Year's Gift* and *New Hope* and also three smaller ships, manning them with the crews from his own 75-ton *Benjamin* and John Hawkins's 120-ton *Hope* and 30-ton *Scout*, which had become unseaworthy and were abandoned. A large but old carrack and twenty or more other ships in the harbour were burned, including a royal galley that was found ashore. *New Year's Gift* was loaded with all the artillery found in Santo Domingo, some 70 guns in total. Drake also set free all the slaves, some of whom – particularly the French and Turkish galley slaves – elected to join him, while many of the Africans went to join Maroon communities in the mountains.

Finally Knollys, still refusing to swear allegiance and demanding 'justice', was removed from command of *Leicester* by order of Carleill and along with his followers put aboard *Bark Hawkins* as passengers with the threat, never carried out, to send them home in disgrace.

On 9 February the English fleet arrived off Cartagena, where the inhabitants had 20 days warning and used it to evacuate women, children and valuables instead of strengthening their naturally strong defences. In particular they failed to contest the very narrow entrance to the outer harbour, which they might easily have done with their three royal guard ships (a galleass and two galleys), supported by shore batteries. Consequently Carleill was able to disembark his soldiers undisturbed on the tidal barrier island of La Caleta while Drake sent Fenner and several other captains in pinnaces under Frobisher's command to attack the entrance to the inner harbour, closed by a chain and covered by the Boquerón fort, which proved too hard a nut to crack. Not so La Caleta, which was joined to the mainland by a sand spit that was

> ... *fortified clean over with a stone wall and a ditch without it, the said wall being as orderly built, with flanking in every part, as can be set down. There was only so much of this strait unwalled as might serve for the issuing of the horsemen or the passing of carriage in time of need. But this unwalled part was not without a very good barricado of wine-butts or pipes, filled with earth, full and thick as they might stand on end one by another, some part of them standing even within the main sea. This place of strength was furnished with six great pieces, demi-culverins and sakers, which shot directly in front upon us as we approached.*

The following map drawn for the *Summarie* by Baptista Boazio, a cartographer who formed part of Carleill's suite, is an unusually accurate representation of the battle by 16th century standards, although the iguana does not do justice to the splendidly wattled and ridged reptiles still to be seen in Cartagena. To avoid flanking fire from the galleys moored to support the 300 defenders at the wall Carleill marched his men along the sea coast, which brought him opposite the weakest section. The agreed signal was the sound of gunfire from the Boquerón, at which the soldiers charged:

Baptista Boazio's map of the assault on Cartagena shows Drake's flagship *Elizabeth Bonaventure* followed by the galliot *Duck* in the foreground. Beyond them the Spanish galleys fire their guns at the flank of Carleill's troops attacking the wall across the tidal neck between La Caleta and the mainland.

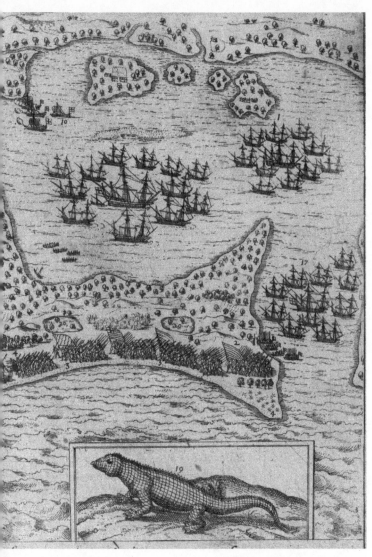

Four phases of the assault are portrayed: the landing at the undefended entrance to the outer harbour; the march across the seaward side of La Caleta; the main anchorage of the English fleet; and, top left, the attack led by Frobisher on the forts and chain barring entrance to the inner harbour.

> *Down went the butts of earth, and pell-mell came our swords and pikes together, after our shot had first given their volley, even at the enemy's nose. Our pikes were somewhat longer than theirs, and our bodies better arm[our]ed; for very few of them were arm[our]ed. With which advantage our swords and pikes grew too hard for them, and they driven to give place. In this furious entry [Carleill] slew with his own hands the chief ensign-bearer of the Spaniards, who fought very manfully to his life's end.*

Amphibious landings are notoriously the most difficult of all military operations, yet Carleill made it all seem easy. If disease had not so greatly reduced his command he would have anticipated Morgan by 85 years and crossed the isthmus to take and hold Panamá, as Drake intended. Cartagena was not an adequate alternative because it would not interrupt the flow of bullion, which by now was the only thing in America that really mattered to Philip II. Cartagena was also more vulnerable to counterattack, and there's no reason to believe Drake wanted to hold it any longer than necessary to extort the maximum ransom – although, as at Vigo, Praia and Santo Domingo, he seems to have stayed longer than necessary to emphasize his dominion.

Drake took up residence at the house of Alonso Bravo de Montemayor, one of the few professional soldiers in Cartagena who had been wounded defending the wall. Through daily contact Drake came to confide in him. Bravo reported that Drake was deeply disappointed to obtain a ransom of only 110,000 ducats, mainly in silver bars, because he had promised the queen a million. Bravo also recorded serious disaffection among Drake's subordinates because he and Carleill enforced their instructions about loot very firmly. 'All the gentlemen', Bravo wrote, 'said he would not again find any to go out with him from England'. Since nearly all of them did a year later, one may deduce that the dissidents who spoke to Bravo were probably Knollys's men.

The dean of the cathedral, another Spanish witness, reported that Drake 'treats his people harshly and hangs many', which is not remarkable when one considers that, to bowdlerize a famous utterance attributed to the Duke of Wellington, they were the scum of the earth enlisted for spoil. On the other hand the dean had particular reason to exaggerate anything to the discredit of Drake because, tiring of burning the town block by block, he finally concentrated the Spanish negotiators' minds by demolishing the partially completed cathedral. Even so, the other religious establishments do not appear to have been as systematically wrecked as they were in Santo Domingo, and overall the occupation of Cartagena was a relatively civilized affair.

The explanation probably lies in the mutual respect between Drake and Bravo, cemented when Bravo's wife, who was at their country estate, sent Drake 'a very rich suit of buttons of gold and pearls and a very fair jewel set with emeralds and another emerald set in a pendant'. She also sent Carleill an emerald brooch and ring, and Frobisher an emerald ring. Shortly afterwards she fell ill and Drake released Bravo to be by her side when she died. When he returned with her body the supposedly rigid Calvinist Drake respectfully attended her funeral, which was conducted with all due solemnity and included a requiem mass.

Drake seems to have had an instinctive liking for Spanish gentlemen, in marked contrast to his distrust of their English equivalents. During the circumnavigation he went out of his way to sugar the bitter pill of defeat for other *hidalgos* he captured, and it's not out of character that he should have exercised restraint in Cartagena out of consideration for Bravo and his late wife. He even remitted his share of Bravo's 6,000 ducat personal ransom, although he was compelled to collect the balance of 5,000 on behalf of the company.

Meanwhile those disabled by the plague continued to die, the Spanish counting over a hundred graves after Drake sailed away – although 30 of them were soldiers killed in the assault on the town. It appears that the contagious stage of the disease was past, as there was no outbreak in Cartagena. Most painfully for Drake, one of his oldest comrades, Thomas Moone, the captain of his own

Francis who had been with him on every voyage since 1571, was killed on 23 February in a skirmish at the entrance to the outer harbour.

On 27 February, in a written reply to Drake's questions about future prospects, Carleill and his land captains advised him that they had only 700 fit men, enough to defend Cartagena against a Spanish counterattack but not to assault Panamá, still less Havana, and that in the light of the relatively poor pickings at Santo Domingo and Cartagena they respectfully suggested he take what was on offer as ransom and return the expedition to England.

Drake knew his business better than they and proved it by obtaining double the amount before the fleet finally sailed on 31 March. Two days later they were back, however, *New Year's Gift* having become unseaworthy. Drake ordered the guns she was carrying distributed among the rest of the ships and, to the relief of the citizens of Cartagena, made no further exactions apart from seizing grain they had brought into town after he left, which he had ground and baked into ships' biscuit.

From Cartagena Drake sailed to the Cayman Islands, where a number of the eponymous reptiles were shot for food, and then rounded Cape San Antonio, the westernmost point of Cuba, on 25 April. Drake's plan was to sail 50 miles/80 kilometres past Havana to Matanzas for water, but was kept out of the bay by contrary winds. The fleet, now seriously short of water, was back at Cape San Antonio on 11 May, where they had to make do with taking it laboriously from a swamp. The anonymous author who took over Bigges's journal recorded his admiration for the example Drake set his men:

> *At this point I must not hold my silence about our General's great vigilance, who here (as he previously did everywhere) urged on the rest by his personal example, bending every effort to gathering water, no less than the men of the lowest ranks. But he handled his fleet with such prudence and care, and often not without risk to his own life, and at all times and places had a care that it be in the*

best order possible, so that, had he been any other man who had obeyed orders in such a praiseworthy manner, he would be deemed worthy of the first place of honour.

The sources are silent about why Drake said he wished to water at Matanzas, where he was likely to encounter opposition, but it requires no great leap of the imagination to fill the gap: unable to assault Havana, he wanted to cause as much alarm as possible and possibly pick up a rich prize. Nor do we know what was said at a general council of captains held at this time, although it's significant that Drake felt compelled to convene one. Presumably in response to pressure from Carleill and Frobisher, he abandoned any further attempts to 'make' the voyage and, after sailing close to the entrance of Havana bay once more, rounded the point of Florida and on 27 May arrived off the Spanish military outpost of San Agustín, which he comprehensively destroyed.

One of the survivors testified to the swashbuckling grandeur with which the Spanish now invested him: 'It was understood that Francis Drake, corsair, was among them because where they set up the artillery in the afternoon there was music of cornets, sackbuts and flageolets'.

The assault on San Agustín seems to have been planned from the beginning, to eliminate the threat it posed to Ralegh's settlement further north. There was also vengeful satisfaction to be had from the fact that the Spanish adelantado was the namesake son of Pedro Menéndez, who had slaughtered Jean Ribault and his men in 1565. Drake also intended to destroy the Spanish outpost of Santa Elena (present day Jacksonville) 36 miles/58 kilometres further north, but found it protected by shoals that reached far out to sea, into which he dared not venture without a pilot.

On 9 June, having continued north towards the English colony, a signal fire was spotted on Croatoan Island. Drake sent boats to investigate and they returned with a group of Englishmen who told him they had been sent by Ralph Lane from the settlement at Roanoke, but who could not guide him through the barrier islands

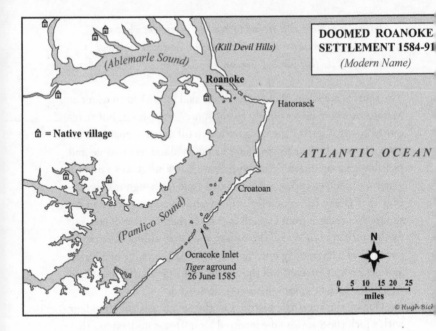

DOOMED ROANOKE
SETTLEMENT 1584-91
(Modern Name)

(Ablemarle Sound)

(Kill Devil Hills)

Roanoke

Hatorasck

🏠 = Native village

ATLANTIC OCEAN

Croatoan

(Pamlico Sound)

Ocracoke Inlet
Tiger aground
26 June 1585

N

0 5 10 15 20 25
miles

© Hugh Bick

to reach it. The fleet anchored off Hatorasck, the closest barrier island, while Drake rowed ashore to confer with Lane. The plan had been to equip the outpost for its predatory mission with his smaller vessels and also to leave 250 black slaves he had 'liberated' in Santo Domingo and Cartagena, but he was quickly disabused of the idea when Lane told him how tenuous the outpost had become. Lane's men had made no great effort to become self-sufficient and their attempts to live off the land had made enemies of the natives. Unless resupply arrived soon, Lane said, they must return home. Soon became immediately because:

> ... the day after we put in a great storm blew up, so that most were obliged to weigh anchor and set sail, some of which returned ... while others sailed straight for England. Here our General made an offer to Ralph Lane, General of the English in Virginia, to provide him and his people with all things most needful, and to leave one ship with a pinnace there, on which he could return to

England if the number of his soldiers (which at the time was only
one hundred and five) were not increased within a month. But
those men were so oppressed and broken by a scarcity of all things
that they wished nothing more than to return home with us as soon
as possible. Thus they were taken into the ships with us, and sailed
from there.

The fleet arrived at Portsmouth on 27 July 1586, unknowingly having crossed paths with a supply ship sent by Ralegh and reinforcements in three ships led by Grenville. Grenville left 15 men with
enough supplies to last two years and with orders literally to hold
the fort until another expedition could be organized. But they had
disappeared when Ralegh's second group of settlers, 115 men and
women under John White, arrived in July 1587. White's group was
supposed to collect the men from Roanoke and then establish a new
settlement further north, in Chesapeake Bay, but they were left at
Roanoke by the Portuguese pilot Simão Fernandes, in whom Ralegh
deposited too much confidence and who repaid his trust by effec-
tively sabotaging the enterprise to seek prizes instead.*

The settlers, who included White's daughter Eleanor Dare and
her infant daughter Virginia, the first English child born in America, sent White back to England to obtain relief, but the Armada
intervened and further acts of faithlessness by captains hired to relieve the colony delayed White's return until August 1590, by which
time no trace of the colony was to be found except the word 'Croatoan' carved into a tree. Bad weather and the plunder-mindedness
of the sailors nominally under his command prevented the frantic
White from checking the barrier island, and the 'Lost Colony' remains a tragic mystery to this day.

The period 1585–86 witnessed what may have been the only
attempt to pursue a strategic approach to waging war against Spain
in America. Of the three components we have reviewed so far, two
of them, Bernard Drake's raid on the Iberian fishing fleet off New-

* The Chesapeake settlement was finally made at Jamestown in 1607, by which time the original
military-strategic rationale was gone. It became the first successful English colony in America.

foundland and Francis Drake's *chevauchée* in the West Indies, harmed the Spanish economy and Philip II's prestige – but they did not represent a serious threat to Spanish power. That could only have been achieved by establishing and maintaining the pretender Dom Antonio in the Azores, an opportunity Elizabeth's ministers were unable to persuade her to seize. Burghley, constrained as courtiers always are by what his monarch wanted to hear, took far too long to admit that his accommodationist policy had failed and that England's opposition to Spanish hegemony must lead to war.

The concept of a base in North America from which to attack the treasure *flotas* was a poor substitute for the Azores, as was John Hawkins's proposal to establish a relay of blockading ships from bases in England. Each required a greater long-term investment than Elizabeth was ever prepared to make in any overseas enterprise, and private investors took their lead from her. The queen's ambition ran to little more than a return on the investment already made in royal ships and a cut of the proceeds from the corsair war, but her senior county officials were too corrupt and incompetent to harvest revenues for her comparable to those generated by Coligny's *guerre de course* for the Huguenot cause.

It's footling to argue that Philip II did not want a war with England simply because he took so long to embark on it. First of all, he did not have the means to attack England until he gained control of the Portuguese navy. As to intent, he adamantly wanted what could only be achieved by war or by a pre-emptive English surrender. Yet, despite a succession of Spanish-sponsored plots against her life, Elizabeth continued to hope beyond reason that somehow it might be averted. In modern parlance she sent signal after signal that she could damage Philip more easily than he could damage her, and that it was no more in his interest than hers for hostilities to escalate to outright war.

The voice in Philip's head told him otherwise, so he gathered naval forces from across his empire to visit God's judgement on the insolent islanders. By doing so he provided the keystone of English patriotism: the belief, sustained in the face of considerable evidence to the contrary, that they were uniquely free and prosperous and that this was evidence of God's particular benevolence. The passage of over four centuries has not dulled the biting edge of that irony.

CHAPTER 10
ESCALATION

If the English state did sponsor and encourage a genuinely strategic response to the rising threat from the Spanish Empire, then the blanket issuance of letters of marque was its principal component. It gave birth to a relentless war of attrition that over the following 19 years devastated Spanish and Portuguese merchant shipping and transferred a considerable amount of wealth from Iberian to English pockets. What it did not – could not – do was alter in any fundamental way the gross imbalance of power between the world-girdling Spanish Empire and the English part of a group of islands off the north coast of Europe. Thus although the means employed were aggressive, the strategic concept could only be preemptive and defensive.

Technically, this resulted in an English commitment to well-armed, agile, small-to-medium sized ships whose guns further reduced the relatively limited space available for stores and cargo – an excellent short-range warship but sub-optimum for long-distance voyages. This was not what Burghley had in mind when he tried to force open the doors to trans-Atlantic trade, which, had it succeeded, might have seen English merchants investing in the larger galleons favoured by the Spanish. Ironically Philip II's determination to maintain his American monopoly at all costs encouraged the English to build instead ships best suited to prey on his subjects, and in due course to defeat his massed naval might in battle.

Tactically, the corsair war did nothing to develop battle techniques to make best use of the new armament. There was no profit to be had from sinking or even seriously damaging a target ship, which had to be sailed to a home port to obtain the full value of the cargo and the vessel itself. The norm was (and remained throughout the sailing ship era) to use the guns to induce surrender or, failing that, to inflict casualties on the enemy crew before grappling and boarding. The English only discovered the best use of their superior gunnery at the end of the Channel battles of 1588 – after which Lord Admiral Howard received a message from the Privy Council demanding to know why the Spanish ships had not been boarded.

Of course the Armada ships were packed with soldiers and boarding would have been suicidal. But even a normal crew could put up fierce resistance. In September 1585 two corsair ships prepared by Sir George Carey, Captain General of the Isle of Wight, Vice Admiral of Hampshire, cousin to the queen and brother-in-law of Lord Admiral Howard, attacked a 300-ton fishing mother ship manned by Spanish Basques in the Bay of Biscay. William Monson, then on his first voyage aged 17, described the battle that followed:

> *All our men with one consent entered her and were left fighting aboard her all night, the seas being so grown that our barks were forced to ungrapple and fall off. The Spaniards betook themselves to their close fights* [fore and after castles] *and gave two attempts by trains of powder to blow up their decks on which we were, but we happily prevented it by fire-pikes. Thus continued the fight till seven in the morning, when the Spaniards found the death and spoil of their men to be so great as they were forced to yield. When we came to take a view of our people we found few left alive but could show a wound they received in that fight.*

Monson thought it unlikely that any other fight in the whole war resulted in so many killed and wounded of the relatively small number of men involved – and all for a cargo of dried fish, to boot. But that was just the beginning. The ship and her cargo were owned by a French merchant who brought suit to the Court of Admiralty, and despite his high political connections Carey found himself obliged to bribe Julius Caesar, Chief of the Court, to make the problem go away. If all prizes had proved such tough nuts, the corsair war would have taken far longer to gather momentum.

The last element in the worldwide assault on the Spanish Empire were two 'reprisals' that were supposed to combine and together replicate Drake's circumnavigation, this time as a *chevauchée*. Both were under letters of marque from the Portuguese pretender Dom Antonio but approved by the queen. The first was also the first such venture prepared by the spendthrift courtier George Clifford, Earl of Cumberland. Cumberland bought the exceptionally heavily armed 300-ton merchant ship *Assurance* and the more lightly armed 130-ton *Bark Clifford*, and sent them out under contract captains. They were accompanied by Sir Walter Ralegh's *Roebuck* and pinnace *Dorothy*, not long returned from the Roanoke expedition. The flotilla sailed from Gravesend at the end of June 1586 and returned empty-handed at the end of September, having turned back without even attempting the Strait of Magellan. The fiasco cost the earl the manor of Cowthorpe.

The second was by the Suffolk gentleman Thomas Cavendish who, like Cumberland, mortgaged property to finance the venture. As soon as he returned from Roanoke, encouraged by Secretary of State Walsingham, he ordered two ships from Ipswich shipwrights, the 120-ton galleon *Desire* and the 40-ton pinnace *Hugh Gallant*. Ralegh's ships were originally to sail with Cavendish but joined Cumberland instead, presumably because *Roebuck* was a much bigger ship than *Desire* and it would have posed command problems for the inexperienced Cavendish if Ralegh's men, under professional captains, outnumbered his own. Apart from Walsingham his investors included Lord Henry Carey of Hunsdon, who was the queen's first cousin and Lord Chamberlain of the Household, also Hunsdon's eldest son Sir George Carey, who contributed the 60-ton *Content*, a syndicate of Ipswich merchants and High Court of Admiralty Judge Julius Caesar, who required Cavendish to post a £2,000 bond to guarantee that he would attack only Spanish ships.

It was an astonishing act of faith in a man with only one sea voyage under his belt. The main political point in his favour was that, like Frobisher, Cavendish was not part of the West Country mafia; but he must also have impressed investors by the thoroughness of his preparations. He collected copies of every chart that might be of use, hired experienced pilots and also a number of men who had sailed around the world with Drake. Among the latter was the Suffolk gentleman Francis Pretty, author of *Sir Francis Drake's Famous Voyage Round the World*. Pretty's account of Cavendish's voyage is the principal source for the circumnavigation.

Pretty sailed in *Hugh Gallant* until she was scuttled on 5 June 1587, so we have no close eyewitness to how Cavendish handled himself during the first year of the voyage. He sailed from London on 10 June 1586, loaded stores at Harwich and then sailed to Plymouth, where he spent 25 days waiting for Cumberland's flotilla. His departure on 21 July, prompted by a desire to avoid contagion from the imminent return of Drake's disease-ridden fleet from the West Indies, caused him to miss the rendezvous with Cumberland's ships by four days.

The missed rendezvous meant that Walsingham's plan for a major punitive expedition was reduced to three small ships and 123 men. In all probability the faint hearts of Cumberland's captains would have prevailed in a combined fleet and nothing would have come of it; but if instead Cavendish had been able to persuade them to follow his lead, Drake's sack of Santo Domingo and Cartagena might have been matched by similar destruction at Valparaiso, Callao, Panamá and maybe also Manila. To put Walsingham's ambition and Cavendish's skill into historical perspective, it was not until 1740–44 that the next officially sponsored British fleet, under George Anson, reduced by disease and storm damage to a single 1,000-ton ship, conducted a more damaging raid into the Pacific.

Cavendish's aggressive intent was shown five days into the voyage, when he fired on a fleet of Spanish fishing ships that escaped in the dark. In Sierra Leone he made a gratuitous attack on a native village that cost him one man horribly killed and several wounded by poisoned arrows. The episodes give the impression that Cavendish, who had never seen battle before, was seeking to impress his men that he was a suitably bold military leader. After a rapid Atlantic crossing he skulked along the coast of Brazil avoiding settlements until he found an uninhabited bay, where he paused from 1 to 23 November to assemble a pinnace and to make new casks for fresh water.

On reaching Patagonia (Pretty commented on the supposedly very large feet [Sp. *patas*] of the natives, which was thought to have given the area its name), on 17 December the flotilla anchored in a bay Cavendish named Port Desire after his ship – and Puerto Deseado (Port Desired) it remains to this day. There he careened, cleaned and caulked his ships while stocking up on sea lion and penguin meat before sailing to the Strait of Magellan, which he entered on 6 January 1587. The next day he found the wretched remnant of Sarmiento's colony:

> *We took a Spaniard whose name was Hernando* [Tomás Hernández], *who was there with 23 Spaniards more, which were all that remained of four hundred, which were left there three years before, all the rest being dead with famine. And the same day we passed through the narrowest of the Straights, where the aforesaid Spaniard showed us the hull of a small bark, which we judged to be* [Drake's lost ship *Marigold*, commanded by] *John Thomas.*

The other colonists would have been a burden and possibly a danger to his enterprise, so Cavendish abandoned them. Pausing to pick up four cast-iron guns from their abandoned fort, and at another location to shoot a group of natives he thought were hostile, he sailed on until his weather-luck ran out and he spent a month anchored in a bay assaulted by violent tempests and subsisting on shellfish and sea birds. At last the flotilla entered the Pacific on 24 February and a week later was scattered by a storm that blew all three ships and the little pinnace 700 miles/1,100 kilometres north to Mocha Island, where they were reunited on the 15th. Like Drake they encountered the uncompromising hostility of the native Mapuches, which was to keep them free of European domination until the late 19th century.

The flotilla was able to reprovision fully from storehouses at another island that had been conquered by the Spanish, before sailing rapidly up the coast of Chile to Quintero, north of Valparaiso, where Hernández escaped and found that the local authorities had already been alerted. Cavendish assumed Hernández was responsible for the ambush of a foraging party by Spanish soldiers with the loss of 12 men, including the master of *Hugh Gallant*, which was to have dire consequences for a subsequent Spanish captive. His immediate reaction was to conduct a mini-*chevauchée* along the coast of Chile and Perú. In his report to Lord Hunsdon he boasted of destroying 19 ships, and 'all the villages and townes that ever I landed at, I burned and spoiled'.

Carey's corsairs on *Content* began to show their disaffection at this time, separating from the flotilla to raid independently and to fill up her hold with jars of wine, which did nothing to improve their discipline. North of Arica a small ship was intercepted carrying couriers from Quintero to the Viceroy in Lima. They threw the dispatches overboard, but Cavendish 'wrought so with them that they did confess it: he was fain to cause them to be tormented with their thumbs in a wrench, and to continue them at several times with extreme pain'.

For a man anxious to avoid areas of dense habitation, Cavendish's choice for the next place to career his ships left a great deal to be desired. It was near a town and shipyard on Puná Island, which occupies much of the bay of Guayaquil, the principal port of Ecuador. On 2 June 1587 Cavendish's shore party of no more than 20 men was attacked by 'an hundred Spaniards serving with muskets and two hundred Indians with bows, arrows and darts', sent from Guayaquil. The English were driven back to their boats, losing another 12 men but claiming to have killed four times as many. Perhaps they had, because the Spanish force fled when Cavendish counterattacked at the head of 70 men.

> *This done, we set fire to the town and burnt it to the ground,*
> *having in it to the number of three hundred houses: and shortly*
> *after made havoc of their fields, orchards and gardens, and burnt*
> *four great ships more which were in building on the stocks.*

Cavendish was now so short-handed that he had to scuttle *Hugh Gallant* and redistribute her crew before proceeding along the coast of Guatemala and Mexico, sinking ships and burning villages including Sonsonate and Guatulco, where Drake had put ashore Nuño da Silva 10 years before. After raiding Mazatlán he sailed to Aguada Segura ('safe watering place' – today San José del Cabo at the tip of Baja California), close to the great circle route from Manila to Acapulco. So far pickings had been slim, but on 4 November Cavendish 'made' the journey resoundingly by capturing the 700-ton *Santa Ana*, one of two Manila carracks that sailed in 1587, the other having escaped notice in the fog that concealed the approach of *Desire* and *Content*.

It was not a well-handled ship seizure, mainly because *Content* held back and let *Desire* do all the fighting. Although he had no artillery and only two arquebuses, *Santa Ana*'s captain Tomás de Alzola had time to bring up ballast rocks, with which he put up a spirited fight:

> *Now as we were ready on her ship's side to enter her, being not*
> *past 50 or 60 men at the uttermost in our ship, we perceived that*
> *the Captain of the said ship had made fights fore and after, and*
> *laid their sails close on their poop, their mid ship, with their fore*
> *castle, and having not one man to be seen, stood close under their*
> *fights with lances, javelins, rapiers and targets and an*
> *innumerable sort of great stones, which they threw overboard*
> *upon our heads and into our ship so fast and being so many of*
> *them that they put us off the ship again, with the loss of two of*
> *our men which were slain and with the hurting of four or five.*

Cavendish stood off and fired his guns at the carrack, smashing her upper works and killing some of the crew, but his next attempt to board was also beaten off. A third, more prolonged bombardment holed *Santa Ana* below the waterline and after five or six hours, with many of his crew killed and injured and his ship sinking, Alzola surrendered. He and his pilot went aboard *Desire* and knelt before Cavendish, who promised them their lives if they made a true accounting of the value of their cargo. They told him it was 122,000 'pesos of gold' as well as large amounts of silks, satins, damasks, tons of conserves and 'sundry sorts of very good wines'.

Setting the Spanish crew to man the pumps, Cavendish's men sailed *Santa Ana* to Aguada Segura and began to unload her contents into *Desire* and *Content*. There was more than the two ships could load, yet Carey's men mutinied over Cavendish's strict division. Although they were bought off, they were also determined to return to England by what they believed was the shortest route, the mythical Strait of Anian, and sailed into oblivion.

Cavendish declared specie and goods to the value of £90,000 when he got back, which suggests the total worth of the cargo, including what was lost with *Content* and hundreds of tons of cargo burned with the galleon, could have been in the region of £400,000. It was to be the largest loss inflicted on the Manila–Acapulco route in 250 years of operation.

Leaving the Spanish crew and passengers well provided for, Cavendish took with him *Santa Ana*'s pilots, the Portuguese Nicolás Rodrigo and the Spanish Tomás de Ersola, as well as three Filipino boys – and two Japanese brothers who were to accompany him for the rest of his life. He set out on 19 November and, with his weather-luck back, made an astonishingly fast Pacific crossing of 56 days, arriving at the Ladrones (today Mariana) Islands on 4 January 1588.

On 15 January he reached Capul Island in the San Bernardino Strait between Luzon and Samar in the Philippines, where he released the two older Filipinos; the youngest eventually became a page to the Countess of Essex. Rodrigo, the Portuguese pilot, informed him that Tomás de Ersola had written a letter to the authorities that he intended to send ashore with the boys, which being verified Cavendish hanged him.

Unable to do much with such a reduced crew, Cavendish cruised along the coast of Luzon and made sure his presence was known by sending insolent letters ashore, one to the Bishop of Manila. It had the desired effect and the prelate reported the incident in a letter spluttering with outrage:

> *An English youth of about twenty-two years* [actually 27], *with a wretched little vessel of a hundred tons, dared come to my place of residence, defy us, and boast of the damage that he wrought. He went from our midst laughing, without anyone molesting or troubling him.*

The rest of the voyage was something of an anti-climax from a military point of view, although Pretty recorded many fascinating glimpses of native societies in an account of lasting value to anthropologists. *Desire* passed through the Sunda Strait on 1 March and sailed along the coast of Java, stopping to buy supplies from small native settlements, before setting off across the Indian Ocean on the 16th. The Cape of Good Hope was sighted on 11 May but not finally rounded until the 16th, after which Cavendish stopped at the island of Saint Helena from 9 to 20 June to replenish water and supplies.

Pretty reported a beautiful, fertile island with very few inhabitants, to which the Portuguese had imported livestock and fruit trees to serve as a source of fresh food for ships sailing from the East Indies. Once this information was publicized by Hakluyt, enterprising corsairs began to use it as a resupply base while they waited to ambush the Portuguese ships, eventually making it the British possession that it remains.

Cavendish sailed past the Azores on 24 August and on 3 September met a Flemish hulk out of Lisbon, from which he learned about the defeat of the Spanish Armada. *Desire* was almost sunk within sight of home by a 'terrible tempest' that blew out all her sails, and finally limped into Plymouth under jury rigging on 9 September 1588. Although the Armada campaign had stolen his thunder, Cavendish had the wit to rig *Desire* with damask sails and silken ropes when he sailed along the Thames to Greenwich. This was the stuff of ballads and brought a visit from the queen but no knighthood – she was not, after all, one of his delighted investors.

Further evidence of the mean-spirited avarice that was such a feature of Elizabethan England came when Cavendish rewarded his crew generously before distributing profits to the shareholders, thereby incurring the spiteful enmity of Julius Caesar. As Chief Judge of the Admiralty he abused his office to persecute Cavendish, having *Desire* impounded and admitting a false accusation of piracy in order to declare forfeit the £2,000 bond he had insisted Cavendish post before departure. What makes Caesar's malice even less forgivable is that Cavendish made an honest accounting, and the investors a handsome profit. The only obvious explanation is that Cavendish's display of lordly munificence ruffled Caesar's parvenu feathers.

It was Cavendish's further misfortune that through no fault of his own the voyage had been something of a damp squib, a pinprick instead of the brutal blow to Philip II's prestige envisaged by Walsingham, and as a result he did not attract the high level patronage he must have hoped for. Even before the Armada there had been a paradigm shift while he was away, symbolized – if not, as is commonly supposed, caused – by the execution of Mary, Queen of Scots on 8 February 1587.

After Mary was implicated in the Babington plot to assassinate Elizabeth by letters in her own hand intercepted by Walsingham, the Privy Council insisted that she be put on trial for treason – of which, by reason of never having been a subject of Queen Elizabeth, she could not be guilty. Condemned nonetheless, Elizabeth was further prevailed upon to sign her death warrant but then refused to order it carried out. She wanted her cousin dead, but refused to will the means. Burghley persuaded the Privy Council to take the decision for her and for several months she berated him every time she saw him – in public; but there's no evidence he was banished from her private presence.

It may be that his temporary disgrace, even if it was mainly for show, compromised Burghley's ability to prevent an escalation of the naval war, which saw the corsairs moving towards a supporting role after years of being the cutting edge of the naval war. The transition from relatively modest joint-stock ventures in which a few marginal queen's ships might take part as loan investments, to large fleet actions in which she committed some of her best warships and became a major shareholder began with the raid on Cadiz, the main Spanish Atlantic port, led by Francis Drake in April–May 1587.

Sir Francis Bacon, that bountiful source of aphorisms, misleadingly dubbed the Cadiz raid as 'singeing the King of Spain's beard'. It was far more than that – it was a reduced-scale rehearsal of the public–private partnership that was to defeat Philip II's invasion attempt the following year. The terms of association were extremely clear: it was a partnership between the queen and private merchant adventurers, 'ton for ton and man for man', by which was meant that shares in the enterprise would be allocated strictly according to the ships' tonnage and the manpower provided by each of the partners, according to an unstated formula that would require greater mathematical ability than I possess to work out. It marked a break with the fraudulent fiction of loan investment, in which the royal contribution was guaranteed against loss and overestimated in the division of loot: from now on Elizabeth's ships sailed at her own risk and expense.

Elizabeth sent three of her most modern large galleons. They were Drake's flagship *Elizabeth Bonaventure* (rebuilt by Hawkins in 1581 at 448 tons), the vice-flagship of joint Comptroller of the Navy William Borough *Golden Lion* (rebuilt in 1582 at 420 tons), and *Rainbow* (newly built in 1586 at 385 tons) under Sir Henry Bellingham, Vice Admiral of Essex. The other royal ships were the older (1573) 360-ton galleon *Dreadnought* under Drake's West Indies flag captain Thomas Fenner and three new pinnaces, the 45-ton *Makeshift*, 42-ton *Spy*, and 30-ton *Cygnet*. It appears the other partners gallantly connived at the queen's shares being calculated according to the 'tons and tonnage' of her ships, while theirs was calculated according to the lower 'tons burden'.* Accordingly, including the 2,648 men she provided, the queen's share was calculated at 3,120 (40.9 percent) of 7,623 parts.

The list of armed merchant shipowners involved in the raid was a roll-call of London entrepreneurs who had opposed the corsair war until Philip II closed the Iberian market to them, and who became its greatest promoters thereafter. Each of the following was the leader of a sub-syndicate:

- 🕸 Thomas Cordell sent *Merchant Royal* (350 tons) with Robert Flick, who sailed in her as the informal commodore, also *George Bonaventure* (200) and *Thomas Bonaventure* (140);

- 🕸 John Watts sent *Margaret and John* (180) under William Towerson, namesake son of the pioneering Guinea trader, also *Little John* (100), *Drake* (80) and *Examiner* (50);

- 🕸 Paul Bayning sent *Susan* (260) under fellow merchant James Lancaster;

- 🕸 George Barnes sent Cordell's *Edward Bonaventure* (250) under his namesake son;

- 🕸 Simon Boreman sent *Salomon* (170).

Another syndicate comprising former Lord Mayor Sir Thomas Pullison, Robert Cobb and Thomas Starkey sent the large pinnaces *Speedwell* and *Post*. Ships were only part of the investment: the cost of consumables was often as great. Along with Cordell and Bayning the principal capitalists were William Garraway and Edward Holmeden, who did not own any of the ships. Including 894 men, the merchants' share was 2,994 parts (39.3 percent).

---

* See Appendix D: 'Tons Burden' and 'Tons and Tonnage'.

The third component was an 'old guard' of eminent private shipowners. Drake sent his 200-ton *Thomas* (a fireship in 1588) the pinnace *Elizabeth*, and probably held a stake in three or four unnamed pinnaces sent by a Plymouth syndicate. Sir William Wynter (still Surveyor of the Navy and Master of Naval Ordnance) sent his 200-ton *Minion*, Treasurer of the Navy John Hawkins sent his 150-ton *Bark Hawkins* and Robert Crosse, a long-time associate of the Fenners, was appointed captain of land operations. Including 609 men, their share was 1,219 parts (16 percent).

Lastly Lord Admiral Howard sent his 140-ton *White Lion* and 115 men for 290 parts (3.8 percent).

It's not fanciful to see this as the watershed moment after which – headline events apart – the court and West-Country nexus that had driven the naval guerrilla war against Spain until then gave way to the less flamboyant but more businesslike approach of the London merchants. They were men who understood money and played the percentages, voyage after moderately profitable voyage, in contrast to the high-stakes gambles of their predecessors.

Some things remained the same. In the agreement dated 6 December 1587 by which Drake and the major London capitalists bought out the queen's interest in the Portuguese carrack *São Filipe* for £50,000, a pointed comment about cargo taken 'elsewhere' than the warehouses where it was officially inventoried suggests the merchant adventurers prudently covered their costs in advance.

The further novelty of the Cadiz raid lay in the fact that it had a military-strategic objective as its first priority. Previously the damage done to Philip II's ability to make war had been incidental to money-making. Now Drake's instructions were to do as much harm as possible to the shipping and supplies being massed in Lisbon for an amphibious attack on England, and only then to 'make' the voyage. In modern parlance, it was designed to demonstrate the credibility of England's deterrent.

Thus the Cadiz raid can be seen as the last 'signal' in Burghley's policy of trying to convince King Philip that an accommodation with England was in his own interest. Unfortunately

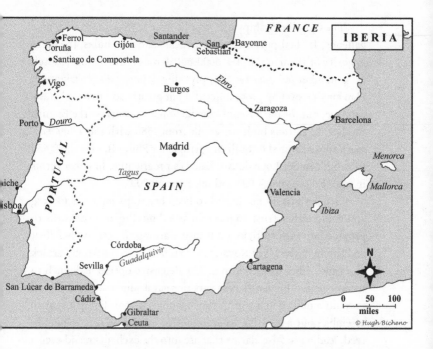

deterrence must fail in the face of a sufficiently determined or ob-sessed enemy, and Philip was both. Since John Hawkins' appoint-ment as Treasurer of the Navy on 1 January 1580, the English deterrent had been strengthened by using the seasoned timbers of six royal carracks and galleasses to construct a like number of 'race-built' galleons. Three new ones had also been built and two ac-quired, one of them (in January 1587) the imposing new flagship *Ark Royal*, accepted from Sir Walter Ralegh as part payment of his large debts to the queen.

In the same period Philip II had acquired not only the high seas navy but also the shipbuilding resources of Portugal, which added twelve large galleons to the royal fleet, while the shipyards of Guipúzcoa, Vizcaya and Cantábria provinces (together known as Cantábrica) had gone into mass production mode from 1582 in re-sponse to a royal disbursement of 60,000 ducats administered by the competent Lope de Avellaneda.

The Cantábrica shipyards supplied the 1588 Armada with nine galleons, 19 dual-purpose *naos* (carracks) and four hulks, the great majority of them in the 300–600 English tons burden range, as well as a number of *pataches* (supply ships) and *zabras* (frigates). Hawkins's recycling programme did not greatly add to Royal Navy tonnage, but for purposes of comparison let's contrast the English total of 4,223 tons built or rebuilt from 1580 with the 4,400 *additional* tons acquired or built in Portugal for Philip II, plus the 9,650 tons built under Lope de Avellaneda's programme. In poker terms it was: 'I'll see your 4,000 and raise you 10,000'.

Elizabeth could not afford to keep her ships on a war footing and could either trust to her ministers' intelligence networks to provide her with sufficient advance warning to activate her fleet and summon the Navy Royal, or else seize the initiative and attack at a time of her own choosing. The defensive option had much to recommend it. England's very superior naval administration proved it could mobilize in a month the resources it took Philip a year to assemble; but a month's accurate notice was by no means guaranteed, leading to false alarms that ate into the exchequer, and even a fully mobilized Navy Royal could not cover Ireland as well as the southern coast of England.

Burghley may have been grudgingly persuaded of the need to even the odds with a pre-emptive strike, but absent Robert Dudley, Earl of Leicester, who had shot his bolt in the Netherlands fiasco, Walsingham was its main proponent. On 2 April 1587 Drake wrote an eloquent letter to the Secretary of State that revealed the degree to which he now regarded himself as a crown servant:

> *This night past came unto us the Merchant Royal, with four of the rest of the London fleet, the wind would permit them no sooner ... I have written to the Justices for the sending of some of those that are run away in our countries, to send them to the gaol ... I have written more largely to my Lord Admiral in this matter, for if there should be no punishment in so great a matter, in this so dangerous a time, it may do much hurt to her Majesty's*

service. I assure your Honour here hath been no time lost, neither
with the grace of God shall be in any other place. I have upon my
own credit supplied such victual as we have spent, and augmented
as much as I could get, for that we are very unwilling to return
arrantless ... The wind commands me away, our ship is under
sail, God grant we may so live in his fear as the enemy may have
cause to say that God doth fight for her Majesty as well abroad
as at home.

The raid was nearly aborted after Philip cleverly fed Elizabeth's tendency to wishful thinking. In a dispatch to Drake dated 9 April, the
Privy Council stated that information received since his departure
indicated that Philip had backed off from his intention and had
begun to disperse the invasion fleet, and had sent a message indicating a desire that the asperities between the two monarchs should
be 'in some honourable sort compounded'. Consequently the queen
commanded (emphasis added):

You shall forbear to enter forcibly into any of the said King's
ports or havens, or to offer violence to any of his towns or
shipping within harbour, or to do any act of hostility upon the
land. And yet, notwithstanding this direction, her pleasure is that
both you and such of her subjects as serve there under you should
do your best endeavour (as well by force as otherwise) to get into
your possession (avoiding as much as may lie in you the effusion of
Christian blood) such shipping of the said King's or his subjects
as you shall find at seas ... and such as shall fall into your hands
to <u>bring them into this realm without breaking bulk.</u>

Apart from the obvious fact that Philip was Elizabeth's master in
the Machiavellian game of Renaissance diplomacy, what stands out
is that even though the queen did not wish to be seen to escalate
the conflict, she still hoped the expedition would resolve her financial difficulties by capturing the annual Spanish treasure convoy.
The underlined reference to 'breaking bulk' refers to the cargo, sup-

posed to be immune from spoil and brought back to England intact for distribution among the shareholders and officers, who would pay royal taxes and the Lord Admiral's tenth on their shares. Needless to say it was a custom (with apologies to Hamlet) seldom observed because there was not even honour in it for the men doing the dirty work, and much profit in its breach.

The dispatch was sent after Drake in a frigate but it never reached him because a week-long storm blew it back to Plymouth. The same storm dispersed Drake's flotilla off the coast of Galicia and sank one of the pinnaces. After the flotilla regrouped, they met two Dutch ships that had just left Cadiz, from whom Drake learned that there was a huge fleet gathered there waiting to sail to Lisbon. This was excellent news, as the bay of Cadiz was a far softer target than the Tagus estuary at Lisbon, where serious artillery forts commanded the few reliable channels through shifting sandbanks.

At midday on 19 April, off Cadiz but still over the horizon, Drake summoned the flotilla captains to a general council and announced his intention to sail into the bay at dusk. As the saying goes, there's always one – this time it was the Vice Admiral, William Borough, a veteran naval commander who had fought several battles against corsairs but had no raiding experience whatever, who objected strongly and tried to insist on entering the bay at dawn the next day. He was ignored and went away fuming. Over the next few days his petulant behaviour put *Golden Lion* at unnecessary risk and finally became indistinguishable from mutiny.

Drake's ships flew no flags and the authorities in Cadiz assumed they were Admiral Juan Martínez de Recalde's escort fleet returning from the Azores. Surprise was complete, as was the panic when the gun ports opened and the guns rolled out to greet the galley carrying Pedro de Acuña, commander of the port guard, when he rowed out from the port of Santa María in the outer bay. Four more galleys rowed out from Santa María to support their admiral but, outgunned, Acuña fell back to a position between the fort at the head of the Cadiz peninsula and a reef of rocks called Los Puercos, from where he could enfilade any direct assault on Cadiz.

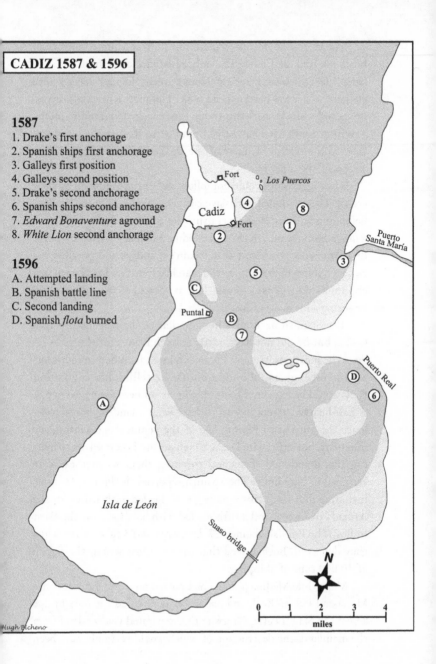

CADIZ 1587 & 1596

1587

1. Drake's first anchorage
2. Spanish ships first anchorage
3. Galleys first position
4. Galleys second position
5. Drake's second anchorage
6. Spanish ships second anchorage
7. *Edward Bonaventure* aground
8. *White Lion* second anchorage

1596

A. Attempted landing
B. Spanish battle line
C. Second landing
D. Spanish *flota* burned

Fort

Los Puercos

④

⑧

Cadiz

①

Fort

②

Puerto Santa María

③

⑤

ⓒ

Puntal

ⓑ

⑦

Puerto Real

ⓓ

⑥

ⓐ

Isla de León

Suaso bridge

N

0   1   2   3   4

miles

Hugh Bicheno

The English found 50–60 merchant ships and numerous smaller boats moored off Cadiz. The only resistance came from a deeply laden 1,000 *toneladas* (maybe 650 tons burden) Ragusan carrack with 40 guns, which was battered and sunk. This must have taken several hours and while Drake's ships were thus engaged four more galleys, two from Santa María and two from Puerto Real in the inner bay, covered the retreat of many of the smaller boats to the shallower waters of the inner bay.

The bigger ships could not follow and were abandoned by their crews. They included a massive carrack (maybe 770 tons burden) belonging to King Philip's cousin Alonso Pérez de Guzmán y de Zúñiga-Sotomayor, 7th Duke of Medina Sidonia, Lord of San Lúcar de Barrameda, the grandest of Spain's grandees and possibly the richest nobleman in Europe, who marched from San Lúcar with several thousand troops as soon as he was advised of the raid. We will be seeing a lot more of him.

The Spanish naturally thought that Drake intended to sack Cadiz, but he did not have nearly enough troops for the job – indeed the mass desertion in Plymouth he had alluded to in his letter to Walsingham followed from Drake telling his sailors that they would be expected to double up as soldiers for no extra pay. A half-hearted attempt was made to send a landing party to silence the guns at El Puntal, one of the peninsulas enclosing the inner bay, but otherwise Drake's men devoted themselves to looting the abandoned ships and torching them when they were stripped to bare hulls. The Spanish reported the loss of 23 ships, including four large 'Biscayners' (*naos*) loaded with stores for the Armada in Lisbon and a fifth loaded with hardware for the West Indies. The English claimed 27 destroyed and 3 taken away when they departed. Both agreed that the total loss was in the region of 10,000 tons of shipping.

Meanwhile Medina Sidonia had posted men and guns at Santa María and Puerto Real, and had strongly fortified the only bridge across the Sancti Petri waterway that separated Cadiz island from the mainland, the destruction of which would certainly have been

Robert Crosse's first priority if the plan had been to occupy the town. When the Spanish did counterattack, it came as a relief to the English sailors, as explained in Hakluyt's *Principal Navigations*:

We found little ease during our abode there by reason of their continual shooting from the galleys, the fortresses and from the shore, where continually they planted new ordnance to offend us with: besides the inconvenience which we suffered from their ships, which, when they could defend no longer, they set on fire to come among us. Whereupon when the flood [tide] came we were not a little troubled to defend us from their terrible fire, which nevertheless was a pleasant sight for us to behold, because we were thereby eased of a great labour, which lay upon us day and night, in discharging the victuals and other provisions of the enemy.

During 30 April the two biggest London ships braved the guns at El Puntal to enter the inner bay, where 40–50 smaller ships were clustered at Puerto Real. *Edward Bonaventure* ran aground within the bay but *Merchant Royal*, followed by Drake in one of the fleet pinnaces, made it through. Neither side reported any great execution at Puerto Real and, presumably after helping *Edward Bonaventure* to warp off the shoal, Drake soon returned to his flagship.*

Meanwhile Borough, who had anchored apart from the rest of the fleet during the looting, moved to a second anchorage in the mouth of the outer bay before coming to look for Drake in his pinnace. While he was away *Golden Lion* came under fire from the main fortress and when he returned he was assaulted by the galleys. Borough was to claim that he took up both positions to guard the fleet, and boasted that *Golden Lion* was the only ship that did any serious fighting.

Drake's view was that by standing aloof from the collective security of the main fleet – which was anchored out of effective range of the shore guns – Borough put *Golden Lion* in harm's way,

* Warp – to move a ship by hauling in cables attached to anchors dropped some distance away by the ship's boats.

and that when he got back from seeking Drake he found the thoroughly unnerved master trying to tow his becalmed ship out of range of the fortress guns with the ship's boats. The exposed boats invited an attack by the galleys, from which *Golden Lion* had to be rescued by Drake in *Elizabeth Bonaventure*. Looking at Borough's own map of the engagement (on which in the absence of any other my own is entirely based), Drake's interpretations seems the more valid.

By this time the venture was 'made' as far as the London captains were concerned. Their holds bulged with looted food, ships' fittings and guns that their owners could sell at a good price. They would also make a profit from the loot in the other ships, which would necessarily be sold on to them because only the London market was big enough to absorb such large volumes of low unit-value merchandise without seriously devaluing the local price. This single fact of commercial life is alone sufficient to explain why London became the dominant force in the corsair war.

In the evening of the second day the wind revived fitfully and the fleet sailed out of the bay, followed by Acuña's galleys whose only success had been to capture five English sailors in an isolated ship's boat – probably from *Golden Lion*. As the chronicler in *Principal Navigations* commented:

> *After our departure ten of the galleys that were in the Road came out, as it were in disdain of us, to make some pastime with their ordnance, at which time the wind turned on us, whereupon we cast about again and stood in with the shore, and came to an anchor within a league of the town: where the said galleys, for all their former bragging, at length suffered us to ride quietly. We now have had experience of galley-fight, wherein I can assure you that only these 4 of her Majesty's ships will make no account of 20 galleys, if they may be alone and not busied to guard others. There were never galleys that had better place and fitter opportunity for their advantage to fight with ships: but they were still forced to retire.*

Intriguingly, a year earlier *Merchant Royal, Edward Bonaventure* and *Susan*, joined by *William and John* (the previous name of Watts's *Margaret and John*) and the 250-ton *Toby* had proved the truth of this assertion. They were engaged in their more usual business of trading with the Levant, sailing from London in November 1585 and remaining in convoy until they passed Sicily, after which they dispersed to Venice, Constantinople and Alexandria. In June 1586 they met again by prior agreement at the island of Zante, and sailed for home in convoy once more.

On 13 July they were intercepted near Panteleria, between Sicily and Tunisia, by 13 war galleys from Sicily and Malta. The galley admiral, Pedro de Leiva, sent a *fragata* to demand they 'acknowledge their duty and obedience to him, in the name of the Spanish king, lord of those seas. Our men replied and said that they owed no such duty nor obedience to him, and therefore would acknowledge none; but commanded the frigate to depart with that answer, and not to stay longer upon her peril'. After five hours of long-range gunfire the galleys withdrew with three of them, including Leiva's flagship, requiring the others to lash themselves alongside to keep from sinking.

Mediterranean war galleys had very big guns indeed, mounted on the centreline in their bows – the account specifies a cannon, which was a 44–48 pounder – yet they were beaten off by English Levanters whose biggest gun was the 15–20 pounder culverin (*Merchant Royal* also had two short-range cannon periers), of which there were four in each ship along with twice the number of 10–12 pounder demi-culverins. Even with the advantage of being able to aim their heavy bow armament very precisely, the galleys wounded just two English seamen in five hours of battle while suffering disabling losses in return. But more to the point, the galleons' firepower prevented the galleys from rowing in to board, which was their principal military function.

After leaving Cadiz, Drake ravaged the south-western Iberian coast for a month, destroying perhaps a hundred small vessels carrying mundane but essential stores to the Armada in Lisbon, most famously about 1,700 tons of barrel hoops and staves, whose lack was to make itself felt in the massive spoiling of Armada supplies packed in barrels of unseasoned wood the following year. At Cape Sagres he had to take some small forts in order to win the harbour for the fleet, and once again summoned a general council to tell the captains what he expected of them. Once again Borough returned to his ship seething, this time to pen a verbose and pompous letter rebuking Drake for informing rather than consulting the council – the immemorial bleat of the professional bureaucrat, more concerned with following procedure than with getting things done.

It was very nearly his last mistake. Drake's well-known fury at having his authority questioned burst out and he stripped Borough of his command. Later the crew of *Golden Lion*, denied spoil at Cadiz, smarting at having become a pariah ship, and many of them ill, mutinied. The captain Drake had sent to replace Borough returned to the flagship and the crew sailed home, enlisting Borough's services as navigator. Had he not been such a useful administrator he would probably have been hanged, a fate he flirted with further when he chose to defend himself by arguing that Drake was unfit for high command, a view bordering on treason since he had been the queen's personal choice. Instead, when the time came to appoint captains for Her Majesty's ships to face the Armada, he was humiliated by being given command of *Bonavolia*, the only royal galley, and left to scull disconsolately around the Thames estuary while the man he had tried to undermine won further glory in the Channel.

Drake sent Robert Crosse home with two prizes and dispatches that, to put it mildly, did not understate the delay he had imposed on Philip's invasion plans. Pausing only to jeer at the Marquis of Santa Cruz in Lisbon for not sailing out to do battle, Drake sailed for the Azores, having learned that a mighty Portuguese carrack was daily expected from the East Indies. He was unable to persuade the London ships to stay with him and they sailed home, but Drake knew that the queen would be less than delighted if all she got from the cruise was tons of indifferent merchandise.

What he did not know was that *flotas* carrying two years'-worth of treasure were due from the Indies. Santa Cruz sent every warship he could to cover their arrival, which in fact inflicted more delay on the Armada preparations than Drake's depredations.

According to Robert Leng, a gentleman aboard the flagship who published his *True Discripcion* of the raid in 1587, with Drake's usual luck the carrack came into sight the same day he made landfall at the island of São Miguel. The remaining nine ships surrounded her, firing at her upper works, and 'our flyboat and one of our pinnaces lying thwart her hawse [grappled to her bow], at whom she shot and threw fire works but did them no hurt, for that her ordnance lay so high over them'. When the carrack surrendered, Drake learned that she was the *São Filipe*, loaded with pepper, Chinese porcelain, bales of silk and velvet, 400 black slaves and £4,000 in gold and silver (as officially inventoried). The account in *Principal Navigations* unambiguously states that those who took the prize 'assured themselves every man to have a sufficient reward for his travel', but fails to mention that the company was wracked by disease and that they were much reduced in number by the time the fleet escorted *São Filipe* into Plymouth harbour on 26 June.

Burghley tried to convince the Spanish that the queen was 'very displeased' with Drake, but they politely told him to pull the one with bells on. With £50,000 from the *São Filipe* alone (no record has been found so far of how the value of the loot from Cadiz was apportioned, but it certainly more than covered the initial investment), Elizabeth must have been delighted. But Walsingham must have been happiest of all – the reactions his agents reported from the chanceries of Europe ranged from frank congratulations to Pope Sixtus V's chuckle that Queen Elizabeth's distaff had prevailed over King Philip II's sword.

The anecdote was far from trivial. On 29 July 1587 the Pope had deposited a million gold ducats with two Roman bankers, which were to be delivered to Philip as soon as confirmation was received that the Armada had accomplished a landing in England. The gold was only on deposit until November and Drake's raid had destroyed all possibility of the Armada sailing in 1587. The agreement was still binding on Sixtus and his successors, but the Vatican excelled at finding unimpeachably pious excuses for not paying its debts.

In order to obtain the commitment from Sixtus's possible successors, Philip II had been compelled to reveal every detail of his 'Enterprise of England' to the College of Cardinals, akin to posting it on the internet today. Cardinal Ascanio Colonna, who owed his elevation to Philip II, appears to have done a very clever damage-limitation exercise by feeding disinformation to his nephew Odo, who believed Sixtus wanted him dead, before he travelled to the Netherlands. Odo sought asylum with the Dutch and told all he knew. The 'confession of Odo Colonna', sent by Count Maurice of Nassau to Walsingham on 9 December 1587, made terrifying reading:

> *He knew from his uncle, the Cardinal, that the pope had made a league against the Queen of England for which he had held three consistories. The pope was chief, and there were also the king of Spain, the dukes of Florence, Savoy, Ferrara, Urbino, Mantua and other Italian potentates, the House of Austria and other Germans. The Venetians wished to stand out, but had at last agreed to give money. The king of France, after several refusals, only entered when the pope threatened to excommunicate him. The king of Scotland will enter on condition that the king of Spain has him crowned king of England and will give him his daughter in marriage. The Prince of Parma to conduct the war by land and Santa Cruz by sea. The Spaniards boast that they will destroy the English fleet if they meet it. When [it was] objected that he took no account of the king of Scotland being of the [same] religion he mocked saying that kings do everything for advantage. Told that the Queen looked for peace and the Prince of Parma was willing to treat, he said she might do what she pleased but she could see if these preparations were for peace. Told that the king of Spain himself had written about it to the king of Denmark he replied that the king of Spain might do this*

to deceive but the war would still go forward in the name of the pope and of the Grand Master of Malta. He knew from his uncle that the funds of which the pope was assured, derived from the said princes and the clergy of Italy whom he had compelled, amounted to 8 millions.

CHAPTER 11
ЈЕНОVАН BLEW
THEM AWAY?

When I set out to analyze the mechanics of the battle of Lepanto in *Crescent and Cross*, I soon discovered that the Venetians had cleverly spun the story to emphasize their strength – artillery – in order to divert attention from the fact that it was a knock-down, drag-out infantry battle. Why? Because most of the soldiers on their galleys came from the Italian *tercios* of King Philip II of Spain. Until relatively recently no such flim-flam obscured the military facts of the 1588 Armada battles; but for the 400th anniversary 'what ifs' proliferated like toadstools in a compost heap.

The emergent consensus was that 'the naval confrontation in the Channel in 1588 and the subsequent disastrous Spanish circumnavigation of the storm-lashed British coastline, helped shape world history from the end of the sixteenth century to the beginning of the twentieth. Spain – the first 'Global Empire' – was bested by Mother Nature and a considerably smaller political power with the result that her imperial pretensions stuttered and England's flourished'.*

'Mother Nature' is the pagan equivalent of Jehovah, who, according to the propagandistic Armada medal issued in 1588, *flavit et dissipati sunt* (blew and they were scattered). England's imperial pretensions did not 'flourish' until the 18th century, when they did so at the expense of France, not Spain. Likewise it was not

* From Robin McPherson's on-line review of Geoffrey Parker's *The Grand Strategy of Philip II*.

Spain's existing global empire but its drive to subject the rebellious Dutch provinces that suffered a fatal set-back in 1588. Lastly, although subsequent armadas sent against England were indeed dispersed by storms, the first one was defeated by what both sides knew was a numerically and technologically superior naval force. Apart from that ...

The concluding sentiment in the splendidly illustrated 400th anniversary book by marine archaeologist Colin Martin and historian Geoffrey Parker is representative of the revisionist view: 'It is always easy to be wise after the event. Only one thing is certain. If, during the second week of August 1588, the army of Flanders had been marching towards London, everyone today would regard the Invincible Armada, despite all its deficiencies, as Philip II's masterpiece'.

Why stop there? It would also have been irrefutable proof that Philip II was indeed God's agent on earth, for it would have required the waters of the Channel to part.

If it were easy to be wise after the event, we would all be well governed. But we are not because personal and collective agendas get in the way, nuances are brushed aside and even the course of past events is often unclear. However, in this case, as even the Martin/Parker book cannot conceal, one thing is indeed certain: the 'deficiencies' that doomed the Spanish Armada reflected the profound religious delusion of Philip II, who micro-managed it. An assessment that teeters on the edge of irony made by an unnamed senior Spanish naval officer, as reported by the Papal Nuncio in May 1588, not only demonstrates wisdom *before* the event but also shines a light on the power of Philip's belief in his divine mission to infect even his more rational servants:

> It is well known that we fight in God's cause. Thus when we meet
> the English, God will surely arrange matters so that we can
> grapple and board them, either by sending some strange freak of
> weather or, more probably, by depriving the English of their wits.
> If we can come to close quarters Spanish valour and Spanish steel,
> and the great masses of soldiers we shall have on board, will make

our victory certain. But unless God helps us by a miracle the
English, who have faster and handier ships than ours and many
more long-range guns, and who know their advantage just as well
as we do, will never close with us but stand aloof and knock us to
pieces with their culverins, without our being able to do them any
serious hurt. So we are sailing against England in the confident
hope of a miracle.

It may be argued that Philip's condition was simply the product of mystical-religious fervour and thus was not, strictly speaking, pathological. However, the fact that he was unable to cope with the crushing burden of his self-imposed duties for several months during the preparation of the Armada, his listlessness during the campaign, and his desire for death after it failed, are all highly suggestive of a personality decompensating under the weight of chronic stress.

We must remember that at a time when only the blissfully ill informed could possibly have believed they really knew what was going on, Philip was the hub of possibly the best intelligence service in Europe. 'Information overload' is not a modern phenomenon, nor is the impulse to act in order to impose some predictability on a cascade of uncontrollable events, as we have seen in the wars of the 21st century. Despite devoting more attention to Philip's personality in the preparation of this book than I did for *Crescent and Cross*, I have found no reason to change the opinion I wrote before:

We may judge him harshly as a king and still feel pity for him as
a man who endured a string of appalling personal tragedies, and
who towards the end of his life had to believe the face of God had
turned away from him, as one after another his enterprises failed.
Yet he still did his lonely duty with dignity and to the best of his
limited ability until his body failed him

'What ifs' invariably hinge on an assumption that only one of the parties might have done things better – but in the case of the Armada, a successful outcome for the Spanish would require a further

ARMADA TONNAGE COMPARISON

Tons burden	Spanish	% of Armada	*Lost*	*Unknown*	English	% of fleet
700–800	5	4	*4*		2	1
600–700	5	4	*2*		1	½
500–600	13	10	*8*		2	1
400–500	22	17	*10*	*1*	9	4½
300–400	26	20	*9*		9	4½
200–300	13	10	*3*	*2*	19	10
100–200	13	10	*1*	*1*	62	31½
Less than 100	31	24	*4*	*7*	93	47
TOTAL	**128**		*41*	*11*	**197**	

CREW AND ARMAMENT OF SELECTED PRIVATE ENGLISH SHIPS*

(based on Kenneth Andrews, *Elizabethan Privateering*,
pp. 47 & 49)

Tons burden	Crew	Demi-culverin	Saker	Minion	Falcon	Falconet	Total guns
200	100	7	10	4			21
160	80	4	8	4			16
150	75	4	4				8
120	60		2	4	1	2	9
100	50		2	5	3		10
80	40		3	4	3		10
45	30			1	3		4
40	20		1	2	2		5
35	20				2	2	4

* Variations could be great. In 1585 the 120-ton *Galleon Fenner* of Chichester, detained on suspicion of piracy, was recorded as having 70 crew, 15 carriage guns, 13 swivel guns and numerous small arms.

assumption that the English would have chosen not to defend the coast of Kent at all. It was not the capital ships of the Royal Navy that represented the principal obstacle to a cross-Channel invasion, but the host of smaller vessels that constituted the bulk of the Navy Royal. A 1582 survey listed 1,455 ships apt for Navy Royal service, of which only 178 had claimed the royal bounty for ships over 100 tons. Thus 1,277, about 88 percent, were under 100 tons (see Appendix E).*

What if Parma had captured a deep-water port in Flanders and the Armada had somehow managed to seize another in England, despite lacking purpose-built landing craft? The problem of getting an army across the Channel and maintaining it on a hostile shore would still have been insuperable. The big English ships could sail rings around their Spanish opponents and the small ships, manned by men experienced in corsair warfare, would have been like a swarm of mosquitoes. Parma's barges and converted coasters would have stood no chance and the Armada's 33 light ships would have been overwhelmed. Meanwhile the larger Armada warships, dispersed to protect both the crossing and the beachhead, would indeed have been 'knocked to pieces' by the superior gunnery of the Royal Navy.

Ah, the 'what if' brigade will cry – but the Royal Navy had run out of ammunition by the time the Armada took off around the British Isles. Well – 'what if' it had not? Besides, the small ships were not engaged in the Channel battles and still had all their powder and shot. So – allowing for all the 'what ifs' bar direct divine intervention, the Enterprise of England, *as planned and directed by Philip II*, was inevitably doomed and the human and material loss the Armada suffered on the long journey home after failing to achieve a junction with Parma's army may have been the least bad of the possible outcomes for Spanish arms.

How could a monarch enjoying the reputation of being 'the prudent king' have set his military commanders such an impossible

---

* I acknowledge again that the Royal Navy/Navy Royal distinction is anachronistic – but I believe it essential for the purpose of differentiation.

task? For the answer we must go back to the Marquis of Santa Cruz's naval victory over Strozzi in late July 1582 and the large and successful amphibious operation he organized and led that conquered Terceira the following year, for which Philip II made him a grandee of Spain. On 9 August 1583 Santa Cruz wrote: 'Victories as complete as the one God has been pleased to grant Your Majesty in these islands normally spur princes on to other enterprises; and since Our Lord has made Your Majesty such a great king, it is appropriate that you should follow up this victory by making arrangements for the invasion of England next year.'

Santa Cruz was impetuous. He commanded the reserve division at Lepanto in 1571 and committed it prematurely to the battle at the centre in support of Juan de Austria, as pointedly remarked in his post-battle report by the Catalán nobleman Luis de Requeséns y Zúñiga, King Philip's lifelong friend, appointed by him to tutor and restrain his young and impetuous half-brother:

> ... if there is any fault to be imputed to [Santa Cruz] it is that
> he charged too soon, because it seems the reserve division he was
> entrusted with should not be committed until the battle is going
> badly, and then to the place most in need of it, but instead he
> charged soon after we did, and better to err on this side than to
> hang back and after all the marquis and his galleys fought most
> honourably.

It's not difficult to deduce why Santa Cruz did not row to support the threatened right wing. If the right was lost the blame could be fastened around the neck of his rival, Gian'Andrea Doria; but if the centre was lost, and with it Juan de Austria, his own career would have been over. Despite Requeséns's feline criticism, Santa Cruz was appointed Juan's successor as Captain General of the Sea, and Gian'Andrea did not inherit his grand-uncle Andrea Doria's title until Santa Cruz died.

Once it became apparent that the informal truce agreed with the Ottoman Empire in 1577 was likely to be renewed for several years, Santa Cruz's focus moved to the Atlantic, where he built on the foundations of the royal oceanic fleet laid by the Cantabrian Pedro Menéndez de Áviles, who died in 1574. Philip II's appointment of Menéndez as Captain General of the Fleet of the Indies twenty years earlier, a post previously in the gift of the monopolists of the *Casa de Contratación* in Seville, had aroused furious resentment, culminating in Menéndez's imprisonment by the *Casa* in 1563.

Philip ordered his immediate release in terms that left them in no doubt about his displeasure at their failure to protect their monopoly against the French corsairs – and the consequent call on the royal exchequer to finance Menéndez's fleet of escort galleons.

Menéndez was a rare example of a senior Spanish commander who owed his position solely to merit. The norm for Philip was to appoint commanders from among his tax-exempt nobles, and to require them to spend their own money in his service. Santa Cruz was somewhere in between: born a *hidalgo* with no family fortune, he was only made a marquis in 1569. Ten years as Captain General of the Sea, however, did wonders for his finances. Some of the galleons that defeated Strozzi were owned by Santa Cruz, built to the two-gun-deck design developed by Menéndez for the Ocean Fleet.

Spanish galleons were broad beamed and round bottomed because they were required to pass over the bar at San Lúcar de Barrameda to reach Seville up the Guadalquivir River. But they also had to be big, because regular long-range operations dictated more hold space for stores and more living room for the crew to reduce the wastage from disease that so often decimated the crews of English ships, which were designed for shorter-range operations. The comparative chart on the next page shows that the 1588 Armada ships were only as crowded as they were because they carried a large number of additional soldiers, and consequently consumed their stores and suffered attrition from disease comparable to the English ships, which had larger standard crews but many fewer soldiers.

Philip II was not immune to Santa Cruz's siren song. After all, along with Portugal and its empire God had granted him the largest

COMPARISON OF TONS PER MAN IN LARGEST WARSHIPS

	SPANISH			ENGLISH			
ne	Type	Men	Tons per	Name	Type	Men	Tons per
Martinho	Galleon	652	1.0	Ark Royal	Galleon	430	1.3
João	Galleon	566	1.2	Victory	Carrack	430	1.3
. del Rosario	Carrack	484	1.4	Elizabeth Jonas	Carrack	490	1.4
idad Valencera	Carrack	468	1.5	Triumph	Carrack	500	1.5
Francesco	Galleon	383	1.6	White Bear	Carrack	490	1.5
zona	Carrack	483	1.7	Golden Lion	Galleon	250	1.7
a Anna	Carrack	462	1.7	Revenge	Galleon	250	1.8
Salvador	Carrack	322	1.9	Vanguard	Galleon	250	1.8
. de la Rosa	Carrack	275	2.2	Mary Rose	Carrack	250	1.9
n Grin	Carrack	305	2.4	Dreadnought	Galleon	190	2.2

navy in the world, and it must be for some holy purpose. Later in 1583 he wrote to Parma asking whether 'it might be advisable to take steps to ensure that the war is not sustained from England'. Even though Parma's campaign was going well and he acknowledged the desirability of cauterizing the English ulcer, he judged it impractical until he had conquered Holland and Zeeland. At that time Philip saw the sense of Parma's view.

As late as 1585 Philip dismissed, on grounds of cost, a suggestion by the newly elected Pope Sixtus V for the invasion of England as something to be undertaken only after the reconquest of the Netherlands. Yet – as we have seen – after 1583 he ordered the mass production of ocean-going warships by the shipyards of Cantábrica and Portugal. Appendix F shows seven medium-sized galleons and two larger ones built under the Lope de Avellaneda programme at Guarnizo (at the mouth of the San Salvador river as it enters Santander Bay), known as El Astillero (The Shipyard) to this day. Perhaps if they had standardized on this very successful design (the only one lost was the result of crew prostration) instead of indulging in gigantism and wasting resources on obsolete *naos* (carracks), things might have turned out differently in 1588.

The surge in naval construction mirrored the recovery of royal finances. As the chart below shows, Philip's income from the royal fifth of treasure from the Indies, which averaged 20 percent of all revenues during his reign, spiked to 40 percent in 1583 with the arrival two years' worth of *flotas*, which had been suspended in 1582. This was the only occasion when Indies revenue alone exceeded military expenditure, which fell sharply after the default of 1575 and the Ottoman truce, matching the lull in the Netherlands war before Parma's offensive.

During this time Philip's ordinary revenues also rose steadily and his outlays were reduced by the completion of the palace-monastery of El Escorial, whose total cost (spread over the two decades 1563–84) greatly exceeded those of either the 1571 Lepanto or the 1588 Armada campaigns. The chart strongly suggests that

MILITARY EXPENDITURE AND INDIES REVENUE 1556–96

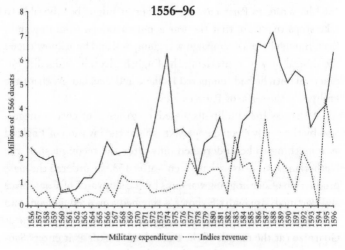

Graph adapted from Mauricio Drelichman and Hans-Joachim Voth, 'Lending to the Borrower from Hell', *The Economic Journal* 121 (December 2011).

Philip embarked on the Enterprise of England as much because he was unusually solvent as for the military-political reasons more commonly advanced to explain it.

Of course these data were not available to Elizabeth's council; but if they had been they would have greatly strengthened John Hawkins's passionate advocacy of a constant naval presence off the Azores. Alas for England, she still could not match the co-ordinated effort of the French entrepreneurs who sent three corsair fleets to the coast of Spain, the Azores and the Caribbean to throttle Spanish transatlantic trade in 1542.

Royal finances aside, Drake's Caribbean raid – or rather his provocative sojourn in Vigo Bay – was certainly the catalyst for Philip's decision. On 24 October 1585, a week after Drake set out across the Atlantic, the king wrote to Pope Sixtus V to accept the suggestion he had rejected earlier in the year and to ask for financial support for an enterprise he estimated would cost at least 3 million ducats. In December he ordered Santa Cruz and Parma to submit fully worked-up plans for the invasion.

Santa Cruz replied within three months in extraordinary detail, evidence that his staff had not been idle since 1583. Like every commander before or since, he put in a bid for more resources than he could have hoped to obtain: 150 major ships served by 400 support vessels at home and 200 purpose-built landing craft, 55,000 troops, bells, whistles – total cost in the region of 4 million ducats. The killer cost arose in part from Santa Cruz's proposal that the invasion be done in two phases – the first a landing in Ireland, followed by consolidation and a final massive lunge along the Channel.

Parma's proposal depended on the maintenance of total secrecy while he assembled a fleet of flat-bottomed barges in the creeks and inlets of the Flanders coast to transport 30,000 men in a surprise crossing to Kent. Even if Parma had been able to shut down the spy network that regularly supplied Walsingham with detailed reports of the duke's dispositions, there was still continuous cross-Channel traffic by English smugglers supplying the Spanish army at premium prices. Furthermore Justin of Nassau's inshore squadron controlled the Flanders coast, so Parma's essential requirement was no less unrealistic than Santa Cruz's cost.

The final plan produced by Juan de Zúñiga, Philip's immensely experienced chief military adviser, sought to correct the fundamental flaws in each of the contributing plans. His solution was to combine the two in an operation that contained its own unstated *sine qua non*, namely the absolute necessity of gaining control of a deep-water port where Santa Cruz's fleet could safely rendezvous with Parma's forces.

Unfortunately for Spanish arms, Philip lost sight of this operational imperative and would permit no discussion of Zúñiga's plan. When Santa Cruz died on 9 February 1588 he was hag-ridden by the certainty that without such a port the enterprise was doomed. This was reported to the king by Martín Jimínez de Bertendona, his most experienced oceanic commander, whose concluding words read much like the previously quoted semi-ironic assessment relayed to Pope Sixtus V by the Nuncio: 'since it is Your Majesty who has decided everything, we must believe that it is God's will'.

The slide to disaster became irreversible only when Philip appointed a wealthy and highly competent administrator to replace the hapless Santa Cruz. In 1586 the Duke of Medina Sidonia, harassed to distraction by the permanent threat to his transatlantic operations by English corsairs, urged prompt action against England: 'let it be understood that it will not suffice simply to oppose what the English send: the fleet will need to go into the Channel.' He advocated maintaining a semi-permanent threat so that the English should look to their defences and be less active off the Spanish coast, and was appalled to be appointed as Santa Cruz's successor, charged with a different sort of enterprise – an actual invasion – that he did not believe himself competent to lead.

By a Herculean effort he assembled a fully manned and supplied fleet of 132 vessels, but this included only four galleys that could serve the purpose of an amphibious assault. In the event the galleys proved unable to cope with oceanic conditions and dropped out in the Bay of Biscay. He did not, therefore, have the means to get his

19,000 soldiers, their artillery and other impedimenta ashore against even limited opposition, and so was necessarily compelled to achieve a junction with Parma and his troop-carrying barges. This was precisely what Philip wished: not content with issuing stringently binding orders, he made certain that the Armada commander *could not* depart from them.

Meanwhile Parma had been ordered under no circumstances even to think of attempting a crossing before the Armada had won control of the Channel. Thus he was outraged to receive royal dispatches in December 1587 that rebuked him for not having done so. 'Your Majesty has the right to give absolute orders, which I receive as special favours and perform,' he replied, 'but for you to write to me now with a proposal that runs so contrary to Your Majesty's previous express orders causes me great anguish. I beg you most humbly to do me the very great favour of telling me what to do next.' Geoffrey Parker believes that Philip was in the midst of a nervous breakdown, which does seem to be the only charitable explanation for this episode – and, indeed, for all that followed.

If we look for evidence of divine intervention in the 1588 campaign, it can be seen as an emphatic warning to both parties that God does not take sides. When the Armada set sail from Lisbon on 30 May it ran into contrary winds, giving the men on board plenty of time to appreciate the ethics of the fleet provisioners. A council of war voted to put in to Coruña to replace the rancid stores, but only the vanguard had entered the harbour before a violent gale scattered the rest far and wide.

Medina Sidonia's chief of staff, Diego Flores de Valdés, had been the naval commander of Sarmiento de Gamboa's catastrophic 1582–84 expedition to colonize the Straits of Magellan. He was also Captain General of the Castilla Squadron but sailed with Medina Sidonia on the Armada flagship, the 640-ton Portuguese galleon *São Martinho*.* The other members of the council were:

---

* The galleons of the Portugal squadron were all listed in the Spanish documents with saints' names in Spanish; I have used the Portuguese equivalents to emphasize their provenance, significant in the battle ahead.

❧ Bertendona, 49 years old, Captain General of the Levante Squadron on the 800-ton Ragusan carrack *Regazona*, the biggest ship in the fleet. He was of a Bilbao ship-building and -owning family, had been at sea since childhood and commanded the in-shore squadron of the Ocean Fleet.

❧ Miguel de Oquendo, 59, Captain General of the Guipúzcoa Squadron on the next biggest ship, the 770-ton Spanish carrack *Santa Ana*. He was of a San Sebastián merchant family, came late to oceanic command but won renown at the battle of São Miguel and the conquest of the Azores.

❧ Juan Martínez de Recalde, 62, was the highly experienced Captain General of the Viscaya Squadron. His flagship was another, smaller *Santa Ana* but he sailed on the 675-ton *São João*, vice-flagship of the Armada. He was of a noble Bilbao family, had charge of the royal shipyards in the Basque country and latterly had responsibility for the transatlantic convoys.

❧ Pedro de Valdés, 44, Captain General of the Andalucía Squadron on the 740-ton Spanish carrack *Nuestra Señora del Rosario*. Born in Gijón, Asturias, he had been the extremely young deputy to Ocean Fleet commander Pedro Menéndez de Avilés for the last 8 years of his life. Twice commander of the Atlantic escort fleet, he also led the Flanders flotilla in the capture of Antwerp.

❧ Hugo de Moncada, Captain General of the four relatively small (380-ton) galleasses of the Naples Squadron, was on *San Lorenzo*. From a long line of Sicilian viceroys, he knew nothing of oceanic warfare and was notable for a level of pride extreme even by Spanish standards.

❧ Alonso Martínez de Leyva, 34, General of the Land Forces and designated successor if Medina Sidonia were killed or disabled, on the 530-ton Genoese carrack *Santa María*, intriguingly known as *Rata Encoronada* – Crowned Rat. He also knew nothing of oceanic warfare, his military experience being limited to the Sicilian galleys and the light cavalry of Milan.

We know little of the relationships among these officers except that Pedro Flores, the duke's chief of staff, nurtured bitter resentment towards his cousin Pedro de Valdés, dating from the preferment shown to him by Menéndez de Avilés. The animosity led Flores to oppose the advice voiced by Valdés, who generally proposed more aggressive action than the letter of Medina Sidonia's instructions permitted. It also led him to recommend the abandonment of his cousin after *Nuestra Señora del Rosario* became disabled, with dire consequences for the Armada.

After another council of war, Medina Sidonia wrote to the king to communicate a doubt that only the grandest of grandees and a royal cousin would have dared to voice. Was it not possible, he wrote, that such unseasonable weather might be a divine warning? Impossible, the king replied with perfectly circular reasoning. Such a possibility could only be contemplated if the war were unjust; since it was just, the Duke should look forward to more good fortune than he could hope for.

On the English side Lord Admiral Charles Howard of Effingham, like Medina Sidonia, had no experience of naval warfare – but it was in his blood. His grand-uncle Sir Edward (1513) and his father Lord William (1554–58) had been lord admirals. He was also given detailed instructions, and the last paragraph was one that should be appended to all political directives in times of war:

> *Lastly, forasmuch as there may fall out many accidents that may move you to take any other course than by these our instructions you are directed, we therefore think it most expedient to refer you therein to your own judgement and discretion, to do that thing you may think may best tend to the advancement of our service.*

Like his opposite number, Howard surrounded himself with the most experienced naval commanders in the realm. Drake was the obvious choice for vice admiral in command of the Western Approaches fleet based at Plymouth. His flagship was the 465-ton galleon *Revenge*, chosen for her speed despite being a notoriously high-maintenance ship. Drake's deputy, Thomas Fenner, was on the newer and no less swift 380-ton galleon *Nonpareil*. Howard's deputy was John Hawkins, who had not been to sea for many years, on the 565-ton carrack *Victory*, while Frobisher was on the 760-ton carrack *Triumph*, the largest ship in the fleet. Hawkins and Frobisher were each to be given independent squadron commands when Howard split up his fleet during the Channel battles.

The rest of Howard's council was made up of relatives who sailed with him. His 24-year-old nephew Lord Edmund Sheffield was on the 730-ton carrack *White Bear*, the second largest ship in the fleet, and his son-in-law Sir Robert Southwell, vice admiral of Norfolk and Suffolk, was on the third largest, the 685-ton carrack *Elizabeth Jonas*. His 27-year-old cousin Lord Thomas Howard was on the 420-ton galleon *Golden Lion*, the unlucky vice flagship of the Cadiz raid. None had previous experience of naval command, although Lord Thomas took to the family business like a duck to water.

Command of the vitally important Narrow Seas fleet, composed mainly of small ships commanded by captains with little respect for authority, was given to the imperious 48 year-old Lord Henry Seymour on the 385-ton galleon *Rainbow*. Seymour had little naval experience and a short temper, not improved by the fact that his shallow-draught ship rolled like a pig. Although Seymour was the step-son of Howard's sister, he must have had other qualities to offset being a younger son of the executed Duke of Somerset and brother of the serial matrimonial offender Edward, Earl of Hertford.

Possibly the intended commander of the Narrow Seas fleet was Seymour's 69-year-old deputy, Surveyor of the Navy Sir William Wynter, on the bigger 465-ton galleon *Vanguard*. Wynter had long experience of naval command, most recently at the 1579 blockade of Smerwick in Ireland, and familiarity with the type, if not also the actual men, who were commanding many of the little ships from his long involvement in the corsair war. However, he had only a few months left to live and may have been ailing, his health not improved when he was knocked down by a dismounted gun during the battle.

Howard's fleet included most of the heavy units of the Royal Navy and the bulk of a powerful squadron paid for by London, with Robert Flick once again the informal commodore, as he had been at Cadiz. They were stationed at the Downs, the roadstead at the confluence of the North Sea and the Channel below the South Foreland on the east Kent coast.

Through April and May Drake clamoured for leave to make a pre-emptive attack, and when Howard joined the chorus the queen granted permission. On 3 June Howard joined Drake's mainly privately owned fleet at Plymouth, leaving Seymour at the Downs to deter any attempt by Parma to cross while the big ships were away.

Jehovah did not smile on the English, either. The demands of the combined fleet soon exhausted the resources of Devon and Cornwall and the arrival of supply ships from London was so intolerably delayed that Howard became convinced there must be treachery involved. Even after the provision fleet finally arrived during the night of 2–3 July and all hands turned out to unload it, he wrote a desperate appeal directly to his cousin the queen: 'For the love of Christ, Madam, awake thoroughly and see the villainous treasons round about you, against Your Majesty and your realm, and draw your forces about you like a mighty prince to defend you.'

Contrary winds kept the combined fleet in port until 4 July and then, after braving storms off the Scilly Isles and Ushant, it ran into a flat calm when in sight of the Spanish coast. When the wind rose again it came from the south-west, ideal conditions for the Armada to sortie. Alarmed by the possibility that the enemy might slip around them, Howard and Drake raced back to Plymouth, arriving on 22 July – the day the re-assembled Armada emerged from Coruña.

After four days of perfect cruising, the wind backed to the north and the Armada had to smash through brutally large waves. The galleys soon fell out, making for the French coast where one was lost. The carrack *Santa Ana*, flagship of the Viscayan squadron, lost a mast and ended up at Le Havre, where she was later destroyed by English corsairs. *San Cristobal*, flagship of the Castilian squadron, was pooped and lost her stern gallery, while Moncada's *San Lorenzo* lost her rudder, the result of a flawed design that was to doom her and two more of the galleasses in the days ahead. Medina Sidonia must have struggled not to think blasphemous thoughts about the fortune God seemed to think he deserved.

After a week of frantic maintenance and resupply the combined English fleet was – just – ready on 29 July when *Golden Hind*, a Southampton corsair pinnace from the screen deployed to cover the western approaches, sailed into Plymouth under full sail and brought the electrifying news that 50 large Spanish ships had been sighted south of the Lizard with their sails struck, 'hovering in the wind, as it seemed to attend the rest of the fleet'.

Howard and Drake's ships may have been ready, but the men of the Royal Navy were at breaking point. On top of short and bad rations their pitiful wages were not being paid and a typhus epidemic had broken out on several ships, notably *Elizabeth Jonas*. Desperate appeals reached Burghley from all three fleet commanders. Seymour wrote to Walsingham begging him to intercede with the Lord Treasurer: 'You shall do very well to help us with pay for our men, who are almost sixteen weeks unpaid, for what with fair and foul means I have enough to do to keep them from mutiny.'

Burghley returned protests that he could not even find the funds to pay the £50,000 outstanding for provisions and wages, and could certainly find no more to cover future costs – this before the first shot was fired. Elizabeth's alleged 'parsimony' is another over-written theme, because Burghley was not lying – 1588 was much the worst year for crown finances since the beginning of Elizabeth's reign. The economy had been in depression since 1586 and she had no access to the financing that Philip II employed to even out the peaks and troughs of his revenues, even on a much-reduced scale. She had nothing remotely equivalent to Philip's Indies revenue and her father had slaughtered the ecclesiastical cow for meat, whereas Philip continued to milk it for the larger part of his income; and with Europe's superpower openly determined to overthrow her, she was a very bad loan risk.

One more general point – there has never been a war in which the expenditure of ammunition did not vastly exceed pre-war estimates. It's not even slightly remarkable that the Royal Navy ran out of powder and shot at the end of a running battle for the Channel which was longer, more intense and involved a far greater number of guns than any previous battle in history. Since nobody had any idea even how such a battle should be fought, it cannot be held against those responsible for arming the fleet that they did not have to hand the enormous amount of powder and shot that proved necessary.

Lord Admiral Howard himself seems to have realized only very belatedly that his ships might need more ammunition than they carried. With a confirmed sighting of the Armada and about to warp out of Plymouth to confront it, he wrote in haste to Walsingham: 'for the love of God and our country let us have with some speed some great shot sent us of all bigness. For this service will continue long; and some powder with it'.

Even though resupply arrangements nearly proved the Achilles' heel of the Navy Royal, it was a fault amply outweighed by other achievements. Low, four-truck gun carriages enabled English ships to reload faster and discharge a far greater weight of fire than their opponents; and those guns were mounted in the agile warships that Hawkins built and – something often overlooked – equipped with flatter sails. It was to be another 140 years before it was established that a sail is pulled by a vacuum in front rather than pushed by capturing the wind like a bag. Hawkins could not know the scientific reason, but experience and intelligent observation had taught him that flatter sails, contrary to contemporary understanding, were not only easier to handle but also more efficient.

However, it was Burghley's administration that enabled Elizabethan England to punch well above its weight. As Rodger points out in *Safeguard of the Sea*: 'Not only did Burghley and his colleagues have more information available about their country's fundamental naval resources than any contemporary government, they had fuller knowledge than any subsequent English government before the twentieth century'.

That knowledge came from several nationwide surveys culminating in a 1582 census of all seagoing ships and their owners, the names of every captain and the numbers of sailors in every parish in England. In the decade before the Armada several partial or total mobilizations were carried out, such that by 1588 England possessed 'an experienced naval administration with a sophisticated mobilization system which allowed England's entire strength to be got to sea at very short notice.'

In contrast the Spanish, with vastly greater resources, and experience in depth of mounting amphibious operations, took two years (the third year of delay can be attributed to Drake's Cadiz raid) to assemble and launch an Armada of slower and less manoeuvrable ships with baggy sails handled by skeleton crews (only 8,000 sailors compared to 19,000 soldiers) and with guns of every conceivable bore and provenance mounted on high, two-wheeled carriages whose long trails obstructed gun decks where untrained troops were supervised by too few master gunners.

As explained more fully in Appendix C, the issue of whether the English favoured culverins and the Spanish cannon is something of a red herring. A breakdown of the guns on the larger, mainly Royal Navy warships for which information is available reveals no particular pattern, although it appears that 380–400 tons burden was the bottom threshold for ships carrying the heaviest guns, mounted in the bow and stern.

Swivel guns could be mounted anywhere, and one would have expected the carracks, built when it was still expected that they would close and board, to have a large number of them; but by 1588, with the exception of the two oldest (*Elizabeth Jonas* and

GUNS ABOARD MAJOR NAVY ROYAL SHIPS IN 1588

p	Built	Tons	Type	A	B	C	D	E	F	G
umph ☞	1562	760	Carrack	4	3		17	8	6	4
ite Bear	1564	730	Carrack	3	11		7	10	–	9
abeth Jonas	1559	684	Carrack	3	6		8	9	9	21
ory ☞	1560	565	Carrack	4	6		12	18	9	3
Royal ☞	1587	555	Galleon	4	4		12	12	6	6
ry Rose	1557	476	Carrack		4		11	10	4	7
enge ☞	1577	465	Galleon	2	6		12	2	6	15
guard (shallow draft)	1586	465	Galleon		8		10	14	2	20
den Lion	1582	420	Galleon		4		8	4	9	3
abeth Bonaventure	1573	400	Galleon	2			4	11	10	5
e	1559	400	Carrack	2	4		9	11	4	18
nbow ☞ (shallow draft)	1586	384	Galleon		8		10	14	2	20
pareil	1584	380	Galleon	2	3		7	8	12	6
adnought	1573	360	Galleon	2			4	11	19	5
sure	1573	360	Galleon		3	2	7	8	12	4
chant Royal (private)	n/a	350	Galleon			2	4	10	6	n/a
elope	1581	340	Galleon				4	13	8	5
sight	1570	295	Galleon				14	8	15	n/a
ard Bonaventure (private)	n/a	250	Galleon				4	9	8	4
ion (private)	n/a	230	Galleon					7	10	4
	1562	220	Carrack					8	2	8
r	1570	200	Galleon				4	8	8	10

Heavy	Medium	Light
A. Cannon (44–48 pounders)	D. Culverins (15–20 pounders)	G. Minions (3–4 pounders), falcons (2–pounders), and swivel guns
B. Demi-cannon (30–38 pounders)	E. Demi-culverins (9–12 pounders)	
C. Cannons perier (24 pounders)	F. Sakers (5–7 pounders)	

Hope), this was no longer the case. Logically, it was Seymour's *Rainbow* and Wynter's *Vanguard*, both galleons designed to operate in shallower water as little-ship killers, that had the largest proportion of light guns.

Apart from Seymour's uniformly armed galleons the ships' armament may have reflected their commanders' experience and preference to some degree. From what we know of the guns on *Jesus* at San Juan de Ulúa it comes as no surprise that Hawkins had a heavy suite of guns on *Victory*, while the 15 light guns on Drake's *Revenge* are suggestive of intent to board.

White Bear was the most massively armed ship in either fleet because she was the flagship of the Royal Navy until Howard transferred his flag to the newly acquired *Ark Royal* in mid-January, delighted by her speed. 'I pray you tell Her Majesty for me', he wrote, 'that her money was well given for the *Ark Ralegh* ... we can see no sail great or small but how far soever they be off we fetch them and speak with them'.

THE *ARMADA* CHARTS

We have reviewed the politics and preparation, the ships, commanders and guns; let's now see how it all came together. Rather than plough the familiar furrow of trying to create a word picture of the Channel battles, the following narrative accompanies the detailed charts commissioned by Lord Admiral Howard, which must be assumed to show the episodes he judged the most important, drawn by Robert Adams, engraved by Augustine Ryther and published circa 1590 as *Expeditionis Hispanorum in Angliam vera descriptio Anno Do: MDLXXXVIII*.

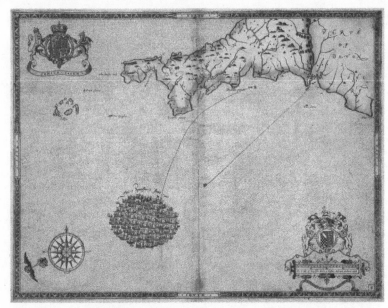

CHART 1: Armada assembly off the Lizard, 29 July.

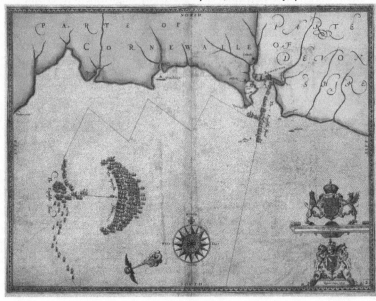

CHART 2: Sortie of the Navy Royal, night of 29/30 July.

Chart 1 shows *Golden Hind* racing into Plymouth to report the Armada assembling south of the Lizard, also the course of the *zabra* sent to reconnoitre the coast, which returned with some terrified Cornish fishermen. They confirmed that the main English fleet was anchored in Plymouth and, with the wind steady from the WSW, conditions were ideal for the Armada to trap the Navy Royal. Medina Sidonia summoned another council in which Pedro de Valdés advocated sending the warships ahead to mount a surprise attack; but he had been doing so unheeded since Coruña and a unique opportunity to force battle on Spanish terms was not taken. The Armada anchored until the hulks closed up and then set off along the Channel in a trailing crescent formation.

Chart 2 shows how the Navy Royal, after warping laboriously out of Plymouth, sailed to gain the weather gauge. Howard took the bulk of the fleet, at night, across the expected path of the Armada on a southerly course pointing into the wind as well as his ships were able. After sailing far into the Channel he turned north to come in behind the enemy fleet. A smaller squadron, led by Drake, tacked west along the coastline.

At dawn on 30 July the Spanish saw the two fleets converging behind them. None of them doubted that the enemy would win the weather gauge, and their formation was designed to counter it. A screen of medium-sized galleons was deployed in the vanguard against the possibility of an attack from the east, but the biggest warships in the Armada were concentrated in the wings of the crescent, such that they could cut off any English attempt to get among the transports in the belly of the crescent.

Howard was nonplussed by the formation and, after sending his pinnace *Disdain* to fire a formal challenge to battle, the first day's action was desultory. Some English captains at the time and many subsequent armchair admirals criticized his caution, but in *History of the World*, written when imprisoned in the Tower, Sir Walter Ralegh wrote a verdict that has stood the test of time:

> *To clap ships together without consideration belongs rather to a madman than to a man of war; for by such ignorant bravery was Peter Strozzi lost at the Azores when he fought against the Marquis of Santa Cruz. In like sort had the Lord Charles Howard, Admiral of England, been lost in the year 1588 if he had not been better advised than a great many malignant fools were, that found fault with his [behaviour]. The Spaniards had an army aboard them and he had none, they had more ships than he had and of higher building and charging; so that, had he entangled himself with those great and powerful vessels, he had greatly endangered the kingdom of England ... But our admiral knew his advantage and held it, which had he not done, he had not been worthy to hold his head.*

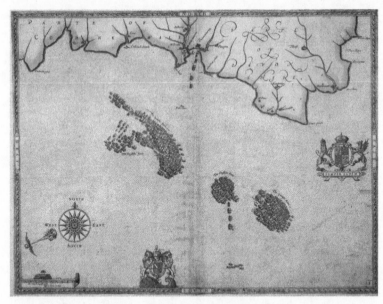

CHART 3: First combat off Plymouth, 31 July.

CHART 4: Drake's capture of *Nuestra Señora del Rosario*, morning of 1 August.

Chart 3 shows that Howard believed the next day's battle drove the Armada away from Plymouth and furthermore caused it to break formation and bunch together. The significant number of ships shown issuing from Plymouth in this and the next chart confirms that the English fleet was not up to strength until 1 August. Logically the big and less weatherly carracks would have stayed behind to cover the port while Howard and Drake took the galleons out to sea on 29/30 July.

The particular value of the Adams/Ryther charts is that they remind us of the importance of the wind in shaping tactical decisions, something that written accounts of battles in the age of sail seldom emphasize enough. To which one must add a reminder that combat among large sailing warships resembled nothing so much as heavyweight boxers standing ankle-deep in molasses.

Several columns are attacking the Armada's northern wing in line ahead, the first appearance of the tactic in naval history. Each ship in turn would fire her big bow-chasers, then turn away with a ripple of fire from the broadside and finally discharge the heaviest guns, mounted in the stern, before sailing out of range to reload. The effect should have been devastating but was not because it was done at too great a range. If logic is any guide they would at this stage have been firing bar shot, hoping to damage enemy rigging and to create stragglers to be secured at leisure.

The two ships selected for particular attention, Recalde's mighty *São João* (which the English may have believed was the Armada flagship) and the inseparable vice flagship of his Viscayan squadron, the huge but relatively lightly armed carrack *Gran Grin*, were not disabled – although *São João* came close, with some stays severed and two shots lodged in her foremast. They were rescued by Medina Sidonia's *São Martinho* and her devoted followers *São Marcos* and *São Mateus*.

Chart 4 illustrates the only, indirect, English success of the day. The bunching of the Armada caused several collisions, the most serious of which damaged the bowsprit and brought down the foremast of Pedro de Valdés's *Nuestra Señora del Rosario*. Probably prompted by Diego Flores, Medina Sidonia decided to abandon one of the biggest and most heavily gunned ships in the Armada, along with her entire crew and the 50,000 gold ducats she was carrying.

Drake, entrusted with guiding the fleet through the night, extinguished his stern lantern and sailed to capture the *Rosario*, which the demoralized Valdés surrendered without a fight (lower centre). At dawn Howard found that he had been following an enemy lantern and was well within the horns of the Spanish crescent, with the rest of the fleet out of supporting range. He did not criticize his subordinate's dereliction in writing – which would have put him in the wrong with the queen, who was desperate for prize money – but the chart is eloquent.

CHART 5: *San Salvador* abandoned; Portland Bill combat begins, 1–2 August.

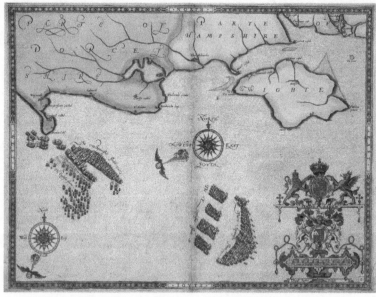

CHART 6: Combat off Portland Bill (note frequent wind changes), 2–3 August.

Another Spanish casualty was the big carrack *San Salvador*, carrying the Armada payroll, which suffered an explosion in her rear magazine that would have sunk a less well-built ship. She was towed until night made it possible to evacuate the money and all except the most desperately injured men, then cut loose. Hawkins came up with the wreck in the morning and ordered her towed to Weymouth. In the region of fifteen tons of gunpowder were recovered from *Rosario* and *San Salvador*, some of which reached the fleet in time to be used against the Armada.

The two charts attempt to tell the story of the battle off Portland Bill, which Howard clearly believed was another crucial moment. What brought it about was a period of dead calm followed by a wind shift of nearly 180°, which gave the Spanish the weather gauge. Howard tried to sail around the Armada on the landward side, found his way blocked by Bertendona's *Regazona* and reversed direction to come around the southern flank. A fierce battle ensued in which the Spanish warships formed a massive line abreast to bear down on the English ships without opening a gap that might be exploited to get among the transports.

While the main battle raged in the centre, with *São Martinho* in the thick of it, as Chart 6 shows, there were separate battles fought by smaller contingents on the two flanks. On the landward side Frobisher's giant *Triumph* and her battle group of London armed merchantmen were cleverly positioned behind the tidal race south of Portland Bill. Medina Sidonia sent Moncada's galleasses against Frobisher, but as they struggled in the current *Triumph* fired bar shot at their oars before using the race to sail away from approaching Spanish reinforcements led by Medina Sidonia.

Howard led a group to attack his opposite number at much closer range than previously. *São Martinho* was lost to view in a column of smoke and by the end of the day one of her officers estimated that she had fired only 80 rounds against 500 fired at her by the English – though to little effect. That evening Hawkins warned Walsingham that the day's rate of fire was unsustainable.

Next morning the wind had swung back to SSW and on the seaward side a small group led by Drake got around the Spanish line, only to run into self-sacrificial resistance by Juan Gómez de Medina, Captain General of the Hulks squadron, on the 420-ton *Gran Grifón*. Drake sailed *Revenge* to point blank range and did serious damage to the hulk, but just as the rest of his group was closing in to finish her off Medina Sidonia sent reinforcements and towed her to safety.

Ironically *Gran Grifón*, a commandeered German hulk whose heaviest armament was four shoddily made demi-culverins, came closer than any other to disabling an English warship. One of her shots hit the mainmast of Drake's *Revenge*, forcing him to drop out of the action.

CHART 7: Off the Isle of Wight, 4 August.

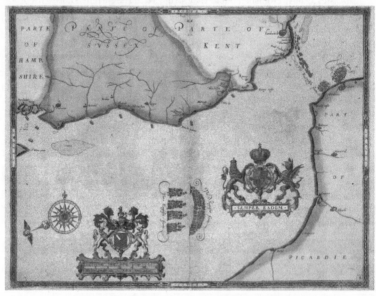

CHART 8: Pursuit to Calais; Seymour's fleet joins, 5–6 August.

THE CARRACK

Minion and *Jesus of Lübeck* from King Henry VIII's illustrated catalogue known as the Anthony Roll (1546).

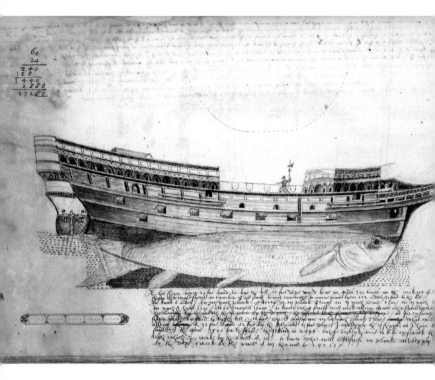

THE GALLEON

Hydrodynamic shape from the manuscript by Master Shipwright Matthew
Baker (1530–1613) known as *Fragments of Ancient Shipwrighting*.

OPPOSITE

SIEGE OF SMERWICK, 1580

Sketch by an officer on *Achates*. *Revenge* has completed her curving attack and
is firing her heaviest (stern) armament as she sails away.

ESPIONAGE

Detailed map sent to Walsingham by a spy in March 1585 showing Parma's
dispositions along the flooded River Scheldt.

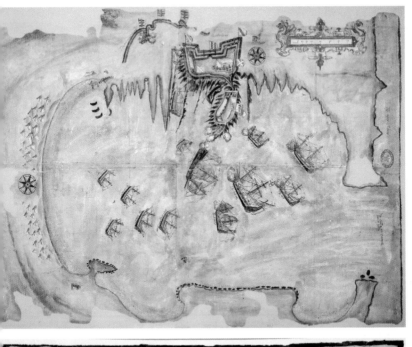

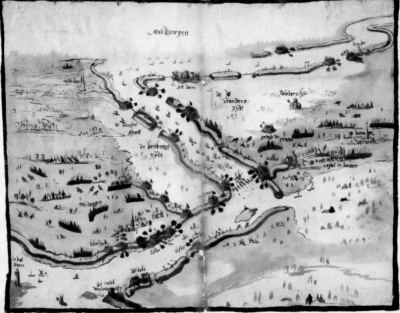

Antdhorpen

DRAKE'S CIRCUMNAVIGATION

Earliest (*c.* 1587) extant map showing the route of Drake's 1577–80 voyage, a
reduced copy of the original given to Queen Elizabeth and subsequently lost.
Note that the route of Drake's Caribbean raid of 1585–86 has been added.

INSETS

(*FROM LEFT*) Drake's reception in the Moluccas (Spice Islands); raising the
Cross of St George on Elizabetha, which Drake believed to be the southern-
most island of the Tierra del Fuego archipelago; the grounding of
Golden Hind on a reef in the Celebes.

DANGEROUS MEN

(*LEFT*) Cornelis Ketel's portrait of Martin Frobisher (1577), (*TOP*) Sir
Martin Gilbert (1584), (*ABOVE*) Sir Richard Grenville (*c.* 1590).

GEORGE CLIFFORD, 3RD EARL OF CUMBERLAND

Depicted dressed as the Queen's Champion by Nicholas Hilliard *c.* 1590.

QUEEN ELIZABETH BORNE BY HER GARTER KNIGHTS C. 1600.

SOMERSET HOUSE PEACE CONFERENCE IN 1604

From the back, the English commissioners on the right are: delegation leader and Lord Treasurer Thomas Sackville, 1st Earl of Dorset; Lord High Admiral Charles Howard, 1st Earl of Nottingham; Charles Blount, Earl of Devonshire; Henry Howard, Earl of Northampton; and at the front Robert Cecil, Viscount Cranborne (later 1st Earl of Salisbury).

Given that the others are so meticulous, the inaccuracy of Chart 7 is highly suggestive. Although Howard had divided his fleet into four squadrons under himself, Drake, Hawkins and Frobisher, the Armada had not been in a crescent since Portland Bill and was now organized into a vanguard and rearguard of warships, with the transports forming a separate group in between.

However, the more significant omission is that the Armada, in fact, continued to sail close to the English coast, not out in the Channel as shown, and the chart does not show the battle fought off the eastern foreland of the Isle of Wight. The only reason that occurs to me for erasing the events of 4 August is that Howard felt he was outshone by his subordinates, whom he may have felt he had honoured enough by knighting Hawkins and Frobisher on 5 August.

He had not made any plan to defend the Solent, even though it was the last place where the Armada could pause before Flanders. When it became clear that Medina Sidonia was contemplating sailing into the roadstead, only Frobisher's group was in a position to stop him. In a repeat of his exploit at Portland Bill, he drew *São Martinho* and her escorts into a tidal race by feigning damage to his ship, before using his boats to tow *Triumph* into the current and sail away. He then joined Howard and Hawkins in an attack on the centre of the rearguard, driving it east.

Meanwhile Drake's squadron made a fierce attack on the seaward flank of the Armada. No account mentions Drake by name and it's possible *Revenge* was still disabled. If so, the attack was led by Thomas Fenner on *Nonpareil*, making him an unsung hero of the Armada epic. The effect was to drive the Armada in on itself and towards the *São Martinho* group, which by now was dangerously close to the Owers Bank (shown off the Isle of Wight foreland in Chart 8).

Relations between Frobisher and Drake or any of his close collaborators were by now so poisonous that we can dismiss the possibility of prior co-ordination; each acted as he did from the indefinable quality known as battle instinct. Revealing the same quality, in the midst of fending off Howard, Hawkins and Frobisher, Medina Sidonia perceived the danger to the rest of the Armada from grounding. Firing signal guns, he led his group SSE, gathering the scattered hulks as he went.

The exemplary bravery, determination and intelligent leadership displayed by Medina Sidonia throughout the Armada saga have seldom been equalled in the history of warfare.

There was no further fighting as the two fleets sailed to anchor off Calais, where Medina Sidonia received the sickening news that Parma's forces would not be ready for another week. From his towering poop deck he could see Seymour's Narrow Seas fleet pouring across the Channel to join Howard, and must have known there was no longer any hope for a successful outcome. Note also in Chart 8 the voluntaries emerging from every little port along the English coast.

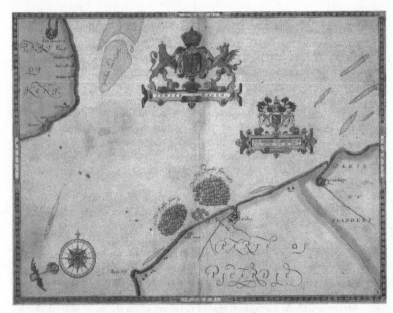

CHART 9: Fireship attack at Calais, night 7–8 August.

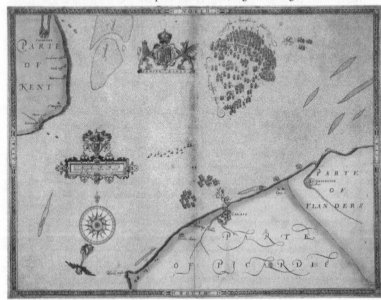

CHART 10: Battles off Calais and Gravelines, 8–9 August.

ELIZABETH'S SEA DOGS

Sir William Wynter claimed the credit for proposing a fireship attack on the Armada at Calais, but the chosen ships were all from Drake's squadron and their well-recompensed owners included Hawkins, Drake himself and some close collaborators, which suggests another author. Medina Sidonia knew they were coming and deployed a screen of boats to turn them aside, but the fireships were much larger than usual (see Appendix F) and only two of the eight were intercepted.

As the burning ships drifted into the anchored fleet, their shotted guns firing as the flames reached them, the nerves of captains who had endured a hellish week finally got the better of them. The Spanish ships all had several anchors down and most of them cut the cables without buoying them, making it impossible to return to the anchorage after the fireships passed through.

At dawn Howard went after Moncada's *San Lorenzo*, which had lost its rudder again and gone aground. He sent his own pinnace *Delight* and *Ark Royal*'s boats, joined by the boats from the London galleon *Margaret and John*, which also ran aground, to seize and pillage the galleass. During the fighting Moncada was killed and after a brawl between the English and a party of French soldiers sent by the governor of Calais to claim the prize, the shore guns opened fire, killing *Delight*'s captain and more English sailors than had fallen during the preceding week.

It was left to Howard's subordinates to do his duty, led by Drake. The indefatigable Portuguese galleons stood against the might of the Royal Navy and bought time for the rest of the Armada to regroup. *São Martinho* and *São João* were riddled but survived thanks to the heroic efforts of their crews. Two, not the three shown, were crippled, not set on fire. *São Mateus* and *São Filipe* ran aground between Ostend and Nieuport, and were looted by Justin of Nassau's cromsters.

Seymour's *Rainbow* and Wynter's *Vanguard*, their magazines full, played a leading role in the battle off Gravelines, fought at point-blank range. Even so, only one other Spanish ship was lost, portrayed top right of Chart 10. This was the isolated carrack *María Juan*, which was mobbed by a pack of armed merchantmen and sank as her captain was trying to negotiate surrender.

Only a lucky wind shift saved the Armada from the Flanders sandbanks, but it also ensured there was no way back. The Armada steered north to sail around the British Isles, followed as far as the Firth of Forth by a reduced English fleet, now out of ammunition. Ordered back to the Downs, Seymour sulked and then resigned, while the hired ships and voluntaries sailed back to their home ports.

The English victory was marred by the death of hundreds of sailors from disease and want, with Burghley refusing to pay for their care, or even their wages. While Howard, Drake and Hawkins did their best to alleviate the suffering, Frobisher could no longer contain his envy and hurled threats at Drake. It was a typically Elizabethan outcome: militarily unsatisfactory and financially sordid.

ARMADA LOSSES BY TYPE

Type	Built	Number	% of Armada	Known lost	% of type
Galleass	**Sicily**	**4**	**3.1**	**3**	**75.0**
Carrack	Mediterranean	11	8.6	8	72.7
Nao	Cantábrica	24	18.7	10	41.7
Carrack	Other	4	3.1	2	50.0
Carrack total		**39**	**30.5**	**20**	**51.3**
Hulk	North European	26	20.3	7	26.9
Urca	Cantábrica	5	3.9	0	0.0
Hulk total		**31**	**24.2**	**7**	**22.6**
Zabra & pinaza	**Cantábrica**	**10**	**7.8**	**2**	**20.0**
Galleon	Portugal *	11	8.6	3	27.3
Galleon	Cantábrica	10	7.8	1	10.0
Galleon	Other	2	1.6	0	0.0
Galleon total		**23**	**18.0**	**4**	**17.4**
Patache	**Cantábrica**	**21**	**16.4**	**0**	**0.0**

* Includes two 110-ton *galeoncetes*.

Off Scotland Medina Sidonia counted 112 ships still with him of the 127 that had formed up off the Lizard on 29 July. The known losses were Valdés's *Rosario*, *San Salvador*, Moncada's *San Lorenzo*, *São Mateus*, *São Filipe* and *Maria Juan*. The 225-ton carrack *San Juan* and two *zabras* are known to have taken refuge in Dunkirk and the other six (of 11 whose fate is unknown) may have been now-empty *pataches* that also took advantage of their shallow draft to reach safety through the sand-banks off the coast of Spanish Flanders. The North European hulks that disappeared from the record may have broken away later to seek refuge in Norwegian ports.

The worst of the Armada's troubles were still to come. Many of the larger galleons and carracks had suffered severe battle damage as a result of stopping English attacks on the transports, with their hulls if not with their guns, which explains why the ensuing losses were so heavily concentrated among the bigger ships (Appendix F). Of the biggest, Bertendona's *Regazona*, Oquendo's *Santa Ana*, Medina Sidonia's *São Martinho*, Recalde's *São João* and the Duke of Tuscany's *San Francesco* got back to Spain only because they had elite crews, and never sailed again. *Santa Ana* burned a few days after arrival, while *Regazona* and *São João* were destroyed during Drake's raid of May 1589.

For the rest, Gómez de Medina's hulk *Gran Grifón* paid the price of her 3 August self-sacrifice and was deliberately run aground on Fair Isle, between the Shetland and Orkney Islands north of Scotland, with nearly all aboard surviving. Only one galleass made it home. They had been in combat more than most, but what doomed them were their curved rudders, which could not cope with severe oceanic conditions. *Zúñiga* made it to Le Havre, where she was abandoned. *Girona*, packed with survivors from other ships including *Alonso de Leyva*, wrecked at Lacada Point, County Antrim. Only nine men survived the wreck, finding refuge at nearby Dunluce Castle, stronghold of Sorley Boy MacDonnell, in whose service they remained.

Apart from the Ragusan carrack *San Juan de Sicilia*, which was blown up by one of Walsingham's agents in Tobermory harbour on the Isle of Mull, and the hospital ship *San Pedro Mayor*, one of the

German hulks, which was run aground in Bigbury Bay, South Devon, the rest wrecked on the coast of Ireland. Nearly all those who did not die in the shipwrecks were killed by the English authorities on the grounds that they lacked the means to incarcerate them and could not take the risk of hundreds of desperate Spanish soldiers making common cause with Irish rebels.

As to Jehovah blowing them away, the Armada did run into very strong winds in the North Atlantic, but this simply eliminated the least seaworthy. Other than battle damage, crew health and pilot skill would have played a part, but the most striking statistic is that so many of the casualties were carracks, particularly those from the Mediterranean (Levante) Squadron. What also stands out is the superior survival rate of the post-1583 Cantabrican ships of all types. The greater loss was the estimated 10,000 men who died, many of them sailors whom Spain could not afford to lose.

It's unwise to extrapolate from the reported losses among the Royal Navy crews to the unreported Navy Royal at large. The Royal Navy was largely manned by the dregs of the population, pressed into service along with their dirt, parasites and diseases, and in some cases commanded by officers who did not know how vital it was to keep their ships clean. Experience had taught the captains and volunteer crews of the private ships the importance of personal and shipboard hygiene, and most would have had little or no contact with foci of pestilence such as *Elizabeth Jonas*.

The commonly cited figure of 6,000 English dead as a result of service in the Armada campaign is absurd. It's only 100 less than the total of all sailors and soldiers on the queen's ships, and from Burghley's acerbic comments it seems that quite a few of those were on the books for accounting purposes only and were not corporeally present. A more realistic figure of 2–3,000 for the entire fleet is still appalling but, sadly, not much worse than usual during long periods of sea service.

The greater victory in 1588 was financial, however cruelly won. The total cost to Elizabeth's exchequer was only £161,185 for land and sea forces mobilized against the Armada, and her total debt in

1589 had increased by only £200,000 despite the severe curtailment of trade since 1585 and even of corsair activity in 1588. Also, consequent on the defeat of the Armada, Burghley could tap into domestic and international credit that had completely dried up pending the outcome.

During the same period Philip spent in excess of 3 million ducats (£1,430,000) on the Armada alone, and was compelled to embark on a crash naval rebuilding programme afterwards. This without counting the opportunity cost of the momentum robbed from Parma in the Netherlands and the large sums disbursed to the French Catholic Leaguers, which did not even achieve friendly control of the deep-water Channel port that was essential for the success of the Enterprise of England.

Non Suffcit Orbis to wage war at a negative attrition rate of 9:1.

CHAPTER 12
THE OLD GUARD PASSES

I n August 1588, before it became apparent that the Armada was
gone for good, Drake wrote 'we much more ought to have regard unto the Duke of Parma and his soldiers than to the Duke
of Medina Sidonia and his ships'. The ailing Sir William Wynter
also warned of the danger that English ships might be trapped in
the Downs by a southerly wind, permitting Parma to slip a vanguard across to be supplied from French ports. English commanders
also voiced the fear that if Spain could get a fleet of galleys to him,
Parma would have the means to land a large force very quickly.

Added to which was the knowledge that Spanish naval power
was likely to recover alarmingly swiftly. After the destruction of
the Ottoman fleet at Lepanto in October 1571, Grand Vizier
Mehmed Sokullu met with Venetian emissary Marcantonio Barbaro
and contrasted the Christian victory with the fall of the last Venetian fortress in Cyprus in August of the same year:

> *You come to see how we bear our misfortune. But I would have
> you know the difference between your loss and ours. In wresting
> Cyprus from you, we deprived you of an arm; in defeating our
> fleet, you have only shaved our beard. An arm when cut off
> cannot grow again; but a shorn beard will grow all the better for
> the razor.*

Although he had no consolation equivalent to Cyprus, Philip II
might have said the same of the partial destruction of the Armada, once he recovered from his post-disaster depression and or-

dered a crash programme of naval construction. Unfortunately he had lost almost all his senior oceanic commanders: Recalde and Oquendo died shortly after returning to Spain, Pedro de Valdés was in captivity and the fate of his venomous cousin Diego Flores de Valdés hung in the balance.* Only Bertendona remained and his expertise appears to have been slighted, probably because whatever faith he had in Philip's divine guidance had not survived the events of 1588.

The council summoned by the king to decide the specifications of the new ships sensibly concluded that they should be galleons. However, they remained wedded to gigantism, presumably because the biggest galleons had made it home despite taking terrible punishment. Of the 'Twelve Apostles' built in the Bilbao and Santander shipyards in 1590–91, four were three-deckers of about 950 English tons burden, four were about 680 and four were about 565. The biggest were at the extreme limit of the design constraints previously mentioned – and indeed the flagship *San Pablo* stranded and lost on the bar at San Lúcar.

They were not lucky ships. The huge *San Simón* was a lemon, never sailed as a warship, proved unsatisfactory even as a merchant ship and was scrapped. *San Mateo* and *San Andrés* were captured, *San Felipe* and *Santo Tomás* burned in Lord Admiral Howard's raid on Cadiz in 1596. Evidence of a decline in the quality of Spanish ships' crews can be seen in the loss at sea of *Santiago* and *San Bartolomé* during the 1597 armada campaign. *San Tadeo* and *San Bernabé* were also lost at sea, *San Pablo* stranded and was lost in the Lisbon estuary, and *San Juan* was lost to fire when being breamed in Havana harbour.

In addition to the Apostles, eight more royal galleons ordered from Cantabrican shipyards in 1589–90 were of the classes that had performed well in 1588: four each of about 480 and 340 tons. The Spanish also started building medium-sized *felibotes* (Eng. flyboats), the shallow-draft carracks developed by the Sea Beggars,

---

* He was condemned to death but the sentence was commuted to life-long exile.

with which to equip corsairs of their own. Operating in the Bay of Biscay and out of Dunkirk, they were to inflict severe losses on English merchant shipping.

Starting earlier and unrelated to the 1589 programme was the development – in Havana – of a brilliant new class of *galizabras*, 320-ton Renaissance pocket battleships designed to outrun what they could not fight and to outgun whatever could match them for speed. They first came into service in 1588, tasked with carrying the main shipments of Indies bullion independently of the annual flotas. No *galizabra* was ever intercepted, yet in a notable example of 'not invented here' bureaucratic malignancy the king's advisers refused to embrace the innovative design and built only seven, when they should have ordered in greater numbers to hunt the enemy corsairs that were strangling Spanish trade.

During the same period 10 new or totally rebuilt galleons joined the Royal Navy: *Mary Rose* (475 tons) in 1589, *Merhonour* (692), *Garland* (532), *Defiance* (440), *Answer* (220), *Quittance* (216), *Crane* (203) and *Advantage* (173) in 1590, *Dreadnought* (360) and *Swiftsure* (333) in 1592. In contrast to the ill-fated Spanish Apostles, only one Royal Navy ship was lost to enemy action and none to storms or accidents for the duration of the war.

This was the context of the Drake–Norreys expedition of 1589, which aimed to destroy Spain's remaining ships and win the naval war outright, which allegedly it might have done had it attacked the majority of the Armada survivors in Santander, as ordered by Queen Elizabeth. Instead, it caused the destruction of just three huge Armada survivors (the badly battered carrack *Regazona* and galleon *São João* and the 630-ton hulk *San Bartolomé*) at Coruña (bizarrely known to the English at that time as 'the Groyne').

The main problem with this interpretation is that it's based on the reports of one of Walsingham's 'intelligencers' in St Jean-de-Luz, just over the border from San Sebastián and Pasajes, which really are in the nethermost leeward groin of the Bay of Biscay and to which only six carracks – the type that suffered most from the great storm in the North Atlantic – returned along with seven hulks

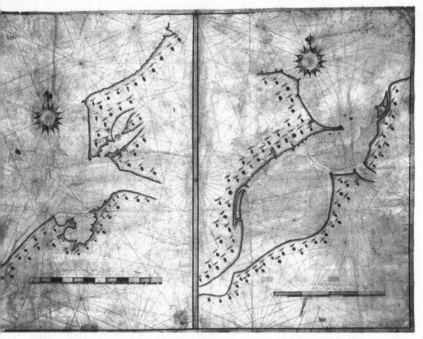

Maps from 1589 of Coruña (bottom left) and Ferrol (top left), and Santander (right).

and *pataches*. No doubt these were 'all unrigged and their ordnance on shore and some 20 men in a ship to keep them' as reported; but it was an unjustified assumption that the warships in Santander were likewise defenceless. It may even have been deliberately false information, as the spy in question was also on the Spanish pay roll.

Along with the heavily damaged great galleons *Sao Martinho* and *San Francesco*, ten more galleons and one *galeoncete* returned to Santander, along with seven carracks and eighteen hulks and *pataches*. A further three galleons and the other *galeoncete*, along with two carracks, the sole surviving galleass and two hulks, made it back to Laredo, 20 miles/32 kilometres to the east. They would have sailed to take advantage of the superior facilities at Santander/Guarnizo as soon as possible. It's not remotely likely that the thirteen intact galleons and two *galeoncetes* would still have been in Santander seven months after their return, when the English fleet might have arrived. They would have been urgently refitted and remanned to resume their essential function of protecting the Indies *flotas*.

The big 'what if' is whether a swiftly mounted English counterattack might have achieved more; to which the answer is surely no. The queen's ships were in no fit state to mount such an attack after a 6–8 month mobilization; but even if they had been turned around rapidly, Santander was a far tougher nut to crack than relatively open Cadiz and Coruña. To enter Santander harbour the fleet would have had to sail around the Magdalena peninsula, bristling with five mutually supporting artillery forts. Then through a narrow channel commanded by the Hano fortress, built after 1570 at the tip of the peninsula, two more forts in the inner harbour and the guns of whatever warships were in port. Also, any damaged ships would have been at Guarnizo, deep at the southern end of the bay.

Could Sir John Norreys have disembarked his troops further along the coast to take Santander from land? Again the answer is no. Santander is set in a singularly inhospitable stretch of coast, but if they had been able to land – perhaps at Laredo – they lacked the siege artillery necessary to take a modern fortification like Hano. Even the medieval walls of the upper town at Coruña and at Cadiz proved too much for them, and unless the fleet could sail into Santander there was no prospect of prizes.

Once Elizabeth had denied the expedition siege artillery, therefore, it follows that Drake never intended to put his head in that lion's mouth, no matter how many ships there were in harbour; which means he was guilty of misleading and disobeying the queen, whose orders were unambiguous:

> *Before you attempt anything either in Portugal or in the*
> *[Atlantic] islands our express pleasure and commandment is that*
> *you first distress the ships of war in Guipuzcoa, Biscay, Galicia*
> *and any other places that appertain either to the King of Spain or*
> *his subjects, to the end that they may not impeach you in such*
> *enterprises as you are to execute upon his dominions, as also that*

> *the said ships remaining entire and undistressed, they may not take*
> *encouragement in the time of your absence to attempt somewhat*
> *against this our realm or the realm of Ireland.*

There's not much doubt what would have happened to the subjects of any other monarch who ignored such explicit orders. Furthermore, Elizabeth had good reason to feel that she had been hustled into backing a much larger and more expensive enterprise than she originally intended. Unaware of the advent of the *galizabras*, her first thought had been to relieve her acute financial distress by sending more modest squadrons to intercept the *flotas* off the Azores, as long advocated by the newly knighted John Hawkins. In 1589 a 14-ship *flota* evaded a squadron mainly paid for by the Earl of Cumberland (who rented the totally unsuitable royal carrack *Victory*) in the Azores and a royal squadron (*Elizabeth Bonaventure*, *Golden Lion*, the pinnace *Advice* and Hawkins's newly built *Repentance*, renamed *Dainty* at the queen's insistence) under Frobisher off the coast of Spain.

Meanwhile the majority of the queen's ships were being cleansed and refitted, and the counter-armada project grew like Topsy. In the end the aim was to: destroy Spanish warships in the northern ports; make a landing in Portugal in the name of the pretender Dom Antonio which was supposed to spark a nationwide revolt against Spanish rule; capture Lisbon and destroy whatever warships there may have been there; open Portuguese dominions to English trade; and finally to intercept the 1589 *flotas* off the Azores.

Philip II erred in defining the strategic mission of the 1588 Armada too restrictively – but the 1589 counter-attack illustrated the opposite extreme. It was a ridiculously over-ambitious project and furthermore would have required an administrator of the calibre (and personal wealth) of a Medina Sidonia even to organize the 130+ ships and 13,600 troops that were eventually involved. Instead it fell to Drake, whose limitations were pitilessly exposed.

Seven of the ships were royal: *Revenge, Nonpareil, Dreadnought, Swiftsure, Foresight, Aid* and the pinnace *Advice*. Only 24 private ships of 95 named in a list made after the expedition returned (three are known to have been lost in action) had also served against the Armada, but they included some of the largest: *Merchant Royal*, *Edward Bonaventure*, *Golden Noble*, *Toby* and *Centurion*. Twelve large Hansa and Dutch hulks were listed but not 30-odd Dutch flyboats commandeered at the last minute, most of which deserted in the Bay of Biscay.

Even though it became yet another public–private joint stock enterprise, it cost the queen £50,000 instead of the £20,000 originally budgeted. Drake later alleged that he attacked Coruña because he received intelligence that a large fleet of Spanish ships was assembled there, but that was a lie to obscure the fact that the raid was made to replenish the supplies paid for by the queen, which the fleet had consumed while sitting in Plymouth. The men put ashore not only found ample stores and wine enough for most to get helplessly drunk, but also looted a warehouse containing the infested clothing of the Armada survivors, thereby spreading typhus through the entire fleet.

Finally, while the fleet was anchored in a dead calm off Cascais, west of Lisbon, 21 Spanish galleys made one of their few successful attacks on an English fleet, cutting out two ships, including William Hawkins's 120 ton *William*, and destroying another. In return Drake's fleet rounded up 60 Hansa and French hulks sailing to Lisbon with grain and naval stores, which would have been a considerable success if the expedition had not aspired to so much more. After re-embarking the remainder of Norreys's landing force, which had marched 120 miles/190 kilometres from Peniche to the walls of Lisbon in the face of a larger enemy army while losing hundreds of men to disease and drunkenness, the fleet was held to the coast of Portugal by strong adverse winds and unable to proceed to the Azores.

Although there were no further ship losses, the human cost was appalling. About 3,000 men deserted in Devon or with the Dutch flyboats before they even reached Coruña, and at least 4,000 of the remaining troops died. Sailors also died in large numbers: of 300 who sailed in *Dreadnought*, 114 died and when she returned there were only 18 still able to work. This time the epidemic also infested the private ships, and the 180-ton *Gregory* of London, which had fought off the galleys at Cascais, had only two men and two boys of her original crew standing when she reached Plymouth, which she was only able to do thanks to the loan of four men from *Bark Bonner*.

The post-mortem conducted by the Privy Council was inconclusive, the proceedings obfuscated by Drake's desperate wriggling to avoid the Scylla of admitting he had lied to the queen and the Charybdis of being found lacking in courage. The latter charge was absurd, but an honest reply would have required him to admit that it would have been suicidal to sail under the guns of Hano at Santander and San Julián at the mouth of the Tagus – and that he knew it before he set out.

He had tried to conduct the operation in the same way he had done successfully on a much smaller scale so often in the past: get to sea by promising whatever was necessary, make an intermediate stop to stock up on supplies at enemy expense and then muddle through, counting on his fabled good luck. He was not entrusted with another expedition until 1595–96, during which his death was perhaps hastened by the bitter realization that Lady Fortune had finally turned her back on him.

So, it seemed, she had on Elizabeth. As the Drake–Norreys expedition limped home in July, news came of the assassination of King Henri III of France and civil war broke out over the succession of the Huguenot Henri of Navarre, he of the archetypically sardonic French visage. The Catholic League went into overdrive and Philip II gave France priority over the war in the Netherlands. In the summer of 1590 Parma marched to relieve Henri's siege of Paris and the able Spanish commander Juan del Águila with 3,000 troops landed and set up a galley base at Port-Blavet in southern Brittany (now Port-Louis, opposite Lorient), a first step towards the deadly threat foretold in 1588.

By August 1591 there were 14,000 English troops on the mainland: 4,000 with Henri's army at the siege of Rouen (relieved by Parma in April 1592), 3,000 with the army of the Prince of Conti and the Duke of Montpensier in Brittany (routed during the relief of the siege of Craon by Águila in May 1592), and 7,000 with the Dutch. Elizabeth and Burghley now felt the regime was secure enough to raise taxes, but it was still warfare on a shoestring and increasingly dependent on financing by the City of London, which was only prospering thanks to a wholesale commitment to the corsair war.

After the Drake–Norreys fiasco, another effort under Frobisher and Hawkins in 1590 returned empty-handed, although the two operations did cause the *flotas* to be held back in Havana. The lure of intercepting the combined *flotas* and relieving the strain on English finances at the expense of the Spanish was irresistible. On 5 April 1591 Lord Thomas Howard left Plymouth bound for the Azores in the new *Due Defiance* with five other royal ships, including Drake's old flagship *Revenge*, now the vice admiral under the command of Sir Richard Grenville. The others were *Elizabeth Bonaventure*, *Nonpareil*, the new *Crane* and the pinnace *Moon*. In the course of the operation *Nonpareil* and *Moon* were sent home with sick sailors and were replaced by *Golden Lion* and *Foresight*.

This was a venture entirely underwritten by the crown, but the changing cast of hired private warships and supply ships that made up the bulk of the fleet included what we might call a *noblesse obligée* contingent from men dependent on royal patronage: four ships belonging to Lord Admiral Howard, two from the Earl of Hertford, and one each from Sir George Carey, Sir Walter Ralegh, his older brother Carew and Sir John Hawkins. It also set out with a commandeered group of powerful armed merchantmen belonging to a London syndicate led by Alderman John Watts, which parted company at the first opportunity to resume its interrupted corsairing venture to the West Indies.

Against which desertion should be set the fact that Lord Thomas's squadron was to be saved from certain destruction by the just-in-time warning brought by the frigate *Moonshine* from the Earl of Cumberland's flotilla of corsairs, which was just about to return home after an unfruitful cruise off the Iberian coast when it sighted

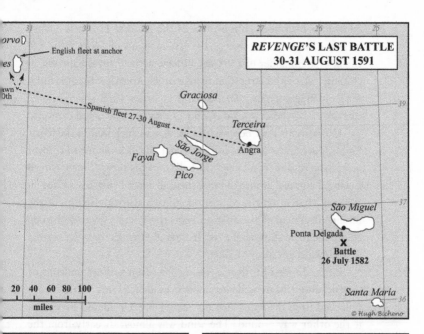

REVENGE'S LAST BATTLE
30-31 AUGUST 1591

English fleet at anchor

Spanish fleet 27-30 August

Graciosa

Terceira

Angra

Fayal *São Jorge*

Pico

São Miguel

Ponta Delgada
X
Battle
26 July 1582

20 40 60 80 100

miles

Santa María

© Hugh Bicheno

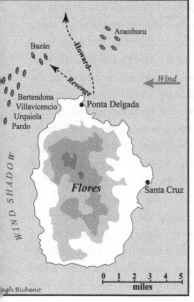

Aramburu

Bazán

Howard

Bertendona
Villavicencio
Urquiola
Pardo

Ponta Delgada

Wind

Revenge

WIND SHADOW

Flores

Santa Cruz

0 1 2 3 4 5

miles

© Hugh Bicheno

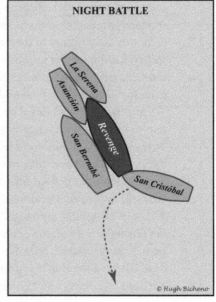

NIGHT BATTLE

La Serena

Asunción

Revenge

San Bernabé

San Cristóbal

© Hugh Bicheno

a large Spanish fleet sailing towards the Azores. This was Alonso de Bazán, younger brother of the late Marquis of Santa Cruz and the new commander of the Ocean Fleet, with 17 royal galleons including two of the largest and three other Apostles, Medina Sidonia's old flagship *São Martinho* and 11 other 1588 survivors, 12 carracks, 9 of the new *felibotes*, and 17 *pataches*, *zabras* and caravels.

Howard, his fleet beset with illness, had anchored in the lee of Flores, outermost of the Azores, to put the sick ashore to recover in fresh air and to 'rummage' the ballast of his ships. This involved rowing the gravel ashore to be washed, so when *Moonshine*'s Captain William Myddelton rowed over on 30 August to advise him of the imminent arrival of the Spanish fleet, there was a great deal to do before the royal ships could sail. It was only thanks to Bazán's errors that Howard got away at all.

Bazán divided his fleet, sending the seven veteran galleons of Castile under Marcos de Aramburu east of Flores while he approached from the west with the main force. He should have done it the other way around. The wind was almost directly from the east and the less weatherly main force had to tack to complete the envelopment. Bazán's second mistake was to have shortened sail to permit running repairs to the broken bowsprit of the Apostle *San Andrés*, flagship of the squadron led by Sancho Pardo, instead of leaving her behind. The delays gave Howard just enough time and space to sail around the head of Aramburu's fast-closing squadron.

As it was, the jaws closed on *Revenge*, by some distance the last ship to leave the anchorage, only because Grenville went berserk. To the admiring astonishment of the Spanish he steered directly at Bazán, all sails set and guns run out. Commanding a squadron in Bazán's group was our old friend Martín de Bertendona, who was not easily impressed. He wrote of Grenville 'advancing towards our fleet with arrogance' as though 'valuing the world as nothing'. In fact Grenville was not, as he may have believed, steering to engage Bazán's *San Pablo*, which had fallen behind because of a damaged topmast, but her sister ship the no-less enormous *San Felipe*, commanded by Claudio de Beamonte. The big galleon proved more nimble than

Grenville expected, took *Revenge*'s wind, rammed her amidships, and a boarding party leapt onto her deck from *San Felipe*'s beak-head.

To the further astonishment of the other Spanish ships a point blank broadside from *Revenge* so damaged *San Felipe* that she fell away, leaving ten very lonely men on the deck of the enemy ship. They sold their lives dearly but only three were left alive when Bertendona played the game winner. Coming up on *Revenge*'s unengaged port side, he swung away at the last moment to come alongside her, bow to bow and stern to stern, hurled grappling irons and then lashed the two ships together. After *San Simón* had proved unseaworthy he had moved his flag to *San Bernabé*, one of the smaller Apostles and only 100 tons larger than the 465-ton *Revenge*; but even so his upper deck gunners enjoyed a crucial height advantage as the light guns of both ships smashed each other's superstructures. The big guns were silent and the usual fire bombs were not thrown because the men on both ships knew that they would share the fate of the other.

Bertendona did not intend to send in his boarders until his gunners had taken some of the fight out of the wild Englishmen, but the inexperienced Aramburu scorned such prudence, sailed his 450 ton *San Cristóbal* into *Revenge*'s stern and sent his boarders swarming up to her tall poop deck. That was when the pressed men of *Revenge*, the dregs of London and Plymouth, began their journey to join the likes of the Spartans at Thermopylae in Valhalla. The elite Castilian marine infantry drove as far as the mainmast, and one of them shot Grenville through the body. But when he ordered his men below deck to clear the line of fire for the guns in the forecastle, the Spanish were shot down in droves. Grenville then led a counter-attack that drove them back to their ship.

Aramburu's rashness had led him to approach from the one quarter he should have avoided at all costs and the bow of *San Cristóbal* was shattered by point blank fire from the heaviest guns on *Revenge*, demi-cannon and full culverins. He had to disengage and, like Beamonte on *San Felipe*, was too occupied with keeping his ship afloat to take any further part in the battle.

Although Bertendona had immobilized *Revenge*, he had also made it impossible for the rest of the fleet to fire their heavy guns at her for fear of damaging *San Bernabé*. The battle would have to be won by boarding, which was supposed to be what the Spanish did best. The next Spanish captain to put this assumption to the test was Antonio Manrique in *Asunción*, one of the medium-sized Guarnizo galleon Armada survivors in the Castile squadron, who drove his ship between the bows of the interlocked *Revenge* and *San Bernabé*. His boarders, too, were thrown back with heavy losses.

The last captain to join the night battle was Luis Coutinho, commander of the fly-boat squadron, in his carrack *La Serena*. Her tonnage is not recorded but he must have reasoned that boarding was what carracks were designed for and charged in with more enthusiasm than skill, holing *Asunción* in the process before settling on the other side of *Revenge*'s bow. This was not a good place to be either. *Revenge* had at least two demi-cannon and two cannon perier mounted in her bow and the broadside culverins nearest the bow could also be swung to fire forward. Hulled repeatedly, *Asunción* sank where she lay, and although *La Serena* disengaged, her crew could not save her either, and she sank next day.

As dawn broke, after fourteen hours of battle with all his masts down and only 80 of 250 men still on their feet, most of them wounded, the dying Grenville ordered the magazines fired to blow up *Revenge* and *San Bernabé*. The dwindling band of survivors prevented the mortally wounded master gunner from reaching the powder store and sent a boat to seek honourable terms from Alonso de Bazán. They were freely granted, to the relief of Bertendona, who did not doubt that the Englishmen would otherwise have complied with Grenville's order.

Sir Richard was taken aboard *San Pablo*, where he died two days later. There are two different accounts of his dying words. One has him cursing the 'traitors and dogs' who had disobeyed him, which is in character. But perhaps we should charitably accept Bertendona's version, which has him saying, 'as I know all that remains is a living death, it will be better to die'.

After the battle, Bazán's fleet was joined by the remains of the combined 1589–90 *flotas* that had been pounded by bad weather during the Atlantic crossing, losing 17 of the 78 ships that had left Havana. The two fleets set out together from Flores to Terceira on 15 September, in perfect weather. At about the midpoint of the crossing they were hit by a sudden and violent storm. Seven more ships were lost including two from the Ocean Fleet, both 1588 survivors: the galleon *Nuestra Señora de la Begonia*, and the carrack *Magdalena*. And the *Revenge* – repaired, re-rigged and lightened by the removal of some of her hugely admired suite of bronze guns – was smashed to pieces on the north-west coast of Terceira.

The failure of Lord Thomas Howard's campaign discredited the blockade strategy advocated by Sir John Hawkins. It can be argued that Elizabeth failed to give it a proper trial, but the narrow escape from disaster at Flores was the last nail. She also had to deal with the wolves nearest her sled following heavy defeats at Craon and Rouen in April and May 1592. The threat posed by the Spanish military and naval presence in Brittany had priority and after Craon she sent Sir John Norreys with 4,000 more troops to the theatre. Over the next 18 months disease and desertion whittled Sir John's command down to about 1,500 men at Paimpol on the north coast of Brittany, facing the Channel Islands, although he continued to claim expenses for 4,000.[*]

Fortunately for Elizabeth 1592 proved to be the high water mark of Spain's recovery and England's strategic outlook rapidly improved thereafter. Parma died in December 1592, aged 47, shortly before he was to be recalled to Spain for failing to achieve the impossible, which his enemies persuaded Philip II was proof of treachery. He was succeeded by 75-year-old Peter Ernst von Mansfeld-Vorderort, and then in 1594 by Philip's 41-year-old nephew Archduke Ernest of Austria, who died in February 1595 before he could get a grip on the situation. The Allied army exploited the lacuna in Spanish command to take Groningen in the north-east

[*] The 1592 Alderney wreck discovered in 1977 (http://www.alderneywreck.com) was carrying arms for Norreys.

and to secure the Dutch Republic's southern flank by gaining control of both banks of the strategically crucial Maas River.

The collapse of Philip II's grand design came about when Henri of Navarre converted to Catholicism in July 1593 and was crowned King Henri IV at Chartres in February 1594. As a result the Catholic League had crumbled even before Pope Clement VIII declared him free from excommunication in September 1595. Apart from the Duke of Mercoeur, determined to make himself prince of an independent Brittany (invoking the rights of his wife, who was a descendant of the historic dukes) with Spanish support, France was united for the first time since 1560.

Although French unity was directed against Spain in the first instance, formally allied with the English and the Dutch, the end of the civil wars that had kept England's traditional enemy weak was not greeted with unalloyed joy in London. Also, Henri IV gave Brittany a low priority (he did not subdue Mercoeur until 1598, shortly before making peace with Spain), forcing the English to take the initiative in dealing with the Spanish presence. Matters were brought to a head when Juan del Águila built the fortress of El León on the Crozon peninsula, 65 miles/105 kilometres north-west of Port-Blavet and commanding the mouth of the great Brest roadstead.

The prospect of a secure Spanish base in France's finest Atlantic port caused the immediate transfer of Sir Thomas Baskerville and 1,000 troops from the Netherlands to join Norreys's men at Paimpol. Meanwhile Norreys had returned to London to beg for more resources and was granted 3–4,000 reinforcements and the royal siege train. Burghley's man Sir Martin Frobisher was appointed naval commander. In August 1594 he sailed in command of the shallow-draft royal galleons *Vanguard* and *Rainbow*, the handy 200-ton *Crane* and the pinnace *Moon*. As he had shown during the Armada campaign, Frobisher was without peer among the Elizabethan naval commanders when given a defined military mission to accomplish.

After delivering Norreys to Paimpol, Frobisher's instruction were to assist Henri IV's local commander Marshal Jean d'Aumont

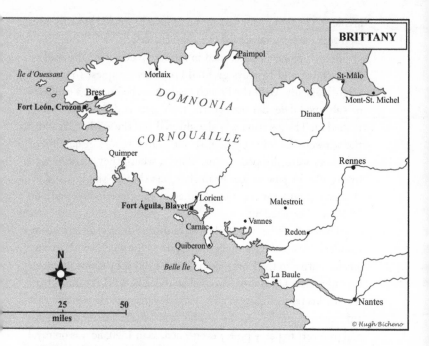

and Baskerville to complete the recovery of nearby Morlaix from the Catholic League and finally to assist in the reduction of the El León fortress at Crozon. On his own initiative Frobisher took the siege train to the Bay of Morlaix, but it proved unnecessary after he induced the Leaguer garrison to surrender by sailing close inshore with guns run out.

The 400-man Spanish garrison at El León was not similarly impressed when he arrived at Crozon on 6 September, and Frobisher spent the rest of the month conducting a siege almost single-handed, landing sailors and guns to close the neck of the peninsula while bombarding the fortress from the sea. Dutch warships brought ammunition and supplies but Norreys and Baskerville did not arrive until 1 October, having been obliged to leave the siege train at Morlaix by Aumont's refusal to let non-Catholics into the town. Even after they arrived, the heavy guns made little impression on the thick walls and succeeded only in silencing the Spanish artillery. The first major assault, on 23 October, failed bloodily after a powder explosion disabled the siege battery.

French pioneers succeeded in mining a section of the wall on 7 November and Norreys granted Frobisher's request to lead the English assault. With the French held up at the breach, a confused or suborned defender opened the main gate and Frobisher's men rushed in. The garrison was slaughtered and those who leapt into the sea were drowned by English and Dutch sailors. A handful of survivors were shipped to Port-Blavet, where they were hanged by Águila for cowardice. Frobisher was shot in the hip and although the bullet was cut out he died of gangrene in Plymouth on 22 November, aged 59.

Thus passed the first of the trio of great Elizabethan naval commanders. He owed his eminence entirely to Burghley's wish to have an alternative to the Devon mafia, and repaid it by showing proper subordination. Unrivalled as a combat leader, he was kept from greatness by his poor education and a crudely larcenous disposition that led him to cheat the queen – and his men – in the matter of rations, and to revert to petty piracy even when, as in 1590, he was on royal business. He seems to have worked well with Hawkins, but his last years were embittered by a corrosive envy of Drake, who was so abundantly endowed with the star quality Frobisher sadly lacked.

Even as Frobisher was dying the last significant public–private expedition was about to be authorized under the joint leadership of Hawkins and Drake. Drake, at 54, was a sadder but not noticeably wiser man after the 1589 fiasco. Hawkins, eight years older, was past his best, worn out by the thankless task of increasing the fighting strength of the Royal Navy at far lower cost than Elizabeth had any right to expect. As he wrote in 1590, the worst of it was the ceaseless back-biting by such as the Lord Admiral, who wanted to replace him with someone more accommodating:

> ... *the matters handled by the office* [of Treasurer] *grow infinite and chargeable beyond all measure and such that hardly any man can make sense of the innumerable businesses that daily grow; yet*

*the mistrust is more troublesome and grievous than all the rest, for
in the answering of the one and the toil of the other there is
hardly any time left to serve God or to satisfy man. The higher
officials who serve in this office have grown so proud, obstinate
and insolent that nothing can please them, and the lesser very
disobedient, such that a man might prefer to die than to live under
the obligation of answering all of their immoderate demands.*

The project was a revival of Drake's old ambition to seize Panamá
and hold it, cutting off the flow of bullion that underpinned Philip
II's ability to finance his wars. It was a nostalgic pipe dream. Leaving
aside the attrition by disease that decimated the expedition, if
Panamá had been taken the Viceroy would have sent every ship and
soldier in Perú to recover it. On its way back to England the expedition was attacked off the Isle of Pines by a fleet of 8 galleons and
13 armed merchant ships under Bernardino de Avellaneda. While
the engagement simply confirmed that the English ships outgunned and out-sailed the Spanish, if the expedition had still been
anchored off Nombre de Dios, as it would have been if Panamá had
been captured, the fleet might have escaped but Sir Thomas
Baskerville's land force would have been lost.

There were unconscionable delays in getting under way, during
which time the Spanish received accurate information on its objectives thanks to the indiscretion of Sir Walter Ralegh, who spoke far
too freely with a captured Spanish officer during his own 1595 expedition to Guiana. Elizabeth was minded to cancel the expedition
but was persuaded to permit it to sail by news that the flagship of
one of the returning 1595 *flotas*, yet another *Nuestra Señora de la Begonia*, had been storm-damaged beyond hope of local repair and
forced to take refuge in San Juan de Puerto Rico with a reported
two and a half million pesos of bullion on board.

No shipments had reached Spain in 1594 and *Begonia*'s cargo
represented not much less than half of what proved to be a bumper
year for the Spanish exchequer. Such a prize alone justified the venture, but while granting permission for the fleet to sail the queen

also insisted that it must return within six months, a clear signal that she did not countenance any long-term plan for Panamá.

Drake sailed in *Due Defiance* (550 tons burden) and Hawkins in *Garland* (532), royal galleons built under Hawkins's modernizing programme in 1590, along with the brand new *Adventure* (275), the hardy perennials *Elizabeth Bonaventure*, *Foresight* and the unreconstructed 1559 carrack *Hope*. The private contingent included a high proportion of newly built large armed merchantmen: *Concord* (330), *Salomon*, *Saker* and *Desire* (all 246 tons burden and built in 1594), *Amity* (200), *John Bonaventure* (200) and *Elizabeth* (194). There were 13 more private ships, ranging from the 1588 supply ship *John Trelawney* (150) down to two small Ramsgate ketches hired for inshore work. The fleet also carried more than two-dozen disassembled pinnaces for the same purpose.

They were supposed to sail straight to Puerto Rico and had they done so they might have achieved their first objective. However, Drake insisted on making an unplanned and completely un-

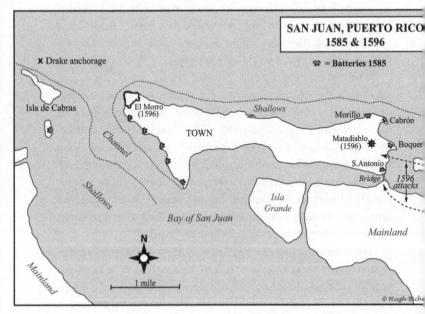

successful amphibious assault on Gran Canaria, and Hawkins caused a further delay at Guadalupe after crossing the Atlantic to 'trim his ships, mount his ordnance, take in water, set up some new pinnaces and make things in that readiness that he cared not to meet with the King's whole fleet'. Stores from the sluggish hired supply ship *Richard* were distributed and she was burned.

By now Hawkins was very ill and he died as the fleet arrived off San Juan, deeply embittered by the constant disputes with his kinsman Drake that had divided the fleet into rancorous factions. One of his partisans, *Elizabeth Bonaventure*'s Captain John Troughton, sent a highly revealing letter to the queen as soon as he got back to England, purporting to report Sir John's dying words:

> *Forasmuch as through the perverse and cross dealings of some in that journey, who preferring their own fancy before his skill would never yield but rather overrule him, whereby he was so discouraged, and as he himself then said his heart even broken, that he saw no other but danger of ruin likely to ensue of the whole voyage, wherein is some sort he had been a persuader of your Majesty to hazard as well some of your good ships as also a good quantity of treasure, in regard of the good opinion he thought to be held of his sufficiency, judgement and experience in such actions; willing to make your Majesty the best amends of his poor ability would then stretch to, in a codicil as a piece of his last will and testament did bequeath to you Highness two thousand pounds if your Majesty will take it, for that as he said your Highness had in your possession a far greater sum of his which he then did also release.*

Evidently Hawkins foresaw some drastic action against his estate by the queen, which suggests a guilty conscience. With reason, according to Thomas Maynarde, a member of Drake's entourage on *Due Defiance* and author of the clearest-eyed narrative of the voyage, who judged that although the characters of the two expedition leaders were completely incompatible, yet:

Agreeing best (for what I could conjecture) in giving out a
glorious title to their intended voyage, and in not so well
victualling the navy as (I deem) was her Majesty's pleasure it
should be, both of them served to good purpose, for from having
the distributing of so great sums their miserable providing for us
would free them from incurring any great loss whatsoever befell
the journey.

The delays granted just enough time for a squadron of 5 *galizabras*,
which left Spain on 25 September under Pedro Tello, to reach San
Juan before the English fleet and retrieve the bullion on *Begonia*.
On the way, off Guadalupe, they captured and sank the 35-ton pinnace *Francis*, which had become detached from the main fleet. From
the surviving crew Tello learned all the details of the English fleet
save one: if they knew, they did not tell him that the ultimate objective was Panamá. With the identity of ships sighted coasting
Guadalupe confirmed, Tello raced to San Juan, where he arrived
on 13 November. His ships were to play a decisive part in the
events that followed.

The narrow entrance to San Juan harbour was covered by 44
guns in shore batteries as well as the heavy bow guns of Tello's *galizabras*, moored across the channel. As Cumberland was to prove in
1598 the western end of San Juan island was weakly defended, but
when the small batteries at El Morrillo and El Cabrón opened fire
on *Due Defiance*, one 'great shot' destroyed the stool on which Drake
was sitting and mortally wounded Sir Nicholas Clifford, second in
command of the land force, and another of the land captains, who
were dining with him.

The fleet sailed back to the main entrance and anchored out
of range at the Isla de Cabras, from which it launched a night attack on 23 November in pinnaces, each holding 50–60 men. Their
orders were to destroy the *galizabras*, but after they succeeded in
setting one alight the illumination made them easy targets for the
shore batteries. Eight or nine boats were sunk and 200 men killed
and wounded.

Departing San Juan, Drake sailed south to the mainland, burning the empty supply ship *John Trelawney* before he left and scuttling William Wynter's shot-damaged 140-ton galleon *Exchange* in the Mona Passage. The three weeks he spent at Rio de La Hacha gave time for Alonso de Sotomayor, a soldier of great experience sent by the Viceroy of Perú, to impose himself on the squabbling Panamanians and to order fieldworks built at some narrows on the Chagre River and on the Camino Real in the Capirilla ravine, both well inland.

To suggest that Drake was idly looting, as many have done at the time and since, is to overlook his *modus operandi* of drawing enemy attention away from his intended target by striking elsewhere. As it was, his sojourn on the coast of Colombia drew the large oceanic fleet sent from Spain under Avellaneda, who sailed to Cartagena after deciding that the (in fact accurate) intelligence he had received of Drake's intention to attack Panamá was disinformation.

The old fox had not lost his cunning, but sadly he had lost his mojo. With the stragglers eliminated and a following wind, the fleet sailed rapidly to Nombre de Dios, only to find that it had been evacuated and all things of value removed. Baskerville disembarked his men, perhaps 600 of the 900-odd he set out with, and made a forced march along the Camino Real until he reached Capirilla Pass on New Year's Day (old style – 9 January Gregorian)*. Despite furious attacks the English could not break through the log barrier, although the Spanish admitted that on several occasions reinforcements arrived just in time. After losing 60–70 men killed and 18 wounded, among them several officers including his brother Nicholas, Baskerville retreated and sent a desperate note to Drake begging for 100–200 men with supplies to meet his starving troops on the way back.

It had been Drake's intention to send reinforcements and supplies with his pinnaces up the Chagre once Baskerville sent word

* See Map, page 114.

that he had crossed the mountains. Now, with his hopes dashed, he still sailed to the mouth of the Chagre and then, aimlessly, back to the harbour at Porto Bello. There, early on 28 January (old style) 1596 he died of cholera, which was sweeping through the fleet. Gian' Baptista Antonelli, a military engineer sent by the king to review the physical defences of the isthmus, reported in May 1596 that its principal defence was how unhealthy it was: 'Of this we have much experience, and lately have observed it upon the arrival of the English this year ... when the principal obstacle they encountered was the evil condition of the country and its waters, which were the reason why the beaches were peopled with dead bodies'.

Although the source (Purchas) is often suspect, a letter he printed from a man identified as 'R M' is generally regarded as an accurate assessment of Drake and Hawkins by a man who had sailed with them both and knew them well:

> They were both of many virtues, and agreeing in some. As patience in enduring labours and hardness, observation and memory of things past, and great discretion in sudden dangers in which neither of them [were] much distempered; and in some other virtues they differed. Sir John Hawkins had in him mercy and aptness to forgive, and true of word; Sir Francis hard in reconciliation and constancy in friendship; he was withall severe and courteous, magnanimous, and liberal [generous]. They were both faulty in ambition, but more the one than the other; for in Sir Francis was an insatiable desire of honour, indeed beyond reason. He was infinite in promises, and more temperate in adversity than in better fortune. He had also other imperfections, as aptness to anger, and bitterness in disgracing, and too much pleased with open flattery. Sir John Hawkins had in him malice with dissimulation, rudeness in behaviour and passing sparing [tight-fisted], indeed miserable. They were both happy alike in being great commanders and grew great and famous by one means, rising through their own virtues and the

fortune of the sea. [But] there was no comparison to be made between their well-deserving and good parts, for therein Sir Francis Drake did far exceed.

CHAPTER 13
REGULAR WARFARE

After Drake died Baskerville assumed command of the expedition and decided to cut his losses. Scuttling two more ships* to distribute their crews among the rest, the disease-ridden fleet sailed back to England, pausing to fight Avellaneda off the Isle of Pines. Avellaneda later captured the fleet's reconnaissance caravel *Help* off the north coast of Cuba, a meagre return for the largest war fleet sent to the Indies during the reign of Philip II. On the other hand the *galizabras* had sailed back with the bullion from *Begonia* as soon as Drake departed San Juan, which was the greater victory for their cash-strapped monarch. It was not enough, however, and in 1596 he had to default on his debts, mainly to Genoese bankers, leading to a drying up of credit for the last two years of his reign.

The factor that precipitated Philip's default was assembling in England even as the ships of the Caribbean expedition limped back. The returning fleet was kept away from Plymouth, where the largest of all the Elizabethan amphibious operations was about to set out under the joint command of Lord Admiral Howard and the manic-depressive Robert Devereux, Earl of Essex, the last and least worthy of Elizabeth's favourites. He stepped into the void in her affections left by the death in September 1588 of his step-father Robert Dudley, Earl of Leicester. The death of Sir Christopher Hatton in 1591 and the disgrace of Sir Walter Ralegh in 1592 (when his secret marriage became known) also cleared Essex's path,

---

* *Elizabeth* and the pinnace *Delight*, whose remains were discovered by marine archaeologists in November 2011.

to the point that for the first time Burghley found himself faced with a rival whose influence over the queen threatened his own.

The infatuation was not limited to the ageing queen. Leicester's last service to Elizabeth had been the carefully choreographed apotheosis ('I know I have but the body of a weak and feeble woman; but I have the heart of a king, and of a king of England, too') at Tilbury during the Armada scare. The aura did not survive her apparent indifference to her people's welfare during the demobilization and the failure of the counter-armada. By the mid-1590s the populace was turning out to cheer Essex as a breath of fresh air. More ominously, he also gained a strong following among professional soldiers exasperated by the queen's chronic dithering and perceived parsimony.

Hindsight supports the charge of indecisiveness, but from Hakluyt to the present day historians have given too much credence to the clamour of Elizabeth's naval and military commanders for more of everything, without regard to her limited means. Yet honest dealing and cost-effectiveness were alien concepts to most royal officers – Christopher Carleill and Sir John Hawkins (in his capacity as Treasurer of the Royal Navy) being among the rare exceptions – and if there's one constant in history it's that military men invariably blame their failures on lack of resources.

Although devastating to Philip II's prestige and precarious finances, the 1596 raid on Cadiz failed to bring home the one thing Elizabeth needed above all: the means to pay for the on-going war, which now extended to a rebellion in Ulster led by Hugh Roe O'Donnell, openly joined in 1595 by his father-in-law Hugh O'Neill, Earl of Tyrone, with stronger Spanish encouragement than practical support. The Cadiz raid was mounted to disrupt the preparations for a new armada, this time aimed at Ireland, but failed to do so because the ships were concentrated in Lisbon and Vigo. However, it did succeed indirectly, because Philip's finances could no longer stretch to opening a new front in the war. New orders were issued to sail instead to reinforce Águila in Brittany, but *Jehovah flavit* with a vengeance and the armada was shattered by a storm off Cape Finisterre in late October.

The 1596 armada was no small undertaking. At Lisbon there were 24 galleons and 53 hired Flemish and German merchant ships carrying nearly 11,000 men, joined by 30 shallow draft *felibotes* with 2,500 men from Seville. A further 41 ships with 6,000 men were assembled at Vigo. The storm sank 14 ships, including 2 pay ships carrying 30,000 ducats. Thirty more were unaccounted.

The Howard/Essex fleet, entirely paid for by the queen, was not much smaller. It consisted of her 13 most powerful galleons in four squadrons led by the Lord Admiral, Essex, Lord Thomas Howard and Sir Walter Ralegh. Distributed among them were a London contingent of 10 armed merchantmen, assorted royal and London pinnaces, and 64 store ships and troop transports carrying 14,000 men. It was joined by a Dutch contingent of three large and 15 smaller warships with six store ships.

Initially hesitant to risk the queen's ships by sailing straight into the bay – as Drake had done in 1587 – the Lord Admiral first tried to land the troops on the western side of the peninsula. As a result he sacrificed the operational surprise he had achieved by a cloud of disinformation indicating that Lisbon was the target (he had only revealed the true objective to his captains once he was at sea). The Spanish were granted time to moor their warships in a line between the Puntal and Matagorda peninsulas, and to move the merchant ships of the outgoing Indies *flota* to the inner harbour.

The battle line included four of the Apostles, two large Portuguese galleons, three medium-sized galleons from the *flota* escort, three of the *galizabras* that had brought back the bullion from San Juan, and two large and heavily armed Ragusan carracks. Eighteen galleys were moored off the city with their heavy bow armament ready to hit the attackers in the flank.

The English should not have been able to break through such a line, but the crews of the Spanish warships were not the men of 1588. They let go their anchors and the biggest, the Apostles and the Ragusan carracks, promptly ran aground. Ralegh observed 'tumbling into the sea heaps of soldiers so thick as if coals had been poured out of a sack, [from] many ports at once, some drowned, some sticking in the mud'. Some remained long enough to set fire to *San Felipe*, *San Tomás* and one of the Ragusan carracks, but *San Mateo*, *San Andrés* and the other Ragusan were captured intact by English boarding parties.

The way was clear to send the smaller ships into the inner harbour to capture the flota, but instead Essex charged ashore and the Lord Admiral, not greatly against his will, was compelled to support him. Cadiz fell surprisingly easily and the entire expedition devoted itself to looting the city. While they were thus occupied, the Duke of Medina Sidonia arrived and ordered the 42 large and uncounted smaller ships in the inner harbour burned. The loss was estimated at 12 million ducats, while Howard and Essex were demanding one percent (120,000 ducats) of that as a ransom for the hostages they had taken. When this was not forthcoming they set fire to the city and sailed away with the hostages.

Furthermore, with their auxiliaries (and not a few of the royal ships) anxious to get home with their loot, they made no effort to comply with the second part of their commission, which was to intercept the Portuguese East Indies carracks or the incoming Spanish *flota* that were due to arrive at the Azores. Instead of being rewarded with enough money to keep the war going indefinitely, the queen was reduced to trying to wring her share from the participants, from whom her commissioners managed to extract a mere £8,359 against her outlay of £50,000.

It almost defies belief that the queen was persuaded to give Essex another naval command, but to some extent circumstances forced her hand. In the investigation that followed the Cadiz raid it became clear that Essex, Ralegh and Lord Thomas Howard had consistently voted in favour of the more aggressive course of action in all the councils of war summoned by the Lord Admiral, and 1597 brought credible intelligence that the Spanish were assembling yet another armada at the arsenal port of Ferrol, located a few miles north-east of Coruña across a broad bay. (See Map, page 267.)

The entrance to the Ferrol estuary was through a narrow, twisting channel commanded by forts on either side, and whatever wind permitted a fleet to enter the harbour would keep it there. Even more than at Santander, the neutralization of the land defences was an absolute prerequisite for any naval attack on the port. Yet the original English plan provided only 5,000 troops, of which 1,000 were experienced soldiers drawn from the Netherlands and the rest untrained levies.

Even if supplied with siege artillery, which they were not, and if there had been a suitable place to land, which there was not, it would have required a landing force considerably larger even than the one sent to Cadiz in 1596 to take the forts and to hold both sides of the mouth of the Ferrol estuary against Spanish counter-attacks. The whole plan was based on a contemptuous under-estimation of the enemy, and magical thinking with regard to the wind and weather conditions required for the operation to have any chance at all of success.

Adverse winds delayed the departure of the expedition, and after it sortied on 10 July a violent storm drove much of it back to Plymouth with masts sprung and yards broken. It became apparent that standards in the royal shipyards had slipped since the death of Sir John Hawkins when ship after ship, including the brand new *Warspite* and Essex's flagship *Merhonour*, developed serious leaks. As the end of the campaigning season drew nearer, the operation was scaled back to the bare core, a charge into the harbour led by the two huge captured Apostles, now known as *Saint Andrew* and *Saint Matthew*, counting on confusion among the gunners in the forts. They were to be followed by a flock of smaller vessels, some of which were to be expended as fireships while the rest would bring off the crews of the Apostles, which would also be burned.

When the expedition sailed again on 17 August, now with only a reduced number of the Netherlands veterans embarked, bad weather disabled the two Apostles and opened a dangerous leak on the newly built *Due Repulse*, Essex's replacement flagship. His orders were to destroy the armada and only then to seek to pay for the expedition by trying to intercept the Indies fleets. The queen could not have been more categorical that under no circumstances should Essex leave the Channel unguarded if he could not first destroy the ships assembled in Ferrol.

So that is just what he did. The loss of the Apostles alone doomed the planned attack, and steady easterly winds – ideal for a Spanish sortie – made a blockade impractical. Instead of returning to England, Essex sailed to the Azores on the basis of the flimsiest intelligence. After dashing off madly in all directions and failing to achieve anything significant he finally set sail for England, came close to running the fleet onto the Isles of Scilly,* and finally reached Plymouth on 26 October.

It would be a considerable understatement to say that he met with a frosty reception. In his absence the largest armada since 1588 – 136 ships, 60 of them warships – had sortied from Ferrol on 9 October towing 20 purpose-built landing craft with which to put ashore a well-equipped army of 8,600 troops. Their objective was to seize the great harbour at Falmouth, where the troopships would remain while the warships sailed offshore to intercept Essex's fleet returning from the Azores. It was a realistic plan and required only for the Spanish to enjoy some long overdue good luck.

It was not forthcoming and the armada was hit by a storm out of the north when almost in sight of Falmouth. Although not as severe as in 1596, losses were disabling (all the landing craft were lost) and the ailing king had neither the will nor the means to try again. Queen Elizabeth had nothing to complain about God's partiality, but she sensibly judged it best not to presume on divine providence any further and turned against any further grand expeditions to concentrate on matters nearer to hand.

A month before his death on 4 August 1598, Lord Burghley had the satisfaction of seeing the queen box Essex's ears after one too many insolences. Shortly before his death on 13 September, Philip II had the slight consolation of learning that Tyrone and O'Donnell

* Exactly 110 years later, during the night of 22–23 October 1707, Admiral Sir Cloudesley Shovell and nearly 2,000 sailors died when HMS *Association*, *Eagle*, *Romney*, and *Firebrand* were wrecked by night on the Isles of Scilly.

had inflicted a stinging defeat on the English at Yellow Ford a month earlier. The outcome of these events was that the queen granted Essex one more opportunity to redeem himself, in Ireland in 1599. As Tacitus once wrote of the Emperor Galba, so Wernham sums up the chasm between theory and practice in Essex's military career: had he not held high command, everyone would have thought him well qualified for it.

After his failure in Ireland (reaching a truce with Tyrone rather than defeating him) and subsequent house arrest, there was no-one left at court to balance the influence of Burghley's son Robert Cecil, Secretary of State since the death of Walsingham in 1590, who in alliance with Lord Admiral Howard dominated the Privy Council to a degree his father had never achieved. There remained only the tragi-comedy of Essex's attempted *coup d'état* and execution in early 1601. The queen had successfully balanced factions throughout her long reign, but she was approaching 70 and in her last bravura speech to Parliament in 1601 spoke frankly: 'To be a king and wear a crown is a thing more glorious to them that see it than it is pleasant to them that bear it'.

In Spain, Philip III came to the throne determined to succeed where his father had failed. Elizabeth wanted peace but did not feel she could leave the Dutch unsupported, although she obtained a commitment that they should pay for the English forces still fighting alongside them and also begin to repay the large sums she had lent them over the preceding 13 years. They could afford to do so because throughout the war they had continued to trade very profitably with Spain.

Nobody ever accused the Spanish Hapsburgs of learning from their mistakes, thus one of Philip III's first acts was to order all Dutch ships in Spanish ports seized and to ban trade between Spain and the Dutch Republic, a ban extended to trade with the Spanish Netherlands in January 1599. The Dutch responded with a ban of their own and, confident that they could succeed where the English had failed, sent a large fleet to raid both the Spanish ports and the Atlantic islands.

It was a complete fiasco but it did help England indirectly. Philip III had prepared an armada against England in 1599, which caused Elizabeth to order a full mobilization of the Royal Navy, but the Spanish fleet was sent instead to deal with the Dutch threat to the Atlantic islands. Oppressed by the heavy cost of maintaining 17,000 troops in Ireland, Elizabeth ordered the demobilization of the fleet as soon as she learned of this. But with attention fixed on the armada that never came, the Narrow Seas squadron left its station off Calais and failed to prevent six Spanish galleys from Santander and their attendant *fragatas* under 28 year-old Federico Spinola from running the Channel gauntlet past Dunkirk to Sluys, the Spanish-held port across the main channel of the Scheldt estuary from the English cautionary port of Flushing.*

Federico was the younger brother of Ambrogio, who was to keep the Spanish cause in the Netherlands alive from 1602 to 1625. After the Dorias, the Spinolas were the second most powerful of the Genoese banking clans that provided the backbone of the Hapsburg Mediterranean galley fleet. They were also owed so much money by the Spanish crown, and had such extensive land holdings in Spanish Lombardy, Sicily and Spain itself, that their interests were inseparable.

Galleys had a wretched record in combat with galleons. In April 1590 a flotilla of Levant Company ships, including Alderman Boreman's *Salomon*, John Watt's *Margaret and John* and Thomas Cordell's *Centurion*, all 1588 Armada veterans, beat off 12 large galleys under the command of Gian'Andrea Doria himself in the Straits of Gibraltar. *Margaret and John* had previously taken part in the July 1586 battle described in Chapter 10. In April 1591, again off Gibraltar, *Centurion* alone defeated five galleys even though they managed to grapple with her and board.

Federico, who had served in the Netherlands for many years under Farnese, was convinced that galleys would be able to regain control of the Flanders coast from Justin of Nassau's cromsters, and

---

* The *fragatas* were not generic 'fast ships' but a specific type of small galley. See Appendix B.

had been petitioning Madrid since 1593 to be permitted to prove his theory. When Philip III became king he gave his assent to a complicated deal involving the Spinolas lending him 100,000 ducats interest free for a year, in return for which the king undertook to provide six galleys and a *tercio* of troops to man them, and to maintain the flotilla to the tune of 81,000 ducats every six months.

Upon the death of Philip II the Spanish Netherlands became a semi-autonomous principality under Cardinal Archduke Albert of Austria, previously the governor-general after the death of his older brother in 1595. Permitted to renounce the purple by Pope Clement VIII, he married Philip III's sister in April 1599. Archduke Albert was a party to the agreement between the Spinolas and Philip III and undertook to provide quarters for Federico's troops, also heavy guns and ammunition for the galleys. The aim was to regain the military initiative in the Netherlands and to force the Dutch and English to negotiate from a position of weakness.

Although Federico Spinola's ambitions extended to seizing a beach-head in England, his first priority was to support Archduke's Albert's renewed offensive against the Dutch enclave around Ostend. In combination with the Dunkirk *felibotes*, and joined by two galleys built there by shipwrights sent from Genoa by his older brother, Federico did such damage to coastal traffic in 1599–1600 that Elizabeth ordered the construction of four 100-ton galleys (all given Anglo-Italian names – *Advantagia*, *Superlativa*, *Gallarita* and *Volatillia*) and even the Dutch, who had never before employed galleys, built three, including the 200-ton *Black Galley of Zeeland*.

Spinola's activities suffered from lack of support from Archduke Albert, who suffered a humiliating defeat after trapping the hypercautious Maurice of Nassau at Nieuport in early July 1600. Further negotiations with Philip III in 1601 saw a revival of the English beach-head project with the promise of eight fully manned galleys to come from Genoa, supported on land by Ambrogio Spinola who would raise 6,000 troops in Italy at his own expense and march them to the Netherlands, where he would take over the active conduct of the war.

Before that, in September 1601, the Spanish at last struck at what had always been England's Achilles' heel in Ireland. Juan del Águila landed with 3,000 troops at Kinsale and a smaller force under Alonso de Ocampo landed at Baltimore. They were about as far away as it was possible to get from rebel-held territory in the north and the idea seems to have been to turn the two ports, already notorious havens for pirates with no regard for English authority, into corsair ports preying on Dutch and English shipping, following the successful example of the *felibotes* operating out of Dunkirk.

Águila was promptly cut off by sea while Sir George Carew, Lord President of Munster, besieged Kinsale by land. When Tyrone and O'Donnell marched south their forces, joined by Ocampo, were defeated outside Kinsale on Christmas Eve by Charles Blount, Baron Mountjoy, Essex's competent successor as Lord Deputy of Ireland. Mountjoy had already torn the heart out of the rebellion with an amphibious landing in the north and a scorched earth campaign on Tyrone's lands.

The suppression of the rebellion was possible only because the Royal Navy established control of the waters around Ireland for the first time. The naval commander was Sir Richard Leveson, one of a new generation of naval commanders in their early 30s who also included Sir William Monson, author of the multi-volume and occasionally accurate *Tracts* that gave historian Michael Oppenheim the hook on which to hang the first detailed history of the 1585–1604 war.

Leveson and Monson came the closest of all Elizabeth's admirals to capturing a silver *flota* off the Azores during the last fund-raising cruise of her reign, in the summer of 1602. It was supposed to be a combined operation with the Dutch but they were late to the rendezvous in Plymouth. Leveson sailed on ahead with five Royal Navy ships while Monson remained behind with four to wait for the Dutch. Within a few days Monson received an order from the queen to sail immediately, as word had reached London that the *flota* had reached the Azores.

It had, and sailed on to Lisbon past Leveson, who attacked one of them unsuccessfully. Monson, delayed by malfunctions on his ships, arrived just too late. They found a consolation prize at the Portuguese port of Sesimbra, south of Lisbon, where on 12 June they fought off eleven galleys to capture the large carrack *São Valentinho*. Her cargo was sold for £44,000, which barely covered the queen's costs, rapidly rising amid the wholesale corruption and shoddy workmanship presided over by Lord Admiral Howard. 'If the queen's ships had been fitted out with care', Monson wrote, 'we had made her majesty mistress of more treasure than any of her progenitors ever enjoyed'.

Three of the galleys at Sesimbra had come from Lisbon under the command of Alonso de Bazán, but the other eight were Spinola's Genoese galleys, which Federico had only just joined in Lisbon to lead on the last part of their voyage to the Netherlands. The galleys had massive 60-pounder cannon in their bows and formed a tight defensive screen in the shallows around *São Valentinho*.

Monson, who had spent a year as a slave on one Bazán's galleys, anchored outside their effective range and bombarded them with the 16 culverins on *Garland* to force them to break formation. When Bazán's galleys did, the shallow draft *Dreadnought* (360 tons to *Garland*'s 532) sailed into the gap and took them on at close range with her 11 demiculverins and 10 sakers. After Bazán was badly wounded his battered galleys rowed away, but Spinola stayed and fought until he had lost two and the rest were in imminent danger of sharing their fate.

Spinola took his six remaining galleys back to Lisbon and with royal consent took oars and rowers from Bazán's galleys. On 9 August the galleys departed, carrying 36 pay chests for the army in Flanders. At Santander he took on a further 400 troops to complete an on-board *tercio* of 1,600 men and reached Port-Blavet in Brittany by mid-September. This time there was no armada to distract attention: the English and Dutch were well informed of his movements and they were ready for him.

Off Dungeness during the night of 3–4 October Spinola ran into the 400-ton *Hope*, launched in 1559 and along with *Victory* the

last unreconstructed carrack in the Royal Navy.* She was the flagship of 29-year-old Sir Robert Mansell, one of the Lord Admiral's
placemen of whom Julian Corbett wrote the damning verdict that
'it is the rise of this man that marks the commencement of a reign
of selfishness and corruption that almost brought the navy to ruin
in the next reign'. Mansell had little naval experience but his excellent flag captain anticipated that Spinola would try to repeat his
1599 tactic of sailing close to the English coast. The carrack savaged
San Felipe before the other five galleys came up in support, and followed them until they rowed over the Goodwin Sands.

When they made a break for the Flemish coast the Dutch inshore squadron was waiting for them and sank *San Felipe* and *Lucera*
by ramming. *Padilla* escaped to Calais, where the French interned
her and used her as firewood. *San Juan* and *Jacinto* made it inside
the Flanders Bank but were too badly damaged and their rowers too
exhausted to do more than run aground near Nieuport. Only Spinola on *San Luis*, carrying the 36 pay chests, managed to row to safety
in Dunkirk.

Queen Elizabeth died on 24 March 1603 and Federico Spinola
survived her by barely two months. Having brought his Sluys
squadron back up to its eight-galley strength, he sortied on 26 May
to attack three Dutch oared ships, including *Black Galley*, which
were accompanied by the 34-gun cromster *Gouden Leeuw* (Golden
Lion). Spinola, standing on the forecastle as his galley led the
charge against *Black Galley*, had an arm shot off and was hit in the
stomach by swivel guns, after which his men lost heart and rowed
back to Sluys.

Sir Walter Ralegh and George Clifford, Earl of Cumberland,
spanned the gap between the wholly royal and wholly private naval
expeditions during the latter years of Elizabeth's reign. As such
they represent the (not very close) English equivalent to the Spinolas as men so indebted or devoted to their monarch that they spent
their own fortunes in her service. Ralegh was a parvenu whose for-

---

* *Hope* was rebuilt in 1603 but Hawkins's old flagship *Victory* was broken up in 1606.

tune came entirely from the favour Elizabeth had shown him. The Barons de Clifford were an old established northern borderer dynasty, but the earldom of Cumberland was created for Clifford's grandfather by Henry VIII as a reward for the family's dog-like loyalty to the Tudors.

Posterity exalted Ralegh, mainly because, thanks to his Roanoke venture, he was seen as the prophet of the British Empire, but also because his five-volume *History of the World*, written when imprisoned in the Tower under sentence of death, was an intellectual *tour de force* that put him on a par with Sir Francis Bacon as the most influential English author of the 17th century. I cannot improve on the conclusion of his *Dictionary of National Biography* entry:

> *Those who came after him, who never met him, have instinctively liked Ralegh, or their version of Ralegh. He was certainly a most astonishing and compelling man, in his writings as in the rest of his life touched by genius and greatness, the focus of legend. It should not be forgotten, however, that many of those who lived in the same small world of the Elizabethan court, after long association with Ralegh, either disliked him intensely or distrusted him profoundly.*

Cumberland's loyalty was sparingly rewarded and mercilessly exploited by Elizabeth. He began to lose his hair early and was not particularly good-looking, but the biggest obstacle between him and the royal favour that cascaded on prettier men may have been that he was too awkward to indulge convincingly in the artifices of courtly love. He was also an inveterate gambler, and although granted the ceremonial role of Queen's Champion in 1590, Elizabeth never gave him a military command or admitted him to the Privy Council. His best-known portrait, a 1590 miniature by Nicholas Hilliard, shows a man dressed in extravagant jousting armour with the queen's jewelled glove pinned to a feathered hat that makes the whole ensemble seem rather ridiculous.

Both men were among the foremost promoters of the corsair war, but neither was solely motivated by the prospect – in Cumberland's case the urgent need – of profit. We have seen Ralegh's attempt to set up an operational base in Virginia from which to interdict the Spanish *flotas*, and Cumberland adjusted his ventures to supplement the Royal Navy's attempt to blockade the Spanish coast, thereby saving Lord Thomas Howard from disaster at Flores in 1591. Of course both hoped for wealth as well as glory, but they would probably have achieved more of the former if they had not also wished to perform some outstanding service in the hope of tangible recognition by the queen.

Both of them built giant galleons that could not possibly pay their way simply as corsairs and must have been intended to supplement the Royal Navy. Ralegh, as we have seen, was relieved of the expense of his *Ark*, which became Lord Admiral Howard's flagship. In 1595 Cumberland built an even bigger (600 tons burden) ship named *Malice Scourge* at the queen's suggestion. In it he led, brilliantly, the largest entirely private military-strategic operation of Elizabeth's reign to take San Juan, Puerto Rico, three years after Drake had failed to do so during his last voyage.

It did nothing to change Elizabeth's opinion of him and after 1598 he was compelled to sell off his fleet. *Malice Scourge*, renamed *Red Dragon*, became the flagship of the new East India Company in 1600. Rather pathetically Cumberland tried to console himself with the thought that 'I have done unto her Majesty an excellent service and discharged that duty which I owe to my country so far as that, whensoever God shall call me out of this wretched world, I shall die with assurance I have discharged a good part I was born for'.

He spent less time at court, curtailed his gambling and devoted his last years to salvaging some of the lands he regretted having 'cast into the sea'. He also made himself useful to James VI of Scotland and, despite having been among those who condemned James's mother to death, was finally made a privy councillor when the king became James I of England. Cumberland died in 1605.

Ralegh's meteoric career stalled after he got with child and secretly married Bess Throckmorton, one of Elizabeth's ladies in waiting. When the truth emerged in April 1592, after the birth of the child, the queen was incandescent. Husband and wife were put under separate house arrests, but after Ralegh grossly misjudged the situation and indulged in some insultingly theatrical expressions of contrition the queen had them both consigned to the Tower. He was let out a month later to salvage what he could of the queen's share of the richest single prize taken during her reign.

This was the great Portuguese East Indies carrack *Madre de Deus*. According to the results of an 'exquisite survey' given in Hakluyt, she was about 1,450 tons burden and in excess of 2,000 tons fully laden.* The model in the Lisbon Museu de Marinha confirms she had a two-storey forecastle and a staggered three-storey sterncastle. With 32 guns, 10 of them sakers or larger firing through main deck gunports, and a complement of 600–700 men, she was a formidable challenge.

How *Madre de Deus* was taken and what followed provides a suitable microcosm through which to explain the corrosive failure of public–private ventures in the English *guerre de course*. Three groups met by chance off Flores in the Azores. With the scandal of his secret marriage hanging over his head, Ralegh made a desperate effort to put together an expedition involving the ever-popular queen's ship *Foresight* (295) under Robert Crosse. The private component was Ralegh's own *Roebuck* (240) under Sir John Burgh, John Hawkins's *Dainty* (200) under Thomas Thompson, *Bark Bond* (56) sent by John Bond and partners of Weymouth under Nicholas Ayers (the previous *Bark Bond* had been used as a fireship in 1588), and a number of pinnaces and frigates.

Ralegh tried to get away on 6 May but, blown back, he was superseded a week later at the queen's command by Sir Martin

---

* Keel length of 100 feet × beam at broadest point of 46 feet 10 inches × hold depth from that point of 31 feet ÷ 100. The bulk cargo of pepper, spices, cochineal and ebony was *alone* estimated at 553 tons. Plus there were countless rolls of high-quality cloth and carpets, boxes of fine porcelain and chests of ambergris, jewels, pearls, and gold and silver coins.

Model of the *Madre de Deus* in the Lisbon Museu de Marinha.

Frobisher in *Garland* (532) and recalled to London. Frobisher may have been accompanied by some unnamed ships grudgingly sent by London merchants in response to the conditional release by the queen of £6,000 on the money due to them for prizes taken by the London squadron in 1591. This was something new: the queen was not only retaining the proceeds of her subjects' ventures as a forced interest-free loan, but was also using it to tell them what to do.

The objective was to intercept five East Indies carracks expected at the Azores in July. Ralegh intended to lead the whole flotilla to the Azores, but Frobisher brought with him instructions for the main component to sail with him to Cape St Vincent while a smaller group under Burgh patrolled the Azores. Frobisher was not one to question orders, but Crosse on *Foresight* and Thompson on *Dainty* knew it was folly to divide the command and slipped away to join Burgh's *Roebuck*.

Cumberland's ships made up the second component, led by John Norton in *Tiger* (170), followed by Abraham Cocke in *Sampson* (260), *Phoenix* (60), the frigate *Discovery* (12) and two other small ships, *Grace of Dover* and *Bark of Barnstaple*. *Gold Noble* (200), owned by the London merchants John Bird and John Newton, was supposed to sail with them but became separated and sailed instead to the coast of Portugal, where it took a 900-ton (presumably 'tons and tonnage') prize.

The third component was two ships returning from an already highly successful West Indies voyage, in which they raided San José de Ocoa and captured Yaguana on Hispaniola, and then cut a prize out from under the guns of the fort at Trujillo and captured Puerto Caballos in Honduras. The syndicate that sent the expedition was headed by John More and included John Newton (again), Robert Cobb and Henry Cletherow, all of London. It was led by Christopher Newport in *Golden Dragon* (130) followed by Hugh Merrick in *Prudence* (70). *Golden Dragon* carried two demi-culverins, six sakers, seven minions and four falcons. She had a crew of 70–80 men with 31 muskets and three arquebuses.

Burgh arrived at Flores on 21 June to learn that he had missed the first of the East Indies carracks, which also slipped past Frobisher during the night of 7–8 July. Immediately afterwards Burgh sighted *Santa Cruz*, pursued by Cumberland's ships. In a dead calm he rowed to examine the carrack, intending to board her next day, but during the night a storm came up and she ran herself aground, where her crew were seen frenziedly unloading the carrack before setting her on fire. Burgh and Norton sent a landing party that routed the Portuguese and captured some of the cargo, as well as the ship's purser, who was coerced into admitting that three more carracks were 15 days behind. He did not know that two of them had already wrecked.

When Newport arrived he agreed to 'consortship' with Burgh, but Norton refused to acknowledge that Burgh's commission from the queen had seniority over his own from Cumberland. Despite this, the two agreed to act in concert and stationed their ships in a screen west of Flores, each ship spaced about 6 miles/10 kilometres from the other on a south–north axis. From the southern (windward) flank the sequence was *Dainty*, *Golden Dragon*, *Roebuck*, *Tiger*, *Sampson*, *Prudence* and *Foresight*.

In the morning of 3 August *Dainty* sighted *Madre de Deus* and attacked her at about midday, followed at two-hour intervals by *Golden Dragon* and then *Roebuck*, joined by *Foresight* – which was either out of station or sailed past Cumberland's ships and *Prudence* – at about 7pm. *Dainty* had her foremast shot away and lost contact for five days. Burgh and Crosse, desperate to prevent the carrack running herself aground, crashed *Dainty* and *Foresight* into her, under her main deck guns, and disabled her by cutting the bow rigging.

After that it was a pell-mell night assault with the crews of *Golden Dragon*, *Sampson* and *Tiger* pouring aboard alongside the men of *Foresight* and *Dainty* in a looting frenzy that nearly resulted in the loss of the ship and all aboard her, as recounted by Purchas: 'The English now hunted after nothing but pillage, each man lighting a candle, the negligence of which fired a cabin in which were six hundred cartridges of powder'.

There never has been honour among thieves. When Thompson's *Dainty* rejoined he asked Burgh for a share of the silks, jewels and coins that now filled the cabins of the other captains. Burgh gave him a seaman's chest that had already been broken open. Norton, who had promised the Portuguese captain that his passengers would not be personally robbed, kept his word and gave them *Grace of Dover* to take them to Flores. But Nicholas Ayers on *Bark Bond* intercepted the pinnace and stripped them naked, collecting hundreds of diamonds, rubies and pearls sewn into their clothing.

The extent of the preliminary looting can be judged from the fact that *Madre de Deus* drew 31 feet when she left Cochin but only 26 when she sailed into Dartmouth harbour on 9 September. There, theft on an industrial scale began with two thousand buyers flocking to the port. When it became apparent that Sir Francis Drake, vice-admiral of Devon and Cornwall, and the other queen's commissioners were taking a decidedly broad view of this, Burghley sent his son Robert Cecil to try to stop the carrack being emptied of all her contents. He reported from Exeter that everyone he met within 7 miles/11 kilometres of the city smelled strongly of pepper, cloves and other spices.

Finally the queen ordered the release of Ralegh from the Tower to recover whatever he could. He managed to have what was left of the bulkier goods to the value of £141,200 loaded on *Garland* and *Roebuck* for transport to London. Elizabeth, whose investment had been a mere £3,000, tried to claim all of it, 'challenging the services of her subjects' ships, which are bound to help her at sea'. The Lord Admiral, anxious to preserve the income from his tenth, persuaded her that 'it were utterly to overthrow all service if due regard were not had of my Lord of Cumberland and Sir Walter Ralegh and the rest of the adventurers, who would never be induced further to venture'.

The point being that the looting had cost the ship owners, promoters and suppliers – who were entitled to two-thirds of the value of the prize – far more than it had diminished the Lord Admiral's tenth and the twentieth due to the queen for customs duties. Nonetheless she took the lion's share of the remainder, arguing that the sailors had already taken much more than they were entitled to and that the adventurers must recover what they could from their ships' crews. Cumberland's syndicate was allowed £37,000, with which he was deeply unhappy but which gave them all a reasonable return. Ralegh and his partners were allowed only £24,000, which was a stinging slap in the face. Against this he had earned the queen's forgiveness, which he must have considered worth the price. But he was still banned from the court until 1597, and never recovered her favour.

The conclusion to be drawn from this episode is obvious. Elizabeth's public–private ventures did severe damage to the subjects of King Philip II and on occasion caused the Spanish monarch acute financial embarrassment. However, she herself gained much less from those ventures than she might have done because she presided over a kleptocratic state and was herself guilty of dishonest dealing. Majesty is the first casualty when a monarch descends to squabbling with her subjects over the division of loot, and it's perfectly clear that it was not just her increasing age that caused Elizabeth's moral authority to drain away during the last decade of her reign.

CHAPTER 14
GUERRILLA WARFARE

E very year between 1585 and the end of the war in 1604 a minimum of 100 ships sailed from England under letters of marque and reprisal, rising to double that number in the years when some grand project increased the sortie rate. It was to be expected that the private promoters of the corsair war should have run their ventures more cost-effectively than the state, but there were also occasions when they undertook military-strategic operations that contrast favourably with the public–private expeditions reviewed in the last chapter. There were several such operations, but two will suffice for the purpose of comparison.

The first was the month-long occupation of Recife, the port from which most Brazilian sugar was exported, in 1595. The expedition was led by the merchant James Lancaster, newly returned from a disastrous expedition to the East Indies plagued by scurvy in which all except one ship, sent home early with the sick, were lost. In October 1594 Lancaster sailed in *Consent* (350 tons) owned by John Watts, followed by Simon Boreman's *Saloman* (170) and *Virgin* (60). It was a joint-stock venture with Watts, Boreman, Paul Bayning, John More and William Shute as the leading investors. On the outward voyage the expedition took several small prizes and was joined by Edward Fenner, owner-captain of *Peregrine* out of Portsmouth and *Welcome* of Plymouth, with a large prize of their own.

Lancaster sailed directly to Recife after he learned that the cargo of an East India carrack wrecked on the Brazilian coast had been taken there, arriving in April 1595. In harbour were three large

Dutch *fluitschips* (see Appendix B) hired to carry the carrack's cargo to Portugal. Lancaster took the town and agreed a fee with the Dutch captains to take a load of looted sugar and brazilwood to England instead, with *Virgin* along to make sure they did. A group of five French corsairs arrived during the occupation and Lancaster agreed to share the spoil with them in return for their assistance in defeating several Portuguese counter-attacks.

It's safe to assume that the month-long pillage of Recife put a smile on the face of every French and English sailor. In addition, the declared value of the bulk goods from the carrack brought back by *Consent* and *Salomon* was £31,000, and the cargo of *Virgin* and two of the *fluitschips* was assessed at £15,000. *Peregrine*, *Welcome*, their prize, and the other *fluitschip* must have carried at least as much, which in total would have represented a tidy £6,100 for the Lord Admiral and £3,050 for the queen.

Leaving aside the glaring anomaly that over-rewarded the Lord Admiral simply for issuing letters of marque on behalf of the queen, this was how the *guerre de course* should have been run, and indeed had been run by Admiral Coligny. He had taken a fifth for the Huguenot cause, but in return ensured that subordinate officials dealt honestly with the corsairs. This was not the case in England, and we may be sure that the real value of the goods brought back from Recife was considerably greater, with the difference shared among the promoters and corrupt port and treasury officials. Merchants also built and supplied their ships themselves, making the investment per ton far lower than it was for royal ships, the costs of which were inflated by corrupt collusion in everything from building materials to fraudulent manning returns.

The second and more spectacular example was the 1598 capture of San Juan, Puerto Rico, mentioned in the last chapter. By this time Cumberland was to all intents and purposes acting as the agent of the London merchants who were his principal creditors and who also joined or backed this venture. Cumberland's expedition can be usefully compared to the private component of Drake's 1587 raid to 'singe the King of Spain's beard' at Cadiz because so many of the participants were the same. The average size of their ships, however, had markedly increased:

🐾 Cumberland himself provided *Malice Scourge* (600), *Sampson* (260), *Guiana* (200, hired from Ralegh), *Anthony* (120), the frigate *Discovery* (12), the pinnace *Scout* and two barges;

🐾 John Watts sent his namesake son as Cumberland's flag captain on *Malice Scourge* and contributed *Alcedo* (400), *Consent* (350), *Galleon Constant* (250), the veteran *Margaret and John* (180), *Affection* (120) and *Pegasus* (80);

🐾 Thomas Cordell sent *Prosperous* (400), *Merchant Royal* (350, jointly with William Garraway), *Centurion* (300) and the pinnace *Bark Ley*;

🐾 William Garraway sent *Ascension* (400) under Robert Flick, commodore of the London squadron in 1587 and 1588, and *Royal Defence* (190).

Bearing in mind that *Merchant Royal* was the largest armed merchantman in the 1588 Navy Royal, the above list shows that Lord Burghley's ambition to encourage private owners to build ships that could serve as a potent naval reserve force had finally been realized.* *Malice Scourge* was as powerful as any galleon built for the Royal Navy since 1588 and *Alcedo*, *Prosperous* and *Ascension* were on a par with all except the biggest. With the exception of Cumberland's squadron, all of them engaged in trade as well as corsairing ventures, often on the same voyage.

This was another joint-stock venture in which, along with the shipowners, the leading capitalists were (once more) Paul Bayning, John More and William Shute, joined by James Lancaster, whose

---

* Between 1560 and 1610 the 100-ton bounty was paid for 510 vessels; 126 (totalling 22,843 tons) were built before 1588, and 384 (totalling 88,604 tons) afterwards, with two-thirds of the latter (255 ships) in the 200–400 ton range.

share of the proceeds from the Recife raid permitted him to graduate from hired captain to investor. The expedition included 1,000 raw troops under Sir John Berkeley, an experienced soldier, and royal permission was obtained to repeat Lancaster's raid on a grander scale. However, the fleet did not sail until March 1598, six months after the queen's commission was granted, by which time Philip II had learnt of it and sent reinforcements to Brazil.

It's highly likely that the story about Recife was disinformation and San Juan was always their target, as it seems most unlikely that the queen and Cumberland's partners would have accepted such a fundamental last-minute change of plan without demur. Cumberland did not tell the other captains about the new destination until they were at sea.

The contrast between the queen's indifference to Cumberland's qualities and the confidence in him shown by the hard-headed London merchants is striking. It was not misplaced. Cumberland first sailed to the mouth of the Tagus hoping to intercept the outgoing *flota* of East Indies carracks, but these were held back and missed their annual journey. An *aviso* was also sent to the West Indies ordering the returning *flota* to stay in Havana, so Cumberland achieved as much as the late Sir John Hawkins could have wished.

After taking a few small prizes Cumberland sailed on to the West Indies, pausing in the Canaries to give Berkeley a chance to drill his men. The crossing was rapid and operational surprise was achieved, followed by tactical surprise when Cumberland landed his troops on the Puerto Rican mainland 12 miles/19 kilometres to the east of San Juan island. (See Map page 282.)

Since 1595 the Spanish had built Fort Matadiablo (Kill Devil) to replace the two batteries that drove off Drake. It also covered the narrow crossing between the island and mainland known as El Boquerón, which was further defended by stakes in the channel. Cumberland and Berkeley, who had hoped to cross in small boats, instead abandoned them and marched inland to attack the causeway linking the island to the mainland. This had a drawbridge covered by another fort, but Cumberland learned from an escaped slave that the channel at this point was fordable at low tide.

Dressed in a full suit of armour he led a storming party across the creek at night and nearly drowned when he tripped at the deepest point and could not get up again. Rescued by Berkeley he pressed on, spewing brackish water as he went. The assault failed and the storming party was forced to retreat to the mainland to avoid being cut off by the rising tide. Undaunted, Cumberland and Berkeley recovered the boats and sent 200 men along the coast to land behind Fort Matadiablo the following night. One of the small prizes was driven aground to fire at the fort from the sea while Berkeley's men fired at it from behind and across the channel. After Matadiablo surrendered, the men at the fort covering the causeway fled and Berkeley was able to march his main force on to the island.

The English had now cut off the retreat of the inhabitants of San Juan and could block the arrival of any reinforcements from the mainland. Leaving a garrison to guard the crossing, Cumberland and Berkeley marched along the island to the city of San Juan to find that the inhabitants had taken refuge in the Morro fortress, which covered the entrance to the harbour. After a show of defiance, on 21 June the governor negotiated a capitulation and all the Spanish were permitted to leave the island unmolested by the English troops, who were on notice from Cumberland that he would hang anyone who laid hands on them. The fleet then sailed into the harbour and took possession of perhaps a dozen small ships and warehouses full of sugar, hides and ginger. An orderly spoiling of the town followed, with the proceeds distributed fairly among the sea and land captains and their men.

But then an outbreak of the 'bloody flux' began to winnow the troops, and the possibility of retaining San Juan as a naval base faded. Cumberland thought he could hold the island with 500 men, but by August he had nearly 400 dead and as many more sick, including Berkeley. Cumberland sailed with his own ships on the 13th, leaving the rest to follow once Berkeley recovered. The fleet reassembled at the Azores but once again had missed the East Indies carracks and so returned home. The return was marred by the loss of *Discovery* off Ushant and *Pegasus* on the Goodwin Sands, both probably due to there being too few healthy crewmen left on board.

The declared value of the goods taken from San Juan was only £16,000, but the notable lack of complaints from the partners suggests that all of them had more than covered their costs, which would have included at least the interest on their loans to Cumberland, before declaring the remainder. Like Sherlock Holmes's dog that did not bark in the night, the absence of acrimony indicates that this was not only the best disciplined and led of all the Elizabethan amphibious operations, but also profitable. It hardly needs stating that the capture of San Juan shows how much more successful an honestly regulated *guerre de course* conducted by private operators might have been than the public–private expeditions led by political appointees we reviewed in the last chapter.

There were other examples, although none on the scale of Cumberland's last venture. Puerto Caballos in Honduras was particularly vulnerable, being taken by Christopher Newport, sailing for Henry Cletherow and John More, in 1592. Walter Ralegh's protégé William Parker, sailing for a Plymouth syndicate, and the French corsair Jérémie Reymond took the town in 1594. Reymond returned to burn Puerto Caballos in 1595 but was trapped and killed shortly afterwards. Another Anglo-French corsair consortium sacked it in 1603. In 1595 Sir Amyas Preston and Sir George Somers took the port of La Guaira in Venezuela and marched inland with 300 soldiers to seize Caracas, which they looted for five days and burned when they departed. Parker took Campeche in 1597 but was driven out and lost the pinnace *Adventure* and her crew. His last raid was on Porto Bello in Panamá, which he seized in February 1601 and came away with 10,000 ducats.

These were simply the more audacious highlights of a grinding war of attrition against Spanish and Portuguese shipping, extended to ships of any other nation carrying goods to Iberia. In this, the London merchants rapidly became dominant. Professor Andrews, drawing on the very partial documentation that still exists, found

70 of the 236 corsair ships known to be active in 1589–91 were from London, including the great majority (17 of 25) over 150 tons. In 1598 it was 43 of 86, including 23 of 28 over 150 tons. Given that about 160 private warships accompanied Essex's 1597 voyage, the figures for 1598, in particular, are much too low – but the trend towards larger ships, based in London, was clear.

Rather than attempt an inadequate précis of the vast and fascinating amount of data in *Elizabethan Privateering*, I will concentrate on two men who epitomize, respectively, the groups of individuals Andrews classifies as 'The Great Merchants' and 'The Professionals'.

John Watts, described by the Spanish Ambassador to the Court of Saint James in 1607 as 'the greatest pirate that has ever been in this kingdom', was born in about 1550 in Hertfordshire, a long way from the sea. His big break was marrying the daughter of Sir James Hawes, a leading figure in the Clothworkers' Guild and Lord Mayor of London in 1574–75, with whom he went into business, mainly with Spain. During the early 1570s Watts may also have moved into the space vacated by the Hawkins brothers in trade with the Canary Islands, and in 1577 he was a founder member of the Spanish Company, which so strongly disapproved of Drake's activities and lobbied successfully against English participation in Strozzi's 1582 expedition to the Azores.

That changed in 1585 when five ships owned by Watts and his partners were among those seized by the Spanish. Issued with letters of marque and reprisal for the amount of £15,000, Watts joined John Bird and John Newton of the Barbary Company to send out *Bark Burr*, *Golden Noble* and *Little John* in 1585–86. By 1587 Watts owned *Margaret and John*, *Little John*, *Drake* and the pinnace *Examiner*, all sent with Drake himself to singe the King of Spain's beard at Cadiz. *Drake* and *Examiner* stayed off the Spanish coast in consort with Thomas Cordell's *George Bonaventure* and John Ridlesden's *Prudence*, taking several prizes that more than compensated Watts for his original loss.

In 1588, as captain of *Margaret and John* Watts led the charge to attack the galleass *San Lorenzo* at Calais, but his other ships were among the few that sailed on reprisal in the Armada year. Thereafter he sent out a growing fleet of corsairs in 1590, 1591, 1592, 1594 and 1597, sometimes in partnership with Paul Bayning but more often alone. He was the foremost sponsor of Lancaster's 1595 raid on Recife, and as we've seen he sent the biggest contingent with Cumberland to Puerto Rico in 1598.

We know from the participation of *Margaret and John* in the battles with galleys in 1586 and 1591 that Watts was trading in the Mediterranean from the beginning of the war, and in 1592 he was elected to the new Levant Company. He became an alderman from 1594, and after building the great ships *Alcedo* and *Consent* in 1595 was certainly among the foremost London shipowners. He was not one of those invited to form the East India Company in 1600, but the omission was quickly corrected and he was the company's second governor in 1601–02.

Watts's career illustrates as well as any that London merchants would not have made the heavy investment in armed ships necessary to open trade with the East Indies if Philip II had not closed the doors to peaceful commerce. They used the corsair war to obtain the goods from ships on the high seas that they previously obtained by trade at Iberian ports, but the staggering wealth taken from *Madre de Deus* opened their eyes to the advantages of by-passing the Portuguese middle men.

Although they did well out of the war the London magnates were happy to see it end, not least because in the final years Spanish corsairs, particularly those operating out of Dunkirk, took a rising toll on English shipping. Thus after peace was declared Watts played a leading role in the re-birth of the Spanish Company and reverted seamlessly to peaceful trade as though he had not spent the intervening 19 years waging war on Spanish commerce.

James I knighted Watts on 26 July 1603, shortly after his coronation, from which we may assume that he had been of financial service to the new king. Evidently the relationship continued, because when Watts was Lord Mayor of London in 1606–07 the king paid him the exceptional honour of dining at his home. This was at a time when the first permanent settlement was made in North America, and as the leading London merchant Watts can fairly be credited with being the godfather of the Virginia Company, of which he was a founder member. Watts was also involved in the development of the tobacco trade with Guiana. He died, very wealthy, in 1616.

Watts's career was interwoven with that of the great sea captain Christopher Newport, for whom the town of Newport News in Virginia is named. Christopher Newport University in that town boasts a wonderful Falstaffian statue that shows Captain Newport with two arms, a regrettable solecism given that he had the right one shot off in 1590 when boarding a bullion ship off the coast of Cuba. This, his first voyage as a commander, was aboard Watts's *Little John* in company with his friend Abraham Cocke on *Harry and John*. To add insult to injury, the treasure ship sank before they could unload it.

The loss of his arm proved no handicap, but it was a step down from the 100-ton *Little John* to the 60-ton pinnace *Margaret* in which he set out early in 1591 for a London syndicate including John More, Robert Cobb, Henry Cletherow and John Newton. He sailed to Morocco (Barbary) to trade and then to the West Indies on reprisal, returning with a modest prize loaded with hides and sugar. It was enough to convince the syndicate, however, and in 1592 he sailed on the 130-ton *Golden Dragon* in command of a 4-ship flotilla. This was the journey during which he captured Yaguana on Hispaniola and Puerto Caballos in Honduras, and rounded it off by participating in the capture of the *Madre de Deus* off Flores. It is to be assumed that as the man entrusted with sailing the carrack back to England, Newport did better than most from the plundering that lightened her load so notably.

For 1593 a letter of reprisal was issued to the More–Cobb–Cletherow syndicate, joined by Sir John Burgh, for *Golden Dragon*, *Roebuck*, *Prudence* and *Virgin*, which indicates either that Burgh had done so well from *Madre de Deus* that he could hire *Roebuck* and *Prudence*, or else he was in partnership with Ralegh and Ridlesden.

There's no record of this venture, but in 1594 Newport sailed in *Golden Dragon* with owner-captain Ridlesden's *Prudence* to the West Indies, taking two prizes with cargoes of hides and timber. The London merchants appear to have been even more litigious than the gentry, and Newport's promoters sued Watts for a share in a rich prize taken at this time by his ship *Affection*, alleging that *Golden Dragon* was in consortship at the time.

In 1595 Newport sailed *Golden Dragon* to the Mediterranean on a trading voyage in consort with a number of other merchantmen and had a share in two Spanish prizes taken on the return. In October his status changed when he married into the Glanfield family, who were leading London goldsmiths. All his subsequent voyages were in command of *Neptune*, newly built for a partnership between Newport and his in-laws, initially with the participation of Ridlesden and Michael Geare, another experienced corsair captain. *Neptune* is variously described as 'powerful', 'formidable' and too big for inshore work, so she was probably in the 300–400 ton range.

Geare was given command of the pinnace built to accompany *Neptune*, but during the first voyage, in 1596, he failed to meet Newport at the agreed rendezvous and made an independent and lucrative voyage while the bigger ship returned empty-handed. Newport and the Glanfields blamed Geare for this and sued him for cheating them of their shares of his prizes. Sailing solely for himself and his in-laws, Newport's next voyage to the West Indies in 1598 was so quickly profitable that they were able to send *Neptune* out again later that year, accompanied by the pinnace *Triton*.

Newport fell ill and the voyage was successfully conducted by *Neptune*'s master, who returned with a good prize but had to sue Newport and the Glanfields not only for his share as acting captain but for the recovery of personal property they had retained and for expenses they had authorized. The Glanfields appear to have been the worst offenders in sharp practice, but from the revealing depositions in Andrews' *English Privateering Voyages to the West Indies* it's apparent that there was no trust among the London corsair promoters, or between them and their employees. The big winner was the Lord Admiral, for whom the High Court of Admiralty was a nice little earner, while the judges graciously accepted gifts from plaintiffs and defendants alike, their consciences no doubt assuaged by the thought that their even-handed venality balanced the scales of justice.

Newport did not sail again until 1599–1600, when he made a rapid voyage to capture and sack Tabasco, not far from Campeche on the Gulf of Mexico, returning with everything removable, including the church bells. In his voyage of 1601–02 he took several modest prizes near Havana, but in 1602–03 he was rumoured to have captured five *fragatas* loaded with gold, variously reported as worth one or two million pesos. There is no record of any such haul being brought back to England, or any significant improvement in Newport's lifestyle, so the rumour is best seen as an indication of Newport's reputation as an outstandingly able and lucky captain.

After the peace treaty he sailed to the West Indies with trade goods, returning in 1605 with two crocodiles and a wild boar for the royal zoo, which he presented to the king in person. In 1606 he was chosen to command the Virginia Company's first expedition. Sailing in *Susan Constant* (120), followed by *Godspeed* (40) and the fly-boat *Discovery* (20), he left London in late December, spent a month waiting in the Downs for a favourable wind, then sailed to Chesapeake Bay via the Canary Islands and the West Indies, arriving in late April 1607. Newport made four more voyages and played a crucial role in the development of the Jamestown settlement.

During the 1609 crossing in the newly (and badly) built *Sea Venture* (300 tons burden), carrying a new governor and 150 settlers, Newport was ordered to take a more direct route and, with the ship foundering after surviving a hurricane, ran her aground on Bermuda. The party spent the winter on the island, cannibalizing the wreck to build two boats in which they sailed to Jamestown. The epic voyage inspired Shakespeare's last sole-authored play, *The Tempest*, and resulted in Bermuda becoming a self-governing colony in 1620, three years before the first English settlement in the Caribbean, on St Kitts.

Newport made his last voyage to Virginia in 1611, and closed his remarkable career in the service of the East India Company, making three journeys to Java during the last of which, in 1617, he died. The following year saw Sir Walter Ralegh's life ended by the executioner's axe after a Spanish settlement on the Orinoco River was sacked during his venture to find El Dorado in Guiana. When preparing the expedition, he discussed the possibility of capturing the silver fleet with Attorney General Sir Francis Bacon. Ralegh replied to Bacon's warning that it would be piracy by asking if he had ever heard 'of men being pirates for millions?'

Perhaps not; but for a man who failed to return with millions at a time when the English and Spanish courts were discussing the dynastic marriage of the future King Charles I and the Infanta María, the outcome was certain. He had been under sentence of death for treason since 1603 and the sentence was carried out on 29 October 1618. In his long valedictory speech from the scaffold he rejected the charges that had brought him there, but confessed to having been 'a man full of all vanity' who had lived 'a sinful life, in all sinful callings, having been a soldier, a captain, a sea-captain and a courtier, which are all places of wickedness and vice'. Indeed — but it was the vanity that killed him.

As to wickedness and vice, he was a babe in arms by comparison with the men who ingratiated themselves with the new king at his expense: Sir Robert Cecil, made Earl of Salisbury in 1605, and the Howards. Lord Admiral Charles was made Earl of Nottingham in 1597, but Lords Henry and Thomas were made Earls of Northampton and Suffolk by James in 1603, before his coronation. Under the new regime their corruption became unconstrained and the Royal Navy went into abject decline; but the seeds of that decline had been planted and nurtured during the last years of Elizabeth's reign.

There were many reasons for this, the most important being the unreformed royal finances. Elizabeth never felt strong enough to risk offending the Protestant gentry who were the mainstay of her regime by modernizing the inadequate, medieval tax structure she inherited. The same consideration inhibited her from clamping down on piracy and the result was the perilous symbiosis of public and private interests in the corsair war, stripped of all pretence and deniability after 1585, and which became a full-scale guerrilla war after the 1588 Armada.

In the following three years more than three hundred prizes were taken with a declared total value of £400,000. It's reasonable to assume the true value was more than twice as much, and the attrition continued at the rate of about £100,000 in declared value every year through the 1590s. Only a small proportion of this came from the spectacular expeditions we have reviewed, and as we have seen the benefit to the English exchequer was in no way commensurate with the damage done to the enemy's economy and shipping – for every prize thought worth bringing back to England at least another was scuttled or burned.

There was also the multiplier effect of causing Spanish and Portuguese ships to set out on oceanic voyages at the wrong time of year. The English captured only three of the great Portuguese East India carracks and caused the captains of another two to burn them to escape capture – but they often forced the rest to sail out of season, increasing their exposure to bad weather. After Philip became king of Portugal the rate of attrition due to natural causes went from one in ten to one in four. The Portuguese merchant fleet was also whittled down by incessant attacks on ships sailing between Brazil and Lisbon with raw sugar and hides, which were taken in such numbers that leather and sugar became cheaper in England than in Iberia.

The effect on Spanish and Portuguese shipping was devastating. From being by some distance the premier oceanic powers even before the union of the two crowns in 1582, they were progressively driven to conducting much of their trade in neutral ships. Thanks to Philip II's insistence that the rebel Dutch were still his subjects and thus free to trade with the rest of his European empire, they occupied the commercial space left when English merchants were shut out of Iberia, and also benefited from the increase in third-party carrying trade brought about by English attrition of the Spanish and Portuguese merchant fleets.

The paradox infuriated the English traders, and laid the foundations for the Anglo-Dutch wars of the next century. Early in 1598, before Philip III declared an embargo on trade with the Dutch Republic, the well-connected gentleman John Chamberlain, whose letters shed priceless light on the period, reported that many in London no longer judged it in their interest to support the Dutch:

> One of the chiefest reasons I can hear for it is a kind of disdain and envy at our neighbours' well-being, in that we, for their sake and defence entering into the war, and being barred from all commerce and intercourse of merchandise, they in the meantime thrust us out of all traffic, to our utter undoing (if in time it be not looked into), and their own advancement, and though the fear of the Spaniards recovering those countries [the Netherlands] and increasing greatness do somewhat trouble us, yet it is thought but a weak policy for fear of future and uncertain danger (which many accidents may divert) to endure a present and certain loss.

It is impossible to say whether Philip III's reversal of his father's policy prevented a breach in the Anglo-Dutch alliance, but it certainly removed a growing source of friction. Even so, as more and more enemy goods were shipped in neutral hulls, the political cost of the corsair war increased.

From about 1597 the volume of complaints from the Hanseatic League, Sweden, Denmark and the Italian states about indiscriminate English predation began to rise steeply. Following the Franco-Spanish Peace of Vervins in May 1598 English attacks on French ships also increased, but the official French response was muted by common strategic concerns and the fact that Henri IV owed Elizabeth a great deal of money. Not so the German and Baltic states, which began to retaliate against English trade. Long before peace was declared the English merchant community had come to see that a prolongation of the war harmed their interests.

Why, then, did it persist? Mainly because the Spanish insultingly over-played their hand at a conference in Boulogne in 1600, but also because, although the Dutch and French feared she might, Elizabeth would not renege on her commitment to the Dutch Republic. Nor would it have been wise to seem forced to make peace because of the Irish rebellion, even though it was eating into her exchequer more than the rest of her military expenses put together. Consequently the tempo of the self-financing corsair war increased and with it, inevitably, the number of offences against neutrals.

Although correlation is not causation, it is suggestive that indiscriminate attacks increased during the last year of Lord Burghley's life. His had always been a voice arguing for moderation in the queen's council, and he had avoided personal involvement in the corsair war. His son, Secretary of State Sir Robert Cecil, was not so scrupulous, and he was now politically joined at the hip with Lord Admiral Howard, now Earl of Nottingham, who had much to gain from an indiscriminate corsair war.

Not content with his tenth of the loot declared by others, Nottingham also sent out corsair ships of his own, which he equipped and perhaps also supplied at the queen's expense, particularly after the death of John Hawkins and his replacement as Treasurer of the Navy by the poet and dramatist Fulke Greville, who knew nothing of ships and the sea. But Howard also made money from the increase in the number of petitions flooding into the High Court of Admiralty and by issuing back-dated letters of reprisal even to notorious pirates. His rationale was that they would otherwise move to Munster or Barbary, which tells us all we need to know about the ethics of the noble earl.

One must assume that his parasitism earned him the secret contempt of the seafaring community, but ironically it strengthened England's negotiating position during the London peace conference of May–August 1604, slightly off-setting the urgent desire for peace signalled by James I, who agreed a ceasefire from 24 April 1603 with the emissaries sent by Philip III and the Archduke and Archduchess of Austria, co-rulers of the Spanish Netherlands, to congratulate him on his accession.

Several corsairing expeditions took place nonetheless, at least one of them to the Mediterranean promoted by Nottingham with Cecil as a silent partner. When the Venetian ambassador complained that claims lodged with the High Court of Admiralty were being ignored, the king swore, 'By God, I will hang the pirates with my own hands, and my Lord Admiral as well'.

The five-man English delegation included Cecil, Nottingham and Henry Howard, Earl of Northampton. The two delegates not clearly identified with the Cecil–Howard interest were the victor of Kildare, Lord Mountjoy, created Earl of Devonshire by James in 1603, and the ailing Lord Treasurer Thomas Sackville, created Earl of Dorset in March 1604. Remarkably, the opening words of the Treaty of London implicitly identified the person of Queen Elizabeth as the *casus belli*:

> *Know all and every one, that after a long and most cruel ravage of wars, by which Christendom has for many years been miserably afflicted, God (who has the disposal of all things) looking down from on high, and pitying the calamities of his people (for whom He was pleased to shed His own blood, that He might bring them peace, and leave it with them) has powerfully extinguished the raging flame by a firm confederacy of the most potent princes of the Christian world, and graciously made the day of peace and tranquillity shine, which was hitherto rather wished for than hoped for by the grace of the omnipotent God, the kingdoms of England and Ireland devolving, for extirpating the seeds of discord, upon the most serene prince, James King of Scotland, and consequently those causes of dissension removed, which so long fomented and nourished war between the predecessors of the most serene princes Philip the III King of Spain, and Albert and Isabella Clara Eugenia Archduke and Archduchess of Austria, Duke and Duchess of Burgundy, &c. and of the said King James.*

Despite the best efforts of Cecil and the Howards, all they could achieve in the matter of trade with the Indies was a declaration restoring the *status quo ante bellum*, which left the issue unaddressed. In effect the informal understanding was the same as that reached by the negotiators of the 1559 Peace of Cateau-Cambrésis between Philip II and Henri II of France: neither party would permit any action by their subjects 'beyond the lines' to compromise the peace. Although the English undertook to support Spanish efforts to uphold their own laws, that was a dead letter for as long as the Earl of Nottingham was Lord High Admiral – which he remained until his death in 1624.

Although the Treaty of London rejected Spanish demands that the cautionary ports be handed over to the Archduke and Archduchess on grounds that James was bound by the terms of the 1585 Treaty of Nonsuch, he did undertake to give no more aid of any kind to Holland and Zeeland, and:

> He promises on the word of a King, to enter into a new treaty
> with the said States, in which treaty his Majesty shall assign them
> a competent time wherein they may receive just and equal
> Conditions of Pacification from the said most serene Princes, his
> dearest Brother and Sister, otherwise, if they shall refuse to do
> this, the most serene King of England, thereby freed from former
> Conventions and Agreements, shall appoint and ordain what he
> shall judge honourable and just concerning these towns – and his
> said most dear Brother and Sister shall be given to understand,
> that he will not be wanting to perform the offices of a Prince who
> is a Friend.

Out of context, the terms agreed in 1604 were those that Philip II sought before the 1588 Armada. The difference was that the Dutch were now more than strong enough to continue the war unaided. In April 1609, two years after the battle of Gibraltar in which the Dutch Navy destroyed a Spanish fleet at sea – something the Royal Navy had never managed – the Twelve Years' Truce agreed by the rulers of Spain and the Southern Netherlands amounted to de facto recognition of the Dutch Republic. The Dutch finally recovered the cautionary towns in 1616, when James was so desperate for money that he accepted £100,000 down and £150,000 in three half-yearly payments to settle outstanding Elizabethan loans totalling £600,000.

In sum, the Treaty of London called off the officially sponsored corsair war that had become an expensive embarrassment for England, and peace was declared because both sides were financially exhausted. As such it represented an admission of strategic defeat by Spain without representing a commensurate victory for England, which saw the fruits of victory plucked by the Dutch not merely in continental Europe but in the Baltic, the Mediterranean, the East and West Indies and even in the North Sea.

They were able to do this because in the midst of a conflict that threatened them far more than it ever did England, they put commerce ahead of all considerations apart from those directly threatening their independence. Beginning with the sack of 1575, the centuries-old commercial expertise of Antwerp transferred to Amsterdam. Under the pressure of a grinding land war with Europe's super-power, the Bank of Amsterdam overcame an acute shortage of specie with the first large-scale issue of paper money in European history, symbolic of a level of trust unthinkable in any of the European monarchies. With the founding of the Wisselbank (Exchange Bank) and the Beurs (Stock Exchange) early in the 17th century, and with the German and Italian banking houses ruined by their symbiosis with the Hapsburgs, Amsterdam became the new financial centre of Europe.

It was not until the Glorious Revolution of 1688 brought William of Orange to the English throne, followed in due course by the offices and expertise of the main Dutch trading and banking houses, that England began to reap the commercial rewards that it might have won a century earlier – if English society had not then been so institutionally backward, predatory and corrupt.

LEGACY

T he Elizabethan era defined English and then British na-
tionhood for as long as it was something valued by the islanders themselves. It appears that is no longer the case,
which takes me back to the theme of my first chapter. As the nov-
elist L. P. Hartley put it, 'the past is a foreign country: they do
things differently there'. It is pointless lamenting what is gone, but
perhaps useful to establish why it went. The most obvious reason
is that nationalism became a dirty word after the appalling bar-
barism of two World Wars. One may seek to differentiate patriotism
from nationalism, but in practice quiet pride in one's own history
and culture lacks the existential force of feeling superior to others.

The English came to that sense of superiority by successfully
opposing the hegemonic pretension of Hapsburg Spain, refined it
by frustrating the imperialism of Bourbon and Napoleonic France,
and finally threw the wealth accumulated over centuries into the
balance against the drive to world power of Wilhelmine and Hitler-
ian Germany. Unsurprisingly, the society shaped by those struggles
has not proved well suited to participation in the latest attempt to
create a united Europe.

Finally there's the demonization of the British Empire, 'acquired in a fit of absence of mind' according to Sir John Seeley, a
key figure in modern English historiography. While Seeley's apho-
rism is true enough if one focuses only on state policy in the 17th
and 18th centuries, the Empire eventually grew out of the overseas commercial expansion – and related growth of naval power –
actively encouraged in the 16th by the far from absent-minded
Lord Burghley.

There are other factors involved, but condemnation of nationalism and imperialism is sufficient to explain why the doings of Drake and Co. are no longer taught in schools. Furthermore, apart from the flamboyant efforts of David Starkey, once a disciple of the great Tudor historian Sir Geoffrey Elton, modern English historiography is dominated by the acolytes of Elton's rival Sir John Plumb, a historian of the 18th century who did not regard the Tudor era as particularly significant.*

There's also the persistence of the view of history as a morality tale with its 'good things' and 'bad things', as brilliantly satirized in *1066 and All That*. The reaction against the late Victorian view of Drake and Co. as good things has, perhaps inevitably, led to them now being condemned as bad things because they were not 'nice' people. Indeed they were not by modern standards; but they were the sharp-edged products of a far more abrasive age.

Within the context of their time, Elizabeth's sea-dogs surpassed their French predecessors mainly because the Wars of Religion aborted the development of the French corsairs as an element of state policy. To avoid exacerbating similar divisions in England, Elizabeth at all times stressed national rather than religious reasons for opposing Spanish hegemony, even though Philip II saw himself as the principal agent of the Counter-Reformation. The queen was remarkably consistent in maintaining that stance despite several Vatican-inspired and Spanish-supported plots to assassinate her.

Elizabeth and Burghley were equally consistent in seeking to avoid open warfare. Her ordinary revenues (customs, feudal dues and the income from crown lands) were insufficient and she was reluctant to summon Parliament to ask for increased extraordinary revenues (subsidies and forced loans). There were only thirteen Parliamentary sessions during her reign, totalling less than three years. Several of them discussed matters that infringed on her prerogative and none of them voted enough extra taxation to cover military expenditure. As we have seen, this forced the queen to sell crown land

* I had the privilege of hearing each give an axe-grinding lecture on the other's centuries.

– and to become an investor in corsairing ventures that increased the risk of war.

There was a well-established tradition of piracy. The essential condition of inexpensive control of discreet harbours and the surrounding countryside was met under a generation of complicit royal officials who owed their preferment to having proved their loyalty to the Protestant cause during Mary's reign, several of them by resorting to commerce raiding under letters of marque from French ports against English as well as Spanish shipping. The tradition thus established died hard – at the end of the long Anglo-Spanish war royal officials gradually became less indulgent, but by then piracy was endemic. Thousands of sailors previously employed in the Royal Navy, or accustomed to making a good living under letters of marque and reprisal, turned to outright piracy.

Great ocean-going captains like John Ward, Sir Francis Verney and Sir Henry Mainwaring became prosperous Barbary corsairs preying preferentially on Iberian shipping – but most English pirates operated around the British Isles. During James I's reign English merchants lost more cargoes and ships to their own countrymen than they had to enemy action during the Spanish war, with the ports of southern Ireland, as they had throughout Elizabeth's reign, continuing to offer alternative havens beyond the reach of royal authority. The height of audacity came in 1610 when the pirate Thomas Salkeld declared himself the king of Lundy Island in the Bristol Channel, requiring an expedition led by Admiral of the Narrow Seas Sir William Monson to depose him.

West Countrymen took the lead in the guerrilla war against Spain in the Caribbean over the following century, most famously in the person of Sir Henry Morgan. They also provided the leading figures in the 'golden age of piracy' following the end of the Spanish Succession War in 1714, which, in a brief echo of the Elizabethan period, flourished thanks to colonial officials acting as accomplices of the pirates. Morgan, Howell Davis and 'Black Bart' Roberts were Welsh and 'Long Ben' Avery was a Devonian. The infamous 'Blackbeard', Edward Teach, was from Bristol, as were most of the characters in Robert Louis Stevenson's *Treasure Island*, from which comes the Hollywood tradition that all pirates must speak with 'Arrr me hearties' West Country accents.

Perhaps the single theme that winds most uninterruptedly from the Elizabethan age through the centuries that followed was the sheer ferocity of the English. Few would question that the last, mad battle of Sir Richard Grenville epitomizes the phenomenon. The men of the *Revenge* sank two and wrecked three more Spanish ships, and killed several times their number in hand-to-hand combat. Their example certainly inspired other Englishmen in similar circumstances and perhaps also disheartened their Spanish opponents – and contributed to a 'can't be beat' moral ascendancy that persisted for centuries.

As I wrote at the beginning – the Elizabethans were not much as we are today. They were not the paladins it suited the proud Victorians to portray, nor the villains denounced today by those with a politico-moralizing agenda. They were men and women of and for their time – let's leave it at that.

Appendix A

SIXTEENTH CENTURY INFLATION, CURRENCY AND EXCHANGE RATES

INFLATION

£1 sterling	Value in 2010 £s	Inflation per cent	Cumulative per cent		Monarch	Wars
1500	486.10		0.00		Henry VII (1485)	
1510	483.77	0.48	0.48			France 1513–14
1520	379.58	21.54	21.91		Henry VIII (1509)	Scotland 1512–2
1530	322.10	15.14	33.73			France 1522–26
1540	307.56	4.51	36.73		Edward VI (1547)	Scotland 1541–5
1550	200.51	34.81	58.75		Mary (1553)	France 1542–46
1560	170.30	15.07	64.97	0.00		France 1549–50
1570	173.89	-2.11	64.23	-2.11	Elizabeth (1558)	France 1557–59
1580	149.31	14.13	69.28	12.33		Scotland 1559–6
1590	125.29	16.09	74.23	26.43		Spain 1585–1604
1600	100.64	19.67	79.30	40.90	James I (1603)	

Source: *National Archives Currency Converter* at: http://www.nationalarchives.gov.uk/currency

ENGLISH CURRENCY

Twelve pence (*d.*) = one shilling (*s.*) and twenty shillings = one pound (£).

Milled gold coins were the sovereign (£1), ryal (15*s.*), angel (10*s.*), half pound (10*s.*), half angel or crown (5*s.*) and quarter angel (2*s.* 6*d.*). Late in Elizabeth's reign a gold pound and silver crowns and half-crowns were issued because the commodity value of the older coins had become greater than their face value.

Milled silver coins were half-a-crown (2*s.* 6*d.*), shilling, sixpence and groat (4*d.*). Hammered silver coins were groats (again), three-pence, half-groat or twopence, three halfpence, penny, three farthings (three quarters of a penny) and halfpenny. Pennies could also be cleaved in two to make halfpennies, or in four to make farthings (a convenient rounded cross was stamped on the reverse side, sub-dividing its area into four and extending around the rim to discourage clipping).

EXCHANGE RATES

The exchange rate among silver currencies did not vary greatly, but the value of silver itself fell steadily after the Potosí mine in modern Bolivia came on-line in the 1550s, with a purchasing power devaluation of 40–50 per cent by the end of the 16th century.

I have found no study of the value of gold either as a unit of account or in terms of purchasing power during the same period, but since no major new sources of gold were discovered it's reasonable to assume that gold coins gained at least the same amount in value relative to silver.

The following is a rough-and-ready guide, intended to permit conversion to pounds sterling of sums in the text denominated in pesos, ducats, and florins, while recognizing that 16th-century merchants and bankers employed different exchange rates depending on the nature of each transaction. The sterling exchange values of gold coins are from the stable decade 1570–80.

Contemporary authors seldom specified whether they were referring to silver or gold ducats. One must guess from the context which unit of account was meant, and the reader's guess is as good as mine. I assume they would normally have been referring to the gold ducat because the difference in sterling value between the peso and the silver ducat is relatively small.

Silver peso/real/thaler/dollar: a coin worth about 4s. 5½d. (so £1 = 4.4 silver pesos).

Silver ducat/ducado: a coin worth about 5s. 6d. (£1 = 3.6 silver ducats).

Gold ducat/ducado: a coin (originally Venetian) worth about 9s. 6d. (£1 = 2.1 gold ducats).

Gold florin/guilder: a coin (originally Florentine) worth about 9s. 8d. (£1 = 2.07 gold florins).

One frequently comes across English references to 'plate' when describing plunder. This is simply an anglicization of the Spanish *plata* (silver), which today (maybe also then) is also used in the sense of 'money', as in the alternative offered to wretched Mexican policemen by narco-gangsters: *plata o plomo* – silver or lead – which is to say accept bribes or be shot.

APPENDIX B

SHIP TYPES

Aviso (Sp.)
A small, fast ship of any type used for carrying urgent messages.

Barge (*c.f.* shallop)
(a) A long rowing boat with up to 20 oarsmen in the forward section and a covered area at the back, used for ceremonial occasions. Also the largest rowing boat that might be carried on board a ship.

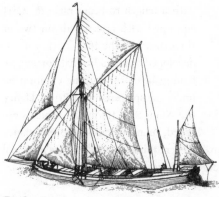

(b) A flat-bottomed, coastal and riverine cargo ketch with a sideboard, spritsail-rigged on the main-mast and gaff-rigged on the small mizzen mast.

Bark
From the Latin *barca*, a generic word for sailing ship of ancient origin, from which derives many nautical terms in several languages. The term was used by English sailors to describe ships of all kinds during the age of sail. When 'bark' was used to describe a specific type of ship in the Tudor period, it may have been something like the busse, used by the annual English fishing fleet to Iceland. These

were ships with two or three short, free-standing masts each carrying a lugsail (irregular quadrilateral sail on asymmetrically set yards, with most of the sail behind the mast). The rig gave good performance both before and into the wind and was easy to handle, requiring only a small crew.

Brigandine/Brigantine

Small, two-masted ship, square rigged on the foremast only. Mainmast may have been gaff- or lateen-rigged. Originally a small Mediterranean sailing ship popular with pirates, hence the 'brigand' of the name. The Barbary corsairs, with access to a large pool of slave rowers, preferred the galiot (*q.v.*).

Caravel (Eng.), *Caravela* (Sp. & Port.)

A medium-sized, shallow-draught ship with a length-to-beam ratio of 3.5:1 equipped with lateen sails on two or three masts. In the 15th century it was developed from traditional Portuguese fishing boats for oceanic exploration under the sponsorship of Prince Henry the Navigator. Its main virtues were speed, manoeuvrability, performance into the wind, and the small crew required to handle it. Its principal drawback was limited cargo space compared to the carrack (*q.v.*).

To improve cargo-carrying the larger and broader *caravela redonda* (round caravel) was developed with a bowsprit carrying a spritsail and square sails on the fore and main masts. *Niña* and *Pinta* in Columbus's 1492 fleet were of this type.

A warship variant had four variously rigged masts, the most common being three with lateen sails and the foremast square-rigged. The hull shape of the warship *caravela redonda* clearly presaged the development of the galleon (*q.v.*).

Carrack (Eng.), *Nao* (Sp.), *Nau* (Port.), *Nef* (Fr.)

Developed by the Portuguese in the 15th century the carrack was the first frame-built design, which permitted the construction of large ships for the first time. Characteristics were a length-to-beam ratio of 2:1, tall aft and fore castles and a strong bowsprit to stay a foremast stepped far forward. The fore and main masts had square main and topsails while the mizzen and, when fitted, the fourth (bonaventure) masts were lateen rigged. Its main virtues were stability in heavy seas and a large cargo capacity, its drawback that it was slow and unwieldy.

As a warship the carrack was optimized for grappling and boarding, with light guns in the aft and fore castles supporting the troops fighting on the well decks between them. The reason why paintings of war carracks commonly portrayed them from behind was that the heaviest guns were mounted pointing aft from the tall, square stern, as the design precluded the possibility of mounting heavy guns to fire forward.

Cromster (Eng.) – from *Cromsteven* (Dutch)

A medium-sized, heavily armed ketch developed by the Dutch to operate in the shoal waters off their coast. It had complex rigging with a square topsail as well as a spritsail on the main mast and a lateen sail on the small mizzen. A very round bow enabled the type to mount four forward-firing guns in a gun-deck instead of in the forecastle. Confusingly the English also called it a hoy (*q.v.*), although apart from both being coasters there was no similarity between the two types.

Fluitschip (Dutch), Flute (Eng.)

A simple and inexpensive cargo vessel of 200-300 tons with a pear-shaped cross section to max-imize cargo space, designed to be operated by a small crew over long distances. It was one of the key factors in the development of the Dutch seaborne empire in the 17th century. It usually car-ried 10-12 guns but was not fast or agile enough to defend itself against a race-built galleon.

Flyboat (Eng.), *Felibote* (Sp.) – from *Vlieboot* (Dutch)

The Dutch name comes from its ability to navigate the shallow estuary of the River Vlie. A two- or three-masted, shallow–draft carrack (*q.v.*) favoured by the Sea Beggars and the Dunkirkers.

Fragata (Sp.)

A term commonly used to describe any fast ship, it was also more specifically a multi-purpose, lateen-rigged equivalent of the smaller type of pinnace/*pinaza* (*q.v.*), used for inshore work and towed behind the parent galley when at sea. In battle it would row around an enemy ship to board on the unengaged side.

Frigate (Eng.), *Zabra* (Sp.)

A fast ship intermediate in size (10–30 tons) to the two types of pinnace/*pinaza* (*q.v.*).

Galleass (Eng.), *Galeaza* (Sp. & It.)

Large hybrid Mediterranean warship with a gun deck added above the banks of rowers but with the heaviest guns still mounted to fire forward in a bow that clearly presaged the galleon. Its oars were set higher and so at a less efficient angle than on the fighting galleys, to compensate for which it had three masts. When lateen-rigged it was superior to the carrack (*q.v.*) into the wind.

Hugo Moncada's squadron of square-rigged Sicilian galleasses employed in the 1588 Armada were an unsuccessful experiment that was not repeated.

Galleon (Eng.), *Galeón* (Sp.), *Galion* (Fr.)

Sixteenth century type that combined the best features of the caravel (*q.v.*), carrack (*q.v.*) and galley (*q.v.*) with a length-to-beam ratio of 3:1 to produce a fast and manoeuvrable ship that could mount a heavy gun broadside in a full-length gun deck as well as in the bow and stern. The tall fore and after castles of the carrack were abolished and with them their large number of lighter guns. The Spanish galleon (illustrated) was a large ship that traded speed and agility for carrying capacity.

French corsairs adapted the galleon by removing a deck (thus *razée* or shaved, from which the English 'race-built') and by a more

pronounced narrowing of the hull from the waterline towards the upper deck (tumblehome) to lower the centre of gravity so that smaller ships could carry the same press of sail. The result could sail rings around a Spanish galleon but had a limited range between stops to load water and supplies. In 1570 John Hawkins began a partnership with Richard Chapman, Peter Pett, and Mathew Baker to build or rebuild warships for the Royal Navy according to the new design, a process that accelerated after Hawkins' appointment as Treasurer of the Navy in 1577.

Galley (Eng.), *Galera* (Sp. & It.), *Galère* (Fr.)

A shallow-draught vessel of 100–150 tons with a length-to- beam ratio of at least 8:1. Propelled by 20 three-man oars per side and with a high centre of gravity it was far from being an ideal sailing vessel; but a large lateen sail set on two long yards bound together along about a quarter of their length, and set on a low mast mounted one-third of the length from the bow, resolved two problems in one. Even a moderate head wind could render forward progress under oars impossibly demanding, but the lateen in combination with quarter rowing (*q.v.*) was most effective into the wind. Limited cargo space and the high water consumption of the rowers demanded frequent stops.

Beyond a certain number the additional mass of extra rowers plus the added drag of a larger hull cancelled out their efforts. The largest galleys (200+ tons) had 25–27 five-man rowing benches per side and mounted an additional mast well forward. No matter what their size, galleys could only mount heavy guns in the bow, making it necessary to point the whole ship at a target.

Galliot (*c.f.* brigantine)

The typical equipment of the Barbary corsairs, it was a medium-sized ship with 14–16 two-man oars per side that retained the length-to-beam ratio of the galley with a deeper keel and higher freeboard to optimize performance under lateen sails on two masts. More seaworthy than its bigger cousin and carrying smaller numbers, it was capable of surprisingly long-range operations.

Galizabra (Sp.)

From *galeón* (*q.v.*) and *zabra* (*q.v.*). First built in the later 1580s as a belated response to the race-built French and English corsairs, it was a medium-sized, fast and well armed galleon designed to carry bullion across the Atlantic in safety. None was ever taken, and a *galizabra* based in Callao helped to run down and capture Richard Hawkins' race-built galleon *Dainty* off the coast of Ecuador in 1594.

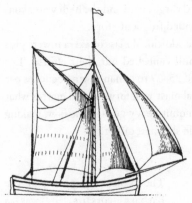

Hoy (but see also cromster, *q.v.*)

A small, single-masted, gaff-rigged ship used for coastal traffic.

Hulk (Eng.), *Urca* (Sp.)

A large merchant ship similar in construction to the carrack but with a simpler sail plan that was the principal type employed by the Hanseatic League throughout the 16th century. King Henry VIII of England purchased several large hulks and converted them to war carracks, the best known being *Jesus of Lübeck*, which was lost at the battle of San Juan de Ulúa in 1569.

Patache (Sp. & Fr.)

Tender or supply ship in a flotilla.

Pinnace (Eng.), *Pinaza* (Sp.)

a) A large, open ship's boat too big to stow on board (unless dismantled) with a single unstepped mast, oars, and swivel guns, used for inshore work and towed behind the parent ship when at sea; in battle it would row around an enemy ship to board on the unengaged side.

b) A small three-masted warship armed with light guns (sakers or smaller) of 30–80 tons.

Quarter rowing
Technique to balance galley and galliots when operating under sail. Half the oars on the leeward side would be employed to point further into the wind and to counter crabbing.

Shallop – from *Chaloupe* (Fr.)

(a) A rowing barge with a covered stern and 6–8 oarsmen.

(b) A small rowing/sailboat with a single, spritsail-rigged mast used for inshore and riverine traffic, sometimes equipped with a sideboard.

Urca (Sp.) – see **Hulk**

Zabra (Sp.) – see **Frigate**

Note: Ship illustrations not to scale.

APPENDIX C

NAVAL ARTILLERY

Numbers in roman are from William Bourne, *The Arte of Shooting in Great Ordnaunce* (1587), those in italics are averaged from several sources. Gun weight could vary greatly depending on whether the gun was iron or bronze, the age of the piece, where it was cast, and how 'fortified' it was.[1]

Name	Bore (in)	Length (in)[2]	Weight (lb)	Shot (lb)[3]	Powder (lb)
Fowler[4]	*½*	*60*	*100*	*2oz*	*1oz*
Robinet	*1*	*60*	*200*	*5oz*	*3oz*
Base	*2*	*60*	*300*	*12oz*	*9oz*
Falconet	2¼	60	360–400	1–1½	1¼
Falcon	2½–2¾	84	550–750	1¾–2½	2–2½
Minion	3–3¼	96	900–1000	3–3?	4
Saker	3½–4	96–120	1,400–1,800	4¾–7¼	5–7¼
Demi-culverin	4¼–4¾	120–144	2,200–3,200	9–12	10–12
Culverin	5–5½	144–156	4,300–4,800	15–20	16–20
Demi-cannon perier	*5*	*88*	*2,500*	*15*	*9*
Cannon perier[5]	*7*	*96*	*3,800*	*24*	*14*
Demi-cannon	5¼–5¾	132–144	5,000–5,500	30–38	23–24
Cannon[6]	8	132–144	7,500	64	42

Some revisionist historians have unwisely argued that 16th-century artillery textbooks did not know what they were talking about. Thus Parker:

It is now known that lengthening a smooth-bore gun barrel beyond a certain point, far from increasing range, actually reduces it. A charge of black powder, when ignited, can only produce a set volume of gas, and when that is expended (or is not being produced quickly enough to maintain pressure behind the rapidly accelerating projectile), any further increase in barrel length will retard its velocity.

Let's start with the law of conservation of momentum (mass x velocity). Apart from the relatively minor factors of inter-related gas loss and friction (the greater the one, the less the other), after the propellant explodes the momentum of the projectile is equal and opposite to the momentum of the gun. For any given momentum, the smaller the projectile mass, the greater the velocity. A smaller projectile also incurs less wind resistance.

Plus – a black powder explosion is not instantaneous. It takes time for the powder granules to burn completely and for the gas produced by combustion to expand and push the projectile out of the barrel. So the longer the projectile remains in the barrel, the greater the energy transfer.

Shorter-barrelled guns reduced the amount of time available for energy transfer, thus to achieve the same momentum as a longer gun they had to fire larger projectiles. Cannon were 16–24 calibre (then a measurement of internal barrel length as a multiple of bore), culverins 24–36 calibre.

The distance within which gravity and wind resistance do not significantly degrade the velocity of a horizontally fired projectile (point blank) is greater for the gun with the longer maximum range, although the difference in point-blank range between culverin and cannon was less than 100 yards. Firing at long range was also wasteful because wind and wave make ships move unpredictably and the effect of such movement on the trajectory of the projectile increases with distance.

A second application of the law of conservation of momentum relates to recoil. The greater the mass of the projectile, the greater the effect on the gun. Since the guns were attached to the ship's hull, the larger the projectile the greater the strain on the ship's structure.

The Spanish officer who predicted that the English would 'knock us to pieces with their culverins, without our being able to do them any serious hurt' overestimated the importance of range in the coming battle, in which long-distance fire proved ineffective, but overlooked momentum (impact) at point blank range and the structural damage done by the repeated recoil even of medium guns to ships not built for it (hulks, Levanters). In that respect it was a saving grace that clumsy Spanish gun carriages and inadequate gun crews prevented them firing more often.

[1] Guns came in three categories depending on how thick the bore walls were cast. Thicker-walled guns could take a larger charge. From heaviest to lightest they were known as 'double-fortified', 'legitimate' and, logically enough, 'bastard'.

[2] Unfortunately this is overall gun, not internal barrel length, so not useful for calculating calibre.

[3] The Royal Navy later standardized on 1, 2, 3, 6, 9, 12, 18, 24, 36 and 48 pounders, and an internal barrel length 24 ? bore.

[4] Fowlers, slings, demi-slings, double bases, robinets, and bases were all iron breech-loading guns set in a fork on a pivot, collectively known as 'swivel guns', that could be mounted anywhere from fighting tops to ship's boats.

[5] A perier was a short, large bore gun designed to fire frangible stone shot (or scrap metal). The lower density of the missile required a smaller charge and so the gun could be cast lighter.

[6] Although some large galleys carried 60 pounders on the centre line, naval cannon were the lighter (6,000–6,500lb) bastard cannon with 44–48lb shot. A pro-rata reduction would make the powder charge about 30lb.

APPENDIX D

'TONS BURDEN' &
'TONS AND TONNAGE'

Y
ou can go mad trying to convert Spanish *toneles machos* (virile tuns) and *toneladas* (tons) to English 'tons burden' and 'tons and tonnage', none of which were directly comparable to modern calculations of displacement.

English 'tons burden' were arrived at by the following formula (in feet of 12 inches)

(Beam [widest point] × Depth from widest point × Length of keel) ÷ 100

'Tons and tonnage' (fully equipped and loaded) was one third greater.

Spanish *toneles machos* were arrived at by the following formula (in *codos* of 22.62 inches)[1]

({Beam ÷ 2 × Depth from main deck × Length of main deck} minus 1/20) ÷ 8

Spanish *toneladas* were arrived at by adding one fifth to the *toneles machos* figure.

For the English I was surprised to find that the tons given in the Armada list for Royal Navy ships (for which measurements are available) were tons and tonnage, whereas for the private ships they were tons burden.[2] Presumably this was to increase the royal share of any public/private venture.

For the Spanish, having different words helps distinguish between *toneles* and *toneladas*, but gross mathematical errors were common using their more complicated formula, and many assessments seem to have been guesstimates. Intriguingly, the *codo* was standardized as a result of having to calculate costs and compensation for the wide variety of ships employed and lost in the Armada.

For the purpose of comparing the Armada ships I converted the Royal Navy ships to tons burden and the Spanish *toneladas* to the same unit by using the formula suggested by R. J. Lander[3] (although he does emphasize, by reference to Frederic Lane's comprehensive but ultimately bewildering work,[4] how inexact any such formula must be) multiplying by 4.5 and dividing by 7 (or × 9/14, or × 0.643).

[1] The *codo* was not standardized until 1590; before that each Spanish province used a different measurement.

[2] See *Three Decks: Warships in the Age of Sail* at http://www.threedecks.org/index.php

[3] Lander, R. J., 'An Assessment of the Numbers, Sizes, and Types of English and Spanish Ships Mobilized for the Armada Campaign', *The Mariner's Mirror*, 63/4 (November 1977), 359–67.

[4] Lane, Frederic, 'Tonnages, Medieval and Modern', *The Economic History Review*, 17/2 (December 1964), 213–33.

Appendix E

1588 LITTLE SHIPS

I *am in no doubt that readers will find errors and omissions in the following data. Substantiated corrections will be gratefully received and incorporated into future editions.*

SPANISH LITTLE SHIPS

29; there were also 2 unarmed *pinazas* (not listed)

Name	Type	Tons	Guns	Crew	Troops	Origin	Squadron	Fate
Miguel de Suso	*Patache*	60	6	25	20	1585 Cantábrica	Viscaya	Returned Guipúzcoa
San Sebastián	*Patache*	50	6	25	10	1585 Cantábrica	Viscaya	Returned La Coruña
Espíritu Santo	*Patache*	50	2	–	–	n/a Cantábrica	Pataches	Returned Santander
Concepción de Castro	*Patache*	50	6	10	–	n/a Cantábrica	Pataches	Returned Castro Urdiales
Concepción de Lastero	*Patache*	50	6	–	18	n/a Cantábrica	Pataches	*Unknown*
N S del Socorro	*Patache*	50	14	15	20	1586 Santander	Castilla	*Unknown*
San Antonio de Padua	*Patache*	50	12	31	20	1586 Santander	Castilla	*Unknown*
Isabela	*Patache*	45	10	29	24	1585 Cantábrica	Viscaya	Returned La Coruña
María de Aguirre	*Patache*	45	6	25	19	1585 Cantábrica	Viscaya	*Unknown*
N S de Fresneda	*Patache*	45	2	0	–	n/a Cantábrica	Pataches	Returned Santander
N S de Guadalupe	*Patache*	45	–	29	19	n/a Cantábrica	Pataches	Returned Santander
Concepción de Carasa	*Patache*	45	5	21	18	n/a Cantábrica	Pataches	Returned Castro Urdiales
San Francisco	*Patache*	45	–	–	–	n/a Cantábrica	Pataches	*Unknown*
San Bernabé	*Patache*	45	9	19	20	1586 Cantábrica	Guipúzcoa	Returned San Sebastián
Espíritu Santo	*Patache*	45	10	15	18	1585 Cantábrica	Andalucía	Returned Santander
N S de Begonia	*Patache*	40	10	24	12	n/a Cantábrica	Pataches	*Unknown*
Concepción de Capitillo	*Patache*	40	10	16	–	n/a Cantábrica	Pataches	Returned Santander
Asunción	*Patache*	40	9	16	19	1586 Cantábrica	Guipúzcoa	Returned Guipúzcoa
N S de Gracia	*Patache*	35	5	25	17	n/a Cantábrica	Pataches	Returned San Sebastián
N S del Puerto	*Patache*	35	8	17	28	n/a Cantábrica	Pataches	Returned Santander
San Jerónimo	*Patache*	35	4	36	–	n/a Cantábrica	Pataches	Returned Castro Urdiales
Trinidad	*Zabra*	–	2	23	–	n/a Cantábrica	Pataches	*Lost Ireland*
Asunción	*Zabra*	–	2	18	–	n/a Cantábrica	Pataches	Returned Santander
San Andrés	*Zabra*	–	2	17	–	n/a Cantábrica	Pataches	Returned Santander
N S de Castro	*Zabra*	–	2	20	–	n/a Cantábrica	Pataches	*Lost at sea*
San Juan de Carasa	*Zabra*	–	2	29	6	n/a Cantábrica	Pataches	*Stayed Dunkirk*
Santa Catalina	*Zabra*	–	2	20	–	n/a Cantábrica	Pataches	*Stayed Dunkirk*
Concepción de Balmaceda	*Zabra*	–	2	23	–	n/a Cantábrica	Pataches	Returned Castro Urdiales

Private warship details mainly from Kenneth Andrews' 1589–91 list of privateers – may well have been different in 1588

In addition to the 52 listed here, records list a further 40 named ships, but with no further details

Name	Captain	Owner	Type	Tons	Guns	Men	Built	Squadron
Achates	Gregory Riggs	Royal	Galleon	95	13	60	1573	Howard
George	Richard Hodges	Royal	Hoy	90		24	1588	Howard
Dolphin	John Maynard	Colthurst Company	Galleon	90				London
Elizabeth (fireship)		Lowestoft syndicate	Galleon	90				Drake
Passport	Christopher Colthurst	Colthurst Company	Pinnace	80	11			London
Anne Fortune (Bristol)		Thomas Howell *et al.*	Coaster	80				Seymour
Gillaume	William Walton	Rye syndicate	Coaster	80				Seymour
Bark Buggins	f.n.u. Buggins		Pinnace	80				Drake
Great Delight	William Coxe (k.i.a.)	Lord Admiral Howard	Pinnace	70				Drake
Charles	John Roberts	Royal	Pinnace	70	16	45	1586	Howard
Disdain (fired first challenge)		Lord Admiral Howard	Pinnace	70				Royal hire
Minion (Southampton)	Thomas Prowse	Prowse family	Pinnace	60				Drake
Moon	Alexander Clifford	Royal	Pinnace	60	13	40	1586	Howard
Fancy (Plymouth)	Nicholas Webb	Andrew Founes	Pinnace	60				Royal hire
Bark Hall	John Langford	William Hall	Pinnace	60				London
John (Chichester)		John Young	Coaster	60				Seymour
Fancy (London)		London Syndicate	Coaster	60				Seymour
Golden Hind	Captain Adams	Edward Lewes	Pinnace	50				Drake
Merlin	Walter Gower	Royal	Pinnace	50	10	35	1579	Howard
Brigandine	Thomas Scott	Royal	Brigantine	50		35	1584	Howard
Moonshine	John Myddelton	John Newton / John Bird	Pinnace	50				London
Makeshift		Royal	Pinnace	45	8		1586	Drake
Spy	Ambrose Ward	Royal	Pinnace	42	9	40	1586	Howard
Sun	Richard Buckley	Royal	Pinnace	40	5	30	1586	Howard
Advice	John Harris	Royal	Pinnace	40	9	40	1586	Drake
Angel (fireship)		Southampton	Pinnace	40				Drake
Lark (London)		Colthurst Company	Pinnace	40				Royal hire

Name	Captain	Owner	Type	Tons	Guns	Men	Built	Squadron
Grace of God	William Grafton	Owner-captain	Coaster	35				Seymour
Hazard		Feversham	Coaster	35				Seymour
Cygnet	John Sheriffe	Royal	Pinnace	30	3	20	1585	Howard
Little Hare (Southampton)		Dennis Rowse	Coaster	30				Seymour
Gift (Topsham)		Robert Sadler	Coaster	25				Howard hire
Black Dog (London)	John Davis	Owner-captain	Pinnace	20	3	10		Royal hire
Katherine (Weymouth)		Robert White	Pinnace	20				Royal hire
Jane Bonaventure (Bristol)		William Walton	Pinnace	20				Royal hire
Great Catherine (Weymouth)		Robert White	Pinnace	20				Royal hire
Pippin		Unknown merchant	Pinnace	20				Royal hire
Chance (Isle of Wight)	David Perrin	Sir George Carey	Pinnace					Drake
Unity (Plymouth)	Humphrey Sydenham	Unknown merchant	Pinnace					Drake
Hearts Ease	Nicholas White	Southampton	Pinnace					Drake
Speedwell (Barnstaple)		Unknown merchant	Pinnace					Drake
Nightingale (London)		Unknown merchant	Pinnace					Drake
Elizabeth Drake (Plymouth)		Unknown merchant	Pinnace					Drake
Elizabeth Founes (Plymouth)		Humphrey Founes	Pinnace					Drake
Diamond (Dartmouth)		Thomas Walton	Pinnace					Drake
Unnamed (fireship)		(f.n.u.) Cure	Pinnace					Drake
Matthew (Weymouth)		Pitt brothers	Coaster					Seymour
Handmaid	f.n.u. Laughton	Bristol syndicate	Coaster					Seymour

Unattached

Bark Sutton (Weymouth)	Mark Bury	(f.n.u.) Brooke	Pinnace	70				Voluntary
Unicorn (Dartmouth)	Ralph Hawes	William Morcomb	Pinnace	60				Voluntary
Margaret		London syndicate	Pinnace	60				Voluntary
Carouse (Southampton)		Roger Page	Pinnace	30				Voluntary

k.i.a. = killed in action
f.n.u. = first name unknown

Appendix F

1588 WARSHIPS

I am in no doubt that readers will find errors and omissions in the following data. Substantiated corrections will be gratefully received and incorporated into future editions.

TOP SPANISH WARSHIPS

(only the five largest *naos*/carracks shown)

Name	Type	Tons	Guns	Crew	Troops	Origin	Squadron	Fate
Regazona ⚓	*Nao*	800	30	80	403	n/a Ragusa	Levante	Returned La Coruña **
Santa Ana ⚓	*Nao*	770	47	120	342	1586 Cantábrica	Guipúzcoa	*Lost San Sebastián*
Gran Grin	*Nao*	745	28	96	209	n/a Cantábrica	Viscaya	*Lost Ireland*
N S del Rosario ⚓	*Nao*	740	46	125	359	1585 Ribadeo	Andalucía	*Lost Channel*
Trinidad Valencera	*Nao*	705	42	87	381	1586 Venice	Levante	*Lost Ireland*
São João ⚓	Galleon	675	50	184	382	1586 Portugal	Portugal	Returned La Coruña **
São Martinho ⚓	Galleon	640	48	161	491	1578 Portugal	Portugal	Returned Santander
San Francesco/Florencia	Galleon	620	52	89	294	1585 Tuscany	Portugal	Returned Santander
São Filipe	Galleon	540	40	116	377	1585 Portugal	Portugal	*Lost Nieuport-Ostend*
São Luís	Galleon	535	38	97	384	1583 Portugal	Portugal	Returned Santander
San Juan Bautista	Galleon	515	31	64	260	1584 Cantábrica	Andalucía	Returned Santander
São Marcos	Galleon	510	33	98	419	1585 Portugal	Portugal	*Lost Ireland*
N S de la Begoña	Galleon	480	24	95	221	1585 Guarnizo	Castilla	Returned Galicia
São Mateus	Galleon	480	34	110	334	1579 Portugal	Portugal	*Lost Nieuport-Ostend*
San Cristóbal ⚓	Galleon	450	36	212	211	1583 Guarnizo	Castilla	Returned Laredo
San Lorenzo ⚓	Galleass	380	50	124*	242	n/a Sicily	Naples	*Lost Calais*
Girona	Galleass	380	50	121*	253	n/a Sicily	Naples	*Lost Ireland*
Zúñiga	Galleass	380	50	104*	226	n/a Sicily	Naples	*Lost Le Havre*
Napolitana	Galleass	380	50	102*	248	n/a Sicily	Naples	Returned Laredo
San Juan Menor	Galleon	340	24	81	238	1584 Guarnizo	Castilla	Returned Santander
Santiago Mayor	Galleon	340	24	103	213	1584 Guarnizo	Castilla	Returned Santander
Asunción	Galleon	340	24	80	184	1584 Guarnizo	Castilla	Returned Santander
San Felipe y Santiago	Galleon	340	24	86	161	1584 Guarnizo	Castilla	Returned Santander
San Pedro Menor	Galleon	340	24	94	201	1584 Guarnizo	Castilla	*Lost Laredo*
San Medel y Celedón	Galleon	340	24	75	196	1584 Guarnizo	Castilla	Returned Laredo
N S del Barrio	Galleon	340	24	86	208	1584 Guarnizo	Castilla	Returned Laredo
Sãotiago	Galleon	335	24	90	314	1585 Portugal	Portugal	Returned Santander
São Cristóvão	Galleon	225	20	80	135	1580 Portugal	Portugal	Returned Santander
São Bernardo	Galleon	225	21	68	179	1586 Portugal	Portugal	Returned Galicia

(Gun numbers in italics = estimates)

Name	Type	Tons	Guns 1*	Guns 2*	Guns 3*	Crew	Troops	Built	Fleet
Triumph ⌒	Carrack	760	7	31	4	340	160	1562 Royal build	Howard
White Bear	Carrack	730	14	17	9	340	150	1564 Royal rebuild	Howard
Elizabeth Jonas	Carrack	684	9	26	21	340	150	1559 Royal build	Howard
Victory ⌒	Carrack	565	10	39	3	304	126	1560 Royal build	Howard
Ark Royal ⌒	Carrack	555	8	30	6	304	126	1587 Royal purchase	Howard
Mary Rose	Carrack	476	4	25	7	174	76	1557 Royal build	Howard
Revenge ⌒	Carrack	465	8	20	15	174	76	1577 Royal build	Drake
Vanguard	Galleon	465	8	26	20	174	76	1586 Royal build	Seymour
Elizabeth Bonaventure	Galleon	448	2	25	5	174	76	1580 Royal rebuild	Howard
Golden Lion	Galleon	420	4	21	3	174	76	1582 Royal rebuild	Howard
Hope	Carrack	400	6	24	18	185	85	1559 Royal build	Drake
Galleon Leicester	Galleon	400	2	24	5	*250*		1578 Earl of Leicester	Drake
Rainbow ⌒	Galleon	384	8	26	20	174	76	1586 Royal build	Seymour
Nonpareil	Galleon	380	5	27	6	174	76	1584 Royal rebuild	Drake
Dreadnought	Galleon	360	2	34	5	150	40	1573 Royal build	Howard
Swiftsure	Galleon	360	5	27	4	140	40	1573 Royal build	Drake
Merchant Royal ⌒	Galleon	350	2	20	?	*175*		n/a London syndicate	London
Antelope	Galleon	340	–	25	5	140	30	1581 Royal rebuild	Seymour
Swallow	Galleon	330	–	25	5	140	30	1580 Royal rebuild	Howard
Mayflower	Galleon	300	–	23	5	*150*		n/a London syndicate	London
Hercules	Galleon	300	–	23	5	*150*		n/a London syndicate	London
Foresight	Galleon	295	–	22	15	130	20	1570 Royal build	Howard
Susan	Galleon	260	–	21	4	*130*		n/a London syndicate	Seymour
Galleon Dudley	Galleon	250	–	20	4	*125*		n/a Earl of Leicester	Drake
Edward Bonaventure	Galleon	250	–	21	4	*125*		1574 London syndicate	Howard
Centurion	Galleon	250	–	20	4	*125*		n/a London syndicate	London
Roebuck	Galleon	240	–	15	4	*120*		n/a Sir Walter Ralegh	Drake
Aid	Galleon	220	–	10	8	106	14	1580? Royal rebuild	Drake

*Guns 1 = cannon, demi-cannon, periers; Guns 2 = culverins, demi-culverins, sakers; Guns 3 = minions or less

SPANISH WARSHIPS OVER 100 TONS (64)

Name	Type	Tons	Guns	Crew	Troops	Built	Squadron	Fate
Regazona	Carrack	800	30	80	403	n/a Ragusa	Levante	Returned La Coruña
Santa Ana	Nao	770	47	120	342	1586 Cantábrica	Guipúzcoa	Lost San Sebastián
Gran Grin	Nao	745	28	96	209	n/a Cantábrica	Viscaya	Lost Ireland
Nuestra Señora del Rosario	Nao	740	46	125	359	1585 Ribadeo	Andalucía	Lost Channel
Trinidad Valencera	Carrack	705	42	87	381	1586 Venice	Levante	Lost Ireland
São João	Galleon	675	50	184	382	1586 Portugal	Portugal	Returned La Coruña
São Martinho	Galleon	640	48	161	491	1578 Portugal	Portugal	Returned Santander
San Francisco/Florencia	Galleon	620	52	89	294	1585 Tuscany	Portugal	Returned Santander
San Salvador	Nao	615	25	90	232	1586 Cantábrica	Guipúzcoa	Lost Channel
Nuestra Señora de la Rosa	Nao	610	26	100	175	1586 Cantábrica	Guipúzcoa	Lost Ireland
San Francisco	Nao	590	21	86	245	1585 Cantábrica	Andalucía	Returned Santander
Trinidad de Sagra	Carrack	580	22	78	346	n/a Ragusa	Levante	Returned Santander
Duquesa Santa Ana	Carrack	580	23	74	225	1585 Flanders	Andalucía	Lost Ireland
Santa Catalina	Nao	570	24	104	193	1586 Santander	Castilla	Returned Santander
Trinidad	Nao	560	24	90	182	1586 Santander	Castilla	Lost Ireland
Juliana	Carrack	550	32	70	340	n/a Venice	Levante	Lost Ireland
São Filipe	Galleon	540	40	116	377	1585 Portugal	Portugal	Lost Nieuport-Ostend
São Luís	Galleon	535	38	97	384	1583 Portugal	Portugal	Returned Santander
San Nikola Prodaneli	Carrack	530	26	80	259	n/a Ragusa	Levante	Lost Ireland
Sta. María Rata Encoronada	Carrack	530	35	82	508	n/a Genoa	Levante	Lost Ireland
San Juan de Sicilia	Carrack	515	26	63	279	n/a Ragusa	Levante	Sabotaged Scotland
San Juan Bautista	Galleon	515	31	64	260	1584 Cantábrica	Andalucía	Returned Santander
São Marcos	Galleon	510	33	98	419	1585 Portugal	Portugal	Lost Ireland
Santa Ana	Nao	495	30	101	311	1586 Cantábrica	Viscaya	Lost Le Havre
Nuestra Señora de la Begoña	Galleon	480	24	95	221	1585 Santander	Castilla	Returned Cangas
San Juan Bautista	Nao	480	24	90	254	1585 Santander	Castilla	Returned Santander
São Mateus	Galleon	480	34	110	334	1579 Portugal	Portugal	Lost Nieuport-Ostend
Santiesteban	Nao	475	26	75	192	1586 Cantábrica	Guipúzcoa	Lost Ireland
La Via	Carrack	470	25	71	241	n/a Genoa	Levante	Lost Ireland
Santa María Montemayor	Nao	455	18	42	158	n/a Cantábrica	Viscaya	Returned Santander

Name	Type					n/a Ragusa?		Fate
Santa María de la Visión	Carrack	430	18	70	255	n/a Ragusa?	Levante	*Lost Ireland*
Santiago	*Nao*	430	25	106	206	1585 Cantábrica	Viscaya	Returned Guipúzcoa
María Juan	*Nao*	430	24	93	217	1585 Cantábrica	Viscaya	*Lost off Gravelines*
Concepción	*Nao*	425	20	69	191	1584 Cantábrica	Andalucía	Returned Laredo
San Juan Bautista	*Nao*	420	24	57	183	1586 Santander	Castilla	*Lost Ireland*
San Lorenzo	Galleass	380	50	124	242	n/a Sicily	Naples	*Lost Calais*
Girona	Galleass	380	50	129	253	n/a Sicily	Naples	*Lost Ireland*
Zúñiga	Galleass	380	50	104	226	n/a Sicily	Naples	*Lost Le Havre*
Napolitana	Galleass	380	50	102	248	n/a Sicily	Naples	Returned Laredo
San Juan de Gargarín	*Nao*	365	16	54	174	1585 Cantábrica	Andalucía	Returned Santander
Santa María	*Nao*	350	20	73	182	1586 Cantábrica	Guipúzcoa	Returned Guipúzcoa
San Juan Menor	Galleon	340	24	81	238	1584 Guarnizo	Castilla	Returned Santander
Santiago Mayor	Galleon	340	24	103	213	1584 Guarnizo	Castilla	Returned Santander
Asunción	Galleon	340	24	80	184	1584 Guarnizo	Castilla	Returned Santander
San Felipe y Santiago	Galleon	340	24	86	161	1584 Guarnizo	Castilla	Returned Santander
San Pedro Mayor	Galleon	340	24	94	201	1584 Guarnizo	Castilla	Returned Santander
San Medel y Celedón	Galleon	340	24	75	196	1584 Guarnizo	Castilla	Returned Laredo
Nuestra Señora del Barrio	Galleon	340	24	86	208	1584 Guarnizo	Castilla	Returned Laredo
Santa Bárbara	*Nao*	340	12	47	135	1586 Cantábrica	Guipúzcoa	Returned Guipúzcoa
Magdalena	*Nao*	340	18	65	193	1585 Cantábrica	Viscaya	Returned Guipúzcoa
Sãotiago	Galleon	335	24	90	314	1585 Portugal	Portugal	Returned Santander
Manuela	Carrack	335	12	48	115	English prize	Viscaya	Returned Santander
Concepción de Zubelzu	*Nao*	300	16	69	153	1585 Cantábrica	Viscaya	Returned Guipúzcoa
Concepción del Cano	*Nao*	270	18	61	176	1585 Cantábrica	Viscaya	*Lost Ireland*
San Buenaventura	*Nao*	245	21	54	154	1586 Cantábrica	Guipúzcoa	Returned Guipúzcoa
São Bernardo	Galleon	225	21	68	179	1586 Portugal	Portugal	Returned La Coruña
São Cristóvão	Galleon	225	20	80	135	1580 Portugal	Portugal	Returned Santander
San Juan	*Nao*	225	21	53	142	1585 Cantábrica	Viscaya	*Stayed Dunkirk*
N.S. del Pilar	*Nao*	195	11	59	114	1584 Cantábrica	Pataches	Returned Laredo
María San Juan	*Nao*	190	12	40	95	1586 Cantábrica	Guipúzcoa	Returned Lisbon
Santa Ana	Galleon	160	24	69	104	1581 France	Castilla	Returned Santander

ENGLISH WARSHIPS OVER 100 TONS (106)

Private warship details from Wernham's 1589 and Andrews' 1589–91 lists – may well have been different in 1588

Name	Captain	Owner	Type	Tons	Men	Guns	Built	Squadron
Triumph	Martin Frobisher	Royal	Carrack	760	500	42	1562	Howard
White Bear	Lord Edmund Sheffield	Royal	Carrack	730	490	40	1564	Howard
Elizabeth Jonas	Sir Robert Southwell	Royal	Carrack	685	490	56	1559	Howard
Victory	John Hawkins	Royal	Carrack	565	430	42	1560	Howard
Ark Royal	Lord Admiral Howard	Royal	Galleon	555	430	44	1587	Howard
Mary Rose	Edward Fenton	Royal	Carrack	475	250	35	1557	Howard
Revenge	Sir Francis Drake	Royal	Galleon	465	250	43	1577	Drake
Vanguard (shallow draft)	Sir William Wynter	Royal	Galleon	465	250	54	1586	Seymour
Elizabeth Bonaventure	George Raymond	Royal	Galleon	448	250	32	1581	Howard
Golden Lion	Lord Thomas Howard	Royal	Galleon	420	250	28	1582	Howard
Galleon Leicester	George Fenner	Earl of Leicester	Galleon	400	250	34	1578	Drake
Hope	Robert Crosse	Royal	Carrack	400	250	48	1559	Drake
Swallow	Richard Hawkins	Royal	Galleon	400	160	30	1580	Howard
Rainbow (shallow draft)	Lord Henry Seymour	Royal	Galleon	385	250	54	1586	Seymour
Nonpareil	Thomas Fenner	Royal	Galleon	380	250	38	1584	Drake
Dreadnought	George Beeston	Royal	Galleon	360	190	41	1573	Howard
Swiftsure	Edward Fenner	Royal	Galleon	360	180	36	1573	Drake
Merchant Royal	Robert Flick	Thomas Cordell	Galleon	350	175	22		London
Antelope	Sir Henry Palmer	Royal	Galleon	340	170	30	1581	Seymour
Mayflower	Edward Bancks	Eldred and Hall	Galleon	300				London
Hercules		Eldred and Hall	Galleon	300				London
Foresight	Christopher Baker	Royal	Galleon	295	150	37	1570	Howard
Susan (London)		Paul Bayning	Galleon	260				Seymour
Galleon Dudley	James Erisey	Earl of Leicester	Galleon	250				Drake
Edward Bonaventure	James Lancaster	Thomas Cordell	Galleon	250		25		Drake
Centurion	John Fisher	Thomas Cordell	Galleon	250				London
Susan Parnell	Thomas Knyvet	John More et al	Galleon	250				Royal hire

Fleet (London)		London syndicate	Galleon	220				Royal hire
Tiger (ex *Sea Dragon*)	John Bostocke	Royal	Galleon	200	30	100	1584	Howard
Toby	Captain Osborne?	Richard Staper	Galleon	200				Howard
Bark Talbot (fireship)	Henry White	Earl of Shrewsbury	Galleon	200				Drake
Golden Noble	Captain Seager	Bird and Newton	Galleon	200				Drake
Virgin God Save Her		Unknown merchant	Galleon	200				Drake
Griffin	William Hawkins	John Hawkins	Galleon	200				Drake
Thomas (fireship)	Henry Spindelow	Francis Drake	Galleon	200				Drake
Red Lion		Thomas Myddelton	Galleon	200				London
Minion	Wiliam Wynter (son)	William Wynter	Galleon	200	21			London
Ascension		William Garraway	Galleon	200				London
George Bonaventure	Captain Barker	Thomas Cordell	Galleon	200				Royal hire
Minion (Bristol)	Edmund Gifford?	H. Alexander/W. Jones	Coaster	190				Howard hire
Edward		Maldon syndicate	Galleon	185				Royal hire
Bull	Jeremy Turner	Royal	Galleon	180	26	100	1570	Howard
Bark Potts		London syndicate	Coaster	180				Howard hire
Anne Frances		London syndicate	Galleon	180				Royal hire
Bonavolia	William Borough	Royal	Galley	180		256	1584	Thames
Margaret & John	John Watts	Owner-captain	Galleon	180				London
Tiger	John Markham	William Halliday *et al.*	Galleon	170				London
Salomon (London)		Simon Boreman *et al.*	Galleon	170				Royal hire
Bark Mannington	Ambrose Mannington	Owner-captain	Galleon	160				Drake
Bark St Leger	John St. Leger	Owner-captain	Galleon	160				Drake
Gift of God	John Taylor?	London syndicate	Galleon	160				London
Royal Defence		William Garraway *et al.*	Galleon	160				London
Nightingale	Captain Trigges	Plymouth syndicate	Galleon	160				Royal hire
Vineyard (London)	Captain Dale	Thomas Myddelton	Galleon	160				Royal hire
Daniel	Captain Pigott	Yarmouth syndicate	Coaster	160				Seymour
Bark Hawkins	Captain Josias	John Hawkins	Galleon	150	8			Drake
Hopewell	Abraham Cocke	John Watts	Galleon	150				Drake
Bark Bonner	Charles Caesar	Plymouth syndicate	Galleon	150				Drake
Bark Bond (fireship)	William Poole	John Bond (Weymouth)	Galleon	150				Drake

Name	Captain	Owner	Type	Tons	Guns	Men	Built	Squadron
John Trelawney	George Drake	Plymouth syndicate	Supply	150				Howard hire
Marigold (Southampton)		John Crooke	Coaster	150				Seymour
Mayflower	Alexander Musgrave	Lynn syndicate	Coaster	150				Seymour
Grace		Yarmouth syndicate	Coaster	150				Seymour
Galleon Hutchins		Unknown seaport	Coaster	150				Seymour
Bark Lamb		Unknown seaport	Coaster	150				Seymour
Bear Young (Chichester – fireship)		John Young	Galleon	140				Drake
Sparke (Plymouth)		William Sparke	Galleon	140				Drake
Crescent	Captain Gifford	Dartmouth syndicate	Coaster	140				Howard hire
Samuel		London syndicate	Galleon	140				Royal hire
Golden Lion		London syndicate	Galleon	140				London
Brave		London syndicate	Galleon	140				London
White Lion	Charles Howard (son)	Lord Admiral	Galleon	140				Royal hire
William	Captain Boyer	Ipswich syndicate	Coaster	140				Seymour
George Noble (Southampton)		Thomas Heaton	Supply	140				London
Tramontana	Luke Ward	Royal	Galleon	130	20	70	1586	Howard
Unicorn	Captain Johnson	Bristol syndicate	Coaster	130				Howard hire
Bartholomew	Captain Rainsford	Exmouth syndicate	Coaster	130				Howard hire
Bark Burr	William Irish	Bird and Newton	Galleon	130				London
Katherine		Ipswich syndicate	Coaster	125				Seymour
Hope (fireship)		William Hart (London)	Galleon	120				Drake
Scout	Henry Ashley	Royal	Galleon	120	10	70	1577	Howard
Antelope		London syndicate	Galleon	120				London
Primrose (Poole)		John Crooke?	Galleon	120	9			London
Salamander (Bristol)		William Walton	Galleon	120				London
Primrose		Harwich syndicate	Coaster	120				Seymour
Elizabeth		Dover syndicate	Coaster	120				Seymour
Rose		Topsham syndicate	Coaster	110				Howard hire
Jewel		London syndicate?	Galleon	110				London
Robin		Sandwich syndicate	Coaster	110				Seymour

Galleon		Weymouth syndicate	Coaster	100	Howard hire
Little John (London)		John Watts	Galleon	100	Howard hire
Pansy		London syndicate	Galleon	100	8	London
Rose Lion		London syndicate	Galleon	100		London
Anthony		London syndicate	Galleon	100		London
William		Colchester syndicate	Coaster	100		Seymour

Unattached

Sampson	*Joined too late*	Earl of Cumberland	Galleon	260	Voluntary
Samaritan (Dartmouth)		R Ofield / T Bramley	Galleon	250	Voluntary
Golden Ryal (Weymouth)	William Myddelton	Thomas Myddelton	Galleon	160	Voluntary
Frances		Fowey syndicate	Galleon	140	Voluntary
Thomas Bonaventure (London)		Thomas Cordell	Galleon	140	Voluntary
William		Plymouth syndicate	Galleon	120	Voluntary
Elizabeth	John Matthews	London syndicate	Galleon	120	Voluntary
Prudence	John Ridlesden	Owner-captain	Galleon	120	Voluntary
Grace of God (Topsham)		Robert Sadler	Galleon	100	Voluntary

BIBLIOGRAPHY

Printed in London unless otherwise specified.

Professor Kenneth Andrews

Professor Andrews' explorations of the English corsair phenomenon (he prefers 'privateer') are so well researched and thoughtfully interpreted that anybody who wishes to explore the subject in depth must start with his impressive body of work. To emphasize my own intellectual debt I start with a chronological list of the books and articles I have consulted.

'Thomas Fenner and the Guinea trade 1564', *Mariner's Mirror* 38 (1952), pp. 312-14.

'Christopher Newport of Limehouse, Mariner', *William & Mary Quarterly* 11 (1954), pp. 28-41.

English Privateering Voyages to the West Indies 1588-1595 (ed.), Hakluyt Society 2:111 (1959)

Elizabethan Privateering: English Privateering during the Spanish War (Cambridge 1964)

Drake's Voyages: a Re-Assessment of their place in England's Maritime Expansion (1967)

'The aims of Drake's expedition of 1577-1580', *American Historical Review* 73 (1968), pp. 724-41.

The Last Voyage of Drake and Hawkins (ed.), Hakluyt Society 2:142 (1972)

'Sir Robert Cecil and Mediterranean plunder', *English Historical Review* 87 (1972), pp. 513-32.

'Caribbean rivalry and the Anglo-Spanish peace of 1604', *History* 59 (1974), pp. 1-17.

'English voyages to the Caribbean 1596-1604: an annotated list', *William & Mary Quarterly* 31 (1974) pp. 243-54.

The Westward Enterprise: English Activities in Ireland, the Atlantic, and America 1480-1650 (ed.) with Canny, N. & Hair, P., (Liverpool 1978)

'On the way to Peru: Elizabethan ambitions south of Capricorn', *Terrae Incognitae* 14 (1982), pp. 61-75.

'The Elizabethan Seaman', *Mariner's Mirror* 68 (1982), pp. 245-62.

Trade, Plunder and Settlement: Maritime Enterprise and the Genesis of the British Empire 1480-1630 (Cambridge 1984)

Online sources

Abreu, Pedro de, *Historia del saqueo de Cadiz por los Ingleses en 1596* (contemporary, first published in 1866): http://www.archive.org/details/historiadelsaqu00ayungoog

Anthony Roll (1546) of King Henry VIII's ships: http://en.wikisource.org/wiki/Anthony_Roll

Bacon, Sir Francis, 'Of the True Greatness of Kingdoms and Estates' in *The Essays or Counsels, Civil and Moral, of Francis Ld. Verulam Viscount St. Albans*, 1625 (1986): http://www.authorama.com/essays-of-francis-bacon-1.html

Biggs, Walter, *Drake's Great Armada*, 1589 (New York 1910): http://www.gutenberg.org/files/3334/3334-h/3334-h.htm

Bourne, William, *The Arte of Shooting in Great Ordnaunce* (1587): http://www.hroarr.com/manuals/other/Bourne_1587.pdf

Casado Soto, José Luis, *Barcos Españoles de la Expansión Oceánica* (1988): http://www.asesmar.org/conferencias/temas/temashistoricos.htm

Clowes, William Laird, *The Royal Navy: a History from the Earliest Times to the Present*, Vol. 1 (1897): http://www.archive.org/details/royalnavyhistory01clow

Corbett, Sir Julian, *The Successors of Drake* (1900): http://www.archive.org/details/successorsofdrak00corbuoft

Corbett, Sir Julian, *Drake and the Tudor Navy, with a history of the rise of England as a maritime power* (1898): http://www.archive.org/details/draketudornav01corbrich

Dee, John, Preface to *The Elements of Geometrie of the most auncient Philospher Euclide of Megara* (1570): http://www.gutenberg.org/files/22062/22062-h/main.html#title_text

Dittmar, J., *Information Technology and Economic Change: The Impact of the Printing Press* (Article dated 17 June 2010 at https://eh.net/eha/files_2/dittmarb.pdf)

Drelichman, M. & H-J. Voth, *Lending to the Borrower from Hell: Debt & Default in the Age of Philip II*: http://www.scribd.com/doc/29318040/Debt-Default-in-the-Age-of-Philip-II-1556-1598

Fernández-González, Francisco, *Spanish Regulations for Ship-Building of the Seventeenth Century* (Annapolis 2009): http://oa.upm.es/1878/1/FERNANDEZ_GONZALEZ_PON_2009_01.pdf

Foxe, John, *The Unabridged Acts and Monuments* 1563, 1570, 1576, 1583 (HRI Online Publications, Sheffield 2011): http//www.johnfoxe.org

Friel, I., *Elizabethan Merchant Ships and Shipbuilding* (2009 lecture): http://www.gresham.ac.uk/lectures-and-events/elizabethan-merchant-ships-and-shipbuilding

García Hernán, Enrique, *Philip II's Forgotten Armada* (refers to 1596 – originally published 2004): http://www.irishinspain.org/archivos/philip_eghernan.pdf

Hakluyt, Richard, *Principal Navigations, Voyages, Traffiques and Discoveries of the English Nation* (1884 edition, incomplete): http://ebooks.adelaide.edu.au/h/hakluyt/voyages

Harrison, William, 'Descriptions of Britain and England' in Holinshed's *Chronicles*: http://www.fordham.edu/halsall/mod/1577harrison-england.html

HMSO, *Calendar of State Papers, Domestic Series, Elizabeth 1581-1603* with Addenda 1547-65 (1865, 1867, 1870): http://extra.shu.ac.uk/emls/13-3/rollcale.htm

HMSO, *Calendar of State Papers relating to Ireland, of the reigns of Henry VIII, Edward VI, Mary, and Elizabeth* (1860): http://www.archive.org/details/1905calendarofstatep10greauoft

Historical Manuscripts Commission, *Calendar of the Manuscripts of the Most Hon. The Marquis of Salisbury preserved at Hatfield House, Hertfordshire* (HMSO 1883): http://www.archive.org/stream/calendarofmanusc01greauoft#page/n3/mode/2up

Hopper, Clarence (ed.), *Robert Leng's 'Sir Francis Drake's Memorable Service against the Spaniards in 1587' and related documents* (Camden

Society 1863): http://www.archive.org/stream/sirfrancisdrakes
00lengrich#page/n5/mode/2up

Hume, A.S. (ed.), *Calendar of State Papers, Spain (Simancas)* 4 vols,
1558-1603 (1892): http://www.british-history.ac.uk/catalogue.
aspx?gid=138&type=3

Johnston, Stephen, *Making mathematical practice: gentlemen, practitioners
and artisans in Elizabethan England* (Ph.D. Cambridge 1994):
http://www.mhs.ox.ac.uk/staff/saj/thesis

Kraus, Hans, *Sir Francis Drake: A Pictorial Biography* (Amsterdam
1970): http://www.loc.gov/rr/rarebook/catalog/drake/drake
home.html. Serves as a vehicle for Library of Congress holdings
of original documents and illustrations concerning Drake.

Laughton, J.K. (ed.), *State papers relating to the defeat of the Spanish
Armada, anno 1588* (1894): http://www.archive.org/details/
statepapersrela00lauggoog

Macpherson, Robin, review of Geoffrey Parker's *The Grand Strategy of
Philip II* (1998): http://www.history.ac.uk/reviews/review/130

Nichols, Philip & Bourne, Nicholas (bookseller), *Sir Francis Drake revived: calling upon this dull or effeminate age to follow his noble steps
for gold and silver* (1653): http://www.archive.org/details/sir
francisdraker00nichrich

Oppenheim, Michael (ed.), *The Naval Tracts of Sir William Monson* (1902):
http://www.archive.org/details/navaltractsofsir00monsuoft

Oxford Dictionary of National Biography: any public library site;
library card number required.

Roncière, C. de la, *Histoire de la marine francaise*, Vol. 4 (Paris 1910):
http://www.archive.org/details/histoiredelamari04larouoft

Roy, Sharat Kumar, *The History and Petrography of Frobisher's 'Gold
ore'* (Chicago 1937): http://www.archive.org/stream/history
petrograp72roys/historypetrograp72roys_djvu.txt

Three Decks – Warships in the Age of Sail (invaluable resource):
http://www.threedecks.org/index.php?display_type=home

Williams, Sarah (ed.), *Letters Written by John Chamberlain During
the Reign of Queen Elizabeth* (1861): http://www.archive.org/
details/letterswrittenb00chamgoog

Printed primary

Colección de documentos inéditos para la historia de España, Vols 89-94 (Madrid 1887-89)

Corbett, J. (ed.), *Papers Relating to the Navy during the Spanish War 1585-87* (reprint 1987)

Donno, Elizabeth, *An Elizabethan in 1582: the Diary of Richard Madox, Fellow of All Souls*, Hakluyt Society 2:147 (1976)

Hawkins, Richard, *The Observations of Sir Richard Hawkins, Knight, in his Voyage into the South Sea. Anno Domini 1593* (1622 – Da Capo facsimile edition 1968)

Holinshed, Raphael, *Holinshed's Chronicles of England, Scotland and Ireland* (1807)

Hortrop, Job, *The rare travails of Job Hortrop, an Englishman* (1591)

Manwaring, G. and Perrin,W., *The Life and Works of Sir Henry Mainwaring*, 2 vols (1920-22)

Nutall, Zelia (ed. & trans.), *New Light on Drake: A Collection of Documents Relating to His Voyage of Circumnavigation 1577-1580*, Hakluyt Society 2:34 (1914)

Penzer, N. (ed.), *The World Encompassed and Analogous Contemporary Documents Concerning Sir Francis Drake's Circumnavigation of the World* (Amsterdam 1971)

Purchas, Samuel (ed.), *Hakluytus posthumus, or, Purchas his pilgrimes* (1625); Hakluyt Society, Extra Series 14–33 (1905-07)

Taylor, E. G. R. (ed.), *The Original Writings and Correspondence of the two Richard Hakluyts*, Hakluyt Society 2:76-77 (1935)

Taylor, E. G. R. (ed.), *The Troublesome Voyage of Captain Edward Fenton*, Hakluyt Society 2:113 (1959)

Vaux, W. S. W. (ed.), *The World Encompassed by Sir Francis Drake*, Hakluyt Society 1:16 (1854)

Wright, Irene (ed. & trans.), *Spanish Documents concerning English Voyages to the Caribbean 1527-1568*, Hakluyt Society 2:62 (1929)

Wright, Irene (ed. & trans.), *Documents concerning English voyages to Spanish main 1569–1580*, Hakluyt Society 2:71 (1932)

Wright, Irene (ed.& trans.), *Further English Voyages to Spanish America 1583-94*, Hakluyt Society 2:99 (1951)

English Secondary (*particularly valuable)

Appleby, J., *Under the Bloody Flag: Pirates of the Tudor Age* (Stroud 2009)

Baker, J., coined the phrase 'an island in law' in his much re-published *Introduction to English Legal History* (1971)

*Beier, A. & Finlay, R. (eds), *London 1500-1700: the Making of the Metropolis* (1986)

☺ Bicheno, H., *Crescent and Cross: the Battle of Lepanto 1571* (2003) ☺

Blake, J. (ed.), *Europeans in West Africa 1450-1560*, 2 vols. Hakluyt 2:86-87 (1942)

Borman, T., *Elizabeth's Women: the Hidden Story of the Virgin Queen* (2009)

Bosworth, C. (ed.), *Iran and Islam* (Edinburgh 1971)

Boxer, C., *The Dutch Seaborne Empire 1600-1800* (1965)

Boxer, C., *The Portuguese Seaborne Empire 1415-1825* (1969)

Caruana, A., *The History of English Sea Ordnance*, Vol. 1: 1523-1715 (Rotherfield 1994)

Cipolla, C., *Guns, Sails and Empires: Technological Innovation and European Expansion 1400-1700* (New York 1966)

Clark, P. (ed.), *The European Crisis of the 1590's: Essays in Comparative History* (1985)

*Connell-Smith, G., *Forerunners of Drake* (1954)

Cunnington, C. W. & P., *Handbook of English Costume in the Sixteenth Century* (1954)

Dietz, F., *The Exchequer in Elizabeth's reign* (Northampton, Mass. 1923)

Earle, P., *Corsairs of Malta and Barbary* (1970)

*Earle, P., *The Last Fight of the Revenge* (1992)

Eliott-Drake, E., *The Family and Heirs of Sir Francis Drake*, 2 vols (1911). Contains John Drake's two accounts of the circumnavigation given to the Spanish after his capture in 1583.

Ewen, C., *The Golden Chalice; a documented narrative of an Elizabethan pirate* (Paignton 1939)

Ewen, C., *Captain John Ward, 'arch-pirate'* (Paignton 1939)

*Fisher, G., *Barbary Legend: War, Trade and Piracy in North Africa 1415-1830* (1957)

Fox, A., *The English Renaissance: Identity & Representation in Elizabethan England* (Oxford 1997)

Furnival, F., *Early English Meals and Manners* (1972)

Fury, C., *Tides in the Affairs of Men: the Social History of Elizabethan Seamen 1580-1603* (2002)

Goodman, D., *Spanish Naval Power 1589-1665: Reconstruction and Defeat* (Cambridge 1997)

*Gardiner, R. (ed.), *Cogs, Caravels and Galleons* (1994)

Glete, J., *Navies and Nations: Warships, Navies and State Building in Europe and America 1500-1860*, Vol. 1 (Stockholm 1993)

*Hanson, N., *The Confident Hope of a Miracle* (2003)

Heywood, T., *The Lives and deaths of the two English pyrats Purser and Clinton* (New York 1971)

Howard, F., *Sailing Ships of War 1400-1860* (1979)

*Hurstfield, J. & A. Smith (eds), *Elizabethan People, State and Society* (1972)

*Hurstfield, J., *Freedom, Corruption and Government in Elizabethan England* (1973)

*Hurstfield, J., *Man as a Prisoner of his Past: the Elizabethan Experience* (Cardiff 1980)

*Keeler, M., *Sir Francis Drake's West Indian Voyage* (1981)

Keevil, J., *Medicine and the Navy*, Vol. 1: 1200-1649 (1957)

Kelsey, H., *Sir Francis Drake: The Queen's Pirate* (Yale 1998)

Kelsey, H., *Sir John Hawkins: Queen Elizabeth's Slave Trader* (Yale 2003)

Kirsch, P., *The Galleon* (1990)

Kouri, E., *England and the Attempts to form a Protestant Alliance in the late 1560s* (Helsinki 1981)

*Lewis, M., *The Hawkins Dynasty: Three Generations of a Tudor Family* (1969)

Lloyd, C., *English Corsairs on the Barbary Coast* (1981)

*Loades, D., *The Tudor Navy: an administrative, political and military history* (Aldershot 1992)

MacCaffrey, W., *Elizabeth I: War and Politics, 1588-1603* (Princeton 1992)

*McDermott, J., *Martin Frobisher: Elizabethan Privateer* (Yale 2001)

*McDermott, J., *England and the Spanish Armada : the Necessary Quarrel* (Yale 2005)

*MacFarlane, A., *The Origins of English Individualism: the family, property and social transition* (Oxford 1978)

McKendry, M., *Seven Hundred Years of English Cooking* (1973)

Manucy, A., *Pedro Menéndez de Aviles, Captain General of the Open Sea* (Sarasota 1992)

Markham, C., *Voyages of Pedro Sarmiento de Gamboa* (1895)

Martin, C. & Parker, G., *The Spanish Armada* (1988)

National Maritime Museum, *Armada 1588-1988: the Official Catalogue* (1988)

Nelson, A., *The Tudor Navy 1485-1603* (2001)

Nolan, J., *Sir John Norreys and the Elizabethan Military World* (Exeter 1997)

*Oppenheim, M., *A History of the Administration of the Royal Navy 1509-1660* (1988 ed.)

Oppenheim, M., *The Maritime History of Devon* (Exeter 1968)

Outhwaite, R., *Inflation in Tudor and Stuart England* (1982)

Parker, G., *The Dutch Revolt* (1977; 2002)

*Parker, G., *The Grand Strategy of Philip II*, (Yale 1998)

*Parker, G., *Empire, War and Faith in Early Modern Europe* (2002)

Platt, C., *Medieval Southampton AD 1000-1600* (1973)

Plowden, A., *Elizabethan England: life in an age of adventure* (1982)

Quinn, D. (ed.), *The Voyages and Colonising Enterprises of Sir Humfrey Gilbert* (1940)

Quinn, D., *The Roanoke Voyages 1584-90* (1955)

Quinn, D. (ed.), *The Hakluyt Handbook* (1974)

Quinn, D. (ed.), *The Last Voyage of Thomas Cavendish 1591-1592* (Chicago 1975)

*Rodger, N., *The Safeguard of the Sea: A Naval History of Britain 660–1649* (1998)

*Rodríguez-Salgado, M. (ed.), *Armada 1588-1988: an International Exhibition to Commemorate the Spanish Armada* (1988)

*Rodríguez-Salgado, M. & Adams, S. (eds), *England, Spain and the Gran Armada* (Edinburgh 1991)

Rowse, A., *Tudor Cornwall: portrait of a society* (Exeter 1990)

Scamell, G., *Seafaring, Sailors and Trade 1450-1750* (Aldershot 2003)

*Scott, W., *The Constitution and Finance of English, Scottish and Irish Joint-Stock Companies to 1720*, Vol. 1 (Cambridge 1912)

Spence, R., *The Privateering Earl* (Stroud 1995)

Stack, P. (ed.), *Rebellion, Popular Protest and the Social Order in Early Modern England* (Cambridge 1984)

*Starkey, David, *Rivals in Power: Lives and Letters of the Great Tudor Dynasties* (1990)

Starkey, David, *Henry VIII: A European Court in England* (1991)

Silke, J., *Kinsale: the Spanish intervention in Ireland at the end of the Elizabethan wars* (Liverpool 1970)

Strong, R., *The Elizabethan Image: Painting in England 1540-1620* (1969)

*Taylor, E., *Tudor Geography 1485-1583* (1930)

*Taylor, E., *Late Tudor and Early Stuart Geography 1583-1650* (1934)

Tenenti, Alberto, *Piracy and the Decline of Venice 1580-1615* (1967)

Thompson, I., *War and society in Habsburg Spain: selected essays* (Aldershot 1992)

Thrower, N. (ed.), *Sir Francis Drake and the Famous Voyage 1577-1580* (Berkeley 1984)

*Tilly, Charles, 'War Making and State Making as Organized Crime' in Evans, P., Rueschemeyer, D. & Skocpol, T. (eds), *Bringing the State Back In* (Cambridge 1985)

Wagner, H. (ed.), *Sir Francis Drake's voyage around the world: its aims and achievements* (San Francisco 1926)

*Waters, D., *The Art of Navigation in Elizabethan and Early Stuart Times*, Vol. 1 (1958)

*Wernham, R., *Before the Armada: the growth of English foreign policy 1485-1588* (1966)

*Wernham, R., *After the Armada: Elizabethan England and the Struggle for Western Europe 1588–1595* (Oxford 1984)

*Wernham, R., *The Expedition of Sir John Norris and Sir Francis Drake to Spain and Portugal 1589* (Aldershot 1988)

*Wernham, R., *The Return of the Armadas: the last years of the Elizabethan war against Spain* (Oxford 1994)

Williamson, J., *The Age of Drake* (1946)

Williamson, J., *Hawkins of Plymouth* (1969)

Spanish and French Secondary (*particularly valuable)

Acerra, M. & G. Martinière, *Coligny, les Protestants et la Mer* (Paris 1997)

Arróniz, O., *La Batalla Naval de San Juan de Ulúa* (México 1982)

Calderón Ortega, J., *El Almirantazgo de Castilla: historia de una institucion conflictiva 1250-1560* (Alcalá de Henares 2003)

*Cerezo Martínez, R., *Las Armadas de Felipe II* (Madrid 1988)

*Delafosse, M., *Les corsaires protestants à La Rochelle 1570-1577* (Paris 1964)

Lestringant F., *Le Huguenot et le sauvage: l'Amérique et la controverse coloniale en France au temps des guerres de religion* (Geneva 2004)

Morales, E., *Aventuras y desventuras de un navegante: Sarmiento de Gamboa* (Buenos Aires 1946)

O'Donnell y Duque de Estrada, H., *La Fuerza de desembarco de la Gran Armada contra Inglaterra* 1588 (Madrid 1989)

(Olesa Muñido, F., *La galera en la navegación y el combate*, 2 vols (Madrid 1971)

Riaño Lozano, F., *Los Medios navales de Alejandro Farnesio 1587-1588* (Madrid 1989)

*Rumeu de Armas, A., *Los viajes de John Hawkins a America 1562-1595* (Seville 1947)

ARTICLES (by journal and chronological)
Economic History Review

Stone, L., 'Elizabethan overseas trade', 2nd series 2 (1949), pp. 31-58.

Fisher, F. J., 'Influenza and Inflation in Tudor England', 18 (Aug 1965), pp. 120-29. See also comment on Fisher's article, 21 (Aug 1968), pp. 361-68.

Fritschy, 'Public finance in Holland during the Dutch Revolt 1568–1648', 56 (Feb 2003), pp. 57-89.

English Historical Review

Mathew, D., 'Cornish and Welsh pirates in the reign of Elizabeth', 39 (1924), pp. 337-48.

Croft, P., 'Englishmen and Inquisition 1558-1625', 87 (1972), pp. 249-68.

Adams, S., 'New light on the "Reformation" of John Hawkins', 105 (1990), pp. 96-111.

Hispanic American Historical Review

Sluiter, E., 'Dutch-Spanish Rivalry in the Carribbean Area, 1594-1609', 28 (May 1948)

History Today

Tong, R., 'Captain Thomas Wyndham', 7 (1957), pp. 221-8.

Journal of Economic History

Brenner, R., 'The social basis of English commercial expansion 1550-1650', 32 (1972), pp. 361-84.

Mariner's Mirror

Taylor, E. G. R., 'More light on Drake', 16 (1930), pp. 134-51.

Lewis, M., 'Armada Guns: a comparative study', 28 (1942), pp. 41-72; 104-107.

Ewen, C. H. L., 'Organized piracy around England in the 16th century', 33 (1949), pp. 29-42.

Stanford, M. J. G., 'The Raleghs take to the Sea', 48 (1962), pp. 18-35.

Glasgow, T., 'List of ships in the Royal Navy 1539-88', 56 (1970), pp. 299-307.

Thompson, I. A. A., 'Spanish Armada Guns', 61 (1975), pp. 355-71.

Gray, R., 'Spinola's galleys in the narrow sea 1599-1603', 64 (1978), pp. 71-83.

Scammell, G. V., 'Manning the English merchant service in the 16th century', 56 (1970), pp. 31-54.

Scammell, G. V., 'European seamanship in the great age of discovery', 68 (1982), pp. 357-76.

Croft, J. P., 'English mariners trading with Spain and Portugal 1558-1625', 69 (1983), pp. 251-66.

Sugden, J., 'Sir Francis Drake: A Note on his Portraiture', 70 (1984), pp. 305-08.

Dietz, B., 'The Royal Bounty and English Merchant Shipping in the 16th and 17th Centuries', 77 (1991), pp. 5-20.

Rodger, N. A. M., 'The Development of Broadside Gunnery 1450–1650', 82 (1996), pp. 301-24.

Proceedings of the Dorset Natural History and Archaeological Society

Ewen, C., 'The Pirates of Purbeck, with particular reference to Thomas Walton alias Purser, Clinton Atkinson alias Smith and William Arnewood alias Arnold', 71 (1949), pp. 88-109.

Proceedings of the Huguenot Society

Dietz, 'Huguenot and English corsairs 3rd civil war in France 1568-70', XIX (1952-58), pp. 278-94.

Transactions of the Devonshire Association for the Advancement of Science, Literature and Art

Drake, H., 'Drake: the Arms of his Surname and Family', 15 (1883), pp. 489-93.

Chope, R. P., 'New Light on Sir Richard Grenville: I. The Projected South Sea Voyage', 49 (1917), pp. 210-246.

Youings, J., 'Drake, Grenville and Buckland Abbey', 112 (1980), pp. 95-99.

Western Antiquary

Drake, H., 'The Arms of Drake', 2 (September 1882), p. 98.

PICTURE CREDITS

Interior Pages: Charles E. F. Drake, MD, 156; National Maritime Museum, Greenwich, London, 250, 252, 254 ,256, 258; Museu de Marinha, Lisbon, Portugal, 303; Rare Books and Special Collections Division of the Library of Congress, Washington, D.C., 192-193, 267; The Bridgeman Art Library/Index, 97.

Colour Pages: Sir Francis Drake © National Portrait Gallery, London; Queen Elizabeth I, © Walker Art Gallery, National Museums Liverpool/The Bridgeman Art Library; Philip II, Prado, Madrid, Spain/The Bridgeman Art Library; Sir William Cecil, Burghley House Collection, Lincolnshire, UK/The Bridgeman Art Library; Sir Francis Walsingham, Getty Images; Robert Dudley, Yale Centre for British Art, Paul Mellon Collection, USA/The Bridgeman Art Library; Robert Devereux, Royal Armouries, Leeds, UK/The Bridgeman Art Library; Sir Walter Raleigh, Kunsthistorisches Museum, Vienna, Austria/The Bridgeman Art Library; Sir John Hawkins, Plymouth City Museum & Art Gallery; *Minion*, Pepys Library, Magdalene College, Cambridge; *Jesus of Lubeck*, Pepys Library, Magdalene College, Cambridge; The Galleon, Pepys Library, Magdalene Cambridge; Siege of Smerwick, The National Archives, MPF1-75; Walsingham espionage map, The National Archives, MPF1-156; Drake's circumnavigation, Yale Centre for British Art, Paul Mellon Collection, USA/The Bridgeman Art Library; Martin Frobisher, akg-images; Sir Martin Gilbert, National Trust Photographic Library/The Bridgeman Art Library; Sir Richard Grenville, The Stapleton Collection/The Bridgeman Art Library; George Clifford, National Maritime Museum, Greenwich, London; Queen Elizabeth I borne by her garter knights, The Stapleton Collection/The Bridgeman Art Library. Somerset House Peace Conference, National Maritime Museum, Greenwich, London.

INDEX

Figures in **bold** type indicate
tables; those in *italics*
indicate illustrations.